PRESENTED TO

_____

ON THE OCCASION OF

_____

BY

_____

STRENGTH
for the
JOURNEY

Books by Joseph Stowell

Following Christ
I Would Follow Jesus
Loving Christ
Perilous Pursuits
Proclaiming Jesus
Revelation
Shepherding the Church
Simply Jesus
The Trouble with Jesus
The Weight of Your Words
Why Its Hard to Follow Jesus

STRENGTH *for the* JOURNEY

*Day by Day
With Jesus*

JOSEPH M. STOWELL

MOODY PUBLISHERS
CHICAGO

Scripture taken from the *Holy Bible, New International Version*®. NIV®. Copyright © 1973, 1978, 1984 by International Bible Society. Used by permission of Zondervan Publishing House. All rights reserved.

Scripture quotations marked NASB are taken from the *New American Standard Bible*®, © Copyright The Lockman Foundation 1960, 1962, 1963, 1968, 1971, 1972, 1973, 1975, 1977, 1995. Used by permission.

Scripture quotations marked NASB 1977 are taken from the *New American Standard Bible*®, © Copyright The Lockman Foundation 1960, 1962, 1963, 1968, 1971, 1972, 1973, 1975, 1977. Used by permission.

Scripture quotations marked NKJV are taken from the *New King James Version*. Copyright © 1982 by Thomas Nelson, Inc. Used by permission. All rights reserved.

Scripture quotations marked THE MESSAGE are from *The Message*, copyright © by Eugene H. Peterson 1993, 1994, 1995. Used by permission of NavPress Publishing Group.

Scripture quotations marked EMPH. NT are from *The Emphasized New Testament: A New Translation*, Joseph Bryant Rotherham, Grand Rapids: Kregel Publications, n.d. (*The Emphasized Bible: A Translation Designed to Set Forth the Exact Meaning, the Proper Terminology and the Graphic Style of the Sacred Original*, by Joseph Bryant Rotherham [Grand Rapids: Krebel, 1959].)

Scripture quotations marked KJV are taken from the King James Version.

Scripture quotations of Psalms and the Book of Proverbs are taken from the *Holy Bible, New Living Translation*, copyright© 1996. Used by permission of Tyndale House Publishers, Inc., Wheaton, Illinois 60189. All rights reserved. *New Living, NLT,* and *New Living Translation* logo are registered trademarks of Tyndale House Publishers, Inc.

"Knowing you," Graham Kendrick. Copyright © 1994 Make Way Music, P.O. Box 263, Croydon, Surrey. CR9 5AP, U.K. All rights reserved. International copyright secured. Used by permission.

"He's Been Faithful" written by Carol Cymbala © Copyright 1989. Carol Joy Music/ASCAP (admin. by ICG)/Word. All rights reserved. Used by permission."He's Been Faithful," by Carol Cymbala © 1990 Word Music, Inc. Printed with permission.

Cover and interior design: Ragont Design

Library of Congress Cataloging-in-Publication Data

Stowell, Joseph M.
    Strength for the journey : day-by-day with Jesus / Joseph Stowell.
       p. cm.
    Includes index.
    ISBN 978-0-8024-5645-8
     1. Christian life—Meditations. I. Title.
    BV4501.3 .S77 2002
    242'.5—dc21   2001052127

Paperback ISBN: 978-0-8024-3312-1

Originally delivered by fleets of horse-drawn wagons, the affordable paperbacks from D. L. Moody's publishing house resourced the church and served everyday people. Now, after more than 125 years of publishing and ministry, Moody Publishers' mission remains the same—even if our delivery systems have changed a bit. For more information on other books (and resources) created from a biblical perspective, go to www.moodypublishers.com or write to:

Moody Publishers
820 N. LaSalle Boulevard
Chicago, IL 60610

1 3 5 7 9 10 8 6 4 2

Printed in the United States of America

With appreciation
And deep affection
This book is dedicated to

Martie

My companion, friend, lover, and confidante
Who through our many years of marriage
Has consistently strengthened my life and ministry
With her love and wise counsel

I shall be forever thankful and indebted to her

*F*or all of us life is a journey. Unfortunately, left to itself, the destination and direction is not guaranteed. For many, life's journey is no more that an excursion through a maze of dead-end experiments. But for those who follow Jesus, the road is clearly signposted with assurances of confidence, strength, courage, and joy. As long as He is in view ahead of us we are never lost and never alone. The choice is yours.

The psalmist rejoiced in the clarity that God's Word brought to his pilgrimage. He pictured God's Word as a lamp to our feet and a light to our path. As such, he identified Scripture as the only reliable source for guidance, comfort, confidence, encouragement, and strength in an often dark and treacherous world. In Scripture, the complexities of life are unraveled, our confusion is clarified, our challenges are put into perspective, and our joys are multiplied. Turning life's journey over to God's wisdom is a choice full of abundant reward. His advice alone makes our lives like trees planted by rivers of water, yielding fruit in season, unwithered in the driest of times, and prosperous regardless of the difficulty we may face. No wonder that the psalmist exclaims,

Oh, how I love your law!
I think about it all day long.
Your commands make me wiser than my enemies,
for your commands are my constant guide.
Yes, I have more insight than my teachers,
For I am always thinking of your decrees.
How sweet are your words to my taste;
They are sweeter than honey.
Psalm 119:97–99, 103 NLT

But staying in the Word is a constant challenge. Our minds are far more susceptible to Satan's deceitful schemes and our hearts are more vulnerable to his temptation when we lose sight of God's perspective. It is vitally important to stay close to the source.

My prayer is that each day God will meet you in the selected Scripture passage as well as in the application of His message to your heart. God has an uncanny way of bringing us the right thoughts at just the right time. May it happen often.

To maximize the effect . . .

- *read the devotional with your Bible open to the text. Before reading the daily thought, read the passage. Better yet, read the verses that surround the text.*
- *read each devotional prayerfully. Pray the Scripture passage back to God in life-related terms. Pray for grace to grow.*
- *take each devotional personally. Ask, "What is God wanting to say to me today?" Keep a notebook handy, and write down personal applications and specific plans to implement the truth that has impacted your heart.*

Throughout the year you will find recurring themes: *the joy and strength we find in Jesus, the glory of God, heaven, hope, comfort, compassion, servanthood, character development, confidence, courage, suffering and trouble, commitment, our search for significance,* and many other topics that are fundamental to our success as followers of Jesus.

In addition, fifty-one psalms have been included. The Psalms are a gold mine of truths about life, about ourselves, and about God. I read them regularly for stimulation, comfort, and just to keep my view of God clear. So once a week there is a psalm for you to meditate on and in which you can find solace and strength.

Years ago, someone recommended that I read a proverb every day. That goal is particularly easy to track since there are thirty-one chapters, one for each day of the month. To help you capture that additional blessing, we have included the entire Book of Proverbs in the back of the devotional.

My prayer is that each devotional will be used of God to give you strength for your journey. As the hymn says so well, He faithfully provides "strength for today and bright hope for tomorrow." May you experience this grace in great measure.

Special thanks to my wife, Martie, for her indispensable editing help and insightful suggestions; to Charlotte Arman and Sonja Goppert for their efforts in transcribing and organizing the material; to Lori Imhof and Sonja Larson, whose capable assistance in my office frees me to write; to Anne Scherich, whose patient and tireless efforts in doing the final edits will be forever appreciated; to Carolyn McDaniel for the excellent work in typesetting the manuscript through several extra edits; and, most important, to our God, whose Word never fails.

STRENGTH FOR THE JOURNEY

"BE STRONG…THAT YOU MAY BE SUCCESSFUL WHEREVER YOU GO."
—Joshua 1:6–7

*K*ids have a wonderful way of colorfully depicting the realities of life. I remember the day that our little Matt came running in from the backyard, flopped breathless and exhausted on the couch, and exclaimed, "I've lost all my power!"

We've all felt that way spiritually. Many times the journey feels long and is fraught with bumps and turns, steep climbs and valleys. We weary of that same old temptation that keeps battering our will. Insecurities drain our souls of courage and confidence. And unsuspected surprises in relationships, finances, and health threaten to exhaust our will to win.

But for determined followers of Jesus, there is an always-available source of strength and renewal. Tapping into it empowers us to keep Jesus first, where He belongs and blesses. When we live in the safety of His strength things like money, relationships, dreams, and desires submit more readily to His perfect will. And gladly; fear, anxiety, and doubt are rendered weak by the courage and peace that only the strong enjoy.

Strength for the journey is drawn from a daily connection to the fullness of God. His presence and power are available for every moment of our day as He waits to meet us with the strength that we need. Actively casting all your care on Him and checking for wisdom and direction at every turn provide a constant reminder that you are not a lonely stranger.

Though Joshua led Israel through the toughest of times, he found his strength by tapping into the reality of his God. As God promised, "No one will be able to stand up against you. . . . I will never leave you nor forsake you. Be strong and courageous. . . . obey all the law . . . that you may be successful wherever you go" (Joshua 1:5–7).

Strength comes to those who instinctively ask, "What is there about God's presence in my life that will give me strength and confidence now? What is there in His Word that turns the lights on in this situation? How should I pray for His wisdom, grace, and strength to move forward in His will?

Be strong! Plan to consciously tap into the power at every turn in the road today!

TOOLS OF DEVOTION

"Ask and It Will Be Given to You; Seek and You Will Find; Knock and
the Door Will Be Opened to You."
>
> —Matthew 7:7

I finally got organized and set up a workroom in my basement. It's
amazing how much more I get done now that I know where all my
tools are. Here are some tools to help you get organized in a daily encounter
with the living God. I have found them to be helpful.

Select a slot on your schedule and a corner of your world, and claim it for
God. For some, the morning may be best. "In the morning my prayer comes
before you" (Psalm 88:13). Others prefer the evening and agree with David's
prayer: "May my prayer be set before you like incense; may the lifting up of
my hands be like the evening sacrifice" (Psalm 141:2). Others prefer many
encounters during the day. The psalmist did: "Evening, morning and noon I
cry out" (Psalm 55:17).

How much time should you take? My advice is to value the quality of the
encounter over the length of the meeting. I suggest that your quiet time last
long enough for you to say what you want and for God to say what He wants.

Read prayerfully. God speaks to you through His Word. Ask God to help
you understand the Bible. "The Helper, the Holy Spirit, whom the Father will
send in My name, He will teach you all things, and bring to your remem-
brance all that I said to you" (John 14:26 NASB). Before reading the Bible,
speak with the author. Don't go to Scripture looking for your idea; go searching for His.

Read the Bible expectantly. Jesus told us, "Seek and you will find"
(Matthew 7:7). God commends those who "chew on Scripture day and night"
(Psalm 1:2 THE MESSAGE). The Bible is not a newspaper to be skimmed but a
mine to be quarried. Look in His Word for wisdom the way you would search
a mine for silver; and if you read for understanding as you would hunt for hidden treasure, you will find it (Proverbs 2:4–5). God is the rewarder of those
who diligently seek Him.

Take time for Him. He is there . . . waiting.

JANUARY 2 / 14

AMAZING LOVE . . . HOW CAN IT BE

Who Loved Me and Gave Himself for Me.

—Galatians 2:20

*L*ife thrives on the crest of good relationships. Particularly relationships that are essential—our relationships to parents, spouses, our children, friends, and other significant people in our lives. I suppose there are some people who could care less about relationships, but they are few and far between.

Recently my dad said that he thought I was doing a good job at Moody. I'm fifty-seven years old and still thrill at the approving statements of my parents. Martie tells me that I am her favorite preacher. And our grown children call on us for counsel. No amount of money or material gain can measure against the rewards that are only found in relationships. As good as the rewards are, the real joy in a relationship is the pleasure of making someone you love the object of your service and adoration. Nothing makes me happier than to serve Martie in ways that make her happy.

Relationships are the backbone of life when you realize the worst day at the office is not that bad, because there is a friend or a family member who believes in you—who, in effect, reminds you that there are things in life more important than the drudgery of unrewarding daily routines that go south.

It is for this reason that I am taken by the way God approaches the matter of connecting with us. It is profound enough that God would even want to connect; but that He desires to connect in the context of a loving relationship is an overwhelming thought. Among the world's great religions, Christianity alone is defined by the reality that the relationship between God and His people is driven and defined by a deep exchange of love. Other religions call their adherents with no thought of love to enter ritualistic contracts of sacrificial performance of duties and oft-repeated rites.

If you ask me, I am delighted to be a follower of Jesus. What amazing grace that He loves us and desires our love in return!

"Amazing love! how can it be that Thou, my God, shouldst die for me."

KNOWING YOU, JESUS

THAT I MAY KNOW HIM.

—Philippians 3:10 KJV

We all know who Jesus is.

We preach about His will and His ways, tell His stories by heart, celebrate Him in worship, and serve Him with enthusiasm. But there is a gnawing sense that there should be more to this relationship. Why is it that He often feels so far away? So historical? So Other? So church related?

The distance between knowing about Him and knowing Him is vast. The space between these two experiences separates the spectators from intimate participants.

It's a pretty safe bet that if you are reading this devotional you probably can recite stories of intrigue from His life and perhaps even spin a few theological paradigms about the nature of His existence. But the unfortunate reality is that most of us stop there. Seemingly satisfied with knowing *about* Him, we have no conception of the deep richness waiting for those who *experience* Him. And so we live our Christianity all dressed up with nowhere to go, keeping all the rules, exchanging clichés of "Bible-speak," and passing the theological tests of orthodoxy—yet never really *knowing* Him.

If that's your story, get ready. The best is yet to come. He intends for you to experience the pleasure and reassuring peace of His presence in our lives. He didn't die for us to simply strike a deal guaranteeing heaven. He died for us to make us His own and to give us the privilege of experiencing Him personally. He lives to connect with the entire you. In fact, He sent us the Holy Spirit to make the total connection possible and He gave us His Word to show us the way. And you can know the pleasure.

The words of my grandmother's favorite hymn capture the privilege: "He walks with me, and He talks with me, and He tells me I am His own, and the joy we share as we tarry there, none other has ever known." Knowing my grandmother, I have the feeling that she had tapped the secret of getting past knowing about Him for the joy of experiencing Him.

Read Philippians 3:7–10.

EXPERIENCING JESUS

That I May Know Him, and the Power of His Resurrection, and the
Fellowship of His Sufferings, Being Conformed to His Death.

—Philippians 3:10

*M*ost of us who have grown up in "church world," particularly of the
evangelical kind, tend to want God to come in neat packages that are
clearly defined and identifiable. He seems safer that way. Don't misunderstand. God is both definable and identifiable. It's just that He is more than
that. There is a mystery about God that escapes the limited definitions of our
finite minds and an experiencing of Him that often escapes our capacity to
describe. If you are longing for more of Him, then you must be willing to seek
Him in places where He can be found, . . . beyond the boundaries of definitions and dogma.

Paul, at the end of his life, declared that it was his passion to know Christ.
Interestingly, he used the word that means to know by experience, which is
noteworthy, since no one has ever experienced Jesus more intimately than
Paul. He had a personal encounter of the Jesus kind on the road to Damascus
and then spent an extended season in the "third heaven" (2 Corinthians 12:2)
with Jesus. Yet he longed for more. Which only proves that you can't get
enough of Jesus.

He tells us his secret. First, he puts all of self away so that his heart is clear
to see Jesus (Philippians 3:4–11). Then he tips us off that he meets Jesus in
three specific places: in resurrection power, in other words, in victory over sin;
in shared experiences with the sufferings of Jesus; and in the surrender that
does whatever Jesus asks us to do, regardless. And here is the mystery. As we
seek Him to deliver us from evil and feel His pain as we experience our own,
and fully surrender . . . Jesus meets us. Not all of us feel it the same way or
can describe it precisely. Yet His presence is manifest in ways that whet our
appetite for more.

As Graham Kendrick wrote, "Knowing you Jesus, knowing you, there is
no greater thing. You're my all, you're the best, you're my joy my righteousness
and I love you Lord."

*Meet Him as He delivers you from evil, in seasons of suffering, and in the
Gethsemane of surrender.*

CHOOSING JESUS

THE SURPASSING VALUE OF KNOWING CHRIST JESUS MY LORD.
—Philippians 3:8 NASB

"Daddy are we famous?" Libby was only six when she asked the question. I was pastoring a church in a small town in the Midwest at the time, and it didn't take me long to respond. "No" was the only legitimate answer. She paused thoughtfully and then replied with confidence and a touch of consternation, "Well, we would be if more people knew about us."

Poor Libby, just six and already concerned with what people thought about us. Wondering where we registered on the Richter scale of people's opinions.

It is something that Libby will wrestle with the rest of her life. All of us end up being caught in the web of self-intrigue. Since earliest childhood we have been aware of and concerned about ourselves. We mastered words like *my* and *mine* long before we knew the word for *friend* or *share*. Growing up doesn't help. What do people think of me? Have I been sufficiently recognized for my accomplishments? How am I being treated? Does anyone care about me? These questions still haunt us.

Books about knowing and understanding who we really are consistently make the best-seller list. Obscene amounts of money go to therapists who offer to guide you on a journey through your inner self. Actually, I can't think of a more unsettling thought: to spend money for an inner journey through me. More important, it is a dreadfully unbiblical thought. If you are in the process of becoming a follower of Christ, life is not about a journey to get to know yourself but an adventure in getting to know Jesus.

Paul knew you can't have it both ways. Your life will either be about self-absorption or about a Savior who is adored. We will either live for the applause of men or the applause of heaven. No wonder that Paul, after listing his stellar accomplishments, would exclaim, "I count all things to be loss in view of the surpassing value of knowing Christ Jesus my Lord" (Philippians 3:8 NASB).

Refocus. Concentrate on getting to know Jesus, and living to know yourself will seem insignificant and shallow by comparison.

PSALM 1

Oh, the joys of those
who do not follow the advice of the wicked,
or stand around with sinners,
or join in with scoffers.
But they delight in doing everything the LORD wants;
day and night they think about his law.
They are like trees planted along the riverbank,
bearing fruit each season without fail.
Their leaves never wither,
and in all they do, they prosper.
But this is not true of the wicked.
They are like worthless chaff, scattered by the wind.
They will be condemned at the time of judgment.
Sinners will have no place among the godly.
For the LORD watches over the path of the godly,
but the path of the wicked leads to destruction.

ALL THAT WE NEED

Jesus Answered Her, "If You Knew the Gift of God and Who It Is That Asks You for a Drink, You Would Have Asked Him and He Would Have Given You Living Water."

—John 4:10

*N*eed something from Jesus today? If you are like most of us, there are some items on your "unanswered prayer" list that you think He's forgotten. In fact, there are times when we feel spiritually abandoned, when He seems to care more about the needs of those who give stunning testimonies of answered prayer—or whose prayers about finding parking places in crowded mall parking lots always get answered.

While traveling through Samaria, Jesus met a village woman at the local well. He asked her for a drink of water. When she answered His request, Jesus said, "If you knew the gift of God and who it is that asks you for a drink, you would have asked him and he would have given you living water" (John 4:10).

Days before, a group of Jews asked Christ to give them a sign to verify His claim to be God. Jesus responded, "Destroy this temple, and I will raise it again in three days." Confused, the Jews replied, "It has taken forty-six years to build this temple, and you are going to raise it in three days?" (John 2:19–20).

The Jewish people thought He was going to rebuild the temple; instead, in three days He rose from the dead to conquer death and hell. The Samaritan woman talked of water from the well; Jesus offered her living water. What Jesus gave people wasn't necessarily what they asked for, expected or, thankfully, what they deserved. Consistently, He had better things in mind.

God gives each of us exactly what we need. And in case you think He has not done much for you lately, think again. With abounding generosity, God has graced us with forgiveness, love, acceptance, security, and substantial healing from the curse of sin . . . and heaven. If He never does anything more for us, He has given us enough to be gratefully praising Him for the rest of our lives—even if we can't find that parking spot!

What specific gifts has He given you to meet your needs today? Resolve to live today with gratitude in your heart for all He has done.

RUNNING TO WIN

Let Us Run with Perseverance the Race Marked Out for Us.
—Hebrews 12:1

*E*ven in the coldest weather, a good runner knows better than to run with a heavy layer of clothing. I can't imagine that in the Olympic games the team from Alaska would run its race in bulging fur-lined parkas.

Running the race for Christ requires that we lay aside every hindering weight and the sin that so easily besets us (Hebrews 12:1). Running for Christ means stripping down to the bare minimum and racing with pure hearts and lives unburdened with willful sin.

Not only do we need to be free to run well, but His race requires perseverance. *Perseverance* literally means to "remain under," to stay under the strain without seeking ways to escape the pressure. Races are flat-out stressful. Don't expect it to be a cakewalk. The ill winds of life get in our faces. The seductions of life at a more leisurely and self-gratifying pace constantly threaten to distract us. We may even get mud kicked in our face by the runner in front of us.

But this race is not run for our own self-satisfaction. It is not even run for our own glory. *We run for Him*—for Christ's glory and for the honor of His name. We run for the advancement of His kingdom, the rescuing of lost souls, the rearing of godly families, and His visibility through our lives on the job.

And so, with eyes fixed on the finish line, we vow to keep a steady, unhindered, undaunted pace. And when we look to see if Jesus is in the stands, we find that He is always there, "the author and finisher of our faith" (Hebrews 12:2 KJV), lifting a nail-scarred hand to cheer us on to the end.

As I shed the weights, it crosses my mind, *If He could run all the way to the cross for me, then surely no cost is too great to run my race for Him.*

Are you on the track? What's that "weight" on your back?

BEYOND 911

ENTER INTO HIS GATES WITH THANKSGIVING AND HIS COURTS WITH PRAISE.
GIVE THANKS TO HIM, BLESS HIS NAME. FOR THE LORD IS GOOD.
—Psalm 100:4–5 NASB

*P*rayer is far more than asking God for what we want or need. Prayer is the way we open our soul for Him to see and hear our heartfelt adoration and gratitude. And, as you no doubt have found, He takes the opportunity to commune with us as well. There have been many times that I have gone to prayer only for Him to remind me of Scripture, His character, and His will. In fact, when I go to Him in prayer with undealt-with sin in my life, He always wants to deal with that before I can go on. Any satisfying relationship needs communication: honest, open, and two-way. Can you think of a relationship that is growing where there is no communication, or worse yet, the only time you talk is when you are asking for something for yourself?

Sadly, many Christians have made prayer a toll-free request line to God. Although it is true that often we "have not, because [we] ask not" (James 4:2 KJV), we are more prone to "worship not because we ask a lot."

When all we do is ask, we stifle our relationship with God. Even self-sufficient secularists turn to God in prayer when they want or need something badly enough. Does that make them friends of God? Of course not.

So just what is it that makes a Christian's prayer unique and effective? There is a simple acronym you can use as a reminder: ACTS. It stands for Adoration, Confession, Thanksgiving, and Supplication. Notice that *asking* comes last.

Of course, this doesn't mean that we should be afraid to approach God with our requests. D. L. Moody said it well: "Spread out your petition before God and then say, 'Thy will, not mine, be done . . .'"

It is easier to ask in the context of His will when we have spent time telling Him how grateful we are for the goodness of His character and the pleasure of His loving grace.

Pray through the ACTS plan. Make it a habit!

A TEMPLE FIT FOR A KING

FLEE FROM SEXUAL IMMORALITY. . . . DO YOU NOT KNOW THAT YOUR BODY IS A TEMPLE OF THE HOLY SPIRIT? . . . THEREFORE HONOR GOD WITH YOUR BODY.

—1 Corinthians 6:18–20

*L*iving in a sensual culture places the follower of Christ in tension with an increasingly seductive environment.

From the subtle erosion of moral sensitivities by a constant dose of the "soaps," to advertisements that push the edges of what is acceptable to sell their products, to the blatant availability of pornography, our generation faces a continual barrage that threatens the very definitions of what is right and wrong. For this we are paying dearly in changed attitudes and the destruction of safe and sane moral boundaries.

Even more important, God's Word notes that when our desires are fulfilled through illegitimate means, we defile the temple of God. That's a heavy charge. When the moneychangers defiled the temple in Christ's day, He turned over their tables and, with a whip, expelled them from the temple. God does not take lightly the defilement of His home. In explaining His actions, Jesus said that His house was intended to be a place of prayer, not a place of sordid gain (Matthew 21:13; Mark 11:17; Luke 19:46). Think of the offense to our Lord when our bodies—His home—are used for sinful pleasure.

What, then, shall we do? We must stand as priests at the gates of our temples to guard against the intrusion of moral defilement. It is our responsibility as royal priests to guard the threshold of our eyes, our ears, our minds, our hands, and our total bodies.

Our motive for refusing the defiling input of our world is not simply because someone told us it was bad. We remain pure because we love God enough to guard against anything that would desecrate His dwelling place. My guess is that if we all wore signs that said, "God Lives Here," we would behave differently and would allow far less impurity to seep into His temple.

Is there a guard who is off duty at one of the entrances to the temple of your life?

SUPPORT THE ARMY

ENDURE HARDSHIP WITH US LIKE A GOOD SOLDIER OF CHRIST JESUS.
—2 Timothy 2:3

I am frequently brought face to face with the everyday struggles of missionaries who serve as soldiers for Christ. It takes many of them years just to get to the front lines because the funds they need are not available. Others feel forgotten and neglected during their stint on the field. When they finally come home, they feel that they somehow don't fit.

I also have the privilege of talking heart to heart with pastors who labor here in the homeland. While some feel loved and supported, others speak of the difficulty they face in trying to focus their church's attention on the advance of the gospel. They tell of bickering and petty agendas that turn the congregation inward and end up dividing and sapping its strength. How tragic that our personal preferences and prejudices should drain support and hinder the eternal cause of Jesus Christ!

Those not called to "ministry" also need support. Slugging it out at work and in our homes can be a daunting challenge.

Soldiers of faith desperately need support troops. An unbridled, enthusiastic show of support for one another would be a great source of encouragement.

Let's put away what is petty and temporal and concentrate on what will advance the cause of Christ. If we pledge to pray consistently and specifically for those involved on the front lines, we will provide vital support. If we put our money where we say our hearts are, we will keep the battle lines well supplied, the troops well fed, and the equipment well maintained.

We are all enlisted as soldiers and called to unashamedly advance the gospel of Christ. At the end of life we should be able to say, with Paul, "I have fought the good fight, I have finished the race, I have kept the faith" (2 Timothy 4:7).

Is there a fellow soldier you can encourage today?

HE CALLS YOU "FRIEND"

No Longer Do I Call You Slaves . . . ; but I Have Called You Friends, for All Things That I Have Heard from My Father I Have Made Known to You.

—John 15:15 NASB

J don't remember much about my mom's decorating, but I do remember the plaque that hung on our dining room wall. It read, "Friends are like melons; let me tell you why: to find a good one, you must one hundred try." Which may explain why I often heard my dad say, "Joe, the greatest treasure in life is trusted friends."

You really can't beat a good friend. Friends care for you regardless. They are there when you need them. They laugh with you and cry with you. They cover your faults and affirm your strengths. They share secrets and keep your confidences. Life is enriched when friends are close.

All of which makes it an amazing thought to hear that Jesus considers us His friends. As He taught His disciples, "Greater love has no one than this, that one lay down his life for his friends" (John 15:13). His death proved not only that He loves us, but that He loves us as a friend.

The thought that God treats me as His friend stuns my needy heart. To think that He "walks with me, and He talks with me, and He tells me I am His own" gets me through a lot of rough water. That He never leaves me and doesn't forsake me secures my anxious soul (Hebrews 13:5–6). That He has experienced every pain and therefore feels my pain comforts me in distress. That He freely supplies abundant grace and mercy in my time of need fills my staggering spirit with fresh resolve (Hebrews 4:14–16).

What a privilege to sing, "There's not a friend like the lowly Jesus. No not one! No not one! None else could heal all our soul's diseases, No not one! no not one! Jesus knows all about our struggles, He will guide till the day is done; there's not a friend like the lowly Jesus. No not one! No not one!"

What a friend we have in Jesus!

Bask in the blessing of His friendship.

PSALM 3

O LORD, I have so many enemies;
so many are against me.
So many are saying,
"God will never rescue him!"
But you, O LORD, are a shield around me,
my glory, and the one who lifts my head high.
I cried out to the LORD,
and he answered me from his holy mountain.
I lay down and slept.
I woke up in safety,
for the LORD was watching over me.
I am not afraid of ten thousand enemies
who surround me on every side.
Arise, O LORD!
Rescue me, my God!
Slap all my enemies in the face!
Shatter the teeth of the wicked!
Victory comes from you, O LORD.
May your blessings rest on your people.

REVERSING THE FLOW

"Blessed Are Those Who Hunger and Thirst for Righteousness, for They Will Be Filled."

—Matthew 5:6

*E*ngineers got the idea that if they could reverse the flow of the Chicago River, the power and resources of Lake Michigan would flow into it. The water from the depths of the great lake would be fresh and clean, and the flow from the greater to the lesser body of water would be a source of long-term satisfaction and strength to the city.

The engineers did just that. They reversed the flow of the Chicago River so that today it is the only river in all of the Great Lakes system that receives its water from the lake. Because of this, the river is clean, strong, and never lacking for a source—unlike tributaries that draw their water from lesser and often unreliable sources, such as rainfall, snow melt, and underground springs.

Unfortunately, some of us are like the Chicago River before its flow was reversed. We have never permitted God's Spirit to restructure our passions nor allowed ourselves to draw our satisfaction from Him and His clean resources. As a result, our passions draw their fulfillment from the world around us, and all we have to contribute is the debris and pollution we have accumulated. Sadly, a bird's-eye view of Christianity looks like that at times, with the pollutants of misplaced passions spilling into the sacred seas of church, home, and friendship.

To reverse the flow means that we need to restructure our longings. We must realize that we have cultivated a longing for lesser, sometimes-impure things. Then, we must repent and turn our hearts toward God and seek to be satisfied in Him and in all that He so wonderfully provides for us. When we do, our hearts sing with the psalmist, "As the deer pants for streams of water, so my soul pants for you, O God. My soul thirsts for God, for the living God. When can I go and meet with God?" (Psalm 42:1–2). Having our deep thirst for God fully satisfied in Him should be the goal of our lives.

What is the source of your satisfaction in life? Is it lesser things or the Living God?

STRONG SPIRITUAL WEAPONS

For Our Struggle Is . . . Against the Spiritual Forces of Evil in the Heavenly Realms.

—Ephesians 6:12

*P*aul states: "Finally, be strong in the Lord and in his mighty power. Put on the full armor of God so that you can take your stand against the devil's schemes" (Ephesians 6:10–11). "Watch out!" is Paul's way of getting our attention. This is no time to relax. He calls us to stand firm and be on guard.

His words are not meant to traumatize our hearts. Instead, they are meant as a wake-up call to our souls.

We all have the tendency to slide into a comfortable Christianity. We attend worship services, participate in ministry activities, interact with fellow Christians, and enjoy the smooth, sometimes predictable, ride. Paul warns us not to get too comfortable. When we least suspect trouble, we can be a target. Our sense of security is only an illusion. We dare not coast through this world in a mirage of safety and happiness. We are involved in a battle.

So what is the answer? Must we live in fear? No. We are to ground ourselves in prayer and in His Word. We must put on the full spiritual armor He has given us (Ephesians 6:10–20).

Our struggle is against the devastating terror of the unseen systems of evil under Satan's control. We must train ourselves to be on guard and alert and to stand firm in the mighty power of the Lord. "You, dear children, are from God and have overcome them, because the one who is in you is greater than the one who is in the world" (1 John 4:4).

Alert. Prayerful. Standing. Declaring. Fearless—but only with the knowledge that the advantage of the all-powerful God is on our side. We have been given mighty weapons to extinguish all of Satan's wicked schemes. In the end, we must use them to be victorious.

Are you living in comfortable Christianity? How might you improve your soldiering skills?

CLEANING AWAY THE CLUTTER

BLOT OUT ALL MY INIQUITIES. CREATE IN ME A CLEAN HEART, O GOD, AND RENEW A STEADFAST SPIRIT WITHIN ME.

—Psalm 51:9–10 NASB

A great cartoon shows a chubby, forlorn figure in a bathrobe and shower cap standing on a bathroom scale. Dejectedly he says, "My body is not my temple; it's my garage." When I saw that cartoon, I immediately thought about my actual garage. It's the place where we put everything for which we have no place. Before long, the clutter is unbelievable. Frankly, there have been times when I have been ashamed to open my garage door. My neighbor fastidiously keeps his garage in order. Our garage doors face each other, compounding my guilt. Sick of the clutter, I sometimes dedicate a Saturday to cleaning it up. By the end of the day, the clutter is gone. I feel so good I would like to leave the garage door open for a week to let everyone see how the Stowells keep their property!

I wonder if God sometimes feels as if He's living in our messy garage when it comes to our hearts and minds. We accumulate a lot of clutter, and we think we can hide it by covering it up with an attractive exterior. But eventually it shows. Garbage in; garbage out. Because our bodies are temples of the Holy Spirit, we cannot wink at an untidy dwelling place. Take a spiritual workday and discard the thoughts of bitterness. Bag and throw away the old patterns of sexual fantasy. Put memories in their proper place. Organize attitudes. Fill your heart with the virtues found in God's Word. Make your spiritual residence clean to the core. Live so that you can leave the door open for all to see.

In fact, figuratively speaking, it might be good to place a sign around our neck that says in big letters, "God Lives Here." I think we would think, act, and react in a new light if that sign were visible for all to see. Can you imagine cultivating an affair while wearing a sign like that? Or attacking someone verbally? Instead, people might see a little more of what Christ really looks like.

What is cluttering your life?

FREE AT LAST

"THEN YOU WILL KNOW THE TRUTH, AND THE TRUTH WILL SET YOU FREE."
—John 8:32

*I*t's not that freedom is so wrong. Scripture validates the pursuit of freedom. Yet it directs that pursuit in a surprisingly different way. As Christ says, true freedom begins with restrictions.

We find this surprising definition of freedom in John 8:31–32, where Jesus says, "If you hold to my teaching, you are really my disciples. Then you will know the truth, and the truth will set you free." Notice the sequence. True freedom is not doing whatever I wish. Freedom is the result of my actualizing Christ's teaching, of restricting my life to that which is right and true.

Restricting my life to that which is true sets me free from the inevitable bondage of addictive and destructive behavior and allows me to know unhindered joy, a clear conscience, growing relationships, and life at its fullest. When I limit myself to honest, biblical business deals, I am free to enjoy a clear conscience without the haunting fear of getting caught at something unethical. When I resist the temptation to do whatever I want and limit myself to meeting my wife's needs and bringing happiness to her, I set our relationship free for growth, intimacy, and long-lasting reward.

Freedom is a result of hard, unflinching commitments to the time-tested ways of the wisdom of God. Freedom is not a right with which we are born. It is a God-given privilege realized only as a result of righteous living. It comes the old-fashioned way—we earn it with an undaunted commitment to truth.

You've probably noticed that our world's pursuit of personal freedom without restrictions has gotten us into a lot of trouble. Broken families, empty lives, crime, and self-destructive addictions are the hefty price we are paying for spending our freedom any way we wish.

"If the Son sets you free, you will be free indeed" (John 8:36).

What "truth" instructions liberate your life?

STRETCHING THE TRUTH

MAY THE WORDS OF MY MOUTH AND THE MEDITATION OF MY HEART BE
PLEASING IN YOUR SIGHT, O LORD, MY ROCK AND MY REDEEMER.
—Psalm 19:14

*H*ave you ever exaggerated to manipulate someone into doing what you wanted them to do? Or have you ever exaggerated to vent your anger? Anger often expresses itself in exaggerated statements to intimidate or humble those we are angry with. I get a chuckle out of King Nebuchadnezzar, who, in his great anger against Shadrach, Meshach, and Abednego, commanded that the furnace be turned up seven times hotter than usual (Daniel 3:19). The fire would have been sufficient just the way it was, but in his anger Nebuchadnezzar had an exaggerated response.

Sometimes we exaggerate to feel better about ourselves and to help others feel better about us as well. The fisherman whose largemouth bass was *just* three pounds ends up telling people that it was *at least* three pounds. The businessman who makes $50,000 a year tells his friend that he's making "something under $100,000 a year." Salesmen face a special temptation in this area. How easy it is to exaggerate the claims of a product to close a sale.

I worked for a carpenter one summer. Occasionally, I cut a board too short. He would say, "Get the wood stretcher." His point was that wood doesn't stretch. Neither does the truth. Some of us want to make Silly Putty out of the truth by stretching it to our own advantage. The problem is that stretching the truth destroys it.

Exaggeration erodes trust and credibility, two building blocks of successful relationships. It is a violation of God's will for us. Yielding our egos to be used to serve God and others instead of our own interests will produce words that help and heal. Then with the psalmist we can say, "May the words of my mouth and the meditation of my heart be pleasing in your sight, O LORD, my Rock and my Redeemer" (Psalm 19:14).

Tell it as it is, not as you want it to be.

GOD'S RICH LOVE

WHOEVER DOES NOT LOVE DOES NOT KNOW GOD, BECAUSE GOD IS LOVE.
—1 John 4:8

You couldn't have asked for a better place to live or for a more perfect spouse. In fact, in this place, intimacy with others and God was deep and pleasurable. It was Eden. A garden where God's best was provided for the lives of Adam and Eve.

Yet, even there, sin and selfishness rose to interrupt the experience.

In the midst of a loss of intimacy and the arrival of aloneness, it is significant to note that God took the initiative toward Adam and Eve and walked back into the Garden of Eden after the Fall. If we didn't know the story and tried to imagine what might happen next, we might have imagined God's exercising a host of options. He could have annihilated everything and started over again. He could have ignored Adam and Eve and let them live with the consequences of rejecting Him, allowing their new scheme of existence to run its degenerative course. Or He could do the unexpected. He could restore the relationship they had so carelessly given up. He could call them back to Himself and to a consistent moral order that would again make possible intimacy with Him and the development of trusted relationships.

And that is just what He did. It is all the more surprising when we realize that God is the only entity in the universe that can be alone and still be fully satisfied and sustained. It may come as a blow to us that God does not need us! But the beauty of it is that, though He can go for eternity without us, He chooses to love us and care for us, which makes His love and concern for us richer still. He doesn't love us for what it will do for Him. Too many of us have been wounded by that kind of love. He loves us because He is love itself and because He created us for the pleasure of our fellowship and the ultimate glory of His name. It was that kind of love and compassion that drove Him to seek to reconnect Adam and Eve to Himself. He offers the same privilege to us today.

Have you accepted God's invitation to intimate fellowship?

PSALM 4

Answer me when I call,
O God who declares me innocent.
Take away my distress.
Have mercy on me and hear my prayer.
How long will you people ruin my reputation?
How long will you make these groundless accusations?
How long will you pursue lies?
You can be sure of this:
The LORD has set apart the godly for himself.
The LORD will answer when I call to him.
Don't sin by letting anger gain control over you.
Think about it overnight and remain silent.
Offer proper sacrifices,
and trust in the LORD.
Many people say, "Who will show us better times?"
Let the smile of your face shine on us, LORD.
You have given me greater joy
than those who have abundant harvests of grain and wine.
I will lie down in peace and sleep,
for you alone, O LORD, will keep me safe.

CHOICES

APPROVE THE THINGS THAT ARE EXCELLENT.

—Philippians 1:10 NKJV, NASB

*O*ne of the most profound pieces of advice I ever received came from a friend who said, "Our lives are not made by the dreams we dream but by the choices we make." It's true. Much of your life today is the sum total of all the choices you have made. So I'm not surprised that God is interested in choices when He directs us to "approve the things that are excellent" (Philippians 1:10 NKJV, NASB).

Granted, restricting our lives to excellent choices can be challenging. We may have to go it alone. We may have to yield comfort, cash, or convenience. But the gain is worth it.

According to Paul, excellent choices render us "sincere and blameless until the day of Christ; having been filled with the fruit of righteousness which comes through Jesus Christ, to the glory and praise of God" (Philippians 1:10–11 NASB). This text delineates three advantages of a life committed to the best choices.

Excellence brings purity. There is nothing better in life than the pleasure of a blameless, clear conscience. Of not having to look over your shoulder to see if someone saw or heard what you did. Excellent choices set us free from the haunting shadow that "I might get caught."

Excellence brings productivity. Think of a life that produces the righteous fruit of the Spirit—love, joy, peace, patience—over the long haul (Galatians 5:22). Think of having a friend like that. Of being married to someone like that. Of being that to others!

Excellence brings purpose. A life of excellent choices brings glory to God, the very purpose of our redemption (1 Corinthians 6:19–20).

What makes a choice excellent? According to Philippians 1:9, it is a living commitment to love, knowledge, and discernment. Love chooses what is best for others, not what is best for me. Knowledge guides every choice by the clear principles of the Word of God. Discernment produces wise application.

When we do what is best for others according to the direction of God's Word, excellence is the product: excellent dads, moms, children, pastors, employers, employees—excellent people!

Remember, your life is not made by the dreams you dream, but by the choices you make.

Plan an excellent choice today!

SUBSTANTIALLY HEALED

ACCORDING TO MY EARNEST EXPECTATION AND HOPE, THAT . . . CHRIST WILL
. . . BE EXALTED.

—Philippians 1:20 NASB

*T*he late Francis Schaeffer called salvation a "substantial healing." He was talking about the reality that though our redemption is fully accomplished in Christ, it will not be fully appropriated until we arrive in heaven. While redemption cancels the penalty of sin and restores us completely to God, it does not as yet free us from the residual effects of sin. We still get sick, struggle with temptation, and, on occasion, fail.

Cooperating with the Spirit's work in our lives means that we consistently grow toward greater healing.

One of the marks of that healing is the desire to live for His glory and not our own. For the more substantially healed, personal significance is no longer something we search for—it has already been secured for us in Him. Those who have not yet embraced this liberating reality remain vulnerable to a whole litany of sins. Greed, lying, boasting, self-centeredness, sexual immorality, gossip, and a dozen other poisons from the pit can be directly laid at the feet of needing to feel more important.

If you are a child of the King, what more could you want in the way of significance? In Christ we have all the worth, identity, affirmation, prosperity, and power we need. As such, we are free to live to magnify Him instead of ourselves. As Paul declared, "I eagerly expect and hope that I will in no way be ashamed, but will have sufficient courage so that now as always Christ will be exalted in my body, whether by life or by death" (Philippians 1:20). He affirmed that since God has "rescued us from the dominion of darkness and brought us into the kingdom of the Son he loves, in whom we have redemption" (Colossians 1:13–14), we are free to serve and celebrate the truth that Christ is the One who deserves the preeminence.

No one can have it both ways. We either live to platform our own significance or live to exalt His.

Do something today that magnifies Christ through your life. Demonstrate the significance of an aspect of His character—love, justice, mercy, grace, truth—and then give Him the credit.

CELEBRATE THE DIFFERENCE

In Christ . . . Old Things [Are] Passed Away; Behold, New Things Have Come.

—2 Corinthians 5:17 NASB

The French are right when they exclaim, *"Vive la différence!"* When it comes to men and women, it's the difference that makes life so wonderful. The unique perspectives, notions, interests, and energies between the sexes challenge, enrich, and bless. In the same way, God has redeemed us to challenge, enrich, and bless the world with our uniqueness in Christ. Our "substantial healing" initiates dramatic, sometimes radical, transformations that stand in vivid contrast to the well-traveled ways of our world. We have been forgiven that we might forgive, loved that we might love, made ceremonially pure that we might become pure, given grace and mercy that we might dispense the same to others. And when we live out these qualities, there is a powerful difference displayed that intriguingly engages an unforgiving, often loveless, impure, and graceless world.

Unfortunately, through the centuries Satan has been surprisingly successful in diminishing the difference. Followers who lived in Corinth and Laodicea, to name two cities, were heavily censured in the Bible for their loss of uniqueness. When the disciples were posturing for the important positions in the kingdom, Christ told them their problem was that they were acting like the typical Gentile. He went on to remind them that He had come not to elevate Himself but to serve—all the way to the cross. If they were to demonstrate the difference that Jesus imprints on a life, they too would be more interested in serving than ruling (Matthew 20:20–28).

Think for a moment of the power of a life that is impeccably honest in its business dealings, self-sacrificing in its relationships, trustworthy, just, and generous in all its dealings. When we live out the uniqueness of Christ, some may just ask us why we are the way we are. It is then that we get to tell them of the difference that only Jesus can make. . . . *Vive la différence!*

What is it that is different about you? Is it a difference that Christ has made?

FORGIVNESS FULL AND FREE

While He Was Still a Long Way Off, His Father Saw Him and Was Filled with Compassion.

—Luke 15:20

*I*t was a defining moment in the Prodigal's life when he abandoned life on his own terms and determined, "I will get up and go to my father, and will say to him, 'Father, I have sinned against heaven, and in your sight; I am no longer worthy to be called your son'" (Luke 15:18–19 NASB). His life was so wasted that his only hope was in the possibility that his father had not abandoned him. He realized, after exhausting all his resources, that what he really needed was a restored relationship. If he didn't have the relationship, he had nothing.

Not quite sure how his father would respond, he left the self-inflicted mire of his life and, with his stomach in a knot and his heart racing, he headed home. Each step closer on what was now becoming a familiar road found his anxiety rising. And with good cause. This boy had deeply offended his father. No Jewish dad would be likely to quickly forgive the embarrassment and squandering of the family assets that he had so wantonly imposed on his family.

But it was wasted anxiety. Jesus notes, "While he was still a long way off, his father saw him and felt compassion for him, and ran and embraced him and kissed him" (v. 20 NASB).

Did his father just happen to notice him a long way off? Or was he keeping a vigil? Had he been keeping his eyes on the horizon, waiting and hoping for the day his wayward son would find his way home? I think so. The son was the object of the forgiving father's love. Shocked, he fell before his dad, stunned by his father's grace and mercy. There was no probation. No lecture. Just a celebration.

So it is for us. Jesus meant this to be a picture of our heavenly Father. The very second we too get up from where we are and repentantly embrace Him as our only hope, He is there. Ready. Waiting.

He's not surprised by your sin . . . He already felt it all on the cross where forgiveness was assured!

CHRIST OR CREDENTIALS

IF ANYONE . . . THINKS HE HAS REASON TO PUT CONFIDENCE IN THE FLESH,
I HAVE MORE.

—Philippians 3:4

*W*hen life has been good to us, it is easy to get lost in the glory of our own accomplishments. There is something magnetic about the line, "If you've got it, flaunt it!" Yet boasting of ourselves is not only seen by God as pride and an affront to His glory through us, but it also inhibits our ability to enjoy intimacy with Jesus.

Listen to Paul rattle off his credentials, which in the crowd he ran with would solicit "wow's" from everyone. "If anyone else thinks he has reason to put confidence in the flesh, I have more: circumcised on the eighth day, of the people of Israel, of the tribe of Benjamin, a Hebrew of Hebrews; in regard to the law, a Pharisee; as for zeal, persecuting the church; as for legalistic righteousness, faultless" (Philippians 3:4–6).

But his choice is clear: "But whatever was to my profit I now consider loss for the sake of Christ. . . . I consider them rubbish, that I may gain Christ and be found in him. . . . I want to know Christ and the power of his resurrection and the fellowship of sharing in his sufferings" (vv. 7–10).

Paul was well aware of the radical choice He would have to make if he were to fully experience the presence and power of Jesus in His life. For Him the decision was clear—he chose Jesus. Granted, he had an edge in that he had literally been in the presence of Jesus at least twice. I doubt that any of us would be interested in a self-absorbed life if we had literally met Him face to face! Fast-food hamburgers lose some of their glow after you have had a killer steak! If we could understand the glory of His greatness our boasting would be our shame and our self-enhancing pursuits would seem embarrassingly trivial.

What makes Paul's decision so instructive is that He had an awful lot to feel good about in terms of glorying in himself. When one who has so much chooses Jesus, it makes a great statement.

It's unsettling to think of losing the bragging rights you deserve. But, then, the Jesus who welcomes us to lose ourselves in Him assures us, "He who loses His life for my sake shall gain it, but he who keeps his life shall lose it."

Losing my life to gain it . . . what an interesting thought.

THE TOUGH TASK

Let This Mind Be in You, Which Was Also in Christ Jesus.

—Philippians 2:5 KJV

*O*ne of the major problems with the pursuit of "stuff" is that the goods that we gain or are hoping to gain often eclipse the value of people in our lives. Our love for people is challenged by our love of things. Though it is sheer deceit, we have come to believe that true happiness, prestige, joy, and fulfillment are the direct result of personal gain. The end result is that things become more significant to us than people. Opportunities to gain things drive us to work longer, which then takes us away from our families, churches, and meaningful time with others. If we see people as a means to the end of gaining more things, we will use people, deceive them, and misrepresent them—all to get and gain.

Of course, putting people in their proper place is not always the most pleasant pursuit. Let's face it; it's easier to manage material goods and the people who work for us than the people for whom we are most responsible. Kids are snotty and often out of sorts. Spouses don't always live up to our expectations and complicate our lives with their expectations. Friends disappoint us, and that guy who doesn't deserve it just got the promotion I deserved. Still others are manipulators, intimidators, or guilt-inducers. We hesitate to get too close lest we get caught in their web.

But, in the face of all of this, Christ still calls us to reach out to others. He is not unaware of the difficulty of the task. He came and loved when it meant great sacrifice to Himself, when it required Him to minister to a world that would rarely reach back and minister to Him—a world that would use Him, misunderstand Him, malign Him, and crucify Him; a fickle world that loved Him and left Him. His example helps us cut through the challenges of our own self-interest and leads us to the toughest, yet most rewarding, of all endeavors . . . the love of our neighbor.

Where do people rank on the list of what is really most important to you?

PSALM 5:1–8, 11, 12

O LORD, hear me as I pray;
pay attention to my groaning.
Listen to my cry for help, my King and my God,
for I will never pray to anyone but you.
Listen to my voice in the morning, LORD.
Each morning I bring my requests to you and wait expectantly.
O God, you take no pleasure in wickedness;
you cannot tolerate the slightest sin.
Therefore, the proud will not be allowed to stand in your presence,
for you hate all who do evil.
You will destroy those who tell lies.
The LORD detests murderers and deceivers.
Because of your unfailing love, I can enter your house;
with deepest awe I will worship at your Temple.
Lead me in the right path, O LORD,
or my enemies will conquer me.
Tell me clearly what to do,
and show me which way to turn.
But let all who take refuge in you rejoice;
let them sing joyful praises forever.
Protect them,
so all who love your name may be filled with joy.
For you bless the godly, O LORD,
surrounding them with your shield of love.

MORE OF ME OR THEE?

BECOME MATURE, ATTAINING TO THE WHOLE MEASURE OF THE FULLNESS OF CHRIST.

—Ephesians 4:13

*W*e all know that spiritual maturity is measured by the extent to which our lives reflect Christ. Yet totally abandoning ourselves to allow Him to emerge through us can, at times, feel threatening. After all, He takes control over who we are and what we want to be. And, to be honest, there are times that we don't want to be totally like Him. After all, He was so demurring, soft, and merciful.

Perhaps we have forgotten that, as the perfect God-man, He was the ideal expression of life as it ought to be. Although He had a compassionate side, He displayed strength and power in balance. He knew how to be tough on charlatans and hypocrites and gentle to those in need. He was strong enough to attract as followers tough fishermen, despised tax collectors, cynics, and members of the underground militia. He was so compelling that people gave up their careers and personal ambitions to follow Him. And, we should add, He was the kind of man with whom women felt safe.

Jesus Christ does not compromise our personhood. When we submit to Him, He emerges through the distinct qualities of our uniquely created selves to create a fuller and richer expression of what a truly good person ought to be. He redefines us by replacing greed with generosity, revenge with forgiveness, self-centeredness with servanthood, and polluted hearts and minds with purity. He takes our instincts to protect, nurture, provide, conquer, and accumulate and helps us point them in productive directions away from ourselves and toward others and the kingdom of heaven.

The apostle Paul wrote, "It is God who works in you to will and to act according to his good purpose" (Philippians 2:13). And, I might add, it is the goal of redemption that we become "conformed to the image of His Son" (Romans 8:29 NASB).

Is there more of Christ or more of "me" in your personality profile?

BELIEVING THE LIE

"HE IS A LIAR AND THE FATHER OF LIES."

—John 8:44

*K*nowing all that we know now, one wonders why Eve ever did what she did in the first place. At the moment that she ate the fruit, all seemed so right, so good . . . and her God seemed so bad.

But if the truth were known, at the time Eve abandoned God for the supposed benefits of her world, nothing about God had changed. All that had changed was her interpretation of the facts she had previously believed. She now saw the generous God, who had given her and Adam everything in the Garden but *one* tree, as stingy and restrictive, keeping her from something she desired. Worse, He was holding her back, oppressively preventing her from sharing in His great knowledge and power (Gen. 3:1–6).

Once we begin to suspect God instead of respecting and honoring Him, we have begun the trek away from Him. Life is full of scenarios where Satan can steal our affection for God by putting his deceitful twist on our experiences. We must remember that he is the spin doctor of hell and—as Christ said—the father of lies. Satan wants to steal our affection from God by using distorted thoughts like these:

- Blaming God for the evil Satan has inspired and superimposed on our lives
- Defining God as a God who has been good to others but not good to us
- Making us feel that we have been good, but God has used us and not rewarded us, leaving our righteousness an empty sacrifice
- Blinding us to the fact that God can take the worst things in our lives and orchestrate them for good and gain
- Convincing us that God's ways and His will for us are unduly restrictive and oppressive

Interestingly, persuaded by Satan that God was less than good and not to be trusted, Eve took life into her own hands and ate the fruit—only to find that Satan slithered off, leaving her inexorably damaged by sin, alone, alienated from her God, and ashamed.

It's important to know whom you can trust and whom you can't.

Have you been harboring such thoughts toward God? Confess them and start again.

IN GOD WE TRUST

But His Delight Is in the Law of the Lord, and on His Law He Meditates Day and Night.

—Psalm 1:2

*A*cross from the Bolshoi Theater in Moscow stands an imposing granite column with a bust of Karl Marx mounted on top. Below the monument is a quotation from Lenin, who said of Marx, "His words will last forever because his words are true." For seventy years, persecuted Christians in the USSR were no doubt tempted to believe that perhaps Marx's words had trumped the power of the Word of God. Yet, in less than a century, his words were discredited by history. What an ironic reminder that the only truth that lasts forever is God's truth.

I am reminded of the psalmist's words: "Why do the nations conspire and the peoples plot in vain? The kings of the earth take their stand and the rulers gather together against the LORD and against his Anointed One" (Psalm 2:1–2). God's response? "The One enthroned in heaven laughs; the Lord scoffs at them" (v. 4).

Throughout history, godless people, movements, and nations have had their day in the sun. We have wondered why their power and pride have prevailed. Yet, in the long view, God and His truth are the only realities that stand the test and turmoil of time. Just ask the oppressed followers of Christ who endured faithfully the *temporary* tyranny of godless Marxism.

The reality is that evil does prosper, but only for a season. Our lives are oftentimes victimized by manipulative and abusive people around us who have climbed to pinnacles of power and prestige. Yet, ultimately, their demise is sure.

Those who live righteously and uncompromisingly advance God's truth and His kingdom will find that when the smoke finally clears, God's Word prevails.

So, while evil will have its day in the sun, it is far more important for us to place our lives and trust in God's Son, whom to know is life eternal (John 17:3).

Few things are of lasting value in this brief existence called life. The only things that lend value and worth to life are those that ultimately endure: life and truth in Jesus Christ.

Choose a "word" from God to cling to today.

HE KNOWS

I Know Your Tribulation and Your Poverty. . . . Do Not Fear What You Are About to Suffer.

—Revelation 2:9–10 NASB

After the evening service at a conference where I was speaking, a couple approached me and asked if we could talk privately. As we went into a side room, it was obvious that they had something deep on their hearts. They told me about their son who was a senior in high school. He loved the Lord and was a leader in their church youth group as well as holding leadership positions at school. They wept as they went on to say that he had been killed two weekends before in a head-on collision. It was one of those times when it seems like there aren't any words in our dictionary to express the grief or to console a broken heart. As I searched for ways to help them see it from God's point of view the boy's mother said, "Our pastor told us that God didn't know this was going to happen and that God was just as surprised as we were that our son had lost his life."

I was shocked. If you want to comfort grieving hearts, that's not where you start. While it may be a valiant attempt to excuse God for not preventing the tragedy, this kind of poor theology leaves us as victims of the careless winds of fate. Thankfully, nothing could be further from the truth. God did know. As Oswald Chambers wrote, "The circumstances of a saint's life are ordained of God. In the life of a saint there is no such thing as chance."

He is all-knowing, and nothing escapes His perception or permission. And although we don't always understand why He permits pain, we do know that we can trust in His character. He is a good, loving, and wise God, and He cannot be unfaithful to Himself.

Take comfort in knowing that God knows; that He is never distracted; that nothing escapes His attention. Thankfully, there is no need for contingency plans in heaven. Working all things together for good is not an insurmountable problem for Him.

He knows! Sometimes that is all we need to know.

TOO GOOD TO CARE

"The Son of Man Came to Seek and to Save What Was Lost."
—Luke 19:10

*I*n Luke 19 we learn that it's possible for really good people—like us—to perform poorly when it comes to compassion for those we consider the "bad" people in our world. The good guys in Matthew 18, the Pharisees, were distraught that Jesus Christ cared for the very people they saw as the enemies of Judaism, the people who shamelessly contradicted all that the Jewish leaders held to be of value and worth. So they grumbled among themselves that Jesus, who claimed to be God, was often found hanging out with what the religious leaders thought was the wrong crowd.

The Pharisees had what I call a "good guys, bad guys" theology. Since God is a holy, perfect, and good God, surely His favor must rest on those who are "good" and not deserving of His judgment. As for those who are "bad," and deserving of judgment, the only thing a righteous God would extend to them would be disfavor and condemnation. That's precisely why Jesus Christ was such an enigma to the Pharisees. How could someone who claimed to be God spend time with prostitutes, tax collectors, and other despised elements of Jewish society? If He were really God, wouldn't He spend His time with the "good guys" and proclaim condemnation on the "bad guys"? The Pharisees were right about God's holiness and justice, yet they failed to see that this holy God was also a God of mercy, grace, patience, forbearance, and love.

If we are not careful, even if our theology is orthodox to the core, it can become distorted and misapplied. When that happens, life and compassion get distorted as well. If doctrines such as the sovereignty of God and election are not held in clear biblical balance, our hearts can easily cool toward the lost and the distraught. Sinners will become His responsibility and not ours. We will grow long on mad and short on mercy and the attitude of grace will be supplanted by grumbling about the wayward sinners of our world.

No one was ever more orthodox than Christ. Yet no one has ever had a longer reach of compassion.

How far does your compassion extend?

TRUE COMPASSION

AND SEEING THE MULTITUDES, HE FELT COMPASSION FOR THEM, BECAUSE THEY WERE DISTRESSED AND DOWNCAST LIKE SHEEP WITHOUT A SHEPHERD.
—Matthew 9:36 NASB 1977

*S*everal words are used in Scripture to translate our English word *compassion*. Their meanings in both Hebrew and Greek are highly instructive.

Two basic words are used in the Old Testament, one of which means "to bear, to become responsible for, to spare someone from trouble." This Hebrew word deals mainly with our actions. The second Hebrew term is more attitudinal. It means "to be soft, gentle." It is sometimes translated "womb" and also means to "be wide" in encompassing others and their needs.

The leading word for compassion in the New Testament means "that emotion aroused by contact with affliction." It is the Greek word used to translate the Old Testament concept of God's loyal, unfailing covenant love. The stress in this particular word is on the action that flows out of our being as we are touched by another's affliction. In fact, the difference between sympathy and biblical compassion is that biblical compassion—true compassion—always leads to action. Compassion is not measured by how we feel but by what we do in response to how we feel.

We might define compassion as our commitment to activate ourselves as channels of God's love, mercy, and grace in tender, thoughtful, understanding acts of help, deliverance, forgiveness, and restoration toward those in need. Compassion really is God's love, mercy, and grace looking for a place to get busy. Compassion asks, "What can I do to help?"

God's compassion offers help to all who are in need. He is not like those who withhold a healing, helping hand behind the excuse of their own interests. It looks at life from the point of view of those who are hurting and refuses to callously walk away, casting blame and guilt on the broken. His compassion never takes sin lightly or discounts His sense of justice. But it never forgets that mercy and grace are gifts of love that offer help and hope before judgment.

I am struck that some of us who have so wonderfully received His compassion are so seemingly uninterested in passing it on to others.

What compassion have you received from Him? What act of compassion could you share?

PSALM 6

O LORD, do not rebuke me in your anger
or discipline me in your rage.
Have compassion on me, LORD, for I am weak.
Heal me, LORD, for my body is in agony.
I am sick at heart.
How long, O LORD, until you restore me?
Return, O LORD, and rescue me.
Save me because of your unfailing love.
For in death, who remembers you?
Who can praise you from the grave?
I am worn out from sobbing.
Every night tears drench my bed;
my pillow is wet from weeping.
My vision is blurred by grief;
my eyes are worn out because of all my enemies.
Go away, all you who do evil,
for the LORD has heard my crying.
The LORD has heard my plea;
the LORD will answer my prayer.
May all my enemies be disgraced and terrified.
May they suddenly turn back in shame.

OUR ULTIMATE PROVIDER

AND MY GOD WILL SUPPLY ALL YOUR NEEDS.
—Philippians 4:19 NASB

When I went into my first pastorate, the small group of believers in the church made a great financial commitment to insure that I could be involved in the ministry full-time. It was a big step of faith for them. What they didn't know was that it meant a 33 percent cut in income for my family. Those were the manna years of our living. Our whole family learned that all we are and have is from God.

I recall coming home from the office one evening and finding on the dining room table a large box addressed to me. It was from a lady in the church where I grew up whom I hadn't seen in years. I eargerly opened the box to find three suits in it. They had belonged to her son, a businessman in Arizona. All three were in perfect condition. They were exactly the styles I liked, and they fit perfectly. No alterations needed!

During those manna years, God clothed our daughter with beautiful, hardly worn hand-me-downs from a family we had met only once. He answered prayer about tires for our car; He kept old cars nearly maintenance free; and He surprised us with unexpected income just when we needed it. In fact, my wife and I used to joke that if a little extra money came in, it was God's advance warning that the washer was going to break down.

Our recognition of God as ultimate provider becomes the joy of a confident heart even in the worst of times. And His provision is not only in material ways. He gives grace to survive, protection to preserve, and wisdom to get us through. In fact the provision of the "daily bread" of our lives is only a reflection of the indispensable provision of His care and love for us. The confidence of living for and serving a generous God translates into the freedom of aggressively becoming all that we can possibly be to the praise and honor of His name without the distraction of accumulating gain for ourselves.

Thank God for making you dependent on Him. He always gives more than He takes!

THE BEGINNING OF THE END?

"I AM MAKING EVERYTHING NEW!"
—Revelation 21:5

*E*ven the most casual observer notices that the more sophisticated and technically advanced our society becomes, the more decadence and despair are evident. Increasingly, I meet followers of Christ who live on the edge of depression about the degenerate forces of society in politics, music, pop culture, and even the church. What we have forgotten is that Jesus warned that we would have trouble in this world . . . but quickly reminded us that He had overcome this world (John 16:33). And that in His time He would create a new world order to replace this sin-seduced planet.

I am not one to jump on faddish bandwagons of speculation, nor am I a date-setter, but I am noticing more than ever that many events begin to come into sync with the return of Christ. History, it seems, has pressed the fast-forward button.

I always wondered how the Antichrist would be able to unify the East and the West. But it's happening—miraculously, as the polarization between long-standing enemies is dissolving economically and politically.

Another indicator of the approaching return of Christ is the rise of supernatural activities. More blatantly than ever, satanism and witchcraft are openly practiced. We should expect the forces of hell to unleash their most blatant attacks when their doom seems imminent. Cultures are descending into decadence as the unrestrained influences of our Western ways infect the world.

The increase of natural disasters may be significant as well. The prophets predicted an increase of such phenomena at the end of the age.

Ultimately, what does this mean for us—fear and despair? No. Christ predicted that the day is coming when He will eternally dwell with us. In that day He will "wipe every tear from their eyes. There will be no more death or mourning or crying or pain, for the old order of things has passed away. . . . I am making everything new!" (Revelation 21:3–5).

Could it be that those words will soon be more than a promise? I certainly hope so. Never before has it looked so much like the end, and never before so much like the marvelous beginning.

Live in this hope!

STABILITY IN THE ROCK

"WHY ARE YOU DOWNCAST, O MY SOUL? WHY SO DISTURBED WITHIN ME?
PUT YOUR HOPE IN GOD, FOR I WILL YET PRAISE HIM, MY SAVIOR AND MY
GOD."

—Psalm 42:5

*H*ope is really a matter of focus. If we focus our attention on the world, its unsettled conditions will have a traumatizing effect on us. If, however, we focus on the Lord and His character, Word, presence, power, and sovereign intentions, there will be hope for the stability we need in this rough-and-tumble world. But, let's face it, most of us are more prone to fret and stew about our world than we are to trust God in the midst of our world. Better yet, some of us are bound and determined to try to change the world.

For those of you who wish to change the world, let me help you. Changing *the* world begins with a willingness to change the only world you can really change—*your* world. As we apply the principles of God's Word to the areas we can change—our values, our attitudes, our families, and our relationships— we bring hope and confidence to our own lives and build a platform from which we begin to influence others for constructive change.

The solid stability of truth uncompromisingly applied to our lives will become evident as people see the light from our lives shining through the darkness of the day. They will inevitably be drawn from their deepening despair to a clear alternative—a hope for God's grace in their own lives. Jesus taught, "Let your light shine before men, that they may see your good deeds and praise your Father in heaven" (Matthew 5:16).

What the world needs is something to hope in. Not the hope that simply wishes something could be true, but a hope based confidently on the reality of a God who is certain and true regardless of the turmoil in our own souls and in the world around us.

As the fabric of the world continues to unravel, our stability must be anchored in the One who does not move: Jesus Christ, the solid rock.

What ray of hope could you bring to your world from the light of your life, Jesus Christ?

THE JOY OF SURRENDER

FLEE THE EVIL DESIRES OF YOUTH, AND PURSUE RIGHTEOUSNESS, FAITH,
LOVE AND PEACE, ALONG WITH THOSE WHO CALL ON THE LORD OUT OF A
PURE HEART.

—2 Timothy 2:22

*G*od has always been interested in knowing what priority He holds in our lives. What we do with our time, money, sensual appetites, friends, family, church involvement, and thought patterns is an expression of whether or not He counts "where the rubber meets the road."

Why would anyone reject the onslaught of youthful lusts? Why would we forgive our enemies, submit to the needs of brothers and sisters in Christ, love our wives, cooperate with our husbands, nurture our children, guard our minds, and pursue holiness . . . if it weren't for Him?

Our Christianity will either be a list of dos and don'ts or a surrender of hearts that are rightly related to Christ. Glad surrender of the heart keeps the fire of righteousness ablaze in our lives. When life is about Him, our actions and reactions are no longer dependent on circumstances, enforcers, peer pressure, or emotions. We love our wives not because they always deserve it, or even because we always feel like it, but because our hearts are set on surrender to Him. We forgive others regardless of the offense, because our hearts are set to love God by forgiving them. We use our money as an expression of our love for Him and His kingdom work. All we do, we do for Him. Nothing else matters. Loving Jesus is the purest and strongest motivation for righteousness.

It makes sense to hear Christ say that surrender to God is the ultimate priority in our relationship to Him. If we love Him, we will surrender to Him. And when our hearts are surrendered to Him, we will do what He bids us to do. This principle has a multiplicity of applications. In fact, it can serve as a first question in discerning right from wrong. When faced with a decision in life, we must begin by asking, What would it mean to lovingly surrender to God at this time? The answer to that question puts righteousness into action.

Is your heart surrendered? How would the people closest to you know?

THE MENACE OF MORE

But If We Have Food and Clothing, We Will Be Content with That.
—1 Timothy 6:8

J recently picked up a paper and read about the marketing of a new cigarette from the R. J. Reynolds Company. "Dakota" is intended to appeal to young "virile females" who like to run with their boyfriends and do what the guys are doing.

The tobacco industry knows that smoking is addictive and deadly. Yet when their research shows that these young women are especially prone to start smoking, they are like predators targeting their prey for the benefit of their profit margin.

This is only one example of our greed-driven culture. Yet in honesty we must admit that the same tendencies often display themselves among those of us who claim to belong to another kingdom.

Think of how often our greed robs from eternity. We spend so much of our time and money accumulating the things that "moth and rust destroy" (Matthew 6:19) that we have few resources and little time left to invest in that which lasts forever. Think of how greed tarnishes the testimony of Christ when we compromise integrity and biblical values to cut a less-than-honorable deal. Or of how greed shreds families when parents devote their best energies to dreams of an extra car, a nicer home, or a better vacation—leaving little strength for rearing children in "the training and instruction of the Lord" (Ephesians 6:4).

Greed contradicts love. It has no regard for values. It gobbles up all that is ultimately precious in life. No wonder Christ told us, "Watch out! Be on your guard against all kinds of greed; a man's life does not consist in the abundance of his possessions" (Luke 12:15).

It's not easy to find contentment in a world in the grip of greed. But we can start by remembering how much we already possess in Christ, whom to have is life abundant. With that truth firmly in hand, we can rid our lives of the love of money and can learn to be content (Hebrews 13:5). And when we are content, we are freed to place loving and caring for Christ, His kingdom, and others above personal gain. May we always treasure that "godliness with contentment is great gain" (1 Timothy 6:6).

Let contentment liberate your heart!

THE HIDING PLACE

"IN THIS WORLD YOU WILL HAVE TROUBLE. BUT TAKE HEART! I HAVE OVERCOME THE WORLD."

—John 16:33

This world is trouble looking for a place to happen. I have a friend who says that the trouble with life is that it is so daily! We all know about Murphy's law. But we might not be aware of O'Toole's law, which says that Murphy was an optimist! Actually, if we understood the depth of the Fall, we would be surprised that anything good happens at all. And when it does, it is an intervention of God's amazing grace.

Christ warned that *in this world* we would have trouble. In the face of that reality He welcomed us to find refuge *in Him.* He told His disciples, "In me you may have peace" (John 16:33). This peace is rooted in the realities of the things that Christ had just told the disciples. Christ gives us five resources for peace: our love for one another, the assured hope of His coming to take us to heaven, the provision of the indwelling Holy Spirit, the wonderful privilege of abiding in Him, and the opportunity through prayer to receive what we need (John 14:1–16:33).

Christ went on to assure us that while He would give us peace in the midst of the world's pain, He also would be the source for our courage and confidence, for He had "overcome the world." Interestingly, the word *overcome* carries the suggestion of a past event that has a continuing effect. Not only has He conquered the fallen world system through His death and resurrection, but He also continues to provide victory for all who will find it in Him.

The believer's hope and confidence are that no matter how tough times get here, Christ's overcoming power guarantees that "in all things God works for the good" (Romans 8:28).

I don't know what you expect from this world, but if you're looking for peace in life, it is found only in Christ. Although this world is our *place,* He is our *peace.* No wonder He said, "Take heart! I have overcome the world."

Have you sought refuge in the things, people, and pleasures of this world? Rest in Him and make His truth your hiding place!

PSALMS 11 AND 12

I trust in the LORD for protection. So why do you say to me,
"Fly to the mountains for safety!
The wicked are stringing their bows and setting their arrows in the bowstrings.
They shoot from the shadows at those who do right.
The foundations of law and order have collapsed. What can the righteous do?"
But the LORD is in his holy Temple; the LORD still rules from heaven.
He watches everything closely, examining everyone on earth.
The LORD examines both the righteous and the wicked.
He hates everyone who loves violence.
He rains down blazing coals on the wicked,
punishing them with burning sulfur and scorching winds.
For the LORD is righteous, and he loves justice.
Those who do what is right will see his face.

Help, O LORD, for the godly are fast disappearing!
The faithful have vanished from the earth!
Neighbors lie to each other, speaking with flattering lips and insincere hearts.
May the LORD bring their flattery to an end and silence their proud tongues.
They say, "We will lie to our hearts' content.
Our lips are our own—who can stop us?"
The LORD replies, "I have seen violence done to the helpless,
and I have heard the groans of the poor.
Now I will rise up to rescue them, as they have longed for me to do."
The LORD's promises are pure,
like silver refined in a furnace, purified seven times over.
Therefore, LORD, we know you will protect the oppressed,
preserving them forever from this lying generation,
even though the wicked strut about, and evil is praised throughout the land.

SEEING HIM

The Heavens Declare the Glory of God; the Skies Proclaim the Work of His Hands.

—Psalm 19:1

When life is far too fast and on the verge of being out of control, it is important to "stop and smell the roses." But when you do, get beyond the refreshing elixir of the smell and the beauty. And, if they are delivered to your door, get beyond the romance. So much of what is around us, while beautiful in itself, is a reflection of the glorious creative hand of a master designer who orchestrated all of it for our pleasure *and* His glory. Even what we make with our own hands and conceive in our own minds is possible because we have been made in the image of a wise Creator-God. From the fountains of the deep to the frontiers of technology, He is in it all!

Look at the star-filled sky and think of Jesus. Bask in the reality that the One who formed the deep and vast universe by the word of His mouth is your Creator and Friend. See Him in the sun that rises each morning, finely tuned to neither scorch nor freeze. Catch the symbol of His hope in the early spring flower that pushes through the crusted snow.

In the Moody Video production *Planet Earth,* astronaut Colonel Guy Gardner, speaking of the marvels of creation he saw in space, pauses and, with tears welling in his eyes, says, "It's very hard to think this must have happened by chance . . . you realize at the same time that there had to be a master designer, a Creator, of this planet.

"To me, that makes life all the more special. Because that tells me that instead of me being something that just came along in the course of time to live and die, that instead of a meaningless existence, I have Someone who cares for me, who has made me and cares about me. Someone I can go to with my troubles, and my cares, and my joys."

You'll never feel far from God when you see Him in all that is around you.

Look for Him . . . rejoice with a grateful heart as you experience His presence.

A HEALTHY SENSE OF SHAME

Godly Sorrow Brings Repentance That Leads to Salvation and Leaves No Regret, but Worldly Sorrow Brings Death.
—2 Corinthians 7:10

At a recent Emmys event, a video history was played detailing the changing treatment of sex on TV. It began with the dad on the old *Father Knows Best* program bidding farewell to his daughter as she leaves for a date. In a smiling exchange, he asks her to be home by 9:30. The video ends with a cut from the current sitcom *Friends,* as two roommates play rock, scissors, paper to see who will take the last available condom on his date that night.

The implication of the presentation can't be missed: This is *progress.*

If we wonder why moral issues don't seem to be important in our leaders' lives and public policy, it may be because we have become a society that no longer is ashamed of sin. Instead, we celebrate our shame.

Our shamelessness should not surprise us. Shamelessness is next to godlessness. Always.

Decades ago, Americans decided that God no longer had a place in our society. When God is banished, so is the morality that holds us accountable for right and wrong. The presence of the divine is what keeps our sensitivities in line.

This makes me wonder about the erosion of shame in the church. When we shamelessly excuse our own sin and tolerate it in the lives of others, it reflects our own godlessness. The erosion of shame does not simply show that we have gotten used to life in America, but rather that we have lost our awareness of the presence of God. When God is close, our sensitivities are sharpened to purity and to living lives that bring Him pleasure. Intimacy with God produces a healthy sense of shame. As God's Word notes, godly shame is the ally that brings repentance (2 Corinthians 7:10), as opposed to a shameless life that is left without restraint.

Before we become too self-righteous about our godless, shameless world, let's measure our own lives. It's time to invite God back to the center, where He belongs.

Is the presence of God a purifying reality for you?

LIVING ABOVE IT ALL

Anyone Who Chooses to Be a Friend of the World Becomes an Enemy of God.

—James 4:4

To listen to some of us, you would think that those who want to adhere to God's moral standards are old-fashioned legalists and grossly out of touch! It is more fashionable these days to be "open-minded" and "able to deal with sinful input" than to flee from or speak out against sin. Yet a life that ceases to differentiate between right and wrong is vulnerable to sin. We have forgotten the clear warning of Scripture, "Do not be deceived: God cannot be mocked. A man reaps what he sows" (Galatians 6:7).

God warns us against partnership with moral decadence (Ephesians 5:7). From movies to the Internet, to music and a dozen other seductions, faithful followers must differentiate between what is good and what is evil. That skill is a measure of our maturity (Hebrews 5:14).

Even sensual speech neutralizes our sensitivity to moral purity, contributes to a sensual mind-set, reflects a lack of self-control, seduces people into believing that we're open to sexual approaches, and robs God of His glory in our speech. Sensual speech tears us down and weakens our resistance to immorality. It does not benefit those who listen. A commitment to words that help others will eliminate sensual speech. Paul tells us that our speech should be "helpful for building others up according to their needs, that it may benefit those who listen" (Ephesians 4:29).

We are children of the light and no longer a part of the darkness (Ephesians 5:8–14). When we revert to old patterns and walk in darkness, we break fellowship with God and violate His will (2 Corinthians 6:14–7:1; 1 John 1:5–7).

What does it take to live out our newness and uniqueness in a sinful, sensual age?

Courage to stand alone when necessary, knowing that He died to purify our hearts. *Humility* to not think of ourselves more highly than we ought and to remember that we too are sinners, saved by grace. *Wisdom* to know what is right and what is wrong. *Desire* to please Him more than ourselves or others. *Passion* to live a life that is clean for maximum use by Him.

"What would Jesus do?" is a question to ask if you want purity and productivity in life.

THIS WORLD IS NOT MY HOME

"In My Father's House Are Many Rooms. . . . I Am Going There to Prepare a Place for You."

—John 14:2

*C*hrist never considered Himself at home here. He knew that He had come from heaven and that He was going back and that heaven was truly home. This left Him free from bondage to this present world and empowered Him to fulfill His mission here unhindered by earthside distractions.

In order to follow Jesus the disciples had to literally become homeless as well. They had given up their homes, careers, familiar places, and families to journey with Christ toward their eternal home. In a very real sense, Jesus Christ had become the disciples' home away from home. As long as they were with Him, they felt safe and secure. That is why they were so traumatized when He told them that He was leaving them.

As Christ instructed them on how to live after He left (John 13–14), they were so traumatized by His impending departure, that they were unable to hear His instructions. So He interrupted His strategic session on survival without Him to patiently answer the testy questions of Peter and Thomas regarding His departure. He took pains to assure them that He was going to His home in heaven to make a home for them (John 14:1–6). As long as they believed this and counted heaven to be their home, they would be able to function here courageously, without distraction or intimidation.

The mission of Christ was never intended to culminate at the cross. The cross and the empty grave were merely means of opening the doors of heaven for us. Home is where you feel comfortable, secure, safe, and at peace. Christ made clear that He came here to take us there. When heaven is home, earth becomes a far different place. It can threaten but not thwart. Trouble but not traumatize. Tempt but not conquer.

Belief in heaven as home has led thousands of martyrs to brave the cruel reproaches of a hostile world and ordinary folk to live victoriously against everyday odds.

In what way does heaven make a difference for you?

THE FREEDOM OF JUST SAYING NO

"You Shall Know the Truth, and the Truth Shall Make You Free."
—John 8:32 NKJV

I recently read an article where the feature writer was marveling that a friend of hers had given up shopping for Lent. Since I have a love-hate relationship with shopping, the comment caught my attention. The writer went on to say that while she always envisioned giving up food for Lent she had never thought of giving up shopping as a legitimate sacrifice. But as I read the article, it wasn't the discussion about shopping that finally arrested my attention. It was the author's reflection on giving up anything at all.

Though not from a "Lent" type of religious background, she admitted that Lent had caused her to think twice about her attitudes on life. She mused about the fact that life ends up controlling us and that we quickly lose the will to control life. She wrote, "I always thought that life was more interesting if I would say yes. But I am learning what Eve never knew, and that is that saying no may be the most liberating thing we can do."

Unfortunately, most people in our world believe that old line from the devil: "Freedom is doing whatever you want to do." And that anything less than the ability to say yes to anything we want oppressively holds us back and robs us of deserved pleasure. Jesus steers us in the right direction when He claims that true freedom is found in being committed to what is true and that when we live in the truth—which involves saying no to the lies of Satan—we experience true freedom.

Nothing could be more true. Show me the drug addict, the victim of broken relationships, the empty regrets of a life ill spent, and I'll show you lives that believed that doing what they wanted to do made them free. But those who have known the truth and have known when to say no are free from debilitating guilt and haunting fear. They are free to enjoy life apart from obsession and enslaving habits.

Enjoy the freedom of "just saying no" in Jesus!

Say no to one thing every day just to stay in shape.

THE FIRM FOUNDATION

BUT SOLID FOOD IS FOR THE MATURE, WHO BY CONSTANT USE HAVE TRAINED
THEMSELVES TO DISTINGUISH GOOD FROM EVIL.

—Hebrews 5:14

*F*oundations are everything. Whether in buildings or in relationships or in families, the foundation is what secures, stabilizes, and anchors us when the storm clouds gather.

Biblical doctrine is the foundation of the church. Today more than ever we need the sure footing of the truth that checks the drift caused by false thinking and teaching in a deceptive world. Lest, as Paul wrote, we be "tossed back and forth by the waves, and blown here and there by every wind of teaching and by the cunning and craftiness of men in their deceitful scheming" (Ephesians 4:14).

We've all heard people say, "The problem with doctrine is that it's so divisive." But that's not the problem with doctrine. That's the problem with how we have handled doctrine—how we have elevated lesser beliefs to the level of core fundamentals.

Doctrine legitimately divides truth from error. That is a divisive element we desperately need in our culture. Hebrews 5:14 describes spiritually mature believers as those who "have trained themselves to distinguish good from evil." Good doctrine, well understood and well applied, helps us to differentiate between the deceit that is inherent in this world and the rock-solid realities that form a firm foundation of truth. We must always remember that Satan started the avalanche of sin's damage when he undercut God's word in Eve's heart and mind.

The worst danger is not for those of us who have witnessed the demise of doctrine in our day. It is for the next generation—those who have been called to the *practices* but have never understood the foundational *principles*.

According to Christ, the wise man built his life on the solid rock of Christ's teachings. The foolish man also built a house, but one without a solid foundation. Only one house stood when the floods came (Matthew 7:24–27).

We need lives that are firmly and uncompromisingly planted on the truth that undergirds our faith.

Choose a doctrine about Christ, salvation, the sovereignty of God, the Holy Spirit, or another topic. What specific stability does this doctrine offer you today?

PSALM 13

O LORD, how long will you forget me? Forever?
How long will you look the other way?
How long must I struggle with anguish in my soul,
with sorrow in my heart every day?
How long will my enemy have the upper hand?
Turn and answer me, O LORD my God!
Restore the light to my eyes, or I will die.
Don't let my enemies gloat, saying, "We have defeated him!"
Don't let them rejoice at my downfall.
But I trust in your unfailing love.
I will rejoice because you have rescued me.
I will sing to the LORD
because he has been so good to me.

PLEASING GOD

So We Make It Our Goal to Please Him.

—2 Corinthians 5:9

*C*ounselors tell us that children who grow up without parental affirmation often become driven to perform, seeking to please someone, somewhere, somehow with some part of their lives. As a result, unhealthy addictions or immoral relationships twist and turn their lives in all the wrong directions. It is easy for those of us still looking for approval to become weak and unprincipled, willing to violate biblical standards if it means we can finally be affirmed.

This intrinsic drive to please significant people in our lives reflects the fact that we were built to bring pleasure to Someone outside of ourselves. And, the highest satisfaction of life is in knowing in our spirits that God is pleased with us. As Paul so beautifully penned, "We make it our goal to please him" (2 Corinthians 5:9).

Before you recoil at the thought of trying to please God because it seems like an impossible task, let me bring you the good news. Unlike some people we know, God is capable of being pleased. The psalmist says that God is bent toward being pleased with us: "The LORD takes delight in his people" (Psalm 149:4). He is pleased when we offer our bodies to Him as "living sacrifices" (Romans 12:1), as well as by our praise and our good deeds (Hebrews 13:15–16). It brings Him pleasure when we show justice, love mercy, and walk humbly with Him (Micah 6:8).

Living to please God reaps the sweet reward of a life that discovers the stability and "all-rightness" that only comes when we walk in the paths of righteousness.

Interestingly, one way we please God is to bring pleasure to others. Paul wrote, "Each of us should please his neighbor for his good, to build him up" (Romans 15:2). He went on to say that Christ "did not please himself" but gave His life so we would have the pleasure of redemption (v. 3).

Make it a daily goal to do at least one thing to please God—start today!

TREASURE FOR ETERNITY

"But Seek First His Kingdom and His Righteousness, and All These Things Will Be Given to You as Well."

—Matthew 6:33

The disciples were no doubt delighted with Jesus' reproof of the man who was rich with earthly goods but poor in that he had no relationship with God (Luke 12). This was a message for the pagans . . . they were off the hook. Until he turned to them and asked why they were so distracted by earthly things and so uninterested in the kingdom.

We have probably heard that living to promote and participate in the kingdom of Christ is important. But what would it mean if we really lived to "seek first His kingdom"?

First, we must understand the essence of the kingdom. At its core is the reality of eternity. Christ hammered home the kingdom truth that there is something significant beyond the grave. This truth guided His view of this life. From Christ's perspective, it made little sense to invest your life only in things you will not be able to take with you. He had a point. I have been to many funerals, and I have yet to see a Brink's truck or a U-Haul following the hearse. A Spanish proverb says, "Shrouds have no pockets." Christ taught that in this life we should live so as to make a difference in eternity.

Just a few verses before Christ gave His call to the priority of kingdom things, He anticipated that point by saying, "Do not store up for yourselves treasures on earth, where moth and rust destroy, and where thieves break in and steal. But store up for yourselves treasures in heaven, where moth and rust do not destroy, and where thieves do not break in and steal. For where your treasure is, there your heart will be also" (Matthew 6:19–21). Someone has paraphrased this statement of Christ by saying, "You can't take it with you, but you can send it on ahead."

Christ commands us to inventory our lives for the future. Think of your children, your money, your strength, and your gifts as investments in your kingdom portfolio. If the kingdom had a national hymn, it would be, "Only one life, 'twill soon be past; only what's done for Christ will last."

What treasures of eternal significance have you stored in heaven?

WORSHIP THE KING

"True Worshipers Will Worship the Father in Spirit and Truth."
—John 4:23

T recently received a letter from a woman who had heard a sermon on worship that changed her life. She admitted in the letter that worship had been narrowly defined in her life as time spent singing hymns in church. She was delighted to learn that worship is actually a lifelong response to the reality of God's grace and goodness in our lives.

"Enter his gates with thanksgiving and his courts with praise" (Psalm 100:4) is preceded by "Know that the LORD is God. It is he who made us, and we are his; we are his people, the sheep of his pasture" (v. 3). There is a profound sequence here.

Worship is a response, not a religious catharsis. It is a response to our knowledge of and experience with the Word and works of God that describe and illuminate His magnificent realities.

One of the most fervent worship experiences in Scripture took place on the banks of the Red Sea just after God had demonstrated His delivering power (Exodus 15:1–21). Experiencing the reality of God's beneficial grace always stimulates authentic worship.

When we go into worship as if it were an event without reference points, it ends up as an exercise that is little more than an emotional ritual. How much better to prepare for worship by meditating on the ways, Word, and works of God so that our hearts are ready to respond rather than recite. In light of this, it might even be better to worship after the sermon.

Some of our great hymns are full of truth about God. They blend edification and enthusiasm into one experience. I love worship choruses. They pull from my heart much of what I feel and know about God. But I also treasure the substance and depth of our hymns.

Whatever mode of worship we choose, true praise is a genuine enthusiasm that grows from knowing Him and experiencing His Word and His ways.

What do you know about God that is worthy of worship? Use it as a springboard for praise throughout the day.

THE PROMISEKEEPER

FAITHFUL IS HE WHO CALLS YOU, AND HE ALSO WILL BRING IT TO PASS.
—1 Thessalonians 5:24 NASB

D. L. Moody often preached his famous sermon, "The Seven 'I Wills' of Christ." Moody explained that "a man, when he says, 'I will,' may not mean much. We very often say, 'I will,' when we don't mean to fulfill what we say; but when we come to the 'I will' of Christ, He means to fulfill it. Everything He has promised to do, He is able and willing to accomplish; and He is going to do it."

Can you remember just a few weeks back to New Year's day? Think about the resolutions you made. How many of your turn-of-the-year "I wills" have you kept? Our intentions are good, but in our human frailty we often fall short of our own expectations. As the days and weeks pass, our determination to carry out resolutions begins to dissolve.

Here's the good news. Jesus Christ possesses none of these human shortcomings. He is able and willing to fulfill every promise He has made. He will never fall short of our expectations. His word is certain. His promises are true.

Scattered throughout the Gospels are what Moody called the "Seven 'I Wills' of Christ." I will never cast you out (John 6:37). I will cleanse you (Luke 5:13). I will acknowledge you before My Father (Matthew 10:32). I will make you fishers of men (Matthew 4:19). I will come to you (John 14:18). I will raise you up at the last day (John 6:40). I will take you into glory, to be with Me where I am (John 17:24). And, in addition, the writer to the Hebrews noted, "I will never desert you, nor will I ever forsake you" (Hebrews 13:5).

When others let you down, think of Jesus! Rejoice in the absolute security you have in His faithfulness. He indeed is the name you can trust. In Him you will find grace and mercy in the time of need (Hebrews 4:14–16), abundant life, and an eternal future of joy in His presence. Count on it.

List the promises Jesus has made to you. Reflect on them often and use them as a springboard to praise and gratitude.

CHARACTER COUNTS

For Those God Foreknew He Also Predestined to Be Conformed to the Likeness of His Son, That He Might Be the Firstborn Among Many Brothers.

—Romans 8:29

*O*f the many things we have lost in the last few years, the belief that character trumps credentials may be one of the most tragic. Credentials are the life targets of many who are searching for significance. Credentials are established through our business cards, home addresses, degrees, cars, clubs, friends, vacation spots, and bank accounts.

While there is nothing wrong with credentials, Christ calls His followers to value character above credentials. And when you think about it, the supremacy of character makes tons of sense. Credentials are transient; character is permanent. Credentials build memories about what we have done; character builds a legacy for others to follow. Credentials are locked into one person; character is transferable. Credentials get us in the front door almost anywhere; character will keep us there. Credentials tend to evoke jealousy; character attracts respect and stimulates others to develop character as well.

Character commits itself to principle over personal gain, to people over things, to servanthood over lordship, and to the long view over the immediate.

Marks of character become a compelling witness. As we grow in character, we offer something that is not only different but of more substance, worth, and value to our credential-mad world.

Those of us who have the privilege of a relationship with Jesus Christ have a distinct advantage: an inner impulse toward character. Scripture tells us that we have been chosen and empowered to become "conformed to the likeness of his Son" (Romans 8:29). Credentials were never a primary concern to Him. Jesus Christ gave up His divine credentials to minister here without earthly credentials. Yet His life was compellingly powerful because of His character.

It is true not only that character still counts, but that character counts over anything else. True character begins with Jesus Christ. It begins with following Him and allowing His life to emerge through ours.

Think of one character quality of Christ that you can live out today, and make a plan to follow through.

NEEDING HIM

"You Say, 'I Am Rich; I Have Acquired Wealth and Do Not Need a Thing.' But You Do Not Realize that You Are Wretched, Pitiful, Poor, Blind and Naked."

—Revelation 3:17

The downside of affluence is that we lose sight of how much we need God. Clothes, food, safety, security, friendship, and fun are all available and affordable. Assuming that we have provided it all for ourselves, we are deluded into a sense of a self-sufficiency that changes our relationship with God from reliance to convenience. When we cease to perceive how much we need God, He soon fades out of sight, then out of mind. He becomes little more than the 911 number of life.

C. S. Lewis wrote, "Everyone has noticed how hard it is to turn our thoughts to God when everything is going well. The statement 'We have all we want' is a terrible statement if that all does not include God." In Deuteronomy 6 God warned Israel about the affluence of the Promised Land. When he gave them "houses filled of all kinds of good things you did not provide . . . vineyards and olive groves you did not plant . . . be careful that you do not forget the LORD" (vv. 11–12).

The tragedy of self-sufficiency is that we end up placing our trust and security in all the "stuff" as though it will last forever. Yet it could all be gone in a moment. God is the only steady, daily, eternal reality that is sufficient for our needs and wants. And, we must remember, all we have is from Him in the first place.

Do we want to be among those who love the gifts and ignore the Giver?

If we, in spite of our affluence, embrace how desperately we need the Giver, we will pray more, seek Him in His Word more often, be more grateful for what we have, and hold all things loosely to be used as gifts with which to serve and worship Him.

List the gifts of His grace to you. Repent of trusting in them, live to need Him, and rejoice afresh in the Giver. Read Revelation 3:14–20.

PSALM 15

Who may worship in your sanctuary, LORD?
Who may enter your presence on your holy hill?
Those who lead blameless lives
and do what is right,
speaking the truth from sincere hearts.
Those who refuse to slander others
or harm their neighbors
or speak evil of their friends.
Those who despise persistent sinners,
and honor the faithful followers of the LORD
and keep their promises even when it hurts.
Those who do not charge interest on the money they lend,
and who refuse to accept bribes to testify against the innocent.
Such people will stand firm forever.

THE POLITICS OF PRAYER

PRAY WITHOUT CEASING.

—1 Thessalonians 5:17 NASB

*A*s evangelicals, we seem to have an unusual interest in politics. We have spent millions of dollars to elect officials who uphold biblical values and have felt anxious, angry, and betrayed because of the rapid national drift from our Christian roots. Ask most Christians and they will tell you that Exhibit A of the loss of a fear of God in our land has been the outlawing of prayer in our public schools. We have lobbied, elected representatives who agree with us, and done everything we can to reverse the law, seemingly to no avail. We are now coming to know what it's like to live in a prayerless nation—which only makes me wonder if this is how God feels about a prayerless church. Or, more personally, about prayerless lives. Let's face it: Prayer in our own lives is far more important than prayer in our schools.

Praying people live in a vibrant connection to the reality and centrality of the transcendent God—the One who is worthy of our prayers and praise (Psalm 148).

More prayer at home would help us rear a generation that also believed in a worthy, caring God. It would expand our children's view of life beyond the confines of Nintendo®. The windows of their hearts would be open to an awareness of their own connectedness to a loving Father, the needs of others, and the lostness of the world.

In churches where it is easier to pay for programs than it is to pray for the empowerment of programs, more prayer would shift our sense of confidence from our own abilities to His (James 5:16).

Prayer opens our eyes to see God more clearly. It opens our hearts to hear from Him more directly. It gives us a greater sense of who we really are—reliant, weak, and needy; and it reminds us of who He really is—the sufficient sustainer and supplier of all we need.

If we all spent more time practicing prayer rather than wringing our hands about prayer in school, we just might have more power in this pagan world.

Do you have a regular and effective ministry of prayer?

LIVING BY THE LAW

"All the Law and the Prophets Hang on These Two Commandments."
—Matthew 22:40

*I*n God's Word there are standards and principles for every situation of life. These "rules" are tools that enable us to distinguish between right and wrong. In a dark world that long ago lost its way regarding righteousness, they become a "lamp to [our] feet and a light for [our] path" (Psalm 119:105). They are principles worthy to be owned at the heart level regardless of environmental influences and pressures. By them we evaluate each perception and decision of life. And we embrace them because our inner flame for Christ seeks to generate a righteousness consistent with His.

But at times it seems that there are so many standards and principles. It's easy to get the feeling that life is overregulated and that it is nearly impossible to be good enough to please God. Well, if you ever feel like that, think of the fact that the Jews in Christ's day had more than six hundred rules and regulations to conform to. It was into this burdensome and overregulated environment that Jesus came and radically simplified the system.

Christ taught that righteousness is birthed from conformity to two foundational commands. Love God and Love your neighbor. Then He said, "All the Law and the Prophets hang on these two commandments" (Matthew 22:40). Slicing through a complex, unrighteous world are two simple yet profound commitments. Commitments that begin with a loving surrender to God and a loving concern for the needs of others.

These rules provide a grid, a set of decision-making standards, for every choice we make. At the crossroads of every decision, temptation, or choice, the follower who is committed to loving God and others measures the moment by these two defining principles. What would be best for God in this matter? And what would be best for others who are impacted by this decision? The answer to these questions is the right thing to do. Every time!

Normally we make choices by the standard of what would be best for "me." More times than not unrighteousness is the result. Master just two rules, and let righteousness flow.

What drives and defines your life? Love for self or love for God and others?

WHO NEEDS TO CHANGE?

IF A MAN CLEANSES HIMSELF . . . HE WILL BE AN INSTRUMENT FOR NOBLE PURPOSES, MADE HOLY, USEFUL TO THE MASTER AND PREPARED TO DO ANY GOOD WORK.

—2 Timothy 2:21

With four years of seminary behind me, I walked into my first ministry with an agenda as long as my arm. I thought, *I'm here to change this place.* It soon became clear that God would use it to change me.

The board members were supportive but relentlessly kept my feet to the fire in administrative details. I needed to know how to work with lay leadership, how to be careful in my work, how to dream with others. I needed to develop those skills so that I would be capable and usable in the days ahead. As unpleasant as it was at the time, that church was God's change agent in my life. I had assumed that I was ready. Competent. Usable.

I took my next pastorate. I asked all the right questions. I knew everything that should be changed. I could see exactly why God had led me there. Boot camp was behind me. It was *my* turn to be the agent of change. I walked in, ready to go—and it was as though God said, "Mug him again."

I often wonder how many times God will have to "mug me" before His message gets through. Before I realize that He is interested in changing me before I can become an instrument of change in others.

I hasten to say that God does not literally mug us. But He does encounter us on the streets of our existence to bring about change in our lives. To change us so that He might use us.

I'm glad God is not finished with me yet. It gives me a sense of confidence to know that He cares enough for me to continue to shape, mold, mend, and stretch me. I want to be useful to Him. Though it sometimes hurts, "the pain is worth the gain." It is His goal to change us into instruments "useful to the Master and prepared to do any good work" (2 Timothy 2:21).

What might God be trying to change in your life today?

TIMES FLIES

*E*very four years we get an extra day on the calendar—a leap year blessing. Think of it, one more day in the year, which is bad or good news depending on what kind of year you are having.

Leap year reminds us that our lives are measured by days, and that every day we tear another sheet off the calendar is a day closer to our last day. When we are young, the unstoppable march of time seems of little consequence. We are bulletproof—we think we'll live forever, or at least for a long time. When we grow old we are much more aware of our mortality. Knees take much longer to heal, faces sag, and memory fades. But even then we try to live in denial, staving off aging with face-lifts and multiple replacement of bones and body parts.

But, regardless of our disdain for the old saying "Time marches on," it really does. And the thought should give us pause. If we lived in the light of the certainty of a limited amount of days, we would live far more wisely. We would love more freely, be kind more readily, serve more graciously, and value people over possessions more passionately. As the psalmist said, if we numbered our days we would live more wisely.

Actually, for all of us who number our days in terms of "three-score and ten," there is always the possibility that we may not get there. The greatest motivation to living wisely in light of the time that flies is the realization that today may be your last day on earth. Little did the people who died in the terrorist attack on September 11, 2001, know that that day would be their last. Think of the difference it would make in how you left home, in what you would have done the night before, how frequently you shared the gospel— and with whom, on what you did with your friends, on what you did with your kids, on how you treated your spouse—if you knew that today was all you had left.

Time flies . . . grab it before it flies by.

HERE IS LOVE

BUT GOD DEMONSTRATES HIS OWN LOVE TOWARD US, IN THAT WHILE WE
WERE YET SINNERS, CHRIST DIED FOR US.

—Romans 5:8

*R*ecently, while speaking at a conference in the UK, my heart was taken
by a song I had never heard before. I asked my British friend where
the song had come from and he told me that it had its origins in the Welsh
revival.

At the beginning of the twentieth century, God put His hand on Evan
Roberts, a common, uneducated coal miner in Wales, and used him to spark
the Welsh revival that eventually swept all the British Isles. The moving of the
Spirit was profound. Bars closed. Dance halls struggled to stay in business.
Even attendance at beloved football matches fell off since most people were in
church. Jails were emptied, and it is said that since the police had little to do
they formed choirs to sing at the daily meetings.

The words of the hymn proved an important point. Revival is fanned not
just by the fear of hell or the consequence of sin, but by the amazing love of
Jesus Christ for the wayward sinner. There may be power in the blood, but
there is unrelenting power in the love of Jesus who loved us and gave Himself
for us.

Think of these truths and see if His love doesn't grip your heart in a fresh
way.

Here is love, vast as the ocean, lovingkindness as the flood,
When the Prince of Life, our Ransom, shed for us His precious blood.
Who His love will not remember? Who can cease to sing His praise?
He can never be forgotten, throughout heav'n's eternal days.

On the mount of crucifixion, fountains opened deep and wide;
Through the floodgates of God's mercy flowed a vast and gracious tide.
Grace and love, like mighty rivers, poured incessant from above,
And heav'n's peace and perfect justice kissed a guilty world in love.

—William Rees (1802–83)

Rejoice that heaven's peace and perfect justice kissed your guilty heart with love!

TOUGH LOVE

"LOVE YOUR ENEMIES AND PRAY FOR THOSE WHO PERSECUTE YOU."
—Matthew 5:44

*A*ll of us have people around our lives who are hard to love. Which makes Christ's command to love our neighbors a particularly tough assignment. Yet when we see the command in context, the secret of how to love the difficult people in our lives is revealed. Christ taught us that the first and greatest commandment was to "Love the Lord your God." He added that the second was to love your neighbor (Matthew 22:37–38). Simply put, if you love God you will show it by your love for others. The best reason to love others is as an act of love toward God. The power of my love for Him crumbles the barriers regardless of how unlovable someone might be.

If we are motivated to meet others' needs for reasons other than our love for God, our love will vacillate and quickly evaporate under pressure. If a wife waits until her husband deserves her love, she may wait a long time. If, however, she is committed to expressing her love for God by how she treats others, she will love her husband regardless. Husbands committed to loving God sensitively meet the needs of their wives. Loving for God's sake keeps us loving wayward children. It even provides the grace and strength to love and forgive those who have heaped injustices upon us. Our love for the Father provides enough motivation to follow Jesus' admonition to "love your enemies and pray for those who persecute you, that you may be the sons of your Father in heaven" (Matthew 5:44–45). While it wouldn't be good to say, "You don't deserve this, but I'm loving you because I love Jesus!" it nevertheless is the way it works.

We must always remember that Christ's love for us was motivated by His loving commitment to the Father. While it is true that He loves us, He came to do His Father's will, and that meant He would love us with His life, which we accept as the highest prize of our existence. Strange, then, isn't it, that we are so stingy with extending that same kind of love to others?

Do something today for someone who has hurt or disappointed you.

PSALM 16

Keep me safe, O God,
for I have come to you for refuge.
I said to the LORD, "You are my Master!
All the good things I have are from you."
The godly people in the land
are my true heroes!
I take pleasure in them!
Those who chase after other gods will be filled with sorrow.
I will not take part in their sacrifices
or even speak the names of their gods.
LORD, you alone are my inheritance, my cup of blessing.
You guard all that is mine.
The land you have given me is a pleasant land.
What a wonderful inheritance!
I will bless the LORD who guides me;
even at night my heart instructs me.
I know the LORD is always with me.
I will not be shaken, for he is right beside me.
No wonder my heart is filled with joy,
and my mouth shouts his praises!
My body rests in safety.
For you will not leave my soul among the dead
or allow your godly one to rot in the grave.
You will show me the way of life,
granting me the joy of your presence
and the pleasures of living with you forever.

PHILOSOPHIES OF LIFE

The school of rational psychology charts the course of decision making in three stages. First, there is the life situation that creates the need for a decision. Next is our philosophy of life, which provides the grid through which we process the decision. Then, in the light of our philosophy of life, the decision is made.

The pivotal issue in the process is our philosophy of life. For instance, if cats make great pets in our philosophy of life, we will respond with openness when we are offered a kitten. But if we view cats as an irritation, the same opportunity will elicit a "You've got to be kidding" response.

It's no wonder that God's Word reminds us that as a man "thinketh in his heart, so is he" (Proverbs 23:7 KJV). Which makes it absolutely critical that followers of Christ put Jesus at the center of their philosophy of life. When our philosophy of life is built on the truth of God's principles revealed in His Word, decisions will be wise and righteous. That is why Proverbs commands us, "Above all else, guard your heart, for it is the wellspring of life" (4:23).

Beware, however. Our hearts are easily deceived by false philosophies of life. Competing for a place in our philosophical "box" will be self, secular philosophies, cultural fads, and a host of other nontruths produced by our world. When we permit them to coexist with God's truth in our hearts, we become "double-minded" and "unstable" in how we live (James 1:8).

Guarding against this instability requires a willingness to let the Word of God form and frame every thought and consideration. We must find ourselves asking on a consistent basis, "What does God teach me about money, friends, lust, enemies, power, purity, pleasure . . . ?" When we find and embrace the answer, it produces a philosophy of life that guides us to righteousness and builds a life of solid character usable in the Master's hand.

Are there toxic thoughts and perspectives in the wellspring of your heart? Let His Word change your mind.

A DISPLAY OF CHARACTER

GLORIFY GOD IN YOUR BODY.

—1 Corinthians 6:20 NASB

I sat in the audience at Moody Bible Institute's Founder's Week and watched as Joni Eareckson Tada told of her deep love for God and her joy in Christ. I found myself wondering what my response to life would be if I had been so severely disabled as a teenager.

Though she is paralyzed from the shoulders down, her face beamed as she sat in her wheelchair. It was clear that God was real, satisfying, fulfilling, and enabling in spite of her lifelong trial. It was a credible statement to the reality and power of God and His grace. Most of us would have been tempted to sink to depths of self-pity and bitterness had it been us. But she obviously knew a secret. And that secret was that life is not ultimately about us but about our privilege to platform the glory and grace of God. Sometimes His glory is best seen in pain instead of pleasure. It is obvious that Joni's response to her problem was to let her life resonate with a love for Him that demonstrates the supporting presence of His grace.

Suffering can be a platform on which the reality of God and His power can be displayed. Sometimes that power is displayed by the grace He gives us to positively endure as we reflect forgiveness and peace during an ongoing, sometimes lifelong, problem.

When trials put us on public display, it is our privilege through God-honoring responses guided by Scripture to turn the tables on Satan's attempt to deface God's glory through our pain. In the midst of our troubles, it is our privilege to demonstrate that He is worthy to be worshiped and trusted regardless of our circumstances and to demonstrate the reality of His presence, power, and peace.

Although we rightly think that our problems are used of God to develop our character (James 1:1–5), it is more important to understand that they are also our opportunities to platform His.

What could you tell the watching world about God in the midst of trouble?

BREAKING DOWN BARRIERS

THE SAMARITAN WOMAN SAID TO HIM, "YOU ARE A JEW AND I AM A SAMARITAN WOMAN. HOW CAN YOU ASK ME FOR A DRINK?" (FOR JEWS DO NOT ASSOCIATE WITH SAMARITANS.)

—John 4:9

*I*n case you think prejudice is no big deal, think again.

In John 4, Jesus Christ did something none of His disciples would have done. Not because they didn't care for lost people, but simply because their culture had instilled prejudices that neutralized their capacity to love a sinner into heaven.

While the disciples went into town to buy dinner, Christ, exhausted after a long day of ministry, sat by a well in Samaria. As He rested, a woman came to that well for water. A multitude of prejudices would have gotten in the way of any of us ordinary folk. First, she was a Samaritan, and Jews had nothing to do with Samaritans, so there was an ethnic barrier. Second, she was a woman, and no Jewish rabbi would permit himself to have anything to do publicly with a woman, let alone a woman of Samaria. Third, Christ already knew that she was a woman whose lifestyle was less than admirable.

Should a rabbi who says He is God in the flesh be caught talking to a Samaritan woman who sleeps around? Probably not. But then Christ was no ordinary rabbi. In a penetrating lesson for us, Christ leaped the barriers of prejudice, saw the need in her heart, and compassionately focused the gospel to meet her right where she was.

We too are saddled with a multitude of cultural prejudices—barriers of class, gender, color, race, region, and status often inhibit our love. Our dismay at certain lifestyles and behaviors makes it nearly impossible for us to separate the sin from the worth of the sinner. Unless we are willing to repent of our prejudices and see beyond the sin to the sinner as Christ did, we will stand at a distance from those who need us most. Compassionless, self-righteous, and often condemning, we will be like those of Christ's day who wouldn't think of extending God's mercy to people like an immoral Samaritan woman.

Today, break through the wall of prejudice, and be like Christ to someone who isn't "your kind."

OUT OF THE SHADOWS

FOR IT IS LIGHT THAT MAKES EVERYTHING VISIBLE. THIS IS WHY IT IS SAID:
"WAKE UP, O SLEEPER, RISE FROM THE DEAD, AND CHRIST WILL SHINE ON YOU."
—Ephesians 5:14

*N*o doubt most of us like the thought of developing an increasingly intimate relationship with Christ. We know we need Him and believe He would be a blessing to our lives. But often we are stuck in places where it seems we can't see Him clearly enough. Along the way, someone stepped between us and blocked Christ from view. Perhaps it was a parent who neglected or abused us yet lived publicly as a respectable Christian. Or perhaps it was a trusted spiritual leader who took advantage of us, or a Christian colleague who cheated or mistreated us, or a friend who, though claiming to be a follower of Christ, blatantly betrayed us.

These failed trusted relationships threaten to eclipse the light of the Son in our lives. When the moon, which ordinarily reflects the light of the sun, gets in the way of the sun, everything turns gray, distorted, and cold. Lost in the eclipse that results when people betray us, we still know the sun—*the* Son—is there, but we can't sense His reality or feel His beneficial power. We can't experience Jesus fully while remaining in the shadow of another person's failings.

It's like sitting in a bad seat at a ball game with an obstructed view. We can hear the sounds, feel some of the excitement, and watch others who see clearly and are absorbed in the game, but we personally feel a helpless sense of detachment.

Christ calls us out of the shadows to see Him as He is. Can you step into the brilliance of His warmth and unrelenting care from the shadow of abuse? Are you tired of being disappointed by others who showed you a distorted view of Christ? Are you ready to see His consistently true nature for yourself?

At first view you will be challenged by the brightness of the Son, but you will soon find yourself basking in His glory and in the confidence of His trustworthy direction for your life.

Is there anyone who blocks a clear view of Christ in your life?

GOD'S FINISHING TOUCH

If We Walk in the Light . . . the Blood of Jesus His Son Cleanses Us from All Sin. If We say that We Have no Sin . . . the Truth Is Not in Us.

—1 John 1:7–8 NASB

*E*arly on in my ministry, I used to occupy the open spaces in my calendar by refinishing antique furniture. It started out not as a hobby but as a necessity, as Martie and I searched through antique shops and used furniture stores to find things we liked that would have value if we fixed them up.

Refinishing good furniture is not unlike God's cleansing work in our lives. The first steps are the most brutal. The cutting of the chemical stripper to purify our souls from obvious and flagrant sin is often painful and radical. But that's not the end of it. It's the continued sanding, varnishing, steel wooling, varnishing, rubbing—until step by step, layer by layer, our lives begin to reflect the brilliant sheen of the glory of Jesus Christ.

That is the nature of progressive repentance. And that is what John had in mind when he spoke of walking in the light of our fellowship with Christ and the resultant ongoing cleansing that His blood assures for us. Paul referenced this pattern of life when he said that in Christ he had nailed all the criminal elements of his life to the cross, leaving him "dead to sin but alive to God in Christ Jesus" (Romans 6:11).

Those who wish to deepen their intimacy with Christ do not wait for the impact of a reproof, an emotional confrontation, or the fear of consequences to bring them up short about their sins. They live in a mode of ongoing repentance, sensitive to the smallest blemish as God works to deepen the luster of our lives.

I worry when I feel that I don't have much to repent of. It's the beginning of self-righteousness and hypocrisy, but, worse yet, it means that I am not close to the light of His purifying presence. The closer we are to Him, the more we see of our short-falling self and the more He is desirous of "fine finishing" our lives.

What "refinishing" does your life require in order to look more like Him?

TRULY RELEVANT

"THEN YOU WILL KNOW THE TRUTH, AND THE TRUTH WILL SET YOU FREE."
—John 8:32

*F*or fear of being outdated or appearing out of touch, we talk a lot today about trying to be "more relevant." But our real problem is not in becoming relevant but in understanding what is truly relevant. In a recent forum, Calvin Miller made this profound observation: "The truth is what is really relevant. For truth speaks about what is always and ultimately real. It is the only hope for meeting our real needs."

Throughout history, the church has done its best work when it stood faithfully for what is true, when it proclaimed it clearly and compassionately, and when it has lived it into the culture—even if that culture resisted it with sword and fire or, more subtly, by falsely defining truth. As Christians, we can be marginalized and even maligned, yet remain relevant if our lives are unflinchingly in sync with the truth.

Truth stands the test of time. And only truth has the power to transform a life. God Himself is "the God of truth" (Psalm 31:5). Jesus was "full of grace and truth" (John 1:14). The truly relevant follower of Christ affirms truth at home, in the office, in relationships, in what we say, in attitude and in character. We affirm truth by living out the specifics of the biblical principles that govern each area of our existence. And what is good about all of this is that truth works. While the world shapes its lives by Satan's false assumptions, those who conform to truth have better homes and relationships, and a stronger sense of personal sanity and stability.

Abiding in truth is the only way we can remain effectively relevant. While the world may say that our adherence to truth is old-fashioned, in time all will know that the only relevant reality of history and eternity is Jesus Christ and what He taught.

Scripture affirms, the day is coming—even for those who have denied the truth in their quest for relevance—when "every knee will bow . . . and . . . every tongue will confess that Jesus Christ is Lord" (Philippians 2:10–11 NASB).

Have you compromised truth in some area of your life in an attempt to become relevant?

PSALM 18:1–6, 25–36, 46

I love you, LORD; you are my strength.

The LORD is my rock, my fortress, and my savior;

my God is my rock, in whom I find protection.

He is my shield, the strength of my salvation, and my stronghold.

I will call on the LORD, who is worthy of praise,

for he saves me from my enemies.

The ropes of death surrounded me; the floods of destruction swept over me.

The grave wrapped its ropes around me; death itself stared me in the face.

But in my distress I cried out to the LORD; yes, I prayed to my God for help.

He heard me from his sanctuary; my cry reached his ears. . . .

To the faithful you show yourself faithful;

to those with integrity you show integrity.

To the pure you show yourself pure, but to the wicked you show yourself hostile.

You rescue those who are humble, but you humiliate the proud.

LORD, you have brought light to my life; my God, you light up my darkness.

In your strength I can crush an army; with my God I can scale any wall.

As for God, his way is perfect. All the LORD's promises prove true.

He is a shield for all who look to him for protection.

For who is God except the LORD? Who but our God is a solid rock?

God arms me with strength; he has made my way safe.

He makes me as surefooted as a deer,

leading me safely along the mountain heights.

He prepares me for battle; he strengthens me to draw a bow of bronze.

You have given me the shield of your salvation.

Your right hand supports me; your gentleness has made me great.

You have made a wide path for my feet to keep them from slipping. . . .

The LORD lives! Blessed be my rock! May the God of my salvation be exalted!

GOD WITH US

"NOW THE DWELLING OF GOD IS WITH MEN, AND HE WILL LIVE WITH THEM."
—Revelation 21:3

*T*hroughout history, God has desired to dwell with His people. Don't let that thought get lost. Put this book in your lap and consider the reality that the almighty God desires your company.

In case you doubt it, the proof is abundant. From the very first it was unhindered fellowship in the Garden of Eden. After Adam and Eve fell, God reentered the scene and sacrificed to restore the broken relationship. After Israel left Egypt, God instructed the people to build a portable tabernacle where His presence would dwell in their midst. Under Solomon, a permanent home for Him was built in Jerusalem. Then Christ came and "pitched his tent among us" (John 1:14 EMPH. NT). When Christ was about to ascend to heaven, He claimed that the time was coming when God would "temple" in us (see John 14:15–17). Ultimately, God will establish a new heaven and a new earth where "the dwelling of God is with men" (Revelation 21:3).

Why would He want to be in our midst?

He dwells in our hearts to glorify His name through us (1 Corinthians 6:19–20). He dwells with us to help us live fruitfully and to empower our prayers (John 15:7–8). The Holy Spirit dwells within us to teach us the truth (John 16:13). He dwells in us to convict in the world (John 16:7–11). He temples in us to produce righteousness through our lives in an unrighteous world (Galatians 5:16–23). And, finally, God dwells in us to strengthen us for works of power and love (2 Timothy 1:7).

How privileged we are to have the unfathomable honor of God in and with us. Yet earthly friends and the cares and distractions of this world often get more space in our lives. If we aren't careful, He can become little more than just another guest of our lives—and often a guest without honor at that.

Can you find time for Him? Can He occupy *the* place of honor in your heart? What have you done to entertain this guest with your love lately?

What can you do today to recognize and reward His presence in your life?

SUBSTANTIVE WORSHIP

We . . . Worship by the Spirit of God.

—Philippians 3:3

*I*n congregations across our land, we see an increasing multiplicity of worship styles. Younger generations relate to music and worship styles that differ from what earlier generations are accustomed to. Our temptation is to attach spiritual meaning to styles and to forget that the substance of worship, not the style, is what interests God.

I doubt if it makes much difference to God whether the choir sways or herald trumpets play from the balconies of a cathedral. What He cares about is that we worship "in spirit and truth, for they are the kind of worshipers the Father seeks" (John 4:23). He cares that we honor Him with our hearts. To hypocritical religious worshipers Jesus said, "These people honor me with their lips, but their hearts are far from me" (Matthew 15:8). He cares that we worship with thankfulness, good deeds, and a generous spirit. In fact, He compares this kind of worship to the bringing of a pleasing sacrifice before Him (Hebrews 13:15–16). And He inhabits the praises of His people—not just the kind of praises we prefer (Psalm 22:3 KJV).

The real issue is not whether or not we like a particular kind of worship. The real issue is whether our Lord is pleased with our worship. True worshipers prepare their hearts to worship purely, free from pettiness and self-absorption. Generation Xers shouldn't write off more traditional worship styles. Nor should we old-timers dismiss the newer forms. Substance is the issue. Worship should be measured by its conformity to the truth and to the spirit in which it is done. Worship needs to fit God's preferences, not our own. Worship that is engaged in to please ourselves, parade our gifts, or impress other worshipers focuses on the created, not the Creator.

As you worship, God measures your heart, listening for resounding echoes of sincerity and truth to fill His throne room so that His pleasure might be full.

Can you turn your attention inward and skyward as you prepare to worship, or has worship become a matter of who is doing what and whether or not it makes you happy?

HANGING IN THERE

AND LET ENDURANCE HAVE ITS PERFECT RESULT, SO THAT YOU MAY BE
PERFECT AND COMPLETE, LACKING IN NOTHING.

—James 1:4 NASB

*U*nfortunately, some of us seem to have more confidence in our doctors than we do in God. Let me explain. If your physician diagnosed a serious health problem, you would ask him to tell you what should be done. He might tell you that immediate surgery is imperative. Even knowing that the process was going to be inconvenient, painful, and disruptive to your life and perhaps your budget, my guess is that you would yield to the trouble for the sake of the outcome.

Spiritually, however, when life begins pressing us, our normal response is "Get me out of here! Lord, solve this problem. Now!" The test comes when God says no. Trusting in God means not trying to wiggle out of the problem but rather clinging tenaciously to God, His Word, and His character. This kind of hanging-in-there faith produces endurance. Staying under the pressure with a good spirit is a necessary part of the divine process as He works toward His productive end in our lives.

In times of trouble, it is important to hang on to specific realities about God that relate to the struggle. Listing Scripture passages that underscore or illustrate the truth in which you are putting your faith is helpful. Memorizing portions and praying through these sections of Scripture will anchor your heart and mind. A pledge to wait for God to fulfill the truths in your life while you unflinchingly obey and trust Him is the essence of endurance. Look with anticipation for grace and growth, and rejoice in any indication that the process is working in your life. Regularly check your commitment. Have you started trusting in your own ways? Are you beginning to feel antsy, angry or resentful? Or are you by faith confident in the wisdom of God and submitted to the process?

"Consider it all joy, my brethren, when you encounter various trials, knowing that the testing of your faith produces endurance. And let endurance have its perfect result, that you may be perfect and complete, lacking in nothing" (James 1:2–4 NASB 1977).

Rest in Him and find peace to your soul.

CELEBRATING THE BOUNDARIES

HOW SWEET ARE YOUR WORDS TO MY TASTE, SWEETER THAN HONEY TO MY MOUTH!

—Psalm 119:103

*R*obert Bork, in *Slouching Towards Gomorrah,* wrote "Our modern, virtually unqualified, enthusiasm for liberty forgets that liberty can only be 'the space between the walls,' the walls of morality and law based upon morality. It is sensible to argue about how far apart the walls should be set, but it is cultural suicide to demand all space and no walls."

Isn't it interesting that Eve didn't know shame and alienation until she believed the adversary, who called God's boundaries into question (Genesis 3:1–7)? In all the years that I have worked with people, I have yet to meet someone whose life was in disarray because he had been faithful to the boundaries of God's Word and God's ways. On the other hand, we all know of lives that have been shattered by the consequences of living as though there were no walls.

As God's people, we should have a distinctly different view of boundaries. Those of us who trust God refuse to believe that boundaries are God's way of taking the pizzazz out of life. We know that His boundaries are actually fences constructed with wisdom and love at the perimeters of life to help us avoid the treachery of our naïveté.

I love the psalmist's perspective when he affirmed that the truly blessed person is the one whose "delight is in the law of the LORD, and on his law he meditates day and night." He went on to describe the one who celebrates the boundaries as one who is "like a tree planted by streams of water, which yields its fruit in season and whose leaf does not wither. Whatever he does prospers" (Psalm 1:2–3).

In Psalm 119 you can almost feel the exuberant affection the writer had for God's boundaries. "Oh, how I love your law! I meditate on it all day long. . . . How sweet are your words to my taste, sweeter than honey to my mouth!" (vv. 97, 103).

While our world scorns the boundaries, the truly free know better—we bless the boundaries.

Bless your boundaries in a prayer of gratitude.

TRUE LOVE

GOD IS LOVE. WHOEVER LIVES IN LOVE LIVES IN GOD, AND GOD IN HIM.
—1 John 4:16

We love God by giving ourselves willingly to Him, His Word, and His will. "This is love for God: to obey his commands" (1 John 5:3). But loving God is also expressed by extending love toward others. In fact, loving others is the proof of our commitment to Christ (John 13:34–35). These upward and outward directions of love are brought together in Christ's command that we are to first love God and then our neighbors as ourselves (Matthew 22:34–40).

The opposite of love is not always hate. It is more often self-centeredness rooted in a fear of loss, of being taken advantage of, of being misunderstood, of becoming vulnerable, or of losing control of our own destiny. Fear turns our attention inward. It thrives on self-centeredness—on our concern for our own welfare. When we are fearful, we refuse to surrender to God's control and are afraid to reach out to others.

Yet John reminds us that "perfect love drives out fear" (1 John 4:18). Love loves in the face of our fears and expels fear from our hearts. When I trust God to protect and prosper me, I have nothing to fear and am free to love. I am free to yield lovingly to God regardless of my circumstances and to unconditionally love others without seeking to protect my own interests. Paul helps us understand how foreign fear is to authentic faith: "For God has not given us a spirit of fear, but of power and of love" (2 Timothy 1:7 NKJV). A conscious commitment to true love will dispel fear and help drive out other fear-inspired enemies, such as anger, jealousy, and hatred.

A loveless life is often a life that has been victimized by fear. Trust Him to cover your fears and risk an act of love that tells Him how much you love Him. Reach "up" to Him in trust and "out" to others.

Start to love today by choosing one concrete way to express your love to God by loving someone you know who is in need.

SEEK AND FIND

RESIST THE DEVIL AND HE WILL FLEE FROM YOU. DRAW NEAR TO GOD AND HE WILL DRAW NEAR TO YOU. CLEANSE YOUR HANDS. . . ; AND PURIFY YOUR HEARTS.

—James 4:7–8 NASB

*M*y childhood memories still ring with the excitement I used to feel when I played hide and seek. Hearing the "seeker" count down as I hunkered in the best hiding place I could find often found my heart beating fast as my pursuer would approach. Hoping he would pass by, every muscle was poised for the moment I could break free and rush to home base shouting "Home free all!"

I've always been glad that God doesn't hide when we seek Him. In fact His assurance is that He is a rewarder of those who seek Him (Hebrews 11:6). But to many of us, tasting of this reward seems so elusive. Could it be that we simply don't know how to seek Him or where He is to be found?

I'll never forget the frustrating experience early one Sunday morning when I was supposed to pick up an elderly relative who was coming to Chicago by train. I was there on time, but she wasn't where I thought she would be. With increasing anxiety I scoured the early morning loneliness of Union Station— to no avail. Thinking that she had missed her train I was about ready to leave when I happened to glance down a hallway toward the baggage area. There she was, luggage at her feet, patiently waiting for me to arrive. She had been there all the time. And to my chagrin, it was right where she should have been. I had been looking in all the wrong places.

The great news is that Jesus is there, patiently waiting for you. In fact, He not only waits, but is in this very moment busily pursuing you (Revelation 3:20). The fact that you are reading this page on this day is no accident. It is just another one of the countless ways that He hopes to get your attention. His saving grace has put you in the station. It's time to connect.

Draw near by resisting every advance of Satan; keep your "hands" clean and your heart pure, and you will find that He has been there all the time waiting for you.

PSALM 19

The heavens tell of the glory of God.

The skies display his marvelous craftsmanship.

Day after day they continue to speak; night after night they make him known.

They speak without a sound or a word; their voice is silent in the skies;

yet their message has gone out to all the earth, and their words to all the world.

The sun lives in the heavens where God placed it.

It bursts forth like a radiant bridegroom after his wedding.

It rejoices like a great athlete eager to run the race.

The sun rises at one end of the heavens and follows its course to the other end.

Nothing can hide from its heat.

The law of the LORD is perfect, reviving the soul.

The decrees of the LORD are trustworthy, making wise the simple.

The commandments of the LORD are right, bringing joy to the heart.

The commands of the LORD are clear, giving insight to life.

Reverence for the LORD is pure, lasting forever.

The laws of the LORD are true; each one is fair.

They are more desirable than gold, even the finest gold.

They are sweeter than honey, even honey dripping from the comb.

They are a warning to those who hear them;

there is great reward for those who obey them.

How can I know all the sins lurking in my heart?

Cleanse me from these hidden faults.

Keep me from deliberate sins! Don't let them control me.

Then I will be free of guilt and innocent of great sin.

May the words of my mouth and the thoughts of my heart be pleasing to you,

O LORD, my rock and my redeemer.

"DO RIGHT"

THE PATH OF THE RIGHTEOUS IS LIKE THE FIRST GLEAM OF DAWN, SHINING
EVER BRIGHTER TILL THE FULL LIGHT OF DAY.

—Proverbs 4:18

*L*et's face it, it's a challenge to walk righteously in such a seductive culture. The menu of choices that our world offers appeals to every desire
and dream that lurks in our hearts. We are urged to do what we want to do,
what is right in our own eyes, or what is culturally correct. Unfortunately,
there is little on the menu that pleases God. What is really troubling is that
many who fashion their lives after the "if it feels good, do it" philosophy of
life seem quite happy and free. It's easy to wallow in self-righteous pity with
the psalmist who complained as he saw the wicked prosper, "Surely in vain
have I kept my heart pure" (Psalm 73:13).

But before you get too down on righteousness, remember that the righteous who resist the deceitful lure of the world find their lives refreshed like
that tree "planted by the rivers of water" (Psalm 1:3 KJV).

What does it mean to be righteous? "He whose walk is blameless . . . who
speaks the truth from his heart" (Psalm 15:2).

Unfortunately, few of us naturally make choices based on what is right and
true. We are far more likely to launch the decision-making process with questions such as, What is best for me? What do I want to do? Will it make me
happy? What is the most convenient and comfortable thing to do?

When the focus of our lives is on our own desires, our decision making
inevitably becomes self-centered, which inevitably yields the unstable fruit of
the flesh (Galatians 5:19–21).

At each intersection of life, the righteous followers step back from the
immediate circumstances and self interests and measure what the right thing
is to do before God.

When that happens life comes into conformity with God's standards and
our lives to enjoy the purity of it all. As an old time evangelist often said, "Do
right till the stars fall."

Enjoy righteousness in every area of your life, no matter how large or small.

CATCHING THE WORLD'S EYE

KEEP YOUR BEHAVIOR EXCELLENT AMONG THE GENTILES, SO THAT . . . THEY
MAY ON ACCOUNT OF YOUR GOOD DEEDS . . . GLORIFY GOD.

—1 Peter 2:12 NASB 1977

*E*ven a casual observer notes the dramatic shift in our culture. Our forefathers lived in a world governed by the consensus that God's laws and the teachings of Christ were the appropriate rules for life and relationships. But that is quickly becoming history. The remaining question is how we as followers are to live in a godless age. Should we stand on the rim of the arena of our society waving our Bibles in the air and shaking our fists in angry condemnation toward those who aggressively advocate all that is wrong?

The strategy of the New Testament church, whose environment was more hostile than ours, should be our model for triumph. In the face of the emperor's claim that he was to be worshiped as the god of the Roman Empire, Christians claimed that Jesus was their God and that their allegiance was first to Him.

As a result, Christians were persecuted so severely they often had to leave homes and vocations. They were fed to lions to entertain the crowds. They were covered with pitch and tied to lampposts, then set on fire to light the night. Yet after three centuries of pressure, oppression, and persecution, the undaunted commitment of the early church to the excellence of Jesus and His ways was so compelling that the more they were persecuted, the quicker the church expanded. Finally, Constantine, the emperor of Rome, embraced Christianity and proclaimed it the official religion of the Empire.

How do we catch the attention of our world? A world that is hostile, yet increasingly hungry, needing desperately to know the redemptive cleansing of Jesus Christ? Scripture says that it is through *lives so well lived* that a watching world cannot help but notice the compelling stories told through the excellence of our lives regardless of the pressure. Lives that have hope in the midst of hopelessness. Families that find joy and love in each other. People who radiate peace in the storms of life. This is the power of light in a dark and unrighteous world.

Has your life caught the attention of an unbelieving world?

GOD'S INTERRUPTIONS

THE LORD HAD SAID TO ABRAM, "LEAVE YOUR COUNTRY, YOUR PEOPLE AND
YOUR FATHER'S HOUSEHOLD AND GO TO THE LAND I WILL SHOW YOU."
—Genesis 12:1

I've always felt that life would be a great experience if it weren't for the
interruptions. The only redeeming factor when life is intersected by
some dilemma or disaster is that God is not surprised and in fact manages
every interruption for His glory and our good. Just in case you think He doesn't
understand, think of Jesus Christ, whose own glory in heaven was interrupted
as He followed the eternal decree that sent Him to this fallen place for thirty-
three years to be misunderstood, maligned, and ultimately martyred on a rugged
cross. All for the purpose of casting a victorious ray of light down through the
centuries to my life and to yours.

Throughout biblical history when people have surrendered to the interruptions God was imposing on their lives by saying, "God, I am willing to let
You use this interruption to transition me to Your intended purposes," God
has used that interruption to accomplish things far beyond themselves.

Consider those whose lives were interrupted for great things: Abraham,
Moses, Joseph, Job, Mary, and Joseph—and the list goes on. God knows what
He is doing. My pastor mused in a sermon recently about what would have
happened if Abraham had said, "I don't do trips," or if Noah had said, "I don't
do boats," or if Moses had said, "I don't do crowds." Think of what it would
have been like if Joseph had said, "I don't do rescue operations in Egypt," or
if Job had said, "I don't do sorrow," or if Mary had said no to the angel, or if
Christ had said, "I don't do crosses." Where would we be today?

The issue in God's interruptions is, "Am I willing to let this interruption
in my life be used for things beyond myself—to be used for *His* glory, *His*
gain, and *my* good?" Can we trust enough to stop resisting life's interruptions
and welcome them as God's unscheduled opportunities?

When the interruptions come, look and live for the opportunities.

TAKING UP CROSSES

... "If Anyone Wishes to Come After Me, He Must Deny Himself, and Take Up His Cross and Follow Me."
—Mark 8:34 NASB

We might initially think that following Jesus should be a cakewalk. Having given ourselves to Him we could easily expect Him to bless us with comfort and ease. But thoughts like this quickly fade when we are called to bear a cross. Crosses are hewn from the reality that the cause of Christ is being carried out through our lives in an imperfect world that is hostile to the One we follow. The rejection, alienation, marginalization, and, ultimately, the crucifixion were not mere inventions of a divine playwright to dramatize the messianic scene. They were the direct result of the fact that Christ came to do His work in alien territory that was dead set against His success.

Every aspect of Christ—His character, His teaching, His attitudes and responses to situations—is a threat to the reign and realm of the god of this age. The very essence and expression of authentic Christianity is a lethal stroke to the grip Satan has on this world.

The inevitability of crosses is grounded in the reality that followers live out the truth and the principles of Christ in a fallen world. Our actions and attitudes become a source of conviction to those who have rejected Jesus. The alternative expressed in our lives is often a reproof to their way of living. Rarely do the people around us respond by falling down in abject repentance; on the contrary, their response is likely to take the form of discomforting and unsettling intimidation. It takes cross-carrying, Christ-following courage to be rejected and maligned, yet remain confident, courageous, and compassionate.

Sound heavy? How heavy was the cross that He bore for you?

Feel deprived? Don't. He's gone to prepare a place for you.

Is there a cross in your life? Did you discard it, or do you bear its weight as a Christ follower?

PRAYING FOR KINGS

I Urge, Then, First of All, that . . . Prayers . . . Be Made for . . . Kings
and All Those in Authority, that We May Live Peaceful and Quiet
Lives in All Godliness and Holiness.

—1 Timothy 2:1–2

*W*ell, we may not have kings to pray for, but as the verse says, we do have people who are in authority over us. It's easy to construct the prayer list. Our president, other government officials, our boss at work, policemen, our parents, teachers, and a host of others who can pull rank on our lives. I don't know how you feel about the "rulers" in your life, but it would be safe to say that praying for them may not be your first impulse. Yet one of our Lord's interests in our prayers to Him is that we keep authority figures on the list regularly.

How should we pray for leaders? We should pray for what they need. Wisdom, freedom from graft and deceit, a genuine interest in doing what is best for those who are under their authority but, most important, governing in a way that would enable us to live "peaceful and quiet lives in all godliness and holiness" (1 Timothy 2:2). The early church lived out its commitment to Christ in the context of authorities who were often treacherous and threatening toward believers. The Christian's only hope was in the protection that God could provide. Which brings me to my point. Consistently praying for those who lead us is an ongoing reminder of two things. First, that it is our calling to live peaceful lives "in all godliness and holiness." If we prayed that every day, we just might make some progress in that area. Second, these kinds of prayers remind us that our hope is not in earthly kings but in the King of kings, who alone has ultimate power and authority over even the most powerful rulers. For too long we have put our trust for protection, prosperity, and peace in earthside rulers.

As the psalmist said, "Some boast in chariots and some in horses, but we will boast in the name of the Lord, our God" (Psalm 20:7 NASB).

Pray for those in authority daily.

GETTING BETTER, NOT OLDER

BUT THE FRUIT OF THE SPIRIT IS LOVE, JOY, PEACE, PATIENCE, KINDNESS, GOODNESS, FAITHFULNESS, GENTLENESS AND SELF-CONTROL. AGAINST SUCH THINGS THERE IS NO LAW.

—Galatians 5:22–23

According to Ephesians 4:11–15, growing older in Christ means becoming more like Him. Why is it, then, that with age we tend instead to become more crotchety, intolerant, unloving, and resistant to change? It's an indictment on the church that we are full of so many grumpy old saints. But it doesn't have to be that way. Had we been tracking with Him all along, we would be growing rich in character rather than cold in heart.

Thankfully, growing older in Christ is unlike growing older physically. The older we get, the better we can actually become. I'm not ancient, but I can already feel the deterioration in my joints and memory. Unfortunately, there isn't a thing I can do about it! But, in Christ, regardless of age, we can still be deepening in character and demonstrating the fruit of the Spirit in richer measure: "Love, joy, peace, patience, kindness, goodness, faithfulness, gentleness and self-control" (Galatians 5:22–23).

If spiritual aging involves the process of becoming more like Christ, then we should reflect these attitudes of Christ, including the giving up of our own rights to serve and celebrate the rights of others (Philippians 2:5–11). Maturing believers also grow in their capacity to discern the difference between good and evil. If we are aging in Him, we no longer need someone to tell us what is right and wrong, because we have consistently exercised our own understanding of scriptural principles (Hebrews 5:12–14). Periodically, I meet believers who mistakenly assume that age in Christ enables them to live with greater freedom in questionable behavior. To the contrary, true maturity shuns evil and lives for what is good.

When I was a little kid, I couldn't wait to grow up. Now that I am growing old, I am still enjoying the pleasure of growing up! In Christ, getting older is getting better and nearer.

In what ways would you say you are better in Christ today than you were six months ago? A year ago? What are your plans for the future as you get older in Christ?

PSALM 23

The LORD is my shepherd;
I have everything I need.
He lets me rest in green meadows;
he leads me beside peaceful streams.
He renews my strength.
He guides me along right paths,
bringing honor to his name.
Even when I walk
through the dark valley of death,
I will not be afraid,
for you are close beside me.
Your rod and your staff
protect and comfort me.
You prepare a feast for me
in the presence of my enemies.
You welcome me as a guest,
anointing my head with oil.
My cup overflows with blessings.
Surely your goodness and unfailing love will pursue me
all the days of my life,
and I will live in the house of the LORD forever.

SERVANTS WANTED

"My Father Will Honor the One Who Serves Me."
—John 12:26

*A*t Moody Bible Institute, we have a set of elevators with stainless steel doors that quickly accumulate handprints and fingerprints. Our housekeeping staff does a great job of keeping the doors clean. One day, I got on the elevator and noticed one of our housekeeping staff members tackling the task. The problem was, she was so short she couldn't reach the top part of the doors. I could have said to myself, *Isn't it a pity that someone else didn't get on to help her? Certainly the president is not called to a task like that.*

I knew better, of course. So I asked if I could help her reach the top of the door. Surprised, she handed me the cleaning cloth. Just as I reached toward the top of the doors, the elevator stopped, the doors opened, and several of our employees got on. There I was with the cleaning equipment in my hands, busy about the task. My instinctive urge was to hand the cleaning materials back to the housekeeper and look a little more "presidential" as the people entered the elevator.

Sometime later, I was walking down the hall and saw this housekeeper. I jokingly asked her how the elevators were coming, and she beamed. "Great!" she said. "In fact, lots of people are helping me with the doors now."

None of us is exempt from servanthood. In fact, it's contagious. And we catch it from Christ. Though holding the highest position in the universe, He chose the identity of a servant and washed the disciples' feet, while they were arguing over who would be the greatest in the kingdom (Luke 22:24–26; John 13:5; see also Philippians 2:5–11).

As He served His Father, He was also a servant to people in need. Our service needs to have this same dual focus. First and foremost, we are servants of our Lord Jesus Christ. There's never a problem here, because He is always worthy of being served. But when we step forward as His servants, He sends us out to serve Him on behalf of the needs and interests of others.

Plan at least one act of servanthood today.

A LIFE OR A LEGACY?

"BUT SEEK FIRST HIS KINGDOM AND HIS RIGHTEOUSNESS."
—Matthew 6:33

You've no doubt heard people sarcastically recommend that you "Get a life!"

Recently I received a letter from a woman in a church I had pastored some years ago in Detroit. Mary wrote to tell me her dad had passed away. I loved her dad. He was a quiet, deep man whose life I held in the highest regard. It was easy to respect Larry. Most who knew him felt the same way. Most significantly, his family felt that way.

Larry and his wife had moved to Louisville to retire near one of their married daughters. Over a period of time, three of Larry's daughters and their husbands moved to live near them. The whole family loved Larry. In fact, one of Larry's sons-in-law said that he wanted his four children to grow up knowing their grandfather.

As he became ill with a cancerous brain tumor, the men in the family—all of whom considered him their best friend—cared for him.

Mary wrote that even though her dad had become quite immobile toward the end, he still knelt before God in prayer each night. It took two people to get him back on his feet again and into bed. Though he knew little else, he still knew his Savior.

Larry walked the streets of Detroit during the race riots of the sixties ministering to those who were injured. His love for people, especially the downcast, led him to encourage Mary to take a job teaching in the inner city sixteen years ago.

What struck me in the letter was what a friend said at the funeral. "It hurts so much because the world has lost a righteous man, and that is no small thing."

I have often wondered what people will say about me when I am gone. What friends and family say is a commentary on the legacy we leave behind. Most of us have been so busy getting a life for ourselves that we have forgotten that life is really about building a legacy for God and others.

Is your life a legacy in the making?

LONGING FOR HIM

As the Deer Pants for Streams of Water, so My Soul Pants for You, O God.

—Psalm 42:1

*W*e all have longings. Longings for sleep, food, friends, safety, pleasure, and enough money to be comfortable. The list is long and seemingly without end. But if you were to list an honest accounting of what you really long for, I wonder if longing for God would be at the top. Or would it even have made the list?

If you like fishing, you know that casting out a line and pulling it back is essentially what it's all about. It is not going through the routine that counts, but how you do it. Doing it well takes the lure deep into the territory where the fish feed. Or you can yank the lure back quickly and simply skim the surface. Lots of expended energy with no satisfying results.

After a fast-paced first half of ministry life, I have an unquenchable desire to slow down and go deeper in my walk with Christ. I want to meet Him in the depths of my soul, away from the stress and press of everything on top. I want Jesus to fulfill my deepest longings. We are built for a relationship with God. All of life is about searching to fill the void that sin and separation from Him have created within. Filling the emptiness with piles of things, earthly friendships, and short term satisfying experiences, ultimately proves to yield less than what we had hoped for. Jesus is the only One who fits.

Underneath the layers of stuff, self-centered pursuits, and substitute satisfactions is a longing to know more of Him—to relate more fully, more intimately, more experientially with Him. Slow down. Pull back the layers and ask yourself in the depths of your being if it isn't a closer walk with Him that you really desire. Let your heart sing, "As the deer pants for streams of water, so my soul pants for you, O God. My soul thirsts for God, for the living God. When can I go and meet with God?" (Psalm 42:1–2).

What would it take to get more in touch with the Satisfier of your soul? Slowing down? More time in prayer and the Word? Dealing with the sin that separates?

FOLLOWING FOR A CHANGE

"COME, FOLLOW ME," JESUS SAID, "AND I WILL MAKE YOU FISHERS OF MEN."
—Matthew 4:19

*M*ost of us would readily admit that we are "followers of Christ." But my guess is that many of us would have a hard time clearly defining what that means in the everyday routines of life. Scripture helps us clarify the profile of a follower. In Matthew 4, when Jesus calls Andrew, Peter, James, and John to follow Him, there are two defining descriptions.

First, when Jesus said, "Follow Me," He used a word that literally means "come after Me." It defines following as a *relationship*—a relationship that redirects one's life. Instead of pursuing our dreams, desires, and plans, we yield to His dreams, desires, and plans to chart the course for our lives.

Second, when Matthew noted that they "left their nets and followed him" (v. 20), he used a different word for following. This word reflects two basic nuances. First, as we have noted above, it means that a follower is one who has a growing and deepening relationship to the one they follow. Followers do not characterize their following as a task or project. It is first and foremost a relationship to the person being followed. But there is more. This word also carries the meaning that a true follower is in the process of a *radical reformation* because of the influence of the leader. True followers do not remain the same once they start following. When we tell Him that we will follow, He immediately begins to change our lives. A follower looks to the leader for reformation in character and conduct. Followers become imitators of the one they are following. You know a follower because he acts and reacts like the one who is leading his life.

Following Jesus should make a difference in every aspect of life. If we claim the privilege, let's back it up with our practice. Followers of Jesus are marked by a relationship that transforms us to look more and more like the One we follow.

Follow Jesus for a change!

ONE AMERICAN AT A TIME

"THEREFORE GO AND MAKE DISCIPLES OF ALL NATIONS."
—Matthew 28:19

We long to see the day when America returns to its moral foundations. Yet, as wonderful as a reclaimed America would be, if it were simply a political victory that reinstated rules of better behavior, America would not be better off. As Ravi Zacharias has noted, "If we succeed in making America more moral, then what we will have is more lost moral Americans." In *The Pilgrim's Progress,* Pilgrim gets sidetracked into a layover in the village of Morality, where all is morally correct. He finds, however, that morality without the Cross can't alleviate his burden of sin.

Unfortunately, we have often been led to believe that political triumph over the enemies of godliness is the best strategy. Yet, a political solution is a seductive sidetrack. It tempts us to shift our eyes away from what must be the focus of true followers—concern for the lost and for the growth and development of believers in Jesus Christ. Some of us can identify with the woman who approached me recently before a meeting. She told me that for the past two years she had been so deeply involved in political causes that she had neglected her growth in Christ and her commitment to her local church in both time and giving. She had even come to see those on the other side of the political fence as enemies rather than as ones for whom Christ died. She admitted that during this time her intimacy with Christ had dimmed. She was convicted about how quickly her political adrenaline had eclipsed her passion for things of Christ and eternity.

While it may be energizing and exciting for us to believe that we are disposing of our Christian duty by marching, politicking, protesting, and supporting groups that do these things, it may well distract us from the most important task—glorifying God through Christlikeness and an unwavering commitment to the eternal destinies of friends and enemies alike.

The best way to win America is to care about Americans . . . one at a time!

What have you done recently to advance the cause of Jesus?

STRENGTH TO STRENGTH

GOD HAS ARRANGED THE PARTS IN THE BODY, EVERY ONE OF THEM, JUST AS
HE WANTED THEM TO BE. IF THEY WERE ALL ONE PART, WHERE WOULD THE
BODY BE?

—1 Corinthians 12:18–19

Think of the potential for division that is inherent simply in the diversity of gifts. Someone endowed with the gift of mercy finds it hard to deal with the prophetic gift that sees sin clearly and demands that people buck up, or pack up. The mercy person hurts with the fallen; the prophet is repelled by the seeming softness on sin that is reflected in the mercy giver. Visionary leaders are often irritated with those who have gifts of administration. Administrators love details; they ask all the hard questions and can be viewed as obstructionists to the visionary, whose primary concern is the outcome. Teachers fault exhorters for lacking depth of content; exhorters fault those with the gift of teaching as being dull, cognitive, and irrelevant.

Yet in Christ we learn that each gift needs the other in a complementary relationship in which weaknesses can be overcome and strengths magnified. Paul taught us in 1 Corinthians 12 that Christ is the Head and we are the body. Christ uses each part of the body so that it can do the work set before it. Can you imagine if the whole body were an eye? Try to envision a bunch of eyeballs rolling into church and plopping down in the pews.

Mercy people need prophets to strengthen their views of truth and sin. Prophets need mercy people to teach them about compassion. Leaders need process people—without them nothing would ever get done completely or well. And administrators need leaders to give them a goal to manage. Helpers need the analytical types to teach them about helping where it is important and to save them from the drain of overcommitment. The analytical need aggressive helpers to teach them to get busy in the lives of others.

Christ has uniquely built each of us to advance His cause . . . together. Know your gift and celebrate those whose gifts complement your strengths.

Is there a gift type that irritates you? Think of how you can affirm the place of that gifted person in your life and let him know of your support.

PSALM 24

The earth is the LORD's, and everything in it.
The world and all its people belong to him.
For he laid the earth's foundation on the seas
and built it on the ocean depths.
Who may climb the mountain of the LORD?
Who may stand in his holy place?
Only those whose hands and hearts are pure,
who do not worship idols and never tell lies.
They will receive the LORD's blessing
and have right standing with God their savior.
They alone may enter God's presence
and worship the God of Israel.

Open up, ancient gates!
Open up, ancient doors,
and let the King of glory enter.
Who is the King of glory?
The LORD, strong and mighty,
the LORD, invincible in battle.

Open up, ancient gates!
Open up, ancient doors,
and let the King of glory enter.
Who is the King of glory?
The LORD Almighty—
he is the King of glory.

THE UNSUSPECTING FOOL

THE FOOL HAS SAID IN HIS HEART, "THERE IS NO GOD."
—Psalm 14:1

*Y*ou're such a fool!" is the last thing I want someone to say to me. I can't imagine a more demeaning, deprecating insult. I would far rather be thought of as savvy and be respected for good advice and wise behavior. No doubt most of us see ourselves as being anything but fools. Fools are what other people are.

When we measure our lives by God's standards we may be surprised.

- "He who spreads slander is a fool" (Proverbs 10:18).
- "The way of a fool is right in his own eyes, but a wise man is he who listens to counsel" (Proverbs 12:15)
- "A wise man is cautious and turns away from evil, but a fool is arrogant and careless" (Proverbs 14:16).
- "A fool rejects his father's discipline" (Proverbs 15:5).
- "A fool does not delight in understanding, but only in revealing his own mind" (Proverbs 18:2).
- "Better is a poor man who walks in his integrity than he who is perverse in speech and is a fool" (Proverbs 19:1).
- "Keeping away from strife is an honor for a man, but any fool will quarrel" (Proverbs 20:3).
- "A fool always loses his temper" (Proverbs 29:11).

But the most damning accusation was written by the psalmist who said, "The fool says in his heart, 'There is no God'" (Psalm 14:1). Lulled into believing that the intelligence we have in our high-tech world exempts us from the label of "fool," we strut our stuff on the brief stage of our own existence and never dream that without God we are of all men most foolish. I'm reminded of the successful entrepreneur who celebrated his smashing success with a party only to have God arrive and say, "You fool, this night your soul shall be required of you. Then whose shall these things be?" (Luke 12). And he wasn't a fool because he had a lot of stuff. He was a fool because he had all the stuff but didn't have God. How poor he really was!

In case we feel we are off the hook on this last one . . . how often do you live as though there were no God?

GROWING GOD'S WAY

FOR WE ARE . . . GOD'S FIELD.

—1 Corinthians 3:6–9

*I*n my spare time I love to garden. I have a history of farmers in my heritage, so it may even be genetic. What frustrates part-time gardeners like me is getting things to grow the way we want them to. Since my life is so hectic, I haven't got the time to prune, cultivate, water, weed, and fertilize as I should. Healthy gardens take time and attention. Healthy followers of Jesus are the same.

True followers of Christ look as if they have received a lot of attention from the gardener of our souls by bearing a striking resemblance to Christ in character and conduct. True followers grow in healthy ways and are constantly grooming their lives in surrender to the gardener's will. And, we must remember, "weedy" lives are also a reflection on Jesus.

Yielding to Him is the key. Let me suggest some ways you can welcome Him in to do His work.

Make a *short* list of the areas of conduct and character in which you would like to grow. Think of strategic areas—family, attitudes, thought life, your job, and relationships. Review the list with a "follower" friend who knows you well and solicit his prayers and encouragement.

Focus on these areas as priorities in your life. Paul exhorted Timothy, "But you, man of God, flee from all this, and pursue righteousness, godliness, faith, love, endurance and gentleness" (1 Timothy 6:11).

Pray these issues back to God, repenting when necessary and pleading for God's grace in your life to grow in these areas and to seek forgiveness from those who have been hurt in the past by your conduct and character faults.

Study and memorize Scripture passages where the issues on your list are most clearly addressed. Spend time with others who reflect more of His character and conduct so that you can find motivation and hope to grow as they have.

Realize that growth takes time and is best cultivated in the ground of a growing intimacy with Christ. And while you're at it, let Him weed your heart often.

As you grow in one area, go back to the beginning and add another to your list. It's satisfying to grow!

A MATTER OF PERSPECTIVE

SINCE . . . YOU HAVE BEEN RAISED WITH CHRIST, SET YOUR HEARTS ON
THINGS ABOVE, WHERE CHRIST IS SEATED AT THE RIGHT HAND OF GOD.
—Colossians 3:1

*A*s believers, we have an important edge when it comes to attitudes toward tragedy and prosperity. Paul writes of this advantage: "So we fix our eyes not on what is seen, but on what is unseen. For what is seen is temporary, but what is unseen is eternal" (2 Corinthians 4:18). We, thanks to His saving grace, have more than just the here and now. All of life here must be seen in the context of what is yet to come. Peace in troubling times and wisdom in prosperity come not from our own short-term ingenuity but from seeing all of life from God's point of view—from an eternal perspective.

Focusing only on what is "seen" ultimately creates anxiety and confusion. We either get lost in the frustrations of our problems or see our prosperity in terms of how we can use our gain to our own advantage.

Joseph was instructed not to focus on the embarrassment of Mary's pregnancy. Job was reminded not to focus on his pain and loneliness. Noah was not to focus on the overwhelming task of building an oversized boat. The Christians at Laodicea were reproved for their self-sufficient focus on wealth. Life takes on new meaning when we see it all in terms of that which is "unseen" and eternal. As Scripture tells us, "Faith is being sure of what we hope for and certain of what we do not see" (Hebrews 11:1).

What long-term gain might He be working out through your pain? What could you do for eternity with the wealth of your energies, talents, possessions, and finances? Is there an aspect of His will for you that in the short term seems unreasonable and risky? By faith, rest in the reliable character and love of your Father in heaven and with great resolve make sure that the goodness of God in your life is reinvested in that which is of lasting value.

Are you focusing too intently on something that is keeping your eyes off the things of heaven?

FROM CURIOSITY TO COMPASSION

"Neither This Man nor His Parents Sinned," Said Jesus, "but This Happened so that the Work of God Might Be Displayed in His Life."
—John 9:3

The disciples who first followed Christ were dreadfully out of step with His heart when they pointed out a blind beggar and asked Christ who sinned—the man's parents or he in his mother's womb—that he should be born blind (John 9:2). No doubt they had seen this beggar many times before and may have reacted with the same kind of standoffish, theological curiosity. What they saw in Christ's response was hardly standoffish, and it clearly demonstrated the distance between Christ and His followers in regard to responding to people's needs. His was a response of compassion, not curiosity and judgment. He marshaled His resources to grant sight to the beggar and claimed that the blindness was actually intended to provide a moment when God could be magnified through Christ's compassionate touch.

We are so like those detached disciples! When we hear of trouble in someone's life, we are far more interested in the details and an analysis of what, why, when, and where than we are interested in finding out what we can do to reach out and help.

It is amazing what a listening ear, a season of prayer, a note, a hug (with no lecture about the sovereignty of God), a meal, or some free baby-sitting can mean to those who are suffering. I have had the pleasure of pastoring churches that were full of followers who went beyond curiosity to Christlike compassion. What I learned was that unsaved relatives and friends were consistently impressed with the uniqueness of a caring community. No doubt they wondered who would rally to their support if similar fates were to befall them. If we would only learn to see tragedy as a platform for the kind of compassion that reflects the power of God's glory through us, we could have a far greater impact on our world.

Anyone can be curious. Followers are curiously compassionate.

Plan an act of compassion today!

BEYOND THE CIRCUMSTANCES

TRUST IN THE LORD AND DO GOOD; DWELL IN THE LAND AND ENJOY SAFE PASTURE.

—Psalm 37:3

The trouble with trouble is that it is so inevitable. As one of Job's comforters observed, "Man is born for trouble as surely as sparks fly upward" (Job 5:7). So the challenge for all of us is to not expect a problem-free existence but rather to know how to deal with trouble effectively.

God's Word time and again instructs us not to focus on our circumstances or ourselves but rather on God and on His divine oversight of our lives. I am reminded of Corrie ten Boom's story.

As a young woman, Corrie and her family faced the horrors of the concentration camps after they were caught hiding Jews from the Nazi police. Certainly, World War II and the Holocaust could be listed among the world's most devastating catastrophes.

Corrie and her sister Betsie were taken to a work camp with thousands of other women. Forced to work at hard labor from daybreak until late into the night, they would fall onto their hard, wooden bunks exhausted beyond belief only to discover that the thin mats on which they slept were infested with fleas. Betsie thanked God for the fleas, to Corrie's horror. Corrie protested, "He doesn't expect thanks for this."

But Betsie insisted, "There has to be a plan, Corrie." Sure enough, what the sisters did not realize was that God was using those fleas for His divine purpose, in a plan not immediately apparent to those looking through earthly lenses.

As Corrie tells it, she found out later that the prison guards, repulsed by the fleas, refused to enter the barracks. So in that flea-infested space, the women found peace and quiet and the freedom to hold Bible studies unhindered by the prison guards. God used those fleas—those unwelcome, "interrupting" pests—for His divine purpose.

In life's most unwelcome interruptions, God is doing something above and beyond our immediate circumstances. Trusting Him, regardless, enables us to remain positive, believing that He uses what seems horrid at the time to accomplish what otherwise would not be possible in and through us.

Will you trust God enough to be faithful and grateful in times of testing?

THE TROUBLE WITH PLEASURE

I Thought in My Heart, "Come Now, I Will Test You with Pleasure to
Find Out What Is Good." But That Also Proved to Be Meaningless.
—Ecclesiastes 2:1

*A*s ironic as it may seem, the pursuit of pleasure can often be the source
of great unhappiness. James asks, "What causes fights and quarrels
among you? Don't they come from your desires that battle within you?"
(James 4:1). Pleasure agendas often clash when two pleasure seekers seek to
build a relationship. For example, the desire to please self is always a one-sided
affair—usually at someone else's expense. "I want to play tennis" clashes with
"I want to talk with you." "I want to be free" clashes with "I want the pleasure of your company."

The pursuit of pleasure distorts and dulls our prayer life. James goes on to
say, "When you ask, you do not receive, because you ask with wrong motives,
that you may spend what you get on your pleasures" (v. 3). While this is true
of much of what we ask for, it is especially true of the heretical "health, wealth,
and happiness" gospel. Prayer is not a manipulative weapon to force God to
grant us pleasure. It is a means by which we worship Him and a means by
which we find peace in the midst of pain and grace and mercy to help in the
time of need.

The pursuit of pleasure also leaves us empty. In Ecclesiastes 2, Solomon
verified the hollowness of pleasure when he wrote: "I thought in my heart,
'Come now, I will test you with pleasure to find out what is good.' But that
also proved to be meaningless. 'Laughter,' I said, 'is foolish. And what does
pleasure accomplish?'" (vv. 1–2).

Solomon went on to explain that he tested the pleasures of wine, great
accomplishments, gardens, and much livestock, silver, and gold. He denied
himself nothing he desired. Yet he found it all to be empty (v. 11).

Pleasure is an empty pursuit without God, who alone is the primary source
of satisfaction and fulfillment. Those who find true pleasure find it in a life
bent on pleasing God (2 Corinthians 5:9).

Focus the pursuit of your heart on true pleasure producers (1 Timothy 6:6–11).

PSALM 25:1–18

To you, O LORD, I lift up my soul. I trust in you, my God!

Do not let me be disgraced, or let my enemies rejoice in my defeat.

No one who trusts in you will ever be disgraced,

but disgrace comes to those who try to deceive others.

Show me the path where I should walk, O LORD;

point out the right road for me to follow.

Lead me by your truth and teach me, for you are the God who saves me.

All day long I put my hope in you.

Remember, O LORD, your unfailing love and compassion,

which you have shown from long ages past.

Forgive the rebellious sins of my youth;

look instead through the eyes of your unfailing love, for you are merciful, O LORD.

The LORD is good and does what is right;

he shows the proper path to those who go astray.

He leads the humble in what is right, teaching them his way.

The LORD leads with unfailing love and faithfulness

all those who keep his covenant and obey his decrees.

For the honor of your name, O LORD, forgive my many, many sins.

Who are those who fear the LORD? He will show them the path they should choose.

They will live in prosperity, and their children will inherit the Promised Land.

Friendship with the LORD is reserved for those who fear him.

With them he shares the secrets of his covenant.

My eyes are always looking to the LORD for help,

for he alone can rescue me from the traps of my enemies.

Turn to me and have mercy on me, for I am alone and in deep distress.

My problems go from bad to worse. Oh, save me from them all!

Feel my pain and see my trouble. Forgive all my sins.

TELL ME THE OLD, OLD STORY

ALL SCRIPTURE IS . . . USEFUL FOR TEACHING, REBUKING, CORRECTING AND TRAINING IN RIGHTEOUSNESS.

—2 Timothy 3:16

*T*here's a danger with children's Bible stories. The problem, of course, is not with the stories themselves. It is rather with our attitude toward them. For believer and unbeliever alike, they tend to be perceived as simply Sunday school fare.

One of the hardest persons to reach with the gospel is the one who views the Bible as merely a "harmless" set of morality tales for children. Although these people readily agree that the Bible's accounts of giants and floods and people being swallowed by great fish are interesting, they quickly dismiss their historical and spiritual validity. To them, the Bible is something a person simply outgrows, like the cartoons they watched as children.

More subtle still is the notion that even we as Bible believers outgrow these stories and go on to "deeper," more "doctrinal" levels of spiritual pursuit. While it is true that going deeper and delving into the intrigue of doctrine is abundantly profitable, abandoning the significance of the "stories" is a big mistake. As Paul noted, the stories of the Old Testament were written for our instruction (1 Corinthians 10:11; see also 2 Timothy 3:16 KJV).

There are profound lessons in Moses' life. Think of what we learn from Noah, Samson, David, and Jonah. Think of the simple yet profound stories Jesus told. Bible stories reveal the tensions that we inevitably face when we merge God's will and ways into the realities of our lives. They teach us of the treachery of sin, the damaging nature of sensuality, our frailty, our desperate need for God, and the reliability of His Word.

We need to remind ourselves that these accounts were not written with a "For Children Only" tag on them. They are part of the teaching, correcting, and training that God's Word is designed to accomplish in all of us. One good way to avoid this perceptual trap and tap into the Bible's spiritual riches is to retell the Bible stories we learned and loved as children, with our adult eyes and hearts open to what God's Spirit wants to teach us through them today.

Think of a familiar Bible story. What lesson for life can you draw from it for today? Read it again.

TAKE IT TO THE STREETS

THEREFORE, AS GOD'S CHOSEN PEOPLE . . . CLOTHE YOURSELVES WITH
COMPASSION.
                                        —Colossians 3:12

*I*n case you wondered why Jonah didn't want to go to Nineveh, it was
because he knew that God was a compassionate God willing to forgive
the Ninevites—whom Jonah preferred to be exterminated (Jonah 4:2). He
had no interest in being a middleman in a compassion transaction between
God and those he despised.

Sometimes it's easy to feel like that toward those who offend our sense of
righteousness. Mustering up compassion for those who promote the sins of
homosexuality or abortion on demand or for those who pass out condoms in
the schools is a tall order.

Yet Christ died for them and told shocked religious folks who were offended
at His interest in tax collectors and "sinners" that He had, after all, come "to
seek and to save what was lost" (Luke 19:10). The authentic follower of Christ
gets his heart in line with the compassion of Christ. But how?

First, we must remember that "while we were still sinners, Christ died for us"
(Romans 5:8). We can then pray that God will bring godly influences into lost
lives to let them know of their sin and lead them to focus on the Savior. We can
also pray that the Christians they meet will deliver a truly compassionate witness.

Granted, not all of us are called or able to be frontline people on the streets.
But many are already there, stunning neighborhoods with the grace of God, waiting for people like us to bring robes, rings, and shoes for prodigals who are repenting. We can be those who provide resources to—the middlemen who are busy
conducting compassionate transactions with people we can't possibly relate to.

The body of Christ today is blessed with a myriad of churches and Christian organizations that minister to AIDS patients, homosexuals, street people,
prostitutes, gang members, the homeless, the poor, the disadvantaged, and the
physically disabled. Crisis pregnancy centers and adoption agencies are compassionate alternatives to abortion. City ministries continue to effectively
reach the needy for Christ.

If you can't be a frontliner, you can be a partner. And no gift of compassion, no prayer, no check or volunteer time is too small.

What could you do to partner with a compassion ministry?

WHAT MIGHT HAVE BEEN

DEMAS, HAVING LOVED THIS PRESENT WORLD, HAS DESERTED ME.
—2 Timothy 4:10 NASB

*I*t was a cold December morning. Dressed in a white execution gown, he was led to the wall of the prison courtyard with the others. Blindfolded, he waited for the last sound he would hear: the crack of a pistol echoing off the prison walls. Instead, he heard fast-paced footsteps, then the announcement that the czar had commuted his sentence to ten years of hard labor.

So intense was that moment that he suffered an epileptic seizure—a malady he would suffer the rest of his life.

Fyodor Dostoyevsky was sent to prison, where he had only a New Testament to read. In it he discovered something more compelling than his socialistic ideals. He met Christ, and his heart was changed. Upon leaving prison, he wrote to a friend that Christ was so dear to him that if he were to find out that Christ were not in the realm of truth, he would rather have Jesus than the truth.

Dostoyevsky returned to civilian life. He wrote feverishly and produced his prison memoirs, *The House of the Dead,* and then *Crime and Punishment,* followed by many other major works.

The sorrowful end of this story is that he never grew as a Christian. His church attendance was sporadic. He neglected Bible study and the fellowship of other believers. He began to drink heavily, and gambling left him penniless. He had left prison with his heart aflame for Christ, but he died with nothing more than smoldering embers.

As a writer, Dostoyevsky left a legacy that places him among the literary greats. One wonders what impact Dostoyevsky's life could have had if he had stayed faithful to Christ. In the words of the poet John Greenleaf Whittier, "Of all sad words of tongue or pen, the saddest are these: 'It might have been!'"

Keeping on track for Christ in good times and bad is the only way to finish life and face eternity with few regrets.

Is there anything that has sidetracked your passion and enthusiasm for Christ?

ALL THAT THRILLS MY SOUL IS JESUS

"I AM THE WAY AND THE TRUTH AND THE LIFE."
—John 14:6

*L*ife has a way of becoming complex, confusing, and often disappointingly flat, which makes the entrance of Jesus into our lives so refreshing. Into our dull routines and disappointing days, Jesus makes this hope-filled claim, "I am the way and the truth and the life." It's an offer of the truly good life to those who follow in His way.

When life gets cluttered with a cacophony of voices, and conflicting advice is everywhere, only His voice carries weight with followers. He simplifies the complexities of life and unravels our confusion. There really is only one way! All that counts is what He tells me to do. Solutions and strategies for the best in life are offered on every talk show and in every magazine, but His ways are always best. They always work. And better yet, they are filled with the gift of grace which enables us to succeed.

Following Christ not only simplifies life, but it also fills the follower with a riveting sense of wonder and awe. Jesus is a most intriguing person. He will take us to places we have never been and unveil perspectives that are new. His compassion knows no stranger. His disdain for empty tradition and meaningless ritual is refreshing. Followers are awestruck by Christ's unlikely tolerance for—and interest in—scoundrels such as "sinners" and tax collectors.

Equally intriguing is His intolerance of hypocrisy and pride. His cleansing of the temple and His ministry of humble sensitivity show sides of His character that seem at once contradictory and compelling. His clarity of truth and arresting wisdom captivate our hearts and minds.

The fact that He chose to come to our earth as a servant instead of a king is an extraordinary paradigm.

He is our awesome God. Following Him as the all-compelling center of life is the starting point. Staying on the road with Him will reward you with a constant sense of adventure and awe.

Have you spent enough time with Christ to be struck with the awe of His person? Is your life tuned to hear His voice, and His alone?

SUNDAY BRUNCH

THEN HE CALLED THE CROWD TO HIM ALONG WITH HIS DISCIPLES AND SAID:
"IF ANYONE WOULD COME AFTER ME, HE MUST DENY HIMSELF."
—Mark 8:34

J will never forget the time when, early in my ministry, a couple in our small, newly planted church brought their neighbors to a service. They were thirty-something and had several children—just the kind of family you'd like to see come to Christ and help build your church. They sat in the second row in rapt attention. The message on that Sunday was about the creation of Eve for Adam. The text lends itself to some intrigue and humor given the dynamics of Adam's waking up and seeing this beautiful provision of God standing there in the Garden of Eden.

After the sermon, the neighbors said they enjoyed the service and enthusiastically said they would be back the following week. And they were. Right in the second row again, with faces full of anticipation for the next sermon. The problem, however, was that the next section of Genesis deals with the Temptation, the Fall, sin, accountability, and a call to nonnegotiated righteousness in our lives. The experience was not nearly as pleasurable for them. The theme of the proclamation was that God requires us to abandon our instincts and whims about life and liberty and to obey Him at all costs. The lesson was clear. If we do not conform to God's standards, there will be consequence, shame, and judgment.

The neighbors were polite as they left, but I could tell that their attitude had completely changed. We never saw them in church again. For them, if following Christ meant the weight of confrontation with sin and unqualified obedience to Christ, they would seek spiritual pleasures elsewhere.

How many of us are like that family? Treating the Word of God like a Sunday brunch, picking and choosing what pleases our taste buds but leaving what is less palatable behind? The journalist and humorist Finley Peter Dunn joked that the newspaper "comforts th' afflicted" and "afflicts th' comfortable." That description applies to God's Word. It is not a buffet. It is a diet. Take it all and grow in good health.

Is there a requirement or principle of Scripture that you have refused to deal with? Take it personally today.

BE HAPPY

WHAT DOES MAN GAIN FROM ALL HIS LABOR AT WHICH HE TOILS UNDER
THE SUN?

—Ecclesiastes 1:3

When Solomon searched for the meaning of life, he discovered in the
end that it was all futility. The lesson we learn from Solomon, who
by the way, had it all and knew the empty ring of life, is helpful for us today.

R. C. Sproul says, "Modern man has an aching void. The emptiness we
feel cannot be relieved by one more gourmet meal or another snort of cocaine.
We carry water in a sieve when we try to fill the empty space with a better job
or a bigger house."

Given everyone's hunger for fulfillment and happiness, I do not know of
a stronger testimony to the reality of Jesus as the "satisfier" than for we who
are His followers to prove the point.

The Bible says a great deal about happiness. God not only created us to be
happy; He has also shown us how to get there. The Old Testament word closest
to our concept of happiness is the word most English versions translate "blessed."
The Hebrew word for blessed has several nuances to it, but basically it means
a life without the clutter that litters our souls with guilt and unresolved anxi-
eties. True happiness, the kind that God supplies, is that wonderful sense that
everything is OK down deep inside. Some of us think of happiness as a twenty-
four-hour smile, but that's an awfully shallow definition. It is, in fact, impossible. What we actually crave is a sense of inner peace and joy in spite of adverse
circumstances. God's kind of blessedness, His happiness, stays intact even
when tears are running down our cheeks and hearts are broken.

When God thinks of your happiness, He wants to create that sense of well-
being in the deepest part of your soul. That your conscience is guilt free. That
you are yielded completely to the One who works all things together for good.
That no matter what happens, He will never leave you or forsake you. This is
the happiness for which Solomon searched—the biblical happiness that only
God can offer. Biblical happiness is the deep, settled sense of "God-all-right-
ness" in your soul.

Is it well with your soul?

PSALM 27

The LORD is my light and my salvation—so why should I be afraid?

The LORD protects me from danger—so why should I tremble?

When evil people come to destroy me,

when my enemies and foes attack me, they will stumble and fall.

Though a mighty army surrounds me, my heart will know no fear.

Even if they attack me, I remain confident.

The one thing I ask of the LORD—the thing I seek most—

is to live in the house of the LORD all the days of my life,

delighting in the LORD's perfections and meditating in his Temple.

For he will conceal me there when troubles come;

he will hide me in his sanctuary. He will place me out of reach on a high rock.

Then I will hold my head high, above my enemies who surround me.

At his Tabernacle I will offer sacrifices with shouts of joy,

singing and praising the LORD with music.

Listen to my pleading, O LORD. Be merciful and answer me!

My heart has heard you say, "Come and talk with me."

And my heart responds, "LORD, I am coming." Do not hide yourself from me.

Do not reject your servant in anger. You have always been my helper.

Don't leave me now; don't abandon me, O God of my salvation!

Even if my father and mother abandon me, the LORD will hold me close.

Teach me how to live, O LORD.

Lead me along the path of honesty, for my enemies are waiting for me to fall.

Do not let me fall into their hands.

For they accuse me of things I've never done and breathe out violence against me.

Yet I am confident that I will see the LORD's goodness

while I am here in the land of the living.

Wait patiently for the LORD. Be brave and courageous.

Yes, wait patiently for the LORD.

NETS THAT ENTANGLE

THEN THE WORD OF THE LORD CAME TO JONAH A SECOND TIME: "GO TO THE GREAT CITY OF NINEVEH AND PROCLAIM TO IT THE MESSAGE I GIVE YOU."
—Jonah 3:1

*S*cripture tells us that early followers of Jesus "at once . . . left their nets and followed him" (Matthew 4:20). Followers are netless believers. What are the nets? A net is anything that inhibits or prohibits our nonnegotiated commitment to follow Christ. None of us is exempt from getting ensnared in our nets. It is surprising to note how many nets entangle our lives and thwart our followership. These can be nets of relationships, plans, a willful heart, greed, immorality, bitterness, fear, impure habits, and more. Nets come in all colors and sizes.

Here's a defining story about nets and following.

He was God's best man. God had groomed and appointed him for spiritual leadership. If you were looking for a follower in that day, you would have known that Jonah qualified for the honor—until God said, "Follow Me . . . to Nineveh." The net of his compassionless prejudice (Jonah 4:1–3) gave him second thoughts. At the crossroads of decision, he concluded that he would do just about anything as a follower except go to Ninevah. So he boarded a boat for Tarshish, the exact opposite direction from Nineveh (Jonah 1:3). Interestingly, he felt at peace about the whole deal, so much so that he was found down in the hold of the ship fast asleep in the midst of a life-threatening storm.

Feeling at peace about a net in our lives is not a gauge of the correctness of the course we are on—at least not always. Our capacity to rationalize and excuse ourselves is too powerful to trust anything except our surrender to the call of God. Regardless of the cost.

Followership is not just something for which we volunteer. It is why He saved us. It's what He expects. His work and glory depend on our responsiveness. Therefore, He doesn't blink and look the other way when we balk at following; He relentlessly pursues us until we drop the net and get back on the road with Him.

What's that net in your hands? Can you drop it for Jesus?

NETLESS LOVE

*I*f we are true followers, we, along with those first disciples, have left our nets and followed Christ. As we have seen, as long as we cling to our prized nets, we are going nowhere with Jesus. The pilgrimage of fully devoted followers should be littered with the nets we have dropped along the way. In fact, you can tell where followers have been by the nets they've left behind.

Following Christ is not only about keeping our eyes on Him in surrender. It is also about the nets of our attitudes and actions toward fellow followers. Scripture teaches us that unity is a primary signature of our followership. Christ intended that our pilgrimage be marked by followers who, hand in hand and arm in arm, form a massive unified movement for Him. Followers are known by their active commitment to loving, encouraging, supporting, and motivating one another on the journey.

Christ said, "A new command I give you: Love one another. As I have loved you, so you must love one another. By this all men will know that you are my disciples, if you love one another" (John 13:34–35). In His last prayer, Christ said, "For them I sanctify myself, that they too may be truly sanctified. My prayer is not for them alone. I pray also for those who will believe in me through their message, that all of them may be one, Father, just as you are in me and I am in you. May they also be in us so that the world may believe that you have sent me" (John 17:19–21).

Like misbehaving children in the backseat of the car, the nets of our individualism and self-centered ways often create an ugly scene on the road behind Christ. The nets in our hands—those of pride, arrogance, gossip, slander, critical attitudes, bitterness, and the pursuit of personal agendas at the expense of others—make it impossible to love and walk as one. Yet the netlessness of mutual love is precisely what marks and empowers us as followers before a watching world.

Is there a net in the way of your expressed love to a brother or sister?

LOOK A-LIKES

"COME, FOLLOW ME," JESUS SAID, "AND I WILL MAKE YOU FISHERS OF MEN."
AT ONCE THEY LEFT THEIR NETS AND FOLLOWED HIM.
—Matthew 4:19–20

When I was in seminary, I could almost always tell what a fellow student's major was by listening to him talk or watching his gestures and mannerisms. He had become so enthralled with his major professor that he used words, phrases, and styles of thinking and speaking that were mirror images of his admired mentor.

One nuance to the word used in Matthew 4:20 to describe the disciples' commitment to follow Christ indicates that those who would be known as followers were so impressed by their leader that they often ended up replicating his traits in their lives. This issue is deeper than conduct. It relates to character. Therefore, when the Epistles speak of "followership," they usually use the word *imitate*. Followers of Christ are clearly enamored with Him, and as such our lives should begin to emulate Him. The expanding character of Christ in our lives becomes the most important mark of the authenticity of our claim to be followers of Him. Unlike travelers on the crowded byways of our world who celebrate competency and credentials, a follower of Christ is known by compassion; zero tolerance for hypocrisy; patience; righteousness, justice, love, and forgiveness. If we see it in Jesus, it should increasingly be seen in us.

Christ's power lay neither in competency as the world saw it nor in the kind of credentials that would give Him rank and privilege among the elite. His competency, in earthly terms, extended to His simple skills as a carpenter; His lack of credentials placed Him as an outsider both politically and religiously. Yet He impacted this planet more than any other person. It was His unique and compelling character that made the difference. And, we should remember, it is His character expressed through our conduct that empowers us to have an incredible impact on our world as well.

Has your heart been stolen by the seductive allure of living for competency and credentials?

List the character qualities you see in Christ. Use these as a growth guide and a point of accountability.

THE TROUBLE WITH ME

I Count All Things to Be Loss in View of the Surpassing Value of Knowing Christ.

—Philippians 3:8 NASB

*K*nowing more about me is not always a pleasant experience. Self-introspection often compounds my insecurities and doubts. Trips into my inner self often expose memories of past failures and resurrect fears of the future. That's why spending time getting to know Jesus is of such great value.

In fact, living to know Him is the key to understanding and making peace with ourselves. Trying to discover self-worth? You have it in Him—He died for you! Plagued by failure and guilt? He does what no one else will or can do for you—He forgives and forgets, kills the fatted calf as heaven rejoices, and clothes you with the best robes of His righteousness. Searching for significance? Search no more . . . you are His child. There is no greater significance than that. Trying to figure life out and wondering if there is any purpose for you to take up space on this planet? The mystery is unraveled in Him as He scripts your life to be lived for His glory and to reflect the reality of His character through your life. Let's face it, you'll never finally or fully make it on your own. Self is forever inadequate to satisfy your soul and is inept to solve the restless searching of your heart.

But until we learn that lesson, we will continue to discover that the trouble with self-focused living is that it is never resolved. Just when you think you know all about yourself you'll do something that surprises and disappoints you. Like the gerbil, who spends considerable amounts of time running in his wheel, self-absorbed people rarely get to resolution.

Life must be about more than getting to know ourselves. In fact if your are determined to spend a great deal of time preoccupied with yourself, life is bound to bore you to tears. None of us is that special.

Live to know Jesus.

PAIN THAT'S WORTH THE GAIN

In This You Greatly Rejoice, Though Now for a Little While You May
Have Had to Suffer Grief in All Kinds of Trials.
—1 Peter 1:6

A while ago I went to the store to buy a new garage door opener. I
shopped, found the right one, paid for it, and took it home. It came
in two boxes. I unboxed it, assembled it, hung it, and wired it. In the process,
there was a lot of banging on its parts to get them to fit. A lot of tightening
of its screws and bolts.

It's like that with God. He accepts us just the way we are. But He then
wants to make us usable. He may need to take us out of our comfortable,
neatly packaged boxes. Hammer on us. Tighten us here and loosen there.
Whatever it takes.

The key to getting properly assembled is to cooperate with God's intentions in our lives. God's goals need to become our goals. If it is our goal to be
conformed to the image of His Son—to be righteous, to find our sufficiency
in Him, to serve Him with our whole hearts, to be made capable and usable—
then we will willingly endure *whatever* if it leads us to the goal. Embracing the
goal helps us remember that the pain is worth the gain. If, however, our goal
is to be happy, healthy, wealthy, and comfortable, we will resist the trials of life
and become bitter and brittle in the Master's hand. We must agree with God
at the outset. Our prayer should be, "Lord, I want to be capable and usable
for You. Regardles of what it takes, I am ready."

Stop now and ask yourself the question, "Am I becoming better or brittle
as He seeks to glorify Himself through me?"

*Will you pray now to transition the goals of your life and the expectations of this
day to be in line with our Lord's desires and expectations for you? Be specific in
your prayer about goals and expectations you are willing to submit your heart to.*

PRAYER CHANGES ME

PRAY CONTINUALLY.

—1 Thessalonians 5:17

J love reading the Psalms. The psalmist is so straightforward with his complaints about life, his enemies, and God's seeming inattentiveness to life's predicaments. Though he complains and whines, in the end his heart transitions into an instrument of praise regardless of how life is treating him. The lesson? Prayer has a wonderful way of getting us to see life from God's point of view. When we do, our perspectives are radically altered. But prayerlessness in times of trouble leaves us to the deceptive jeopardy of our own fallen perspectives.

When David felt God had abandoned him, prayer caused him to realize that he could trust in God's lovingkindness, rejoice in His ultimate salvation, and sing in gratitude for all the good that God had done for him (Psalm 13).

When Asaph was deep in a pity party about the wicked, who seemed to prosper, and grumbling that evidently he had cleansed his heart in vain, he took the complaint directly to God. When he did so, he realized that ultimately God will judge the wicked and that heaven was his sure reward. By the end of the psalm, his self-pity turned to praise as he lifted his voice in this moving anthem: "Whom have I in heaven but Thee? And besides Thee, I desire nothing on earth. My flesh and my heart may fail, but God is the strength of my heart and my portion forever. . . . But as for me, the nearness of God is my good" (Psalm 73:25–26, 28 NASB 1977).

When you can't quite figure out what on earth went wrong, when you can't seem to find your way, lift your eyes toward heaven and pray. Pray out loud if you need to. Turn to the Psalms and pray His Word back to Him. Write out a prayer. But always remember that, when we don't know how to pray, the Spirit makes intercession for us before the throne (Romans 8:26).

Stay at it. Don't abandon the process. Your connectedness to God will change your perspective, and intimacy with Him will be your reward.

Prayer may not always change things, but it will always change you . . . for the better.

PSALM 30

I will praise you, LORD, for you have rescued me.

You refused to let my enemies triumph over me.

O LORD my God, I cried out to you for help,

and you restored my health.

You brought me up from the grave, O LORD.

You kept me from falling into the pit of death.

Sing to the LORD, all you godly ones!

Praise his holy name.

His anger lasts for a moment,

but his favor lasts a lifetime!

Weeping may go on all night,

but joy comes with the morning.

When I was prosperous I said,

"Nothing can stop me now!"

Your favor, O LORD, made me as secure as a mountain.

Then you turned away from me, and I was shattered.

I cried out to you, O LORD.

I begged the Lord for mercy, saying,

"What will you gain if I die, if I sink down into the grave?

Can my dust praise you from the grave?

Can it tell the world of your faithfulness?

Hear me, LORD, and have mercy on me. Help me, O LORD."

You have turned my mourning into joyful dancing.

You have taken away my clothes of mourning and clothed me with joy,

that I might sing praises to you and not be silent.

O LORD my God, I will give you thanks forever!

TRUE PROSPERITY

"I Know Your Tribulation and Your Poverty (but You Are Rich)."
(Jesus to the Church at Smyrna.)

—Revelation 2:9 NASB

*H*ave you ever envied the prosperity of the wicked? Particularly if in your commitment to righteousness you have not prospered as others have? As a child I enjoyed "3-D" comic books. A special set of glasses with colored plastic lenses and cardboard frames came with them. Without the glasses, the books were blurred and unclear. With the glasses, they came alive with action and color.

Seeing life through God's glasses will always provide an accurate assessment of life around us. From God's point of view, the wicked are not in an enviable position. As the psalmist said, "Surely you place them on slippery ground; you cast them down to ruin. How suddenly are they destroyed. . . . As a dream when one awakes, so when you arise, O Lord, you will despise them as fantasies" (Psalm 73:18–20). Or to put it another way, what difference does it make to have a big inning and lose the whole ballgame?

Is it a sign of prosperity to stand before God and hear Him say, "Depart from me, you who are cursed, into the eternal fire prepared for the devil and his angels" (Matthew 25:41)? As Christ said, "What good will it be for a man if he gains the whole world, yet forfeits his soul?" (Matthew 16:26).

In Luke 12 Christ told of a wealthy man who was so prosperous that he had to tear down his old barns and build new ones. He said to himself, "'You have plenty of good things laid up for many years. Take life easy; eat, drink and be merry.' But God said to him, 'You fool! This very night your life will be demanded from you. Then who will get what you have prepared for yourself?'" (vv. 19–20).

True prosperity is not measured in cash or commodities but in our privileged relationship with the ever-present God. That is why we can sing with Fanny Crosby, "Take the world, but give me Jesus."

Would you be willing to define prosperity in terms of God's unfailing presence in your life and His provision for an eternal experience with Him? (See Psalm 73:23–28.)

LONG-TERM COMMITMENT

PERSEVERE SO THAT WHEN YOU HAVE DONE THE WILL OF GOD, YOU WILL
RECEIVE WHAT HE HAS PROMISED.

—Hebrews 10:36

*A*lthough the impact of our good works may occasionally be more immediate, for most of us the influence of our faithful labor will be told in years and not in days, perhaps in the next generation, long after we are gone, in the lives of our children and grandchildren.

Which makes living in a world of immediate gratification, ready cash, and instant Internet access a real challenge to authentic Christianity. Much of God's work calls for stick-to-itiveness over the long haul. Raising a godly family demands long-term commitment. Witnessing to a lost friend is rarely an overnight success. Discipling new believers is about long-term growth. Think of God's perseverance and patience in your life and mine. How long has He been at work—and we aren't even close to finished yet! We too need to be people of routine faithfulness over the long haul to see the fruit of our labor.

Effective Christianity is not a snapshot. It's a feature-length film whose conclusion is played out in eternity.

For believers who lived in the former Soviet Union, it took seventy years of faithfulness in the midst of phenomenal oppression, persecution, and martyrdom to have the story of their lives used to lift the lid of oppression and open the gates of an atheistic empire to the good news of Jesus Christ. In a meeting with top-level bureaucrats concerning the disintegration of their economy, Gorbachev asked, "Why do we oppress the people who do not absent themselves from work, who are not alcoholics, and who give us a good day's work?" The Russian regime found it hard to argue with lives so well lived. It was finally the moment for triumph. Finally . . . after seventy years.

We are called to be faithful to a nonnegotiated, persevering obedience. Unwavering commitment is our task. The outcomes are God's responsibility . . . in His time and His way.

Be not weary in well doing . . . your labor is not in vain in the Lord. (1 Corinthians 15:58)

APRIL 23 / 126

PLEDGING ALLEGIANCE

I URGE . . . PRAYERS . . . FOR KINGS AND ALL THOSE IN AUTHORITY, THAT WE
MAY LIVE PEACEFUL AND QUIET LIVES IN ALL GODLINESS AND HOLINESS.
—1 Timothy 2:1–2

*S*ometimes, to hear Christians talk, you'd think that it is the government's responsibility to advance righteousness and to be the steward, upholder, promoter, and protector of biblical truth and values. Actually, as American Christians we have lived in an unusual season of history. We've had a government that, although led for the most part by people who were not authentically Christian, was built on the fundamental tenets of a biblical heritage. But that has now changed. In fact, it is helpful to remember that most Christians through the ages have lived under hostile, oppressive, pagan systems. Quite frankly, Christians have often done their best in those environments.

God never assigned government the task of upholding scriptural truth. Scripture assigns government the responsibilities of safety, stability, peace, and justice (Romans 13:1–5; 1 Timothy 2:2). We give the wrong impression of the biblical mandate for government when we feel betrayed because it is no longer an advocate for truth and righteousness. The advancement and proclamation of godly values is assigned to our lives, our homes, and our churches. We don't have the luxury of hoping that government will help us in the process.

Early Christians, during times of ruthless political regimes, took the responsibility to uphold their faith under great cultural pressure. They, not their governments, were the light of the world.

It was to these Christians that Paul delineated our responsibilities toward government. We are to honor those in authority over us, pray for them, and pay our taxes. Thankfully, Scripture doesn't say that we have to vote for them; but since they are ultimately placed in authority by God, we are commanded to give them due respect (Romans 13:1–7). This biblical perspective recognizes God's sovereign oversight, realigns our attitudes, and releases us to get on with the business of being the torchbearers that He intended us to be.

Pray today for those in authority over you. Make it a habit—and write to them and let them know.

IS THERE A SERVANT IN THE HOUSE?

"WHOEVER WISHES TO BECOME GREAT AMONG YOU SHALL BE YOUR SERVANT."
—Matthew 20:26 NASB

*J*n Matthew, the disciples James and John came to Christ with their mother. She filed this request: "'Command that in Your kingdom these two sons of mine may sit one on Your right and one on Your left'" (Matthew 20:21 NASB), which being interpreted means, "Could my sons have the most powerful and influential positions in the new government?" The text goes on to say that when the other ten heard about her appeal they were "indignant." Probably for a lot of reasons. But, no doubt, the real rub was that they *all* wanted the big spots in what they assumed would be the soon-to-arrive kingdom. If they had a choice, none of them wanted to play the lesser part.

Christ reproved them for their advanced cases of "big-shot-itis" and went on to tell them that if they were to be authentic followers, they would have to pursue servanthood as a life goal. In fact, He noted that those who would be considered great in His kingdom would be those who served. God wants followers who are willing if necessary to play the small part, the unaffirmed part. As for those whom He has given visibility and clout, He is looking to see if they manage their leadership from a servant's perspective.

After all, God was willing to stoop low enough to serve us all the way to the painful injustice of a cross. The thought that some things are beneath us, that we deserve better, that we really should be served instead of serving, denies the very essence of Jesus and our identity in Him. If we are striving to be like Him, no task is too small, no venue too unnoticed, no legitimate sacrifice too great. Because He served, we gladly live to serve. And we do it all the way home to heaven whether anyone notices or not. Knowing all the while that He notices and will say to us when we arrive, "Well done, thou good and faithful servant" (Matthew 25:21 KJV). Which is a recognition worth not being recognized for!

What serving role do you play—parent, Sunday school teacher, prayer warrior? Keep it up. It's so much like Christ!

BEYOND HAPPINESS

PURSUE RIGHTEOUSNESS, GODLINESS, FAITH, LOVE, ENDURANCE AND
GENTLENESS.

—1 Timothy 6:11

*I*n its May 1996 issue, *American Scientific* magazine unmasked a myth
about happiness: "People have not become happier over time as their
cultures have become more affluent. Even though Americans earn twice as
much as they did in 1957, [the number of] those who are 'very happy' has
declined from 35 to 29 percent."

Happiness has little to do with wealth and the accumulation of things. According to the study, four traits characterize truly happy people. They "like themselves . . . feel in personal control . . . are usually optimistic . . . are extroverted."

Interestingly, these qualities are most deeply enjoyed by those who are
maturing as followers of Jesus. Guiltlessness and unconditional acceptance
enable believers to feel gratefully right about themselves. Followers of Christ
also escape the controlling influences of evil and enjoy the blessing of self-
control. Amid the pervasive despair in our society, we have an assured optimism
in the ultimate victory of Christ and the glory of an eternity with Him. And,
followers care about other people.

It should be no surprise that the article goes on to note that "religious"
people have a greater tendency toward happiness. This only underscores that
the sources of happiness are found not in the temporal gain of this world or
its comforts, but in a growing relationship with God. Though our world does-
n't quite get it, happiness is not a pursuit—it is a reward.

That is exactly what Paul had in mind when he encouraged Timothy to
pursue righteousness, faithfulness, servanthood, contentment, justice, and
compassion (1 Timothy 6:6–11). It is the pursuit of those qualities that will
bring happiness. Happiness cannot be the life goal of the follower of Christ.
God and His Word must be our passion. When this is the case, we will follow
Him whether or not we are "happy." And it is only then that we will discover
that it is He who ultimately gives us true happiness as a gift of His grace.

Do you live to be righteous or happy?

A PURPOSE BEYOND OURSELVES

"For the Pagan World Runs After All Such Things. . . . But Seek His Kingdom, and These Things Will Be Given to You as Well."
—Luke 12:30–31

*I*t's amazing how many of us have become disoriented by the seduction of success. Even those of us who have little and have been unable to make a big splash in this world often live with the regret that life didn't turn out as well as we had hoped.

It's time for us to get a biblical life!

The late Ted DeMoss, former chairman of the Christian Business Men's Committee, tells of a friend, John Herman, whose lifelong ambition had been to meet the brilliant criminal lawyer Clarence Darrow of the Scopes "monkey trial" fame. It was arranged for the two men to meet. Sitting in the attorney's living room, Herman asked Darrow, "Now that you've come this far in life and you're not doing much lecturing or teaching or writing anymore, how would you sum up your life?" Without hesitation, Darrow walked over to a coffee table and picked up the Bible. This took Herman by surprise, since Darrow was an atheist who had spent much of his life publicly ridiculing Scripture.

"This verse in the Bible describes my life." Darrow turned to the fifth chapter of Luke, the fifth verse. He changed the "we" to "I": "I have toiled all the night, and have taken nothing" (see KJV).

He closed the Bible, put it back on the coffee table, and looked Herman straight in the face. "I have lived a life without purpose, without meaning, without direction. I don't know where I came from. And I don't know what I'm doing here. And worst of all, I don't know what's going to happen to me when I punch out of here."

Take it from those who have cut their own wake and arrived in the fantasy-land of fame and fortune without God: We need something more in life than we can supply. Our hearts long for something beyond ourselves, for a cause that can give meaning and value to life.

What is the cause that drives your life? Of what significance will it be at the threshold of eternity? Do you need to refocus?

PSALM 31:1–8, 14–17, 19b-21a, 23-24

O LORD, I have come to you for protection; don't let me be put to shame.

Rescue me, for you always do what is right.

Bend down and listen to me; rescue me quickly.

Be for me a great rock of safety, a fortress where my enemies cannot reach me.

You are my rock and my fortress.

For the honor of your name, lead me out of this peril.

Pull me from the trap my enemies set for me, for I find protection in you alone.

I entrust my spirit into your hand. Rescue me, LORD, for you are a faithful God.

I hate those who worship worthless idols. I trust in the LORD.

I am overcome with joy because of your unfailing love,

for you have seen my troubles, and you care about the anguish of my soul.

You have not handed me over to my enemy but have set me in a safe place. . . .

But I am trusting you, O LORD, saying, "You are my God!"

My future is in your hands. Rescue me from those who hunt me down relentlessly.

Let your favor shine on your servant. In your unfailing love, save me.

Don't let me be disgraced, O LORD, for I call out to you for help.

Let the wicked be disgraced; let them lie silent in the grave. . . .

You have done so much for those who come to you for protection,

blessing them before the watching world.

You hide them in the shelter of your presence,

safe from those who conspire against them.

You shelter them in your presence, far from accusing tongues.

Praise the LORD, for he has shown me his unfailing love. . . .

Love the LORD, all you faithful ones!

For the LORD protects those who are loyal to him,

but he harshly punishes all who are arrogant.

So be strong and take courage, all you who put your hope in the LORD!

GOOD AND EVIL

LIVE SUCH GOOD LIVES AMONG THE PAGANS THAT, THOUGH THEY ACCUSE YOU OF DOING WRONG, THEY MAY SEE YOUR GOOD DEEDS AND GLORIFY GOD ON THE DAY HE VISITS US.

—1 Peter 2:12

*S*trange, isn't it, that America has changed so radically that those who do evil prosper and the righteous end up being the "bad guys" of society. Just raising objections to abortion, homosexual behavior, or sexual promiscuity makes us look like close relatives of Attila the Hun.

It's important to note that Peter reminds us that we would be slandered as "evildoers" (1 Peter 2:12 KJV). Because early Christians called their celebrations of the Lord's Table "love feasts," rumors abounded that they were involved in sexual orgies. And because those feasts involved sharing in the body and blood of Christ, they were said to have cannibalistic tendencies. The early Christians were also known as destroyers of families, since those who struck an allegiance with Christ often broke with the pagan traditions of their kin. Most seriously, they were a threat to the cohesiveness and continuity of the Roman empire, as they expressed allegiance to the God of the universe rather than to Caesar. For all of this and more, Christians were often portrayed as the evil element of society.

There is a sense in which we can identify with being labeled as the evildoers in our culture. When we hold society accountable for righteousness and articulate what is right and wrong from God's point of view, we are increasingly seen as a threat to actual agendas. Agendas like abortion and gay rights are viewed as part of a progressive society that has finally unshackled itself from the chains of a restricted, puritanical past.

Yet no matter what people say about us or how they portray us, Peter instructs us to live in such a way that they can't avoid noticing the outcome of righteousness in our lives—our good deeds. When the consequences of their sin leaves them broken and without hope, they will notice the stability and peace in our lives, which just may give us the opportunity to tell that it is Jesus who's made the difference.

Is your life full of "good deeds"? Do unbelievers notice?

A LIFE WELL LIVED

*O*n a recent vacation, my wife, Martie, and I took a side trip with a group of people we had never met before. I sat next to a man who obviously has never met a stranger. Immediately he and I—an unrepentant people person myself—struck up a conversation. To our surprise, we found that we grew up in the same town, went to the same high school, and graduated the same year. We spent much of the conversation comparing notes regarding mutual friends and memories. In the course of that conversation, he said to me, "Did you say your name was Stillwell?"

I said, "No, it's Stowell."

He said, "Oh, I know a man in northern New Jersey by the name of Stillwell."

I said, "His name wouldn't be Art Stillwell, would it?" (Art Stillwell was a member of my dad's church where I grew up; he operates a major car dealership in north Jersey.)

He said, "Yes, as a matter of fact it is! I am an attorney, and I care for his legal affairs. Art Stillwell is like no other client I have." When I asked what he meant, he said, "Most of my clients want me to keep them out of trouble no matter what it takes. But when Art Stillwell is in a difficult situation and he calls on me to unravel it, I always ask, 'Art, what do you want me to do?' and his reply is always the same: 'Do what is right.' I have no other client who responds like that."

It's hard to argue with a life so well lived.

If that attorney from northern New Jersey ever gets to heaven, it will be in part because he had one client who was completely committed to righteousness, who refused to compromise, even in the tough times. Art's life told a compelling story. His righteousness rose like the light of a city set on a hill.

Let your light shine!

SALT AND LIGHT

You Are the Salt of the Earth . . . the Light of the World.
—Matthew 5:13–14

*W*hen Jesus summarized our mission in this world, He used two familiar metaphors to illustrate the role that we should play. We are to be like salt and light. Salt adds flavor, preserves, and purifies. Light illuminates, guides, and reveals what is otherwise hidden in the darkness. In short, salt and light make a difference wherever they are. They make a difference because they are different. Different from saltless food. Different from all that is dark. It's simple—we are called to be different and to bring that strategic difference to our world through the uniqueness of our lives.

For instance, as we resist the seductions of greed and manage our personal economies according to biblical stewardship, we salt our world with a spirit of generosity. A generosity that stands in stark contrast to a world that lives to accumulate gain and believes that life consists in the abundance of that which can be possessed (Luke 12:15).

When we unflinchingly trust in the loving sovereign control of our God over all of life, we are free to demonstrate peace in the midst of the storm, patience in stress, and the unusual power of a love that reaches all the way to our enemies. Self-centeredness is replaced by servanthood, self-enhancement by living to glorify Christ, and pride by humility.

God calls us to lives so full of salt and so radiantly expressive of the light that He can use us to overcome evil with good and make a difference for His glory.

Carl Henry, theologian and gifted Christian thinker, asked, "Can we take a holy initiative in history? . . . Will we offer civilization a realistic option, or only a warning of impending doom? Will Christianity speak only to man's fears and frustrations, or will it also fill the vacuums in his heart and crown his longings for life at its best?"

May our lives be so lived that people cannot help but ask us about the difference and find their longings fulfilled and life at its best in Christ.

In what ways is your life distinct? Do you have a salt and light uniqueness in your actions and attitudes?

MORE OF CHRIST

"What Good Is It for a Man to Gain the Whole World, yet Forfeit His Soul? Or What Can a Man Give in Exchange for His Soul?"
—Mark 8:36–37

*J*esus calls us to be "rich toward God" (Luke 12:21), but in a world obsessed with acquiring more, we are prone to live for the riches of our present world. Our concerns are intensified by mounting stacks of bills and the shrinking balance in our checkbook. Yet Paul teaches us that "godliness with contentment is great gain" (1 Timothy 6:6 KJV). To watch our lives you would think he had said that godliness with *gain* would make us content.

It's easy to see ourselves in Luke 12:13. As the crowd moved along with Jesus, a man who no doubt had strained to catch Jesus' attention catches Christ's eyes and blurts out, "Teacher, tell my brother to divide the inheritance with me."

Imagine having the opportunity to talk to Christ. You might expect that this man would have chosen some serious theme to probe the depths of Christ's claims. He could have talked with the Savior about deep realities of life and eternity. He could have asked Jesus to bless his frail humanity. Instead, he asked for wealth—for his piece of the pie. He is Exhibit A of how easy it is to be obsessed with consumption.

Jesus' answer was honest and profound: "Watch out! Be on your guard against all kinds of greed; a man's life does not consist in the abundance of his possessions" (v. 15). Jesus said the same thing in Mark 8:36–37: "What good is it for a man to gain the whole world, yet forfeit his soul? Or what can a man give in exchange for his soul?"

There is something far more important than the *more* of this world: It is *more* of Jesus Christ. In Him alone we find true wealth and full contentment. The focus of our contentment needs to be our confidence in Christ, that He is aware of and will supply our needs, and that if we have Him, we have enough.

Do you treasure Jesus and His gifts more than earthly gain? How does it show in your life?

BITTERNESS OR BLESSEDNESS

Do Not Be Overcome by Evil, but Overcome Evil with Good.
—Romans 12:21

I'll never forget an older lady who came to my office and heatedly recited a long list of complaints about her husband, to whom she had been married for more than forty years. I have never counseled anyone to break up their home. But as she went on and on about how miserable she was, I finally said, "Why have you lived with him so long if he's so bad? Did you ever think about just checking out? I'm not advising it, but I'd like to know what you think."

She said, "Oh, no! I'd never walk out of this marriage."

I thought that was an honorable attitude. But as she continued to vent, it became evident that she hated him so much that walking out of the marriage would have meant that she couldn't torment him anymore. For her, that was a reason for staying. Why would she want to give up the opportunity to get revenge at every turn?

Unfortunately, her bitterness had not only ruined her husband's happiness but had made her miserable as well.

God has called us to a better way. God commands that when we are offended by others we are to turn the offender over to Him and let Him deal with the injustice (Psalm 34:1–9; 1 Peter 2:20–25). We are then free to be like our Father in heaven: free to bless those who curse us, free to pray for those who spitefully use us, and free to love our enemies, because we believe the power of God will ultimately deal justly with them.

"Do not take revenge, my friends, but leave room for God's wrath, for it is written: 'It is mine to avenge; I will repay,' says the Lord. On the contrary: 'If your enemy is hungry, feed him; if he is thirsty, give him something to drink. In doing this, you will heap burning coals on his head.' Do not be overcome by evil, but overcome evil with good" (Romans 12:19–21).

Is there anyone in your life whom you have refused to forgive? Consciously and prayerfully give them to God, breathe the fresh air of forgiveness, look for ways to share Christ's love with them.

FROM RESTLESSNESS TO REST

BE STILL, AND KNOW THAT I AM GOD; I WILL BE EXALTED AMONG THE
NATIONS, I WILL BE EXALTED IN THE EARTH.

—Psalm 46:10

J grew up hearing the King James Version of this verse, "Be still, and
know that I am God." I always thought that meant to "be still," as my
mother used to say to me in church (I still have the imprints on my knees
from her hands where she squeezed them as she firmly said, "Joe, would you
please *be still?*"). So I grew up thinking that the verse meant to stop being restless and start listening to God—until I began to study the text and discovered
that the Hebrew word used for "be still" has nothing to do with rapt attention to God. Rather, it has everything to do with relaxing. In fact, the verse
could be translated literally as "Relax, and know that I am God."

The Hebrew word paints a vivid picture. It means to *let go*. Literally, to put
our hands down at our sides. When problems arrive at our doorstep, we
always want to keep our hands on the problem, to manipulate and control it
until it yields the outcome we want. We are like a little child who wants to get
involved in a project with his parent but inevitably messes it up.

God says that when life takes us to ragged edge and we find ourselves out
of righteous options, we have to let go. To let go and let God be God in the
midst of our dilemma. Tough assignment? Only if you don't know about
God's loving interest in working through your life to accomplish His glory
and your good. He is faithful to the end, bigger than your problem, wiser than
your best thoughts, and stronger than your most aggressive enemy. You can
give it all to Him and relax in His care and wise solutions.

When we get a grip on "I am God," we find rest for our souls.

*What is it about God that you can fully trust in regardless of life's blows? Make a
list. Live in the list—and relax!*

PSALM 32

Oh, what joy for those whose rebellion is forgiven,
whose sin is put out of sight!
Yes, what joy for those whose record the LORD has cleared of sin,
whose lives are lived in complete honesty!
When I refused to confess my sin,
I was weak and miserable, and I groaned all day long.
Day and night your hand of discipline was heavy on me.
My strength evaporated like water in the summer heat.
Finally, I confessed all my sins to you and stopped trying to hide them.
I said to myself, "I will confess my rebellion to the LORD."
And you forgave me! All my guilt is gone.
Therefore, let all the godly confess their rebellion to you while there is time,
that they may not drown in the floodwaters of judgment.
For you are my hiding place; you protect me from trouble.
You surround me with songs of victory.
The LORD says, "I will guide you along the best pathway for your life.
I will advise you and watch over you.
Do not be like a senseless horse or mule
that needs a bit and bridle to keep it under control."
Many sorrows come to the wicked,
but unfailing love surrounds those who trust the LORD.
So rejoice in the LORD and be glad, all you who obey him!
Shout for joy, all you whose hearts are pure!

BLESS THE INTERRUPTIONS

MANY ARE THE PLANS IN A MAN'S HEART, BUT IT IS THE LORD'S PURPOSE
THAT PREVAILS.

—Proverbs 19:21

*W*hen our children were little, Martie and I enjoyed taking our kids on surprise trips without giving them any clue as to our destination. While these often unexpected jaunts interrupted their playtime, they never seemed to mind. Lack of information didn't seem to bother them. They never stubbornly folded their arms and said, "We're not going unless you tell us all about it."

Actually, the prospect of a surprise trip sent our kids into a flurry of excitement. They embraced the interruption because they trusted their parents. Should we trust God less?

Some of the great advances in God's work have come through interruptions that were at times traumatic. The angels interrupted Mary's life with the announcement of Jesus' birth. Noah, Moses, and Paul had their otherwise well-ordered lives redirected by God's dramatic intervention.

In Proverbs, King Solomon gives us this sage advice: "Many are the plans in a man's heart, but it is the LORD's purpose that prevails" (19:21). Solomon was right. If we knew the divine potential in what we call "interruptions," we may want to have a few more of them.

Yet, we tend to respond to the interruptions of our well-ordered lives with frustration, irritation, and, if it's serious enough, fear and doubt. Hannah Whitall Smith, in her book *The Christian's Secret of a Happy Life,* points out, "You must remember that our God has all knowledge and all wisdom, and that, therefore, it is very possible He may guide you into paths wherein He knows great blessings are awaiting you, but which to the shortsighted human eyes around you seem sure to result in confusion and loss." She continues: "His thoughts, nor His ways are man's ways, and He who knows the end of things from the beginning. He alone can judge what the results of any course of action may be."

Can you trust that the God of your interruptions knows what He is doing?

WHOSE SERVE IS IT?

FOR WE ARE GOD'S WORKMANSHIP, CREATED IN CHRIST JESUS TO DO GOOD
WORKS, WHICH GOD PREPARED IN ADVANCE FOR US TO DO.
—Ephesians 2:10

Dallas Seminary professor Howard Hendricks likes to chide us when he says that the body of Christ is like a football game: twenty-two men on the field desperately needing rest and eighty thousand people in the stands desperately needing exercise! There's some truth to that. A few people do most of the work in the average church.

But it's not just church work that God is interested in, although that is a priority. It goes much further than the place where we worship—it extends to all of life. The basic question is, Are we saved to *serve* or to be *served?* To sit and bask or to make a definite contribution? Paul informs us that we are all given unique abilities or, as he calls them, spiritual gifts, through which we are to serve fellow believers and the cause of Christ (Romans 12:3–8). Whether it is giving, being merciful, serving, teaching, exhorting, leading, or prophecy, we each have the equipment to make a contribution. Don't wait to discover your gift. Get busy. When you feel joy; when others affirm you in the work; when your service bears fruit; when you have energy in your work, you are probably using your gifts. In *Chariots of Fire*, Eric Liddell says, "God has made me fast and when I run I feel His pleasure." When you serve in the way God has gifted you, His pleasure will be evident in your heart.

To be sure, "it is by grace you have been saved, through faith . . . not by works" (Ephesians 2:8–9), for "he saved us, not because of righteous things we had done, but because of his mercy" (Titus 3:5).

But the Bible is also clear that we are "created in Christ Jesus to do good works" (Ephesians 2:10). Faith expressed in good works of service is God's plan for us. As the great reformer John Calvin so aptly said, "Faith alone saves, but the faith that saves is not alone."

What gifts has God given you? What are you doing with those gifts to benefit others?

WHAT DO YOU EXPECT?

*O*n one occasion when our children were small they asked, "Dad, will you take us to the circus Tuesday night?" Not wanting to appear insensitive, I said, "Maybe," which to their minds was "Yes." Parents know that anything short of an absolute, white-knuckled "No!" is still a possibility.

I remember coming home that Tuesday night. The kids yelled, "Dad's home! Tonight's the night!" "What's tonight?" I said. "The circus! Remember?" "Oh," I said, "we're not going to the circus." Do you think they said, "OK, Dad. No problem," and danced off merrily to do something else? No, of course not. They were crushed.

Unfulfilled expectations are a leading source of despair. We wake up each morning expecting that life will treat us well, that our "to do" list will be accomplished, that our spouse will run the promised errand . . . you know the drill. But as soon as our expectations are dashed, distress and irritation begin to rise.

Paul's report to the church in Philippi contains a most instructive passage about expectations. In chapter 1 he notes that he is in prison (v. 13), that some of the Roman believers were envious and spiteful toward him (v. 15), and that Nero at any moment might decree that his life be taken (vv. 20–24).

Paul had every reason to be lost in despair. After all, he was the lead apostle. He hadn't *expected* that his faithfulness to God would be rewarded like this!

But, in spite of this triple hit against him, he was not lost in despair. He was delighted. How did he get there? He tells us his secret in verse 20: "[It is] my earnest expectation and hope, that I will not be put to shame in anything, but that with all boldness, Christ will even now, as always, be exalted in my body, whether by life or by death" (NASB).

He had one expectation—that Christ be exalted in his life. That is an expectation each of us can fulfill regardless of how badly life gets in our face. Expect to exalt Jesus in every circumstance, and enjoy your day.

Spend the day looking for ways to magnify Jesus regardless.

OVERCOMING EVIL WITH GOOD

KEEP YOUR BEHAVIOR EXCELLENT AMONG THE GENTILES, SO THAT . . . THEY
MAY ON ACCOUNT OF YOUR GOOD DEEDS . . . GLORIFY GOD.
—1 Peter 2:12 NASB 1977

*M*other Teresa was the featured speaker at the February 1994 National Prayer Breakfast in Washington, D.C. With the Clintons and Vice President and Mrs. Gore in attendance, she stood fearlessly at the podium and proclaimed: "I feel that the greatest destroyer of peace today is abortion, because it is war against the child, a direct killing of the innocent child, murder by the mother herself. . . . By abortion, the mother does not learn to love, but kills even her own child to solve her problems. And, by abortion, the father is told that he does not have to take any responsibility at all for the child he has brought into the world. That father is likely to put other women into the same trouble. So abortion just leads to more abortion. Any country that accepts abortion is not teaching its people to love, but to use violence to get what they want. This is why the greatest destroyer of love and peace is abortion."

The crowd rose to its feet in thunderous applause as the Clintons and the Gores remained seated, uncomfortably waiting for the program to continue. Interestingly, as President Clinton began his address to the group, he said, "It's hard to argue with a life so well lived."

It was a strategic moment. This aged, stooped woman, who had no political power or clout, had built a platform with her life that disarmed one of the most influential advocates of abortion.

The dynamic of that breakfast stands as a model of what it will take to catch the attention of a shamelessly sinful society and to fulfill our mandate to "overcome evil with good" (Romans 12:21). It is the model of a life so well lived that it raises a curiosity in others that will open their hearts to the life-changing message of Christ.

What is there in your life that makes a clear statement about the unique difference that only Christ can create? Find ways to express His love and be ready to "give an answer for the hope that lies within you" (see 1 Peter 3:15).

WHOSE AGENDA?

"Do Not Work for Food That Spoils, but for Food That Endures to Eternal Life."

—John 6:27

e live and work in a world focused on status and personal achievement. We raise our children to grow up and "be something." We ask one another, "What do you do?" and this answer often determines our opinion of them. We place a great deal of emphasis on how much we earn and what we have accomplished. Did it ever strike you that all of these considerations are about what we have done and what we have? By contrast, Christ asks us to consider whose we are as more important than what we do and to think of our lives as being used for eternal gain more than for our own.

Jesus Christ was never stuck in social boxes determined by what we do and what we make. Because He was driven by eternity, He crossed boundaries of profession, race, and gender to serve and reach all sorts of people. In turn, this wide variety of individuals was greatly used for His kingdom: a tax collector, a Gentile woman, a doctor, a converted prostitute, an elder in the synagogue, a Roman centurion. These were men and women who served eternity because they were touched by Jesus, who came to work for the "food that endures."

It reminds me of Clayton Brown, the founder and chief executive officer of one of the leading bond houses in Chicago. He told me that although he could sell his business, retire, and be comfortable for the rest of his life, he wasn't ready to do that yet. Why? Because he knew that the day he sold his business he would lose his ministry in the Chicago Loop.

For years Clay held weekly Bible studies in the Loop. Today there are businesspeople who know and live for Christ because of those studies. Young professionals regularly sought Clay's advice on how to mesh business and a commitment to Christ. Clay had clearly surrendered to an agenda beyond himself.

Do you live for an agenda beyond yourself? Allow your life to be a platform for His eternal purpose!

Are you striving for the food that endures or for that which spoils? As you seek your own daily bread, are you using opportunities to reach others with the bread of eternal life?

HE FIXES OUR BROKENNESS

THE LORD IS CLOSE TO THE BROKENHEARTED AND SAVES THOSE WHO ARE
CRUSHED IN SPIRIT.

—Psalm 34:18

*O*ur family was vacationing some time ago when Matthew, our youngest child, fell and broke his wrist. It was a sight. His arm took a sharp left at his wrist and then turned again to the right to resume its normal journey to his hand. It was grotesque.

We rushed Matthew to the hospital, where the doctor began to set his wrist. I watched as the doctor pulled and twisted Matthew's arm. The doctor began to perspire, and I felt like intervening to spare my son pain. But I simply sat and watched. I knew that Matt's arm needed to be restored to its original design and purpose. But I also knew that pain and several weeks of inconvenience would be a part of the process.

We too, broken and hurt by sin and self-will, are in the process of being reset by a good and loving God. Set to become more like His Son Jesus. Set to strengthen our hearts and resolve toward compassion, righteousness, and love. There are times when the process will be inconvenient, even painful. But it is a process of healing and restoration in order that we might be able to serve Him well.

Thankfully, God has the power to complete the project. I love the assurance of the prophet Isaiah, who wrote that God would "comfort all that mourn; . . . to give unto them beauty for ashes, the oil of joy for mourning, the garment of praise for the spirit of heaviness; that they might be called trees of righteousness, the planting of the Lord, that he might be glorified" (Isaiah 61:2b–3 KJV). He is able to restore the years that "the locusts have eaten" (Joel 2:25). And, David assures us, He is "close to the brokenhearted" (Psalm 34:18).

I find great encouragement in the truth that He who has begun a good work in us will complete it. (Philippians 1:6)

Is there a brokenness that you have not submitted to the Healer of your soul? Do you see your trials as processes of resetting and healing so that you can be useful to Him?

PSALM 33

Let the godly sing with joy to the LORD, for it is fitting to praise him.

Praise the LORD with melodies on the lyre;

make music for him on the ten-stringed harp.

Sing new songs of praise to him; play skillfully on the harp and sing with joy.

For the word of the LORD holds true, and everything he does is worthy of our trust.

He loves whatever is just and good, and his unfailing love fills the earth.

The LORD merely spoke, and the heavens were created.

He breathed the word, and all the stars were born.

He gave the sea its boundaries and locked the oceans in vast reservoirs.

Let everyone in the world fear the LORD, and let everyone stand in awe of him.

For when he spoke, the world began! It appeared at his command.

The LORD shatters the plans of the nations and thwarts all their schemes.

But the LORD's plans stand firm forever; his intentions can never be shaken.

What joy for the nation whose God is the LORD,

whose people he has chosen for his own.

The LORD looks down from heaven and sees the whole human race.

From his throne he observes all who live on the earth.

He made their hearts, so he understands everything they do.

The best-equipped army cannot save a king,

nor is great strength enough to save a warrior.

Don't count on your warhorse to give you victory—

for all its strength, it cannot save you.

But the LORD watches over those who fear him, those who rely on his unfailing love.

He rescues them from death and keeps them alive in times of famine.

We depend on the LORD alone to save us.

Only he can help us, protecting us like a shield.

In him our hearts rejoice, for we are trusting in his holy name.

Let your unfailing love surround us, LORD, for our hope is in you alone.

THORNS

—2 Corinthians 12:7

Thorns come in many shapes and sizes. A thorn can be something *physical*, as it might have been for Paul. It could be a *sickness* or a *bodily limitation*. It could also be something *emotional* or an *insecurity* that keeps you close to the Savior. For example, Charles Haddon Spurgeon, London's greatest preacher of the last generation, often felt heavy weights of despondency that deepened his sensitivity to Christ and the crises of others. It may be the feeling of *sorrow that lingers from a past sin,* a feeling that keeps you from committing it again.

A thorn might be *circumstantial.* A businessman recently told me how there seemed to be little possibility of a promotion for him in his company. He related how frustrating that was until he realized that it was of God. He said that he was intense and aggressive in his work and that he had a struggle with materialism. "I'd sell my soul to the company if I was moving up quickly. God has done this to focus my attention on the priorities of my family and my relationship to the Lord. He keeps me from the danger of making my business, money, and things a god in my life."

A thorn can be something *social,* perhaps a person—an in-law or a headstrong child. God has always seen fit to periodically place in my life someone who has been uniquely used of Him to reduce the risk of carelessness, slothfulness, and pride.

Actually, a "thorn in the flesh" is any trouble that enables God to work more effectively in us and through us. It is anything that refines us and keeps us sharp for His glory. It is anything that keeps pride, arrogance, self-sufficiency, immorality, or any other lust of the flesh in check so that God's strength can be made strong without our getting in the way. A thorn is anything that reduces self and enables the power of Christ to engage His purpose in your life.

Do you have a thorn? How is God using it in your life? Read 2 Corinthians 12:7–9.

BLESSED INSECURITY

"... To Keep Me from Exalting Myself ..."

—2 Corinthians 12:7

Insecure? I would have never guessed it of him. He is a well-known communicator and an effective teacher of the Word. And now he was telling his congregation that he often feels insecure. I was surprised, but I could identify with the feeling.

I too find insecurity a frequent companion. It gnaws at me and internally humbles me. It plagues my heart with questions. Did I preach an effective sermon? Was I misunderstood? Will that special person accept me for what I am? What am I doing here? Shouldn't I be a better father? Am I as sensitive as I should be to my wife?

I dislike insecure feelings intensely. But as much as I dislike their intrusion into my life, I realize that they have tremendous value. When I feel insecure, my heart flies to the Lord for strength. I seek Him for perspective; I search His Word for comfort. Not only does insecurity keep me close to God, but it also keeps me from the distortion of a proud spirit. It reminds me of how truly insufficient I am in and of myself. It reminds me how much I need God. I find that insecurities make me more sensitive to others.

If we never felt insecure, we would be plagued by the worst enemy of all, self-sufficiency. As C. S. Lewis said, "It is not a good thing to say we have all we need if that 'all' does not include God."

The truth is that I am a risk to God's effective work through me. We all are. Pride, insensitivity, self-sufficiency, and a host of other potential snipers lurk under the surface of our lives. God often uses insecurity to turn pride into authentic humility, self-sufficiency into a trust in God, and insensitivity into a useful and empathetic sensitivity to others.

Look under the cloud of anxiety. The silver lining is that it provides an honest look at yourself and a productive reliance on God. God's power is made perfect in weakness (2 Corinthians 12:9).

PROSPERITY IN PERSPECTIVE

For I Envied the Arrogant when I Saw the Prosperity of the Wicked.
—Psalm 73:3

When the psalmist complained about the apparent prosperity of the wicked, God reminded him that their prosperity was at best temporary and that soon their day in the sun would turn to judgment by the Son. "Surely thou didst set them in slippery places: thou castedst them down into destruction" (Psalm 73:18 KJV) was his ultimate conclusion.

Our family often vacationed in Florida when our kids were young. We loved the sand and the ocean. When we arrived, my plans were to hit the beach and relax. My children's plans were to play in the water and build sand castles. They usually succeeded in dragging me to the water's edge, where the beginnings of a phenomenal sand castle took form. I would begin reluctantly to help but soon found myself excitedly absorbed in the project. In fact, about halfway through, the kids would be off somewhere else as I designed and built the most spectacular sand castle on the beach. Seaweed formed ivy on the walls. Towers were topped with flags. People would stop and inquire. Some would say, "Who built that?" and I would nod proudly. Then it was time to go home, leaving the labor of my hands, the crowning glory of my own creativity behind. The next day my sand castle was gone, washed out to sea. The tide had done me in.

So it is with the fleeting nature of earthly prosperity in the tide of God's judgment. From God's point of view, the wicked are not in an enviable position.

Yet why should they prosper even now? I am convinced their prosperity is living proof of God's patience and grace. What a picture of God's willingness to withhold judgment and give them what they don't deserve. And, lest we forget, the same grace has covered us with His cleansing love and shielded us from the wrath to come. We are the truly prosperous.

Focus your heart on the goodness God has extended to you. Be specific and grateful. Leave the "wicked" to Him.

OUR WORTHY GOD

"Though He Slay Me, yet Will I Hope in Him."
—Job 13:15

A friend of mine officiated at the burial of a baby. As the mourners walked up the hillside to the grave, the minister admitted that he really didn't know what to say. The mother of the child, with tears on her cheeks, said quietly, "The Lord gives and the Lord takes away. Blessed be the name of the Lord" (from Job 1:21 KJV). In her grief, she knew the truth: Our good God is *sovereign over all of life.*

Job knew as well that God was *sovereign even in death.* In the face of death, Job said, "Though he slay me, yet will I hope in him" (Job 13:15). It is as though Job said, "Lord, even if You take my life, I will still affirm my trust in You. Nothing, not even death, will sever my loyal allegiance to Your name." (Compare Philippians 1:19–24.)

Job knew that God was *sovereign in wisdom and in power.* Near the end of his testing, Job teetered in his confusion and agony. God met him and stabilized his failing heart by reminding Job of His infinite, unchallenged wisdom and power (chaps. 38–41). God asked, "Were you there when I created the heavens and the earth? Did you ever see their cornerstone? Where are their foundations laid?" (see Job 38:1–7). The text goes on and on, question after question. God was driving home His point. He is so vastly superior to us in wisdom and power that anything less than submission to His plan for our lives is foolish. In all that God does—though it may be painful, though it may escape our understanding—He is wise and worthy.

Affirming God's wise sovereignty in life or in death means saying with Job, "God, I trust You." In the midst of excruciating circumstances, Job proved the point that God is worthy of our trust and praise regardless. He shamed Satan, who had accused God of having to bless people to gain their loyal worship (Job 1:9–11), and he glorified the matchless name of God. I love him for it. He's my hero.

Do you so trust God that you count Him worthy of trust and worship, regardless?

THINKING CHRISTIANLY

Do Not Conform Any Longer to the Pattern of This World, but Be Transformed by the Renewing of Your Mind.
—Romans 12:2

The mind is our only place of total personal privacy. It is that territory no other person can invade. As a result, we tend to be very much ourselves in our minds. We do not have to put up a façade to anyone. It is where immoral fantasies and schemes can play out in intimate detail. Thoughts of revenge, jealousy, lingering anger, and envy can have unchecked freedom. In contrast, our mind can be the place where we seek to enjoy the pleasures of purity and devise plans to serve, help, and heal. It is where we can embrace memorized Scripture and meditate on His Word and His ways. Our minds can pray and commune with the Lord on a constant basis. Our thoughts can be a temple where we offer sacrifices of praise and worship to our Lord. Our minds are a powerful force for good or evil.

It is no wonder God's Word teaches us that a changed life begins with a changed mind. Paul wrote in Romans 12:2, "Be transformed by the renewing of your mind." All of life begins and is defined by how we think, what we think about, and what we decide in the confines of our thoughts. God wants our minds. He calls us to think His thoughts after Him and to conform our thoughts to His will and His ways.

Paul is actually calling us to "think Christianly." To make a deliberate break from the decadent mind-set of a decaying society and reorient ourselves toward God. Brain first! Never have God's people needed this more than we do today.

Paul wrote to the Philippians, "Whatever is true, whatever is noble, whatever is right, whatever is pure, whatever is lovely, whatever is admirable—if anything is excellent or praiseworthy—think about such things" (Philippians 4:8).

As Proverbs says, ". . . as He thinks within himself so he is" (Proverbs 23:7).

Start the discipline of thinking God's thoughts after Him. Ask yourself, "What would God think in a moment like this?"

FAMILY VALUES

TRAIN A CHILD IN THE WAY HE SHOULD GO, AND WHEN HE IS OLD HE WILL NOT TURN FROM IT.

—Proverbs 22:6

When we talk about "family values," we usually mean that we want our children to grow up in an environment where they learn to love, respect, and desire what is good and proper, to value what we value and more important, to value what God values.

Our challenge is that we live in a culture that puts these goals at phenomenal risk. Divorce is rampant. Gangs, drugs, sex, and materialism target teenagers. America is no longer the idealistic, wholesome, *Leave It to Beaver* society that it once was. Just look at what is available on the Internet and what sells on TV.

Billy Graham once said, "The family is the most important unit of society. It would be well if every home were Christian, but we know that is not so. The family and the home can never exert their proper influence while ignoring the biblical standards. The Bible calls for discipline and recognition of authority. If children do not learn this at home, they will go out into society without the proper attitude toward authority and law. . . .

"The only way to provide the right home for your children is to put the Lord above them, and fully instruct them in the ways of the Lord. You are responsible before God for the home you provide for them."

The Bible's statement "Train a child in the way he should go, and when he is old he will not turn from it" is a wonderful promise! In this confusing world where traditional values are being trashed, Christian parents have the advantage of filling their homes with the ways of the Lord and His Word. Biblically solid music, books, videos, and DVDs are widely available. Children who see their parents reading God's Word and living out its principles are indelibly impressed. As the psalmist affirmed, "How can a young man keep his way pure? By living according to your word. . . . I have hidden your word in my heart that I might not sin against you" (Psalm 119:9, 11).

Plan now to take steps toward a Word-centered home.

PSALM 34:1–18

I will praise the LORD at all times. I will constantly speak his praises.

I will boast only in the LORD; let all who are discouraged take heart.

Come, let us tell of the LORD's greatness; let us exalt his name together.

I prayed to the LORD, and he answered me, freeing me from all my fears.

Those who look to him for help will be radiant with joy;

no shadow of shame will darken their faces.

I cried out to the LORD in my suffering, and he heard me.

He set me free from all my fears.

For the angel of the LORD guards all who fear him, and he rescues them.

Taste and see that the LORD is good. Oh, the joys of those who trust in him!

Let the LORD's people show him reverence,

for those who honor him will have all they need.

Even strong young lions sometimes go hungry,

but those who trust in the LORD will never lack any good thing.

Come, my children, and listen to me, and I will teach you to fear the LORD.

Do any of you want to live a life that is long and good?

Then watch your tongue! Keep your lips from telling lies!

Turn away from evil and do good. Work hard at living in peace with others.

The eyes of the LORD watch over those who do right;

his ears are open to their cries for help.

But the LORD turns his face against those who do evil;

he will erase their memory from the earth.

The LORD hears his people when they call to him for help.

He rescues them from all their troubles.

The LORD is close to the brokenhearted;

he rescues those who are crushed in spirit.

EVIDENCE

HE REPLIED, "WHETHER HE IS A SINNER OR NOT, I DON'T KNOW. ONE THING
I DO KNOW. I WAS BLIND BUT NOW I SEE!"
—John 9:25

*G*od seeks to use our lives as living evidence of the reality of His claims. Evidence so compelling that those who observe us will seek out the Savior they see in us. A couple in my first ministry spent time and effort to put their difficult marriage together on God's terms. The dramatic change caught the attention of their neighbors, who asked what it was that made their marriage different. They were told that Jesus had changed their lives. That night the neighbors opened their hearts to Christ as well.

But we should not be deceived into thinking that all who see the reality of Jesus in and through our lives will come to seek the One expressed in our lives. The story of the blind man in John 9 gives us the range of responses that we might expect.

Some will see God's works and remain silent. In this story, the blind man's parents feared they would be excommunicated from the synagogue (vv. 18–23). Today, many fear the price of claiming Christ as Savior. What will He demand? What will they lose in gaining Him? So they silently watch. They take notes in their hearts.

Then there are those who will set their hearts against what they see. No one knew more about this event than the Pharisees. They interviewed the blind man twice (vv. 13–17, 24–34) and his parents once (vv. 18–23). Yet the Pharisees refused to accept the clear evidence. Some people are so set against God they refuse to seek Him regardless of the evidence. Think of what our world did to Christ, who was a walking catalog of evidence. In the face of the dramatic display of God's credibility through Christ, they crucified Him.

We should never assume that all people will come to Christ when they see Him expressed in unique ways in our lives. We should only expect to provide the evidence and to let God do the rest.

What evidence is there in your life that God can use?

LEST WE FORGET

"When Your Children Ask Their Fathers in Time to Come, 'What Are These Stones?' Then You Shall Inform Your Children, Saying, 'Israel Crossed This Jordan on Dry Ground.' . . . That All the Peoples of the Earth May Know That the Hand of the Lord Is Mighty."
—Joshua 4:21–22, 24 NASB 1977

*H*ad you been there, you would have remembered the day for the rest of your life. God not only kept a centuries-old promise, but He did it in a way that few people had ever seen.

After years of wandering in the wilderness, the people of Israel were poised to enter the Promised Land. Just one problem stood in the way: a raging river. It was harvesttime, and the Jordan was at flood stage. How could they possibly cross into the Promised Land when its boundary was so dangerously impassable? How could God have brought them this far only to face an impossible barrier to the experience of His reward?

They were soon to find out that God delights in doing the impossible to bless those whom He loves.

No sooner had the priests carrying the ark of the covenant stepped into the shallow edge of that torrent than the river ceased to roar. The riverbed dried, and the people finally completed their incredible journey to the land God had promised. Safe. Dry. Cared for.

Then God told Joshua to do one more thing before the priests and the ark left the riverbed. Twelve men—representing the twelve tribes of Israel—were each to gather a large stone from the middle of the riverbed. God wanted them to build a memorial so that when future generations asked the question, "What do these stones mean?" they could tell their children what God had done for His people.

God wants us to remember His gracious acts on our behalf. Right now, take a moment to jot down the major events that are worthy of a memorial to God's work in your life, and come up with a tangible way for you and your loved ones to remember them. Plant a tree, make a simple plaque, or declare your own "Memorial Day" each year. Lest you forget!

If you are having trouble remembering something, think of the Cross.

THANK GOD FOR RULES

WALK IN ALL THE WAY THAT THE LORD YOUR GOD HAS COMMANDED YOU, SO THAT YOU MAY LIVE AND PROSPER AND PROLONG YOUR DAYS IN THE LAND THAT YOU WILL POSSESS.

—Deuteronomy 5:33

*D*id you ever wonder why God made rules?

It would be easy to think that at some point in eternity past God contemplated how He could make life difficult for us and made up the Ten Commandments. On the contrary, the Ten Commandments are not arbitrary rules given by a maliciously detached divine being. They are actually the revelation of God's righteousness in human terms (Romans 3:21). They reflect what it means to be like God in the sphere of our existence. For example, we are not to commit adultery, because God is a faithful God and is loyal to His covenants and promises. Lying is wrong, because God is a God of truth and cannot lie. If He were here, He would not covet, because He is a self-contained entity and needs nothing; hence we should not covet, because He is always with us ready to supply our needs (Philippians 4:19; Hebrews 13:5–6). God is righteous, so He is our standard for "right living". His commandments reflect the standards of His character and therefore serve as strategic goals for character in our own lives.

God's commandments are also given for our personal safety and prosperity (Deuteronomy 5:33; 1 John 5:3–4). Because God has created us, He knows what does and does not work. His commands keep us on track. They keep us safe and out of trouble.

The tremendous outbreak of social diseases today is a clear illustration of this truth. God knows that sexual promiscuity, unfaithfulness, and homosexuality will cause severe medical problems. He knows that our chemical makeup cannot cope with the perversion of His creation, so He gave us laws for our own protection. Loving our neighbor and not coveting his prosperity keeps us from experiencing self-inflicted, eroded relationships. Truth telling builds trust.

God's laws are an expression of His love. Unfortunately, Satan, the liar from the beginning, has always taught that rules are oppressive and restrictive. Rejoice that Jesus teaches that they make us truly free.

Are you living in His way of safety and blessing?

WHOSE APPLAUSE?

"IF YOU BELONGED TO THE WORLD, IT WOULD LOVE YOU AS ITS OWN."
—John 15:19

The impact of Satan's system is coming into full bloom in America. In the past, life here was guided by the laws of Moses and the teachings of Christ. Honesty, integrity, character, purity, generosity, chastity, kindness, and hard work prevailed. Adultery, homosexuality, and abortion were unthinkable. For nearly everyone, divorce was not an option. Over the past four decades, the restraints of our national virtues have been declared out of style, and the absolutes of righteousness are no longer welcome in the public arena.

The trouble for kingdom travelers is that, as people of truth, our presence is a source of reproof. The light is less than welcome in a world that loves darkness. As torchbearers we have been marginalized by a world system that is now in control of American culture. The Creator has been drummed out of education as secular theories of humanism and evolution explain the origin and purpose of life. Music, the media, movies, documentaries, and sitcoms paint Christians as incompetent, bigoted, nerdish, and thoughtless. Those of us who live under kingdom truth are often mocked and avoided by the world at large, and the pressure to conform creates considerable tension for us.

Fewer things are more unsettling than the realization that our righteousness will inevitably cause us to face moments of rejection, discomfort, and in some parts of the world physical pain and even martyrdom. Yet, this is what it means to identify with Christ: "If they persecuted Me, they will also persecute you" (John 15:20 NASB). And in Matthew 16:24 He warned, "If anyone wishes to come after Me, he must deny himself, and take up his cross and follow Me" (NASB).

Followers need to make up their minds early on as to whose applause they want to hear. Will it be, as Max Lucado says, the "applause of heaven," or will it be the applause of this fallen, soon-to-be-judged world? What will it be for you?

If faithfulness even in the face of rejection or ridicule is your choice, bow your head and ask Jesus for grace to be a cross-bearer when necessary for the worthy name of Christ.

EXPERIENCING GOD

DRAW NEAR TO GOD, AND HE WILL DRAW NEAR TO YOU.
—James 4:8 NASB

*S*tep one in pursuing intimacy with God is to deal with our disconnectedness from Him. Scripture teaches that sin and self-sufficiency keep our hearts at a distance from Him. Intimacy is destroyed by unconfessed sin. And living as if you have life pretty well cared for on your own only compounds the problem. Who needs a close relationship with someone you don't really need? When we understand the picture of Christ knocking at our heart's door, we see clearly that He is looking for repentant, radically reliant hearts with which to fellowship (Revelation 3:17–20).

Having resolved to repent and rely, the pilgrimage toward intimacy with God requires time with Him in the Word and communion with Him in prayer. Maintaining an awareness of His presence and a spirit of worshipful obedience all through the day keeps the relationship fresh and real. When we are faithful about the process of connecting to God, He is faithful to reward us in His time and in His way. He really is the rewarder of those who seek Him (Hebrews 11:6).

Don't compare notes. He doesn't meet all of us in the same way. Some of us experience God more fully in our emotions, others in our intellect; all of us meet Him in the temple of our hearts. The brilliance of a sunlit sky may trigger deep connectedness to God in some, while the rich harmony of a symphony may draw another heart toward the One who has created music and harmony. God meets us where we are and not where someone else is.

The ultimate question is, Am I moving closer to Him today than I was last week, last month, last year? Am I dealing with my sins? Cultivating daily reliance? Living in gratitude and rejoicing in His grace?

Draw near and enjoy the pleasure of His presence.

Recall your intimate moments with God. Rejoice in them—they are unique to you alone!

THE WILL TO RUN

Let Us Fix Our Eyes on Jesus . . . Who for the Joy Set Before Him Endured the Cross.

—Hebrews 12:2

*L*iving out our Christianity is not an easy assignment. Even the simple everyday graces, such as patience and forgiveness, are challenging. Yet Scripture encourages us to stay at it like a runner who endures to win. Hebrews 12:1 pictures us running in a Roman arena filled with a "great cloud of witnesses." Looking ahead, the track is an obstacle course, full of pitfalls. We see more buffetings than blessings and say, "I can't do it! Not me, Lord."

As we turn to leave, our eyes catch a glimpse of the crowd that fills the arena. They have all finished triumphantly by faith.

We see Abel, killed for righteousness. Joseph and David are there. So is Job. Moses, who forsook the pleasures and treasures of Egypt for God's sake, is there. There are Jeremiah and the prophets, who were rejected and stoned. Peter, crucified upside down in Rome. Stephen. The five missionaries murdered by the Auca Indians. They are all calling, "Keep on keeping on! Do your part! Complete what we through suffering have begun. Run, run!"

Encouraged to finish the race, we remember that in every Roman arena there was an emperor's box. An athlete coming onto the field would always look to see if the emperor was watching. And so we look, and He is there. It is Jesus, "the author and finisher" of our faith, the One "who for the joy that was set before him endured the cross" (Hebrews 12:2 KJV). He too urges us on.

And so we run. Shedding the sin that so easily besets us and the encumberances that distract us (v. 1). We join the generations of the faithful and pray for grace to finish well.

David Livingstone, the pioneer missionary who walked more than twenty-nine thousand miles through Africa, whose wife died at home in England, who faced stiff opposition from his Scottish brethren, wrote, "Send me anywhere, only go with me. Lay any burden on me, only sustain me. Sever me from any tie except the one that binds me to Your service and to Your heart."

Do you tend to focus on the obstacles or on Christ?

PSALM 37:1–9, 16–19, 23–28

Don't worry about the wicked. Don't envy those who do wrong.

For like grass, they soon fade away. Like springtime flowers, they soon wither.

Trust in the LORD and do good. Then you will live safely in the land and prosper.

Take delight in the LORD, and he will give you your heart's desires.

Commit everything you do to the LORD. Trust him, and he will help you.

He will make your innocence as clear as the dawn,

and the justice of your cause will shine like the noonday sun.

Be still in the presence of the LORD, and wait patiently for him to act.

Don't worry about evil people who prosper or fret about their wicked schemes.

Stop your anger! Turn from your rage!

Do not envy others—it only leads to harm.

For the wicked will be destroyed,

but those who trust in the LORD will possess the land. . . .

It is better to be godly and have little than to be evil and possess much.

For the strength of the wicked will be shattered,

but the LORD takes care of the godly.

Day by day the LORD takes care of the innocent,

and they will receive a reward that lasts forever.

They will survive through hard times;

even in famine they will have more than enough. . . .

The steps of the godly are directed by the LORD.

He delights in every detail of their lives.

Though they stumble, they will not fall, for the LORD holds them by the hand.

Once I was young, and now I am old.

Yet I have never seen the godly forsaken, nor seen their children begging for bread.

The godly always give generous loans to others, and their children are a blessing.

Turn from evil and do good, and you will live in the land forever.

For the LORD loves justice, and he will never abandon the godly.

IN THE MIDST OF DOUBT

IMMEDIATELY JESUS REACHED OUT HIS HAND AND CAUGHT HIM.
—Matthew 14:31

*H*ave you ever held back from obedience because you were afraid of failure and full of doubt? Jesus wants to help you. But His help is most readily available when we are willing to step out and obey. Moses had to step into the Red Sea before it parted, and Peter also knew that obedience preceeds empowerment.

We first meet Peter when Jesus asks him to put the boat into deeper waters and let down the nets. Peter is quick to respond with doubt but also with obedience: "Master, we've worked hard all night and haven't caught anything. But because you say so, I will let down the nets" (Luke 5:5). And you know the rest of the story. Though doubting, he obeyed, and Jesus met him there.

Do you remember when he walked on water? Seeing a ghostly figure approaching from a distance, the disciples were terrified until they heard their Lord's voice: "Take courage! It is I. Don't be afraid." Peter doubtfully replied, "Lord, if it's you, tell me to come to you on the water." Jesus said, "Come." Peter stepped from the boat. Imagine the courage it took to obey at that moment!

When the winds began to blow, Peter shifted his gaze from Jesus to the troubled waves and began to sink. But Jesus was there. Reaching out His hand to Peter, He caught him. "You of little faith," He said, "why did you doubt?" (Matthew 14:25–31).

The lesson is not in Peter's failure and doubt. It is rather that he was willing to do what seemed unlikely and dangerous. Most of us would not have thrown the nets one more time into the sea, and more certainly would not have stepped out of the boat. But Peter did, and in the midst of his doubt and lapse of faith, Jesus was there to reward and instruct.

Get busy! As long as you are moving in the right direction, He will help you get past your fears and failures and lead you to experiences of fruitful joy.

What is stopping you from full surrender? Give it up and meet Jesus in His fullness as you obey.

A DISCERNING HEART

BUT SOLID FOOD IS FOR THE MATURE, WHO BECAUSE OF PRACTICE HAVE
THEIR SENSES TRAINED TO DISCERN GOOD AND EVIL.

—Hebrews 5:14 NASB

I'd like to have a five-dollar bill for all the times I have heard Christians
back away from condemning evil by saying, "I don't think it's right to
judge others." Although it is indeed wrong to live with a judgmental, holier-
than-thou attitude, it is nevertheless imperative to cultivate a discerning heart.

The ability to clearly discern between right and wrong marks us as mature
believers (Hebrews 5:11–14). Discernment is not developed through following external codes but rather is brought about through the discipline of a heart
that applies the revealed principles of God's Word to each life setting. It makes
us wise and keeps us pure.

Unfortunately, there are many false standards that destroy discernment.
Sincerity is often thought to be the most important thing in determining right
from wrong. Love, by many definitions, is considered to be the chief instrument in discernment. But neither love nor sincerity is at the core of wise and
pure choices. They function as godly motivators but do not train our hearts
in discernment. When I was a student, I answered many test questions very
sincerely, thinking I was right—only to find later that I was sincerely wrong.
Helping a child tie his shoes every morning may be an expression of love, but
ultimately it will hinder him if he becomes the only college freshman in his
class who does not know how to tie his shoes. Love can be well meaning but,
left to itself, it can lead us astray.

Sincerity and love are valuable to discernment only when they encourage
us to do what is truly right. A discerning heart is fine-tuned by making consistently clear and courageous applications of what is true (1 Corinthians 5:8).
Love energizes us toward wise and pure choices when it abounds "more and
more in knowledge and depth of insight, so that [we] may be able to discern
what is best and may be pure and blameless until the day of Christ"
(Philippians 1:9–10).

*Is your discernment based on what you know to be true or on how you feel about
a particular moment or choice?*

THAT DRAGON IN OUR DENTURES

THE TONGUE IS A SMALL PART OF THE BODY, BUT IT MAKES GREAT BOASTS.
. . . THE TONGUE ALSO IS A FIRE, A WORLD OF EVIL AMONG THE PARTS OF
THE BODY.

—James 3:5–6

*J*ames tells us that our tongue "is a fire," small but able to set a whole
forest ablaze! To make his point clear, he concludes that the tongue is
"set on fire by hell" (3:6). If Satan has a scorched-earth policy in his warfare
against the Christians, then the tongue is the front line of attack. James rings
a clear warning. A transformed tongue must be a top priority for those on the
growing edge of discipleship.

James's warning takes on added weight when we realize that many of us are
desensitized to the problems of destructive speech. Sins of the tongue are like
stealth sins that fly under the radar of our consciences. Just listen to us excuse
one another with rationalizations like "Well, it's the truth, isn't it?" or, "If they
didn't want people to talk, they never should have done it." The most subtle
excuse among Christians is "Let me share this with you that we might pray
more intelligently." This desensitization has opened the floodgates to verbal
destruction of reputations and trusted relationships.

Sins like deceit, lying, and false witness need to be understood from God's
point of view. Social sins of the tongue, such as gossip and slander, must be
checked. Verbal ego trips, such as boasting, flattery, and exaggeration, are
clearly out of bounds. The cancer of a murmuring, contentious tongue needs
to be removed.

By making careless speech an acceptable part of our lives, we assume that
a carnal tongue is par for the spiritual course. When that happens, our churches,
schools, homes, friendships, and relationships with God are all victimized.

We should remind each other that Satan is "the father of lies" (John 8:44)
and "the accuser of our brethren" (Revelation 12:10 KJV). Jesus is not only
truth, but also our advocate, and defender. Whose work will you do?

Put your tongue in check. Don't say it until the Spirit approves it!

DON'T TELL

The Words of a Gossip Are like Choice Morsels; They Go Down to a Man's Inmost Parts.

—Proverbs 18:8

The late R. G. LeTourneau, who owned a large earthmoving equipment company, told this story: "We used to have a scraper known as the model 'G.' Somebody asked one of our salesmen one day what the 'G' stood for. The salesman was pretty quick on the trigger. . . . He replied, 'Well, I guess the "G" stands for gossip, because, like gossip, this machine moves a lot of dirt, and moves it fast!'"

Both the Hebrew and the Greek words for gossip are picturesque. The Old Testament word for gossip in Proverbs 11:13 has the meaning of "going about from one to another." Hence our word *talebearing*. The concept of "whispering that is damaging" is the essence of the word as it is used in Proverbs 16:28; 18:8; and 26:20–22.

The New Testament word continues the thought of whispering. One lexicographer describes it as "secret attacks on a person's character." When you pronounce the Greek word for gossip, you begin with the sound "p-s-s-s." "P-s-s-t" is often how we characterize hushed communication.

Though whispering is not always bad, it is always used in a negative context in Scripture. It denotes confidential information, nonpublic information, exclusivism, secretive behavior, and shame. In Scripture, whispering becomes a figurative expression for the sin of gossip.

God's Word teaches that a gossip is untrustworthy and cannot keep a secret (Proverbs 11:13). Gossips often betray confidential information. Their information is not worthy of trust because they tend to add "frills" to the story to make it more interesting.

The person who gossips is to be avoided (Proverbs 20:19). When we hear gossip, we add unneeded information to our mental notebook. These negative thoughts often give Satan a foothold in our lives. Hearing soon becomes telling. For some, "gossip in" means "gossip out"! And, as our text notes, gossip goes down to our inward parts, where it is lodged and not forgotten.

Gossip is the sharing of confidential or negative information with someone who is not a part of the solution. If you have to tell someone . . . tell God in prayer!

Commit your lips to only sharing information that helps and heals.

THE COMPELLING LIFE

MAKE IT YOUR AMBITION TO LEAD A QUIET LIFE, TO MIND YOUR OWN
BUSINESS AND TO WORK WITH YOUR HANDS.

—1 Thessalonians 4:11

*S*aint Francis of Assisi said, "Preach the gospel every day; when necessary, use words." It's like the old adage, "If you can't walk the walk, don't talk the talk," or, "Your life is the only gospel some people may ever hear." It's the sense of Paul's note to the Corinthians when he wrote, "You . . . are our letter, . . . known and read by everybody" (2 Corinthians 3:2).

In Paul's second letter to the Thessalonians, he makes an even more specific appeal to the public example of our lives. In 1 Thessalonians, he urges Christians to keep living the gospel before others, to keep on living well. He wrote, "Yet we urge you, brothers, to do so more and more. Make it your ambition to lead a quiet life, to mind your own business and to work with your hands, just as we told you, so that your daily life may win the respect of outsiders and so that you will not be dependent on anybody" (1 Thessalonians 4:10–12).

What a great goal—to live to earn the respect of a watching world.

The Thessalonians were living good lives. But Paul knew that lives rarely stay on track without some attention and accountability. He also knew that though they were doing well, there was still room for growth. So he urged them not to be satisfied or to slide into patterns of complacency. Instead he urged: "Do so more and more." Keep increasing in your Christlikeness, in your love for one another. Keep striving for holiness. And aim to live a quiet life. I love that thought. Christians do better when they are less mouthy, less bossy, less intrusive. Did you ever notice how quiet light is? It is often better to let Jesus shine through you than it is to make a speech on His behalf.

Let's set the standard high. Let's encourage one another to live for Jesus in ways that show Him off for what He really is.

What area of your life could be grown into a greater measure of testimony that those around your life could appropriately respect?

EYES TO THE SKY

I DESIRE TO DEPART AND BE WITH CHRIST, WHICH IS BETTER BY FAR.
—Philippians 1:23

*M*y friend Bud Wood is the founder and developer of what has become one of the finest homes in America for mentally challenged children and adults. Shepherds Home, located in Union Grove, Wisconsin, ministers to many who are afflicted with Down's syndrome. The staff at Shepherds makes a concentrated effort to present the gospel to these children. As a result, many have come to believe in Christ as Savior and in a heaven that will be their home.

Bud once told me that one of the major maintenance problems they have at Shepherds is dirty windows.

I asked, "Why?"

"You can walk through our corridors any time of the day," Bud explained, "and you see these precious children standing with their hands, noses, and faces pressed to the windows, looking up to see if Christ might not be coming back to take them home and make them whole."

We should be asking ourselves, *When was the last time we glanced toward the sky to see if this might not be that long-awaited moment when we finally see Him face-to-face?* Perhaps our lack of longing for heaven says something about our lack of earthside fellowship with Him.

When Paul said being in heaven was "better by far," he wasn't talking about streets of gold. He said it in the context that heaven meant being with Christ. Heaven is the reward of a heart that has loved Jesus enough to long for Him. It was to shaken disciples, struggling with the prospect of losing the One they loved, that Jesus said, "Let not your heart be troubled. . . . I will come again, and receive you unto myself; that where I am, there ye may be also" (John 14:1, 3 KJV).

The joy of Eden for Adam and Eve was their unhindered fellowship with their Creator. It was their source of unlimited pleasure and fulfillment. Heaven is Eden restored. God looks forward to our arrival (Psalm 116:15). He died to guarantee it.

The question is, do we share the enthusiasm? He has a crown for those who "love his appearing" (2 Timothy 4:8 KJV).

Are there smudges on the windows of your heart?

PSALM 38

O LORD, don't rebuke me in your anger! Don't discipline me in your rage!

Your arrows have struck deep, and your blows are crushing me.

Because of your anger, my whole body is sick;

my health is broken because of my sins.

My guilt overwhelms me—it is a burden too heavy to bear.

My wounds fester and stink because of my foolish sins.

I am bent over and racked with pain. My days are filled with grief.

A raging fever burns within me, and my health is broken.

I am exhausted and completely crushed. My groans come from an anguished heart.

You know what I long for, Lord; you hear my every sigh.

My heart beats wildly, my strength fails, and I am going blind.

My loved ones and friends stay away, fearing my disease.

Even my own family stands at a distance.

Meanwhile, my enemies lay traps for me; they make plans to ruin me.

They think up treacherous deeds all day long.

But I am deaf to all their threats. I am silent before them as one who cannot speak.

I choose to hear nothing, and I make no reply.

For I am waiting for you, O LORD. You must answer for me, O Lord my God.

I prayed, "Don't let my enemies gloat over me or rejoice at my downfall."

I am on the verge of collapse, facing constant pain.

But I confess my sins; I am deeply sorry for what I have done.

My enemies are many; they hate me though I have done nothing against them.

They repay me evil for good and oppose me because I stand for the right.

Do not abandon me, LORD. Do not stand at a distance, my God.

Come quickly to help me, O Lord my savior.

PICTURE PERFECT

BEING CONFIDENT OF THIS, THAT HE WHO BEGAN A GOOD WORK IN YOU WILL
CARRY IT ON TO COMPLETION UNTIL THE DAY OF CHRIST JESUS.
—Philippians 1:6

*H*ow many times have we said, "Well, it turned out all right after all!"?
If, in the normal course of life, things that seem disappointing, difficult, and defeating can be transformed into that which is good and significant,
how much surer is this process in the hand of a wise and powerful God, who
always guarantees the outcome? It is a great comfort to know that He only
permits what He intends to turn to His glory and our good.

Romans 8:28 assures us that "in *all things* God works for the good of those
who love him" and "have been called according to his purpose" (italics added).
And don't miss the notation in the next verse: That purpose to which we are
called is to reflect the likeness of Jesus. The "good" in our "all things" may be
His work to create the character of Christ in us.

In her book *Affliction*, Edith Schaeffer told of a child who fell off a cliff to
his death and of another who slipped through the ice into a frozen lake. While
it is true that these kinds of tragedies occur because we live in a fallen place
and are a part of a fallen race, they do not escape the awareness of God, whose
powerful, creative hand takes tragic settings like these and works them all to
good, regardless.

Often our lives seem like a thousand disassembled pieces of a jigsaw puzzle
—confused, disoriented, senseless, and tragic. But God is in the details . . .
carefully, wisely, in His way and in His time putting the pieces together to
form a complete and perfect picture. If He can turn the agony of the cross into
an empty tomb and ultimately our salvation, He can manage the lesser trau-
mas of our lives toward His ultimate purpose.

Cling to the forever unchanging truth that He indeed works all things for
good.

*Instead of resisting the inevitability of trouble, look for His hand and envision
what good He is doing in the midst of your pain.*

BLESSED ARE THOSE . . .

"Rejoice and Be Glad, Because Great Is Your Reward in Heaven."
—Matthew 5:12

To look at modern Christians you would think that the national anthem of the kingdom is the reggae tune, "Don't Worry, Be Happy." Happiness is beyond a doubt the priority pursuit among worldlings, but it was never intended to be the first desire of followers of Jesus. It's not that He doesn't want us to be happy. It is that He wants us to seek and serve Him regardless and let Him reward us with the blessedness that only He can give. He wants us to live in the realization that He, not life, is the source of ultimate happiness is the message of the Beatitudes.

The poor in spirit have no choice but to fix their hearts on the prosperity that the King provides eternally. Since they have confidence in Christ, and Him alone, theirs is the kingdom of heaven. Those who mourn are confident that throughout eternity they will know the comfort of God. That is certainly superior to a griefless life here and an eternity of mourning. The gentle here are those who respond in grace and forgiveness to their offenders. As such, they will inherit possessions that cannot be taken from them.

In a world where people thirst to satisfy their lusts with evil, Christ said it is those who thirst for righteousness who will ultimately find satisfaction. The merciful will find mercy. In contrast to those who live in sinful ways, Christ elevates those who are pure, for they shall know intimacy with God (Matthew 5:8).

Rather than using intimidation to gain selfish ends, Christ said that those who live to make peace are known throughout eternity as sons of God, since God Himself is the ultimate peacemaker.

Those who have defined their lives by the virtues of the kingdom and have suffered persecution from a world that hates the principles of paradise will remain unshaken, because heaven will be eternally theirs.

It's no wonder that Christ concludes the promise of true blessedness with, "Your reward in heaven is great" (Matthew 5:12 NASB).

In times when life seems less than happy, do you focus on Jesus and look for your reward in Him?

CONTENTMENT

I Am Not Saying This Because I Am in Need, for I Have Learned to Be Content Whatever the Circumstances.

—Philippians 4:11

*C*ontentment is a gift. It is being at peace with life the way it is. It's knowing that we have enough even when we have little. Yet this marvelous gift is up against strong forces that seek to replace it with the gnawing restlessness of dissatisfaction and desires that cannot bring peace. Consumerism and the circumstances of life are the enemies of a contented heart.

Paul knew about the futility of searching for contentment apart from Christ. He wrote to the church at Philippi and thanked them for the money they had sent to him, explaining that he had not longed for more, but rather, "I have learned to be content whatever the circumstances. I know what it is to be in need, and I know what it is to have plenty. I have learned the secret of being content in any and every situation, whether well fed or hungry, whether living in plenty or in want. I can do everything through him who gives me strength" (Philippians 4:11–13).

Contentment is planted deep within when we place our confidence in the fact that having Jesus is having all that we need. And that all that we need will be supplied by Him. Or that what is withheld is for our best. As Paul said, it is doing everything "through Him," as though all of life should be lived through the grid of the reality of His presence, power, and provision. It is living with the confidence that Christ is all He says He is, that He is aware of and attentive to our needs, and that if we have Him, we have enough.

It's not that we should never want to buy something or feel that we have to live in abject poverty to prove our contentment. It is simply that our wants and desires don't rule our hearts. Jesus does.

If in His generosity He enables you to prosper, live in grateful praise for His grace. When you don't prosper, praise Him for the goodness of His presence.

THE NEGLECTED BRIDE

I WILL BUILD MY CHURCH; AND THE GATES OF HELL SHALL NOT PREVAIL
AGAINST IT.

—Matthew 16:18 KJV

*C*hurch. Just the mention of it conjures up myriad mixed feelings and points of view. And not all of them complimentary. Church-bashing is a popular sport these days. As one author wrote, "Americans used to ask 'which church?' Now they are asking '*why* church?'"

It's easy to understand why the world would take a dim view of church. But for the life of me, I can't understand why we who are Christ's followers do. Obviously, there are things that need to change at church. It's full of imperfect people. As someone well said, "If you find the perfect church, don't go there—you'll ruin it!" What we need to understand is that the church is the bride of Christ . . . the very people He shed His blood to redeem.

I've grown up in the parsonage, pastored three churches, and now spend many weekends preaching in all kinds of churches across the country. I've counseled both pastors and parishioners about deep and troubling problems in the church. I think I've seen it all. And while this has not dimmed my love for the church—it has altered that love. I no longer love the church for what it is but for whose it is. It is Christ's, and as such it deserves my love and attention. Seeing it as His encourages me to love it for His sake and to do my part to reduce its imperfections to the barest minimum. I have found that hanging in there with the church has deepened and matured my faith.

This perspective has also altered my view of the people at church. Every church has just a few really unique individuals. As a friend says, "The light always attracts a few bugs!" But, seeing everyone as redeemed souls that are precious to God is a liberating thought. If they are precious to Him, precious enough to die for, then they too must be precious to me.

What are you doing to make His bride in your town the most beautiful bride yet?

Do something this week to beautify your church.

DIVINE RESCUE

ALL DISCIPLINE FOR THE MOMENT SEEMS NOT TO BE JOYFUL, BUT SORROWFUL; YET . . . AFTERWARDS IT YIELDS THE PEACEFUL FRUIT OF RIGHTEOUSNESS.

—Hebrews 12:11 NASB

*I*n a quiet subdivision in Lake in the Hills, Illinois, a rare blue heron stumbled into a steel trap designed to catch invading muskrats. Nancy Monica, a nearby neighbor, came to the heron's rescue, holding the bird still while a rescue worker freed its broken leg from the jaws of the trap.

What Nancy did not realize was that herons are very unpredictable in nature and, when cornered, will attack whatever is nearest. The injured bird began to peck at its rescuers with its razor-sharp beak. Thanks to the efforts of Nancy and the rescue worker, the bird was free to recover from its injured leg. Nancy Monica, however, sported a black eye.

Like that frightened bird, we sometimes do not recognize the One who has come to set us free. Scripture teaches us that God is busy seeking to relieve us from the entanglements of sin. He uses the reproofs of life and the consequences of sin to catch our attention. Like a loving father, He disciplines us to turn our hearts back to Him and His ways. To the church at Laodicea, Jesus said, "Those whom I love, I reprove and discipline; therefore be zealous and repent" (Revelation 3:19 NASB). Yet we tend to resist the reproofs and despise the discipline. It is easier to blame others for the consequences of our sin than it is to admit that God is trying to reach us and free us from our faults. It's not until we submit to the reproofs and surrender to the discipline that we will begin the process of yielded repentance that leads to freedom and purity.

Don't think that His gracious pursuit of you will go away. He is determined to finish the work that He began in our lives (Philippians 1:6). He was battered and bruised by our sin at the cross, and if He didn't give up there He is not going to now. He wants to feel us ceasing to struggle and to repentantly yield to His loving work.

Can you think of a reproof in your life? Think carefully—and surrender and repent.

HOUND OF HEAVEN

BEHOLD, I STAND AT THE DOOR.

—Revelation 3:20 NKJV

*F*rancis Thompson was a poet of modest reputation in Victorian England. He studied medicine at Owens College in Manchester but soon left his practice for the intrigue of London. Unable to support his life through his literary efforts, he became disillusioned and eventually enslaved to opium.

He had been reared in a godly home and never lost sight of God, though he steadfastly refused to follow Him. After a friend rescued him from the streets, Thompson gave his life back to Christ. In his poem "The Hound of Heaven," he reveals that in spite of Christ's constant pursuit, he thought that if he followed Jesus he would lose control and be left with less.

I fled Him, down the nights and down the days;
I fled Him, down the arches of the years; . . .
I fled Him, down the labyrinthine ways
    Of my own mind; and in the mist of tears I hid from Him. . . .
        Up vistaed hopes I sped;
        And shot, precipitated,
Adown Titanic glooms of chasmèd fears,
    From those strong Feet that followed, followed after.
        But with unhurrying chase,
        And unperturbèd pace,
    Deliberate speed, majestic instancy,
        They beat—and a Voice beat
        More instant than the Feet
"All things betray thee, who betrayest Me." . . .
(For, though I knew His love Who followèd,
    Yet was I sore adread
Lest, having Him, I must have naught beside.)

Then Thompson concludes with these wonderful words of invitation that Christ extends to all who flee Him:

    "Rise, clasp My hand, and come! . . .
    Ah, fondest, blindest, weakest,
    I am He Whom thou seekest!"
Thou dravest love from thee, who dravest Me."

When will we learn to clasp our hand in His and surrender to Jesus' throne, which our hearts seek?

PSALM 40:1–11

I waited patiently for the LORD to help me,
and he turned to me and heard my cry.
He lifted me out of the pit of despair, out of the mud and the mire.
He set my feet on solid ground and steadied me as I walked along.
He has given me a new song to sing, a hymn of praise to our God.
Many will see what he has done and be astounded.
They will put their trust in the LORD.
Oh, the joys of those who trust the LORD,
who have no confidence in the proud, or in those who worship idols.
O LORD my God, you have done many miracles for us.
Your plans for us are too numerous to list.
If I tried to recite all your wonderful deeds,
I would never come to the end of them.
You take no delight in sacrifices or offerings.
Now that you have made me listen, I finally understand—
you don't require burnt offerings or sin offerings.
Then I said, "Look, I have come.
And this has been written about me in your scroll:
I take joy in doing your will, my God, for your law is written on my heart."
I have told all your people about your justice.
I have not been afraid to speak out, as you, O LORD, well know.
I have not kept this good news hidden in my heart;
I have talked about your faithfulness and saving power.
I have told everyone in the great assembly
of your unfailing love and faithfulness.
LORD, don't hold back your tender mercies from me.
My only hope is in your unfailing love and faithfulness.

LIFE ON PURPOSE

YOU HAVE BEEN BOUGHT WITH A PRICE: THEREFORE GLORIFY GOD IN YOUR BODY.

—1 Corinthians 6:20 NASB

I'm reminded of the time that Lucy and Charlie Brown were on the deck of a cruise ship. Lucy unfolded her deck chair and philosophically said, "Some people unfold their deck chairs to look at all that is to come. Others set their chairs to see all that is now, while others set them to see all that is behind." To which Charlie dejectedly responded, "I can't even get my deck chair open."

Unfortunately, many of us tend to be like Charlie Brown. Clueless as to what our purpose in life should be. Without a clear view, our purpose vacillates like a meandering stream depending on who we've been with and what we have read lately.

Thankfully, God helps us unfold the deck chair of life according to His wise design. We are called to live to glorify Him. It is the reason for our redemption (1 Corinthians 6:19–20), the all-consuming focus of our existence, and the measure of our maturity (1 Corinthians 10:31; 2 Corinthians 3:18).

Basically, glorifying God means reflecting His nature. Glorifying God means being image bearers who mirror the love, mercy, power, righteousness, and justice of God. It means giving visibility to His *invisibility* and *credibility* to His existence in a world that finds Him hard to believe.

The privilege of living to bring Him glory is profound. God uses many means to reveal His glory. The sun, moon, and stars reveal His power and creativity. God said of His people, "Israel my glory" (Isaiah 46:13 KJV). Israel revealed what God was like to a stunned world as He opened the sea for them and defeated armies far beyond their ability. Christ was God's glory in the flesh. The Bible reveals the glory of God. And . . . think of this . . . we are added to the list. That puts us in significant company. Glorifying God is a high privilege and a purpose worth living for.

If you asked a close friend what he saw of God in your life, what would he say?

THE WISE WEAVER

REJOICE IN THE LORD AND BE GLAD, YOU RIGHTEOUS; SING, ALL YOU WHO
ARE UPRIGHT IN HEART!

—Psalm 32:11

The psalmist David knew what it meant to feel that life was a series of detours. Imagine being called in from the field to be annointed by Samuel as the next king of Israel. He'd been given the promise of a wonderful future. Yet the road to kingship was not without its detours. There was Goliath. Saul's wrath. A forced broken relationship with his best friend, Jonathan. For years he lived in caves as he fled from the armies of Saul with a wretched group of outcasts. I am certain he must have wondered: "God, what happened to the plan?"

We need to remember that God's plans are bigger than ours. Bigger and better. He knows what He is doing with our lives. You've probably heard that God's plan for our lives is like a beautiful needlework tapestry. If you look at the back of a tapestry, it is a jumble of knots and tangled thread. But viewed from the front—from the proper perspective—the threads compose a beautiful picture. It is like that with our lives. Events that through our earthbound lenses we see as unexpected and unwelcome detours are used by God to lead to better destinations. It was the God of David who said through the prophet Jeremiah, "I know the plans that I have for you . . . plans for welfare and not for calamity to give you a future and a hope" (Jeremiah 29:11 NASB).

In Psalm 32:8–11, God assures us, "I will instruct you and teach you in the way you should go; I will counsel you and watch over you. Do not be like the horse or the mule, which have no understanding . . . the LORD's unfailing love surrounds the man who trusts in him. Rejoice in the LORD and be glad, you righteous; sing, all you who are upright in heart!"

Trust Him and find your heart singing, "Where He leads me I will follow, I'll go with Him . . . all the way."

Believe that His ways are best, and rejoice in every turn and twist in your path.

DIRECTED DESIRES

THEN JESUS WAS LED BY THE SPIRIT INTO THE DESERT TO BE TEMPTED BY THE DEVIL.

—Matthew 4:1

We all have instincts that drive our behavior. In fact, if we didn't have instincts, we wouldn't want to eat, procreate, succeed in our work, or relate well to others. A life without these impulses would be a life of severe vegetation.

The problem with our instincts is not that we have them. It is that this world's system encourages us to use them solely for our own pleasure and gain, with disregard for the context in which they were intended to be enjoyed.

Followers of Christ are different. We are not to be controlled by our sensual urges but to bring them under the control of the Spirit, who guides them to productive ends for His glory and our gain. And as a bonus, we find fulfillment and joy without the guilt and destructive erosion that takes place in our souls when we spend our passions on ourselves.

Nowhere did Christ more dramatically demonstrate the virtue of living under the Spirit's control than when He came face-to-face with the king of darkness in the wilderness—at a time when His basic instincts were most vulnerable (Matthew 4:1–11). After Christ had fasted for forty days, Satan attempted to lure Him to satisfy Himself with food, self-authentication, power, fame, and position. Yet Christ put Himself under a higher moral authority than Satan and used the power of the Word of God to direct His responses. As a result, He said no to His impulses so that He could say yes to the honor and glory of His Father.

The issue for those of us who seek to follow is, to whom will we be loyal, regardless of the inner impulses? Will it be the prince of this planet, our own inner urges, or the clear Word of God that directs our desires and protects us as we travel toward home?

The virtue of a Spirit-controlled life stands as a clear kingdom mark in the face of the phenomenal pressure of the sensuality of our day.

Is there an "urging" that you need to give to the Spirit?

WAITING

BE PATIENT, THEN, BROTHERS, UNTIL THE LORD'S COMING.
—James 5:7

*L*ike everything else in the Christian life, patience is a learned spiritual art, perhaps one of the hardest ones to find active in our lives. Patience is the skill of waiting well, of yielding our timetables to others . . . to the Lord. I like the term *patient waiting* because patience is nothing more than the art of learning to wait! *Webster's Dictionary* agrees. For the word *patient,* it offers this definition: "The will or ability to wait."

And it's not just waiting for others. Ultimately, it is about waiting for God. Waiting to experience answers to prayer, the realization of His promises, the cessation of trouble—and the list goes on. The psalmist encourages us to "rest in the Lord, and wait patiently for Him. . . . Wait on the Lord, and keep His way, and He shall exalt you" (Psalm 37:7, 34 NKJV). Patience is about how much we trust God. The quicker we become antsy about life and our predicaments, the less we really believe that He is with us and in control.

The apostle James knew something about waiting—and not just waiting for something desired, but waiting on the Lord and trusting Him during times of intense adversity. In his letter to the scattered and persecuted Jewish Christians of his day, he used various forms of the words *wait, patience,* and *perseverance* ten times. Besides these occurrences, the idea of patient waiting is woven throughout the book. It takes much patience, for example, to be "quick to listen, slow to speak and slow to become angry" (James 1:19)!

James was the right person to deliver a message of patient endurance in trial and patient waiting for the return of Christ. Because James was the half brother of the Lord Jesus (Matthew 13:55), some might have thought he would be eligible for special treatment. But James knew the reality of persecution, and he never tried to claim special privilege. Instead, he identified himself simply as a "servant" of Christ (James 1:1). To a group of people badly in need of wise counsel, James offered not an escape route but a path to spiritual maturity . . . waiting for the Lord. You'll discover that He's worth waiting for.

Yield to God's timetable . . . His timing is always superb!

LOVING GOD

WE LOVE BECAUSE HE FIRST LOVED US.

—1 John 4:19

When a Pharisee asked Jesus what the most important commandment was, Jesus replied, "Love the Lord your God with all your heart and with all your soul and with all your mind. This is the first and greatest commandment" (Matthew 22:37–38). Loving God is priority number one. But what does that mean?

First, loving God means more than feeling good about Him. This is welcome news. There are times in our lives when we don't feel good about much of anything. New Testament love, *agape* love, means choosing to yield to God. We express our love when we yield ourselves—the totality of our being—to Him. And self is important in the process. God never intended that we think badly about self or relegate self to the lowest rung of our existence. Self is only degraded when we spend self on self. Self is intended to be a treasure we give completely to our Lord as an expression of love. Love means giving the gift of "me" . . . willingly and gratefully. Love is total surrender.

The second piece of good news about loving God is that while it is a responsibility, it is more than just that. It is a response to His matchless love for us. It's not a matter of "bucking up" and loving Him but rather of getting a grip on how much He loved us. Once we realize that we are among the "forgiven much" we will *desire* to love Him much.

We all know this dynamic. When someone performs a loving act in your behalf, your first instinct is to repay that with an act of love in return. And just in case you don't think He has done much for you lately, think again. If He never does anything else but save us, indwell us, protect and preserve us and prepare a place for us, He has already done more than we deserve. Enough to keep us looking for ways to express our love in return for the rest of our earthside lives.

God wonderfully loves us far beyond what we deserve. We should be honored that He desires our love in return.

What one thing can you do today to demonstrate your love for God?

IN THE BEGINNING GOD . . .

In the Beginning God Created the Heavens and the Earth.
—Genesis 1:1

The Bible opens with three familiar words, "In the beginning." But it's the next word that should rivet our attention: "In the beginning *God* . . ."

Genesis 1:1 establishes the most significant fact about Creation, that the beginning of all beginnings was the result of the creative word and power of God. And even when sin entered and spoiled the created, it was God initiating the eternal plan that satisfied our need for a Redeemer. In Genesis 3:15, God began again by announcing a plan that would culminate in another great beginning: the coming of Jesus Christ to bear our sins. Thankfully, our Lord is a God of new beginnings. Where would you be today if it weren't for the new beginning of salvation?

Between Creation and Calvary, God's Word records a number of incredible accounts of important beginnings that shaped individual lives and entire nations. In fact, our lives today are greatly affected by all of the events of the Old Testament, for the Old Testament is the story line of the coming of Jesus, our Redeemer. But this is more than just history. Every direct intervention by God into history is intended to be read and heard for our benefit. The apostle Paul reminds us in 1 Corinthians 10:6 that "these things," the events of the Old Testament, happened for our instruction.

God's Word is not intended just to help us fill gaps in our historical understanding but to help us learn from the mistakes and victories of the past. Many of the great beginnings you'll read about were the direct handiwork of God: the Creation, the Exodus, and the call of Abraham. Some were the result of human sin: the expulsion from the garden, Babel, the divided kingdom. But each is significant in the life of God's people.

Thankfully, throughout our lives God continues His work of new beginnings. In the face of our failures He begins again with forgiveness and an assurance of victory. In trouble He begins to refine and refocus us. And in death He begins to wipe away every tear for the ultimate beginning of eternity with Him.

What new beginning is God seeking to begin in your life?

PSALM 42

As the deer pants for streams of water, so I long for you, O God.

I thirst for God, the living God. When can I come and stand before him?

Day and night, I have only tears for food,

while my enemies continually taunt me, saying, "Where is this God of yours?"

My heart is breaking as I remember how it used to be:

I walked among the crowds of worshipers,

leading a great procession to the house of God,

singing for joy and giving thanks—it was the sound of a great celebration!

Why am I discouraged? Why so sad?

I will put my hope in God!

I will praise him again—my Savior and my God!

Now I am deeply discouraged, but I will remember your kindness—

from Mount Hermon, the source of the Jordan,

from the land of Mount Mizar.

I hear the tumult of the raging seas

as your waves and surging tides sweep over me.

Through each day the LORD pours his unfailing love upon me,

and through each night I sing his songs, praying to God who gives me life.

"O God my rock," I cry, "Why have you forsaken me?

Why must I wander in darkness, oppressed by my enemies?"

Their taunts pierce me like a fatal wound.

They scoff, "Where is this God of yours?"

Why am I discouraged? Why so sad?

I will put my hope in God!

I will praise him again—my Savior and my God!

AUTHORITY CRISIS

HUMBLE YOURSELVES, THEREFORE, UNDER GOD'S MIGHTY HAND.
—1 Peter 5:6

I recall as a kid often saying to other kids, "Who made you the boss?" It was an early reflection of my propensity to reject outside authority. In our world it is not uncommon to hear, "You are in charge of your universe. You are your own authority." However, in God's scheme of things, nothing could be further from the truth. God alone is the authority.

When I was in the pastorate, a couple came into my office asking for help with a thorny problem in regard to another family in the church. When I heard their story, it was evident that God's Word spoke clearly to the problem. They were dealing with a matter of litigation, and it involved taking a brother to public trial.

We opened the Bible to 1 Corinthians 6 and read what God's Word said. I explained what some of the biblical alternatives were. We prayed together, and as they got up to leave, I said, "Thank you for coming. I'll be praying for you as you seek to apply God's Word to your life." They turned and said, "Well, thank you—but we really aren't sure we're going to do that." For this couple, the Word of God was an optional resource. It obviously had escaped them that we will all be held accountable for our response to His Word and that breaking His Word always brings consequences. But what surprised me most was that they were long-standing members of the church, and they still had not resolved the issue of who should be in charge of life.

God has spoken not to give us another option but to bring us under His good and wise authority. It's like a divine diet to which we restrict ourselves faithfully that we might trim off the extra pounds of flesh and become conformed to the likeness of His wonderful Son.

The issue is whether we will live under the good and productive rule of His Word or choose to rule ourselves . . . which, in the light of the track record of most of us, is a scary thought.

Are there areas of your life where you are rejecting God's authority?

THE GREAT PHYSICIAN

Jesus Said, "It Is Not the Healthy Who Need a Doctor, but the Sick."
—Matthew 9:12

*O*f all the titles given to Jesus, I have to admit that I am taken with the thought that He is the Great Physician. Doctors are highly respected and their advice and counsel carry great weight. When we have a medical problem, where do we go to find help? The doctor. We are willing to undergo great pain and inconvenience to follow his orders. We even go to the edge of death's door in surgery because we trust his wisdom and skill.

And so it is with Jesus . . . all of the above. Yet Jesus often gets less respect and cooperation from us than our local M.D. In His day, people were amazed by His healing power and continued to come to Him as He preached from one city to the next. Jesus recognized their needs, both physical and spiritual, saying, "It is not the healthy who need a doctor, but the sick. . . . For I have not come to call the righteous, but sinners" (Matthew 9:12–13).

Here was a Doctor who offered more than a temporary escape or a purely physical solution to their problems. He offered healing and understanding that probed far beyond their physical ailments. He cured the most troubling problem of all. He came to save us from our sins, to bring eternal life and contribute hope where before there was hopelessness and utter despair.

He was unique. He was not what people expected—from His humble entry into the world, to His victorious triumph as He conquered the grave; He was a Physician who could not only heal the masses but who Himself conquered death and secured eternal life for everyone who would believe.

Is there any doubt that our world today is in desperate need of the Great Physician? That our lives on a daily basis still need His healing, His direction and advice?

Are there areas in your life where you need to follow "the Doctor's orders?"

REJOICE!

REJOICE IN THE LORD ALWAYS. I WILL SAY IT AGAIN: REJOICE!
—Philippians 4:4

I remember seeing a new student walking toward our Sunday school class wearing a whole chain of perfect attendance awards pinned to the lapel of his suit coat. To a group of junior high guys hanging out by the door of the SS room, it was quite a sight. We sneered among ourselves, "Who does he think he is?" And immediately dismissed him as a legitimate candidate to make it into the "in" group. Not one of my finer moments, I must admit, but a good illustration of the human dynamics that come into play when we flaunt our own accomplishments.

When Paul wrote to the church at Philippi, he wrote to weed out that same dynamic. In chapter 3 he speaks forcefully against the Judaizers, who flaunted their keeping of the religious customs of the law. Their attitude was a source of conflict and division in the church. These law-keepers were, in their minds, the blue-ribbon Christians in Philippi. Others were of less spiritual status. Talk about people saying, "Who do they think they are?" It was rampant.

Paul's remedy? Stop rejoicing in your own accomplishments and start rejoicing in the Lord. When he commanded the Philippians to "rejoice in the Lord" (3:1; 4:4), he wasn't calling for glib expressions of "Praise Jesus" falling from our lips at every opportunity. He was calling for something deeper. It was a call to forsake our absorption with things that elevate ourselves and instead live in the attitude of gratefulness for all we have in Jesus. Hence Paul's personal testimony. After listing his own accomplishments, he sees it all "to be loss in view of the surpassing value of knowing Christ Jesus my Lord" (3:8 NASB).

The desired effect among followers is that there are no "blue-ribbon" Christians. There is no spiritual caste system that separates the high performers from the others. There is only Jesus.

Have anything in your life you'd like to brag about? Don't. Brag about Jesus and His wonderful grace in your life. When we all start doing this, we just may enjoy the pleasure of a oneness that eradicates "Who does he think he is?" with "Let me tell you who He is!"

Read Jeremiah 9:23–24.

TO TELL THE TRUTH

—Colossians 3:9

*L*ittle white lies" are so tempting . . . especially when they keep us out of trouble. Fudging on our 1040 seems innocent enough. Doesn't everyone? Why not juice up the cash gain by cheating a little around the edges? Here's why.

When describing those whose lives will be judged in the lake of fire, God includes liars (Revelation 21:8). The psalmist, in aligning his life with truth, affirmed, "I hate every wrong path" (Psalm 119:104). Scripture shows that God desires that truth would dwell within us (Psalm 51:6). But why is truth so important to God?

Alignment. God's intense concern for truthfulness centers in His very nature. He is a "God of truth" (Psalm 31:5) "who cannot lie" (Titus 1:2 NKJV). Jesus Christ is "full of grace and truth" (John 1:14). The Holy Spirit is the "Spirit of truth," and His mission is to guide us into the truth (John 14:17; 16:13). "All the paths of the Lord are mercy and truth" (Psalm 25:10 KJV). "His works are done in truth" (Psalm 33:4 KJV). The truth is the key to our worship (John 4:24). Therefore, our commitment to the truth aligns us with God, His nature, and His mode of operation. It is a matter of fellowship.

Reflection. Our very purpose in existing as God's children is to be "conformed to the image of his Son" (Romans 8:29 KJV). We are redeemed to reflect His character. When we participate in and propagate that which is not true, we abort the purpose of our redemption and tarnish the reflection of His glory through us. If God is truth, then we too must portray truth to accurately reflect God's image in our lives.

Submission. God's Word commands us to speak the truth in love—regardless of the cost. "The righteous hate what is false" (Proverbs 13:5). Paul wrote, "Do not lie to each other" (Colossians 3:9). Nowhere in Scripture does God grant exemption from these commands. They are absolute. Our consciences cannot be clear before God and our joy cannot be full if we get involved with that which is not true.

Are you careful to live, speak, and reflect truth in every part of your life? What needs to change?

BUT LORD, WHY?

"THOUGH HE SLAY ME, YET WILL I HOPE IN HIM."

—Job 13:15

*S*atan reduced Job to the irreducible minimum—Job, his trouble, and his God. That's right where Satan wanted him. How would Job respond? Would he curse God or praise His name? It was a test of major proportions. Amazingly, Job continued to loyally worship God even though he had no idea why his life had so brutally fallen apart.

The theme of the book of Job is not patience, though we learn something of patience from Job's life (James 5:10–11). It is not Job and Satan, nor is it Satan and God. The theme is not suffering.

The theme of the book of Job is *God*. A God who is worthy of our uncompromised allegiance regardless of the circumstances of life. Does God have the right to be God in our lives even when we don't understand? Are we willing to trust His perfect wisdom when everything in life "seemingly" contradicts His goodness? Job answers, "Yes! Yes! A resounding Yes. Yes, in spite of it all!"

Job had an unshakable belief that no matter what happened, God was worthy. In his deepest agony Job said: "The Lord gave, and the Lord hath taken away; blessed be the name of the Lord" (Job 1:21 KJV). What Job didn't know was the *why*. In fact, he never knew that on this earth. When God resolved the tormenting questions in Job's mind at the end of the book, He did not sit down with Job and explain everything. He simply put Job back in touch with who He was as God. Trouble in life always raises the question "Why?" But, it is more important to know the *who* in our trouble. Knowing Him means that we can trust Him with the *why*.

Loving and trusting God is not about what He does for us in life; we must love Him because He is the God of our lives. It is the supreme compliment of our hearts when we let God know that He is worthy of our trust and praise, regardless.

When life turns against you, what is it that you know about God in which you can unflinchingly trust?

SOMETHING SOLID

GOD IS FAITHFUL.

—1 Corinthians 10:13

*S*ince we rarely know why trouble comes or what God is doing in and through our pain, it is important to have something solid and true to which we can attach our faith.

When trouble comes, faith clings to His *promises.* "Never will I leave you; never will I forsake you" (Hebrews 13:5). "And we know that in all things God works for the good of those who love him, who have been called according to his purpose" (Romans 8:28). "Perseverance must finish its work so that you may be mature and complete, not lacking anything" (James 1:4). Even when there's no light at the end of the tunnel, when you are in a deepening darkness and your heart is broken, these promises are true. When they are embraced they provide stability.

When trouble comes, faith clings to His *ways.* His ways are trustworthy and good (Romans 11:33–36). By faith we pray this kind of prayer: "Heavenly Father, I know what Your ways are good. I've experienced what you have done in the past and I know how you have worked in the lives of those who have gone before. Since that's the kind of God You are, I'll hang on to You through this. I will not become bitter or manipulative. I believe that your ways are good and I will wait for You to do Your work in Your time."

When trouble comes, faith clings to His *character.* First Corinthians 10:13 says, "God is faithful." He is not going to show up at the end of your trouble and say, "I'm really sorry, but I've had a busy three weeks. I just couldn't quite get around to your situation." His character is firm and reliable, fully worthy of our confidence. God is loving, just (that helps in terms of our enemies), righteous, gracious, timely, and merciful. And, best yet, all that He is, is not a choice He makes but an intrinsic part of His being. He cannot *not* deny who He is.

Trouble always looks for somewhere to find comfort and strength. Find it in His promises, in His ways, and in His character. All other ground is sinking sand.

What do you know about God that helps you in tough times? Cling to it and don't let go!

PSALM 43

O God, take up my cause!
Defend me against these ungodly people.
Rescue me from these unjust liars.
For you are God, my only safe haven.
Why have you tossed me aside?
Why must I wander around in darkness,
oppressed by my enemies?
Send out your light and your truth;
let them guide me.
Let them lead me to your holy mountain,
to the place where you live.
There I will go to the altar of God,
to God—the source of all my joy.
I will praise you with my harp,
O God, my God!
Why am I discouraged?
Why so sad?
I will put my hope in God!
I will praise him again—
my Savior and my God!

SET THE CAPTIVES FREE

DEFEND THE CAUSE OF THE WEAK AND FATHERLESS; MAINTAIN THE RIGHTS
OF THE POOR AND OPPRESSED.

—Psalm 82:3

*O*ne of the indelible memories I have to this day is the memory of my dad always including his life verses every time he signed his name: Isaiah 58:10–11. In Isaiah's day, Israel was complaining about why God seemed far away even though they were so good. God replied that they had neglected the needs of the poor and oppressed (Isaiah 58:1–12).

It is interesting how quiet we are about the same issues.

Few voices are raised against the racism and its structures that deny privilege, empowerment, worth, and dignity to people of passport or pigment.

We raise our voices against pornography and prostitution because we see them as problems of sexual perversion, when we should be equally concerned about the fact that these perversions harm, abuse, and destroy women and children. The oppression within these evil systems is managed by oppressors who empower and advance themselves on the backs of the weak. Pimps and pornographers brutalize the vulnerable for their own gain. Child abuse—whether sexual, physical, psychological, or emotional—is a heinous expression of the powerful oppressing the weak. The problem of drugs is bigger than its threat to our own children. Drugs are sold and traded in a system that oppressively manipulates the weak in society. Slavery is a blatant expression of injustice. Apartheid is unjust. Ethnic cleansing is a violation of the just rights of humanity.

Yet the church today is strangely silent about these horrible violations of the dignity and value of people who are created in our Lord's image. Perhaps that is why we as a church are so powerless in our day. Followers of Christ must be willing to take a stand, and speak for what is right and just. While we may not oppress others, neither should we sit by silently when others offend God by brutalizing the weak.

The evangelical abolitionist who gave up becoming Prime Minister to eradicate slave trading in Britain said just months before his death, "It shall never be said that William Wilberforce is silent when slaves need his help."

Read Isaiah 58:1–12.

JUNE 24 / 188

TRUE ENCOURAGEMENT

WHOEVER FLATTERS HIS NEIGHBOR IS SPREADING A NET FOR HIS FEET.
—Proverbs 29:5

"Flattery will get you everywhere" is more truth than fiction. There are fewer skills of the tongue that are more manipulative and ego serving than flattery. The problem with flattery is that it often places the hearer in debt to us by verbally commending some action, virtue, or involvement in his life. The commendation may or may not be true, but it usually is exaggerated. Flattery differs from genuine praise or compliment because of its motive. It is a compliment given to manipulate another for our own personal gain. The psalmist includes flattery in a list of the characteristics of the wicked. He writes, "There is nothing reliable in what they say . . . they flatter with their tongue" (Psalm 5:9 NASB).

A flatterer uses his words to gain favor. All of us like to be in good favor with others. But true favor comes by earning another's respect. Unfortunately, some of us think we can worm our way into other people's favor by flattering them.

Flattery also focuses the heart of the one flattered on his own accomplishments and makes him prone to pride. This may have been what the writer to Proverbs had in mind when he wrote, "Whoever flatters his neighbor is spreading a net for his feet" (Proverbs 29:5).

This, of course, does not mean that we should never genuinely compliment, encourage, or praise someone who is deserving or who is in need of a positive word. The key is our motivation. Why am I complimenting this person? If it truly is an act of love, encouragement, and support with no thought of personal gain, then it is a compliment, not flattery. Compliments should focus on character rather than performance. When they do, they stimulate growth instead of pride.

Compliments that give God the glory take the treachery out of flattery. Comments like "I'm thankful the Lord has given you such a desire to help others," or, "God has been good to give me a husband like you," or, "The Lord has given you a special ability to minister to me through song" go a long way to take the flattery factor out of our desire to encourage.

Plan to encourage someone today in a wholesome way.

TRUE PROSPERITY

SURELY GOD IS GOOD TO . . . THOSE WHO ARE PURE IN HEART.
—Psalms 73:1

*I*n Psalm 73, Asaph is devastatingly disillusioned because the wicked prosper and he, in his faithfulness to God, struggles to make ends meet. He admits, "My feet had almost slipped . . . when I saw the prosperity of the wicked" (vv. 2–3). After a long recitation of the blessings bestowed on the lives of the wicked, you can feel his despair as he concludes, "Surely in vain have I kept my heart pure; . . . all day long I have been plagued" (vv. 13– 14). Most of us have been there. A competitor cheats his way ahead and seemingly suffers no consequence. An offender leaves us devastated and goes on to what appears to be a happy and fulfilled life. Unprincipled people catapult themselves forward by unethical schemes, and we are left in the backwater of our commitment to God's principles. When we let this get the best of us, we are easily tempted to go the way of the wicked, since prosperity seems to be their reward.

But everything changed when Asaph went into the sanctuary of God. There he came to understand that in the end the wicked face the devastating judgment of God. It's clear that his pity party has turned to celebration when he triumphantly writes, "Whom have I in heaven but Thee? And besides Thee, I desire nothing on earth. My flesh and my heart may fail, but God is the strength of my heart and my portion forever. For, behold, those who are far from Thee will perish; Thou hast destroyed all those who are unfaithful to Thee. But as for me, the nearness of God is my good; I have made the Lord God my refuge, that I may tell of all Thy works" (vv. 25–28 NASB 1977).

The psalmist has come to grips with the reality that true prosperity is measured in God's presence, protection, guidance, and eternal guarantee of heaven.

It's no wonder that the writer of Hebrews exclaims, "Keep your lives free from the love of money and be content with what you have, because God has said, 'Never will I leave you; never will I forsake you'" (Hebrews 13:5).

What is your definition of prosperity?

OUR MAIN SQUEEZE

DO NOT LOVE THE WORLD OR ANYTHING IN THE WORLD. IF ANYONE LOVES THE WORLD, THE LOVE OF THE FATHER IS NOT IN HIM.
—1 John 2:15

*O*n my way home from the office, I used to regularly pass a florist shop that had a large marquee on its roof advertising special flower deals. I'll never forget passing by one evening and noticing that it said: "Take roses to your main squeeze." I chuckled at the thought of Martie as my "main squeeze." I hasten to add that there are no secondary squeezes!

When it comes to getting things straight in our walk with Christ, the pivotal issue is who will be our "main squeeze." "The Father" should be our eager response. After all, the first and greatest commandment is that we "love the Lord [our] God" (Matthew 22:37). Yet many of us are still in love with the world, living and sacrificing for all it offers. We too easily yield our careers, our cash, our children, and our chastity to the sizzle that this world offers.

Loving the world means to yield to it, to make aspects of it our primary point of allegiance. Clearly, love for the Father is not in us when the world has its grip on our heads and hearts. We can say it, sing it, or even chant about our love for God, but if our choices consistently point to the cosmos rather than the kingdom, the world has stolen our "first love" (Revelation 2:4).

Loving the world puts us at risk. When we are yielded to its allures, we embrace its lies and destructive power. In fact, our loving allegiance to its misinformation is epidemic. Ask the average Christian what success means, and you will hear answers about careers and lifestyle. Ask about life's main pursuit, and you will often hear us answer, "Happiness."

Lovers of God, however, know the difference. For them, success is faithfulness, and the pursuit of life is not happiness but reflecting the glory of God in our lives. Loving Him means yielding to the sound of His voice and living by His Word.

What is there in your life that reflects a love for this world? Deal with it by turning your heart toward Him.

A BRILLIANT STRATEGY

"You Are the Light of the World."

—Matthew 5:14

*A*lthough we need to continue to slug it out in the political arena, there is a more important strategy for impacting our culture. The most powerful weapon we have against the darkness—a weapon that seems to have suffered as we have picketed and politicked as though revival comes through governmental power—is our privileged assignment to be lights in our world. In Scripture, light is the penetrating, revealing, unquenchable force of a personal expression of rightness and truth. It is ignited in lives that are nonnegotiably committed to living biblically.

Interestingly, neither Scripture nor history demonstrates that political advantage accomplishes true spiritual gain, either personally or culturally. Christ called us to the power of productive personal righteousness when He said, "You are the light of the world. A city set on a hill cannot be hidden. Nor do men light a lamp, and put it under the peck-measure, but on the lampstand; and it gives light to all who are in the house. Let your light shine before men in such a way that they may see your good works, and glorify your Father who is in heaven" (Matthew 5:14–16 NASB 1977).

What would this light look like? Well, it would look like Jesus, who Himself was the "light of the world." Letting Him shine through us means that our compassion is broad enough to cover even our enemies. We learn that from the Good Samaritan (Luke 10:25–37). Our love for the lost would be a compelling priority. The world would hear more about mercy and more about the love of the Cross than cross words about their wickedness. We would aggressively care about the poor, oppressed, and victimized and stop marginalizing those who truly are in need with the rhetoric of "Why don't they get a job?" Servanthood would replace self-centeredness. His grace, justice, and righteousness would rule our lives.

Now is the time to challenge the deepening darkness with the light of a new dawn, the light of Christ obviously evident in our own lives.

What particular aspect of Christ's light shines from your life into the darkness? Are there additional rays of light that you could add?

CHRISTIANITY APPLIED

YOU ARE A CHOSEN RACE . . . THAT YOU MAY PROCLAIM THE EXCELLENCIES
OF HIM WHO HAS CALLED YOU OUT OF DARKNESS.
—1 Peter 2:9 NASB

*G*od is rarely embraced simply because the evidence weighs in His favor. Many refuse to admit His reality simply because they don't want Him interfering in their lives. Why do otherwise well-educated people deny that there is a Creator when all the evidence points to an intelligent design? Why do we cling to theories that depend on the unlikely prospect of random chance producing highly sophisticated systems more intricate than anything our technology has been able to produce?

If we accept the Bible as true and the God of the Bible as real, then we must also affirm what He says about us: that we are sinners hopelessly and helplessly guilty before Him. Most of all, we must accept that we need a Savior and that we must humbly repent and gratefully restructure our lives to conform to His ways instead of our own.

What kind of evidence does it take to turn the hearts of sinners to the reality of their need for a Savior? It is here that we can take a page out of the experience of the first-century church. The early church made an impact on its world of unbelief by remaining unintimidated in the face of ridicule and persecution (Philippians 1:27–28). They loved their God more than their world (Matthew 22:37). They were unified in their love for each other (John 13:34–35) and they kept their behavior excellent so that regardless of what people said about them they were above reproach (1 Peter 2:12). The rewarding outcomes of their applied Christianity stood in sharp contrast to the emptiness and despair produced by pagan permissiveness. Christians preached volumes by their willingness to die agonizing deaths for what they had found to be true and by their unshakable belief in a better world to come.

Today we live in similar times. Our world needs to see similar Christians.

Are you impacting your world with observable, rewarding outcomes in your life as a result of applied faith?

PSALM 46

God is our refuge and strength,
always ready to help in times of trouble.
So we will not fear, even if earthquakes come
and the mountains crumble into the sea.
Let the oceans roar and foam.
Let the mountains tremble as the waters surge!
A river brings joy to the city of our God,
the sacred home of the Most High.
God himself lives in that city; it cannot be destroyed.
God will protect it at the break of day.
The nations are in an uproar,
and kingdoms crumble!
God thunders, and the earth melts!
The LORD Almighty is here among us;
the God of Israel is our fortress.
Come, see the glorious works of the LORD:
See how he brings destruction upon the world
and causes wars to end throughout the earth.
He breaks the bow and snaps the spear in two;
he burns the shields with fire.
"Be silent, and know that I am God!
I will be honored by every nation.
I will be honored throughout the world."
The LORD Almighty is here among us;
the God of Israel is our fortress.

THE EXCELLENT WAY

For the Word of God . . . Judges the Thoughts and Attitudes of the Heart.

—Hebrews 4:12

*F*ollowing Christ is about growing to sin less and following Him more. Why is it so tough, then, to pull off that agenda in some areas of our lives? Let me introduce you to an adversary that resides in all of our souls: rationalizations. You've got to love them. They make sinning so easy and poor choices so comfortable.

This "trick of the trade" of sin neutralizes the built-in resistance to sin and leaves us wide open to failure. Rationalization is a mental excuse for an error in life. It is characterized by excuses we all have used: "I know it's wrong, but . . ." "If it weren't for the way my husband treats me . . ." "I can't help myself." "I know a lot of people who are worse than I am." "Let me tell you about the home I grew up in." "This will be the last time I do this."

God calls us to a better way. In fact, He calls us to live out unrationalized choices that are "excellent." And what is the excellent way? Philippians 1:9–10 says, "And this I pray, that your love may abound still more and more in real knowledge and all discernment, so that you may approve the things that are excellent" (NASB). Excellent decisions come from being committed to *love,* the welfare of others; to *knowledge,* the principles of God's Word; and to *discernment,* the application of love and knowledge to a given situation. What is the product of this kind of think right, act right living? It is personal purity ("pure and blameless," v. 10), a productive life ("the fruit of righteousness," v. 11), and the privilege of living to bring "glory and praise" to God (v. 11).

What a startling contrast to the way we are prone to live when we cover our shame with self-deluding rationalizations.

Isolate your favorite rationalizations. What difference would it make if you never used them again?

STAY IN TOUCH

Draw Near to God and He Will Draw Near to You.
—James 4:8 NASB

*Y*ou've probably noticed that life has a way of grinding us down to repeated routines and rituals. We really are creatures of habit. The problem is that if we are not careful a daily sense of connectedness to the Lord somehow gets lost in the shuffle. We end up carrying on as though He weren't particularly relevant to the everyday occasions and encounters of life.

Unfortunately, we get used to life at a distance from God and become resigned to life's not being what it is cracked up to be. We end up thinking that a close, satisfying relationship with God is what only others possess. Even though He has offered us nearness, God seems inaccessibly far away. And so we give up. We're like the person who's lost a limb. We know how much we miss what we've lost, but, having no hope of getting it back, we adjust. Of course, we flee to Him when we get beyond ourselves and we maintain a basic level of religious activity. But God is hardly the throbbing center of our lives.

Yet He needs to be. And until He is, life will always be less than it should be. Sometimes tragically less.

Those of us who want Him close need to draw close to Him. It is such a joy to stay in touch with Him all day long. To ask for grace and wisdom as you pick up the phone . . . or pick the kids up from school. To regularly thank Him for the little things . . . when they happen. To seek His wisdom when you don't know what to choose or to say. To confess immediately when those inevitable slips show you how frail you really are. And to live as if you need Him all the time.

Those who draw near to God *do* find Him drawing near to them. God *is* the rewarder of those who "diligently seek him" (Hebrews 11:6 KJV). Legions could testify to the pleasure of living in His presence. Join them.

Refresh yourself with regular encounters with God.

WHATEVER HAPPENED TO HEAVEN?

EVERYONE WHO HAS THIS HOPE IN HIM PURIFIES HIMSELF, JUST AS HE IS PURE.

—1 John 3:3

*I*t is interesting to note that when Christ came, the disciples were frightfully naive about heaven. One might assume that having been schooled in Judaism they would have a keen understanding of the world to come. Yet their thoughts of a future paradise focused on the dream that a messiah would overthrow the Roman occupation, establish his rule on earth, and restore Israel to its former glory. It was not heaven there but heaven *here* that they anticipated.

In fact, the whole religious environment of Christ's day minimized the thought of heaven. One of the major religious groups were the Sadducees. They were wealthy materially, which made even the thought of heaven superfluous, and their theology actually denied the resurrection and the thought of an afterlife. Both their theology and their affluence made heaven unnecessary. The Pharisees, on the other hand, affirmed the reality of a life to come, yet, as one writer observed, "They were primarily concerned with the ritual dimension of Judaism."

Given these prevailing religious attitudes, it's no wonder that the disciples' view of heaven was dim. As such, it brought confusion to their hearts about Christ's mission and anxiety within when He told them He was leaving.

But all that changed after the Resurrection and Ascension. Heaven was real and compelling to the early church. They could take the flame of the fire and the torture of hungry lions because they knew that all that was better was yet to come. That this was indeed what Thomas Hobbes was to call the "nasty, brutish, and short" world. The idea that heaven was "far better" (Philippians 1:23 KJV) was a realization that enabled them to hold life loosely here and live for Christ regardless of the cost. And, as John said, living in the hope of seeing Jesus face-to-face was a motivation to purity in their lives.

To this day, affluence and a preoccupation with earthside rules and rituals dim our view of heaven. It's only when heaven is in full view that our lives start functioning as they should.

Is heaven in clear view for you on a regular basis? If it were, what difference would it make?

ENCOURAGE ONE ANOTHER

"If You Keep on Biting and Devouring Each Other, Watch Out or You Will Be Destroyed by Each Other."
—Galatians 5:15

*C*ontentious words are the meat cleaver of relationships. I recall watching a butcher prepare a chicken for selling. His sharp cleaver chopped away with well-timed strokes until the bird lay in a pile of pieces. Contentious words are like that. In Proverbs 6 the word for contention is translated "discord" (vv. 14, 19 KJV). It catches my attention when I note that "he that soweth discord among brethren" (v. 19 KJV) makes the infamous list of "six things . . . the Lord [doth] hate: yea, seven [that] are an abomination" to the Lord (v. 16 KJV).

Contentious hearts look for things to criticize, for opportunities to tear a person, program, or idea down. Contentious words make a ready ally for angry, resentful hearts. They divide instead of unify. They do Satan's work for him.

In 1 Corinthians 3:3, Paul faulted the Corinthians for being contentious with each other. Later on, he pictured the church as the body of Christ working as one in cooperative harmony (1 Corinthians 12:12–31). Have you ever seen a body cut into several parts functioning well? Division among the brethren destroys the reflection of God among us and the power of His unity through us.

But it's not just the church. Our relationship with our spouse is God's living illustration of Christ and the church. Christ never divides Himself from His bride, the church. His unconditional love and acceptance are unifying factors. His words to the church promote healing and growth. When contentious words divide our spirits at home, we destroy the God-intended picture of Christ and His church.

Whoever coined "divide and conquer" knew what they were talking about. Division among God's people gives Satan a tremendous advantage in conquering our usefulness, joy, and peace. Let's commit ourselves to exchanging contentious words for words that encourage His people. As Paul said, "Do not let any unwholesome talk come out of your mouths, but only what is helpful for building others up according to their needs, that it may benefit those who listen" (Ephesians 4:29).

Can you be counted on for a good word?

BLOOM WHERE YOU'RE PLANTED

Let Us Run with Perseverance the Race Marked Out for Us.
—Hebrews 12:1

*R*ecently, my daughter Libby ran the Chicago marathon. I was so proud of her for training and staying at it. Needless to say, Martie and I showed up to cheer her along and met her after the finish line with camera flashing and flowers in hand! Watching her run kindled my interest in marathons —those massive, grueling twenty-six-mile endurance tests. As I watched on that day, I noted that friends along the way threw towels and handed runners cups of something to drink. It became apparent that companions like these were essential to the runners' success.

It's like that with perseverance. You can't run the marathon of life without it. Especially in difficult times.

It's no wonder that the author of Hebrews wrote to his readers, who were under severe pressure: "Therefore, since we are surrounded by such a great cloud of witnesses, let us throw off everything that hinders and the sin that so easily entangles, and let us run with perseverance the race marked out for us" (Hebrews 12:1). The race marked out for them was like an obstacle course. It required that they run in spite of rejection, loss of friends, economic difficulty, and daily persecution. Perseverance would need to be their indispensable companion.

The word *perseverance* is literally made up of two words. One means "to remain"; the other means "under." Perseverance is the ability to stay under the pressure of our difficulty with a good spirit until God has finished His work. We usually want to squirt out from under the pressure. To be done. To hurry the sunshine.

God intends that we, in time, will blossom under pressure. Perseverance gives God the time to do His work. Which is why James exhorts us to submit to the trial and let perseverance "finish its work" (James 1:4).

Remember, He is waiting for you at the finish line!

In prayer, ask God for the grace to endure so that He can accomplish His purpose in your life (2 Corinthians 12:7–10).

OH, TO BE ALONE!

WHEN JESUS HEARD WHAT HAD HAPPENED, HE WITHDREW BY BOAT
PRIVATELY TO A SOLITARY PLACE. HEARING OF THIS, THE CROWDS FOLLOWED
HIM ON FOOT FROM THE TOWNS.

—Matthew 14:13

*B*eing alone is a treasure. It is therapy from the busyness and fast-paced confusion of life. Being alone helps us get in touch with our values, our priorities, and ourselves. Every mother knows the treasure of hours—or is it minutes?—when she is alone. While I am an unrepentant people person, I too long for times of being alone. And when we can get alone we shouldn't feel guilty about it.

Christ often went away to find spiritual renewal, solace in times of grief, and rest from the crush and demanding pace of a people-intensive ministry. One of the most touching moments of Christ's humanity was when He withdrew to a place of solitude after He heard of the beheading of John the Baptist. John was Christ's cousin. But more significant, he had given his life on the altar of announcing the coming of Christ. Matthew tells us that when Jesus heard of this savage, cruel tragedy, He was struck by a sense of personal loss and "withdrew by boat privately to a solitary place" (Matthew 14:13).

Interrupted in His solitude by people who followed Him, He took His boat ashore and ministered, healing and feeding the five thousand. The text then says that He sent His disciples to the other side of the sea and sent the multitudes away. Then He "went up on a mountainside by himself to pray. When evening came, he was there alone" (v. 23). It was in these times of being alone that He dealt with His grief and refreshed His reserves to effectively live and serve for another season.

Surviving life and succeeding spiritually demands downtimes when we are alone with God and ourselves. When are you alone? Do you meet God there in the quietness? Life cannot run on empty. God waits to fill our hearts afresh in quiet places.

Each day make it a habit to find a quiet spot in which to speak with God and to hear from Him through His Word.

PSALM 51

Have mercy on me, O God, because of your unfailing love.

Because of your great compassion, blot out the stain of my sins.

Wash me clean from my guilt. Purify me from my sin.

For I recognize my shameful deeds—they haunt me day and night.

Against you, and you alone, have I sinned; I have done what is evil in your sight.

You will be proved right in what you say, and your judgment against me is just.

For I was born a sinner—yes, from the moment my mother conceived me.

But you desire honesty from the heart,

so you can teach me to be wise in my inmost being.

Purify me from my sins, and I will be clean;

wash me, and I will be whiter than snow.

Oh, give me back my joy again; you have broken me—now let me rejoice.

Don't keep looking at my sins. Remove the stain of my guilt.

Create in me a clean heart, O God. Renew a right spirit within me.

Do not banish me from your presence, and don't take your Holy Spirit from me.

Restore to me again the joy of your salvation, and make me willing to obey you.

Then I will teach your ways to sinners, and they will return to you.

Forgive me for shedding blood, O God who saves;

then I will joyfully sing of your forgiveness.

Unseal my lips, O Lord, that I may praise you.

You would not be pleased with sacrifices, or I would bring them.

If I brought you a burnt offering, you would not accept it.

The sacrifice you want is a broken spirit.

A broken and repentant heart, O God, you will not despise.

Look with favor on Zion and help her; rebuild the walls of Jerusalem.

Then you will be pleased with worthy sacrifices

and with our whole burnt offerings;

and bulls will again be sacrificed on your altar.

ALL ARE PRECIOUS IN HIS SIGHT

THERE IS NEITHER JEW NOR GREEK, SLAVE NOR FREE, MALE NOR FEMALE,
FOR YOU ARE ALL ONE IN CHRIST JESUS.

—Galatians 3:28

*E*verybody is so different. And, while the differences between us should enrich us, they more often than not threaten to divide us. There are differences of color, culture, class, gender, and tongue. Distinctions like these have been the cause of wars, excused the shame of slavery, and fanned the evils of pride and prejudice.

Yet oneness across these divides is what Jesus desires and provides for us. As Paul noted, in Christ there is no difference. We are all His children, heirs and joint-heirs with Christ. Which gives us a stunning advantage.

Our world seeks to dissolve the difference by urging us to celebrate diversity. The problem is that the more we celebrate diversity, the more it looks like we are in tribal warfare. When we concentrate on our differences without a unifying factor, we end up scrambling for our place in the sun and fighting for the rights and privileges of our kind.

Hence our advantage. Above the differences among us as followers is the preeminent person of Jesus Christ. He is where we meet each other and find joy in being together with Him. In fact, as we together celebrate our oneness in Jesus, our differences become a blessing. It's enriching to see Jesus worshiped with a choir that sways and to see Him praised with a choir that stands straight and masterfully sings Bach. In Jesus we are no longer red and yellow, black and white. We are brothers and sisters in Christ. As Tony Evans says, "We may have all come over on different boats, but we're all in the same boat now." Whether lawyers or pipe fitters, young or old, well or disabled, we are all precious to Him and therefore precious to each other.

I've often thought that those of us who can't get over our differences here will have trouble in heaven, since some from "every tribe and . . . nation" will be there (Revelation 5:9).

Tony Evans also says, "Our lives here on earth should be a 'sneak preview' for the really big show to come!" Are you doing your part?

POWER TO THE HUMBLE

"FOR EVERYONE WHO EXALTS HIMSELF WILL BE HUMBLED, AND HE WHO HUMBLES HIMSELF WILL BE EXALTED."
—Luke 14:11

*U*nless you know better, it's hard to spot true humility. Quiet, unassuming individuals may sometimes appear to be humble—when in reality they may feel intimidated and be fiercely jealous of others. People with reflective attitudes who rarely laugh, and are pious in speech may be proud of themselves for their piety. Or those who give the "I am nothing" impression may be begging for a compliment or just suffering from an inferiority complex.

On the other hand, authentically humble people may be the last ones you'd expect. They could be the life of the party, who laugh harder than anyone else, and who enjoy life to the fullest. The lesson is that humility cannot be measured in outward appearances and stereotypical temperament profiles.

Humility starts in the heart where two basic attitudes produce true humility. The first attitude deals with who is the final authority in life. Pride resists the reality of God's right to unconditionally call the shots in life. When Moses reproved Pharaoh for not cooperating with God's plans for Israel, he said, "Thus says the Lord, the God of the Hebrews, 'How long will you refuse to humble yourself before Me?'" (Exodus 10:3 NASB). A humble heart is an obedient heart that recognizes God's right to rule (Philippians 2:8).

The second attitude of true humility is the recognition that I am what I am not by my own scheming, skill, and intellect but rather solely by the goodness and grace of God. A proud heart wants to take the credit for our achievements. But God's Word teaches us that position, wealth, health, goods, and abilities are ultimately gifts from God. *Humility gives credit where credit is due.* It gladly claims that I am what I am by God's grace and that apart from Him I would be nothing (see 1 Corinthians 15:10).

It's a sobering thought to be reminded that God resists the proud. But think of this . . . He gives grace to the humble (1 Peter 5:5). Take your pick.

Today, humbly bow your heart in obedience, and look for ways to tactfully give Him the credit.

PILGRIM'S PROGRESS

WATCH YOUR LIFE AND DOCTRINE CLOSELY. PERSEVERE IN THEM, BECAUSE IF
YOU DO, YOU WILL SAVE BOTH YOURSELF AND YOUR HEARERS.
—1 Timothy 4:16

*P*eriodically, I'm asked what my greatest challenge is at Moody. That's not a hard question to answer. The answer does not relate to finances, personnel, management, or even the busyness of my schedule. My greatest challenge at Moody is *me*. When I'm keeping myself spiritually, emotionally, and physically fit, I have a far greater capacity to deal with the challenges at the office. When I keep myself functioning in the context of my gifts and am growing in Christ, I have a special strength, even on the tough days. As the old spiritual says, "It's not my brother, nor my sister, but it's me, O Lord, standing in the need of prayer."

Paul challenged Timothy to do the same: "Do not neglect the spiritual gift within you, which was bestowed upon you. . . . Take pains with these things; be absorbed in them, so that your progress may be evident to all. Pay close attention to yourself and to your teaching; persevere in these things; for as you do this you will insure salvation both for yourself and for those who hear you" (1 Timothy 4:14–16 NASB 1977).

When Paul said to "take pains with these things . . . so that your progress may be evident to all" (v. 15 NASB 1977), he was referring in part to his earlier exhortation that Timothy develop the qualities of love, purity, faith, excellent conduct, and wise speech.

The primary focus of Paul's plan for Timothy's success was Timothy himself. His leadership would rise or fall on how well he managed his personal growth and progress. And I like the fact that Paul called for him to make progress, not perfection. If perfection is required, we might as well quit. We'll never make it. But if progress in character, attitudes, and behavior is your passion, keep at it. That's a goal that you, by His grace, can attain.

Unfortunately, it is easier to become task oriented, throwing our worn-out selves and spirituality into the work. But God needs fit, growing workers in the vineyard. With Him it's always personhood before performance.

Is your life more involved with doing than becoming?

THE CURE

THERE IS NO FEAR IN LOVE. . . . PERFECT LOVE DRIVES OUT FEAR.
—1 John 4:18

*I*s there a cure for the debilitating enemy of fear? Thankfully, yes— replace it with love and trust.

Fear focuses on protecting and preserving "me." At times it can be constructive (fear of fire, fear of wild beasts), but more often it shows its destructive side. Fear inhibits us from witnessing. Fearing the loss of a promotion, we may compromise our ethics to gain business success. When others get in the way of our plans, we may fear that our desires will go unfulfilled, so we intimidate or abuse them to get our own way. This kind of fear is not a friend of growth or grace.

But a genuine love that commits itself to God's will and the needs of others overcomes fear (1 John 4:11–21). In the life of a follower who is committed first to love, fear will become increasingly nonexistent. Love acts for the best interests of others. Fear is all about "me". Jesus had much to fear by surrendering to the cross experience. But His love for His Father and His love for you superseded His fears.

Yet, for us, dispelling fear and expressing unconditional love require an additional ally.

Trust must go hand in hand with love to conquer fear. Trusting in God to watch over me, meet my needs, protect me, and give me His best releases me from the normal fears that hold me back. If I assume that I am solely responsible to protect and preserve "me", then fear will dominate me and love will be impossible. Trusting in God to protect and provide dispels fear (Psalm 56:3–4).

Are you afraid that in your love you will become vulnerable, misunderstood, taken advantage of, or misused? Is your God who He says He is? Then trust Him to work in and through the outcomes of your love and fearlessly turn your attention to His will and the needs of others. Fear wishes to hold you captive to yourself. Love wants to set you free.

Can you trust God enough to love in the face of your fears?

SOMETHING FIT TO WEAR

To Present Her to Himself as a Radiant Church, Without Stain or Wrinkle or Any Other Blemish, but Holy and Blameless.
—Ephesians 5:27

I like to think that the works of righteousness in my life are weaving threads into the beautiful gown that the church will wear on that grand day when we stand before our Lord. As Paul noted, Christ, the Bridegroom, desires a church "having no spot or wrinkle or any such thing; but that she should be holy and blameless" (Ephesians 5:27 NASB 1977).

I'll never forget what life was like in the months preceding our daughter's wedding. There were long lists of things to do, but preeminent on the list was picking out Libby's dress. But it wasn't just about the dress she wanted. Libby was looking for a dress that Rod, her soon-to-be husband, would be pleased to see her in.

And so it is with Christ, the Bridegroom, the lover of our souls. The only fitting way to present ourselves and to bring pleasure to Him is to wear the resplendent beauty of righteousness.

Since the pull of our fallenness and the seduction of nearly irresistible temptations are so real and tempt us so often, finding motivations that keep us pure is of great importance. The Scriptures are full of them. We are to be good for Him because He has been so good to us. We are to love Him with the obedience of our hearts because of His inexplicable love on the cross for us. We are to obey that we might glorify Him in all that we do. Yet the thought that in this life I am preparing to present a pure life well pleasing to Him is equally compelling (1 John 3:1–3).

Let our world scorn a life of righteousness as worthless—the truth is that we are righteous for very good reasons. And among them is the reason that righteousness is the very fabric that adorns the bride that brings Him great pleasure.

Is He pleased?

NAMES IN VAIN

YOU SHALL NOT MISUSE THE NAME OF THE LORD YOUR GOD, FOR THE LORD WILL NOT HOLD ANYONE GUILTLESS WHO MISUSES HIS NAME.
—Exodus 20:7

*N*ames are important. We may choose a name for a child because we like the sound of it, but it is just a name until the child's life begins to give it value. That's why we talk about someone as having a "good *name* in town." Of course we can ruin a name as well. In all my years of pastoring I never knew of anyone to name his child Judas.

This is what makes our taking of the Lord's name in vain so serious. *Jesus* is not just five letters thrown together to identify a great person who lived two millennia ago. It means "savior" and as such carries the weight of His death on the cross. In fact, His name is so significant that at the mere mention of it the whole world will bow in humble admission of His lordship (Philippians 2:9–11).

The name *God* in all of its forms represents the almighty ruler of the universe and a whole host of qualities, including the appropriate terror of His holy righteousness as well as His mercy and grace. The Jews so reverenced His name that they refused to utter it. When they had to write it, they took out all the vowels to minimize the risk of desecrating the power and glory of His name.

Using His name in a casual, flippant way should give us great concern. "Oh, God," "God," and "My Lord" are often used as verbal exclamation points even among His followers. "Praise the Lord" gets thrown around to fill up verbal space as though we couldn't think of anything else to utter. Have you noticed that many Christians get more upset with "four-letter" swear words than with taking His name in vain?

We will know how much we honor His saving work, respect His sovereign authority, and see Him as wholly sacred and worthy when we render the names of Jesus, Lord, and God as precious in our speech.

In what ways do you lift up, honor and defend the name of Jesus?

PSALM 57

Have mercy on me, O God, have mercy!
I look to you for protection.
I will hide beneath the shadow of your wings
until this violent storm is past.
I cry out to God Most High,
to God who will fulfill his purpose for me.
He will send help from heaven to save me,
rescuing me from those who are out to get me.
My God will send forth his unfailing love and faithfulness.
I am surrounded by fierce lions who greedily devour human prey—
whose teeth pierce like spears and arrows,
and whose tongues cut like swords.
Be exalted, O God, above the highest heavens!
May your glory shine over all the earth.
My enemies have set a trap for me.
I am weary from distress.
They have dug a deep pit in my path,
but they themselves have fallen into it.
My heart is confident in you, O God;
no wonder I can sing your praises!
Wake up, my soul! Wake up, O harp and lyre!
I will waken the dawn with my song.
I will thank you, Lord, in front of all the people.
I will sing your praises among the nations.
For your unfailing love is as high as the heavens.
Your faithfulness reaches to the clouds.
Be exalted, O God, above the highest heavens.
May your glory shine over all the earth.

PLEASURE, PRIDE, AND PASSION

SHE CAUGHT HIM BY HIS CLOAK AND SAID, "COME TO BED WITH ME!"
—Genesis 39:12

Those restless, inner energies of pleasure, pride, and passion can be perilous impulses. They threaten to clutter and corrupt our whole world.
And it doesn't help that our world constantly appeals to these inner energies.
From the Internet to sitcoms, from the ease of affairs to the massive availability of soft- and hard-core porn, destructive forces have all of us in their
crosshairs.

A pastor I know was on his way to his hotel room one evening when two
appealing young women on the elevator smiled at him and said, "How about
some fun tonight?" Who would know? He looked away, and when the door
opened, he stepped off the elevator. Alone. As challenging as that may have
been, he took action by walking away from the temptation. Obviously, he had
a management system within that helped keep these three forces in check.

Think of Joseph, who day after day worked with Potiphar's wife—who no
doubt was a "pick of the land," given Potiphar's status in Egypt. What a flattering lift to his pride that *she* would want him. What pleasure for a young
man with hormones in their heyday. What urges of passion he must have felt.
Yet each day Joseph resisted her advances. Finally, when she boldly grabbed
him, he ran from her (Genesis 39:12). Joseph demonstrated an unusual command of the forces of pleasure, pride, and passion.

When he resisted, he told her of the commitments that gave him strength.
He told her that he couldn't be that irresponsible to his boss, her husband, and
that he couldn't do this wickedness against God (vv. 8–9). Joseph had a grasp
on the two great commands: to love God with our whole being and our neighbor as ourselves (Matthew 22:37–39). As Jesus said, keep those two and all the
rest of the law cares for itself (v. 40)! All sins of passion violate love, hurting
those who are closest to us. And they offend God. Keeping relationships with
significant others thriving and staying close to God is God's insulation from
the destructive fires of pleasure, pride, and passion that irreparably scorch our
lives.

Are these three energies focused on your self-fulfillment or on God's best in your life?

HOPE, REGARDLESS

An Inheritance That Can Never Perish, Spoil or Fade—Kept in Heaven for You.

—1 Peter 1:4

*H*ope is a word that belongs in every believer's vocabulary. The hope of the Christian is not a wistful wish for a carefree life but a hope that is active and unthreatened even in the furnace of life's worst trials.

The apostle Peter knew something about this kind of hope. He had lived with both the wistful and the fire-tested kind of hope. At the transfiguration of Christ, Peter hoped out loud that he and the others could build a couple of lean-tos and stay on the mountain with Christ forever (Matthew 17:4).

But Peter had to come down from the mountain, and in the course of his ministry he faced "fiery trials" that refined and purified his faith (see 1 Peter 4:12 KJV). After years of faithful service, as a mature and seasoned apostle, he counseled persecuted believers, "Dear friends, do not be surprised at the painful trial you are suffering" (4:12). Peter reminded them that a world that persecuted and condemned Christ would certainly not give His faithful followers a pass. But even in the midst of the worst adversity, Peter said, we still have a "living hope," which includes "an inheritance that can never perish, spoil or fade" (1 Peter 1:3–4).

The hope that Peter wrote about is not a fingers-crossed wish that trouble will pass, but a hope in the truth that no trial on earth can rob us of all the goodness and grace that we have in Him, including eternity. Peter, along with Paul, was convinced that tribulation, distress, persecution, nakedness, and famine are unable to separate us from the love of Christ! (Romans 8:35). Our temporary trials, supported by this by hope, translate into eternal gain as, undeterred, we live to make an impact for Christ's glory.

That is why Peter could speak about *hope* and *suffering* in the same breath. He had found the only hope that lasts—the one that Paul called "Christ in you, the hope of glory" (Colossians 1:27).

Identify the "hope" that you have in the midst of trouble. Cling to it and don't let go.

GIVING

ON THE FIRST DAY OF EVERY WEEK, EACH ONE OF YOU SHOULD SET ASIDE A SUM OF MONEY IN KEEPING WITH HIS INCOME, SAVING IT UP, SO THAT WHEN I COME NO COLLECTIONS WILL HAVE TO BE MADE.

—1 Corinthians 16:2

Christ taught in His stewardship parables that all we have has been given to us by Him, and we will be held accountable for how we use it (Matthew 25:14–30). That truth is certainly a step beyond the lopsided "10 percent for God; 90 percent for me" formula. That limited view of stewardship actually makes us vulnerable to letting the 90 percent become master of our lives. True stewardship sees all I have as belonging to God. How do I invest it all for Him? By measuring every expenditure in the light of what is best for Him.

For instance, when my children were younger, we lived in a delightful neighborhood where many of our neighbors did not share our faith in Christ. Most of them knew I was a minister. I knew they watched us and that the testimony of Christ was at stake through our lives. Since no one had dandelions in their lawns, I spent money on weed killer so that the Christian on the block wasn't the one to reseed my neighbor's lawns with dandelions. My children needed to be fed and clothed in a way that glorified Christ.

Keeping indebtedness in check is important as well. How can we use our money for the eternal cause of Jesus if we are in bondage to our credit cards? Giving directly to His cause is essential. Not just 10 percent—that would be the minimum—but 12, 15, 20 percent, or more. As God's Word says, we are to give in proportion to how He has prospered us so that we make friends who will welcome us into heaven (Luke 16:9; 1 Corinthians 16:2).

God uses money to test our trustworthiness and commitment to Him. As Christ said, "Whoever can be trusted with very little can also be trusted with much, and whoever is dishonest with very little will also be dishonest with much" (Luke 16:10).

Is He the ruler over all you have?

LOOKING UP

HE WHO SITS ON THE THRONE SAID, "BEHOLD, I AM MAKING ALL THINGS NEW."

—Revelation 21:5 NASB 1977

*I*f you are a realist, you'll readily admit that life on this side of heaven often has a lot we can complain about. But authentic followers are not the complaining kind. In fact, we should be the incurable optimists. Not because we are lost in some fairyland form of religious denial but because we have so much to be realistically positive about. Pessimism is a denial of faith, and optimism is as core as the creeds of the church.

What do we have to be so blatantly upbeat about? Name them. God uses even bad days to make us better. No blindside attack from earthside forces can separate us from the love of Christ. Unwanted interruptions are scheduled by Him as appointments to accomplish things He would not be able to otherwise get done in and through us. And soon He is coming to take us home! Whether at the Rapture or through death, it's a totally optimistic thought that, as the song says, "This world is not my home; I'm just a-passin' through."

The optimistic reality of Christ's return is assured by biblical prophecy from the beginning to the end of Scripture. God promised that through the seed of woman Satan would be dealt a fatal blow (Genesis 3:15). And Scripture ends with the assurance that Christ will fulfill this prophecy and dwell among His people and make all things new (Revelation 21:5; 22:20)!

The sheer volume of detail in the prophecies about Christ is astounding. The place of His birth and its miraculous nature were prophesied, as were His rejection by Israel and betrayal by a trusted friend; His crucifixion, with its awful suffering by thirst and exposure; the piercing of His body; the mockery of onlookers; and even His unbroken bones.

He Himself prophesied that He would rise from the dead on the third day, the event that Christians the world over celebrate on Easter Sunday. If Jesus fulfilled several hundred prophecies at His first coming, how trustworthy are the prophecies of His return? As sure as His Word! Our optimism is on solid ground.

Chin up . . . the best is yet to come!

Had you forgotten how good it is?

JULY 18 / 212

GETTING ALONG

"First Be Reconciled to Your Brother, and Then Come and Present Your Offering."

—Matthew 5:24 NASB

*G*etting along with God and getting along with people are unconditionally linked. In fact, how I relate to and treat other people has a direct impact on and is a clear reflection of my relationship with God. Which is not good news for most of us. We'd much rather write off everybody who has hurt us and excuse away all the times we have hurt others and go blissfully on our way, happy in Jesus. But, unfortunately, it doesn't work that way. If we are not doing well with people, we are not doing well with God.

For instance, the proof of my love for God is that I treat my neighbor well (Matthew 22:34–40). I can't hate my brother and love God (1 John 4:20–21). To be forgiven by God, I must forgive (Mark 11:25). Before I can worship God, I must lay down my gift and make wrongs right (Matthew 5:23–24). If I mistreat my wife, my prayers are hindered (1 Peter 3:7).

God is passionately committed to the well-being of others. He died to prove the point. When we hurt and abuse what He loves, it is clear that we have not only offended them, but Him. He died to forgive even the worst of sinners. When we refuse to forgive, we violate the character of God and refuse to give others the gift that God has so graciously given to us. Don't miss the story Christ told about forgiven people who refuse to forgive (Matthew 18:21–35).

During the time da Vinci was painting *The Last Supper,* he reportedly lashed out in anger at a friend. Returning to his work, he attempted to brush some delicate lines on the face of Jesus. But, unable to continue, he left his tools to look for the man and ask his forgiveness. Only after he apologized could he go back and complete the face of Christ.

The story makes a point. Our relationship with others conditions our fellowship with God. Or is it God who conditions our fellowship with others? It's both!

Is there anyone in your life whom you refuse to love or forgive?

COMING HOME

THIS THY BROTHER WAS DEAD, AND IS ALIVE AGAIN; AND WAS LOST, AND IS FOUND.

—Luke 15:32 KJV

A familiar hymn begins, "I've wandered far away from God, now I'm coming home; the paths of sin too long I've trod; Lord, I'm coming home." Seeking intimacy with God is not just a nice thing to do. It is necessary if we are to be fulfilled at the core of our being. To live life as He meant it to be lived, to be fulfilled as He intends us to be, and to be sustained and secure as He wishes us to be means that we need to begin the rewarding adventure of closing the gap.

The story of the Prodigal Son is a classic picture of a life that is sick and tired of living on its own. Awakening to the prospect of the safety and security of his father's love, he heads for home. As he journeyed, I wonder if the familiar landmarks touched his heart and quickened his steps.

Only one issue remained for the wayward son—what would his father do? He had been so offensive, so careless, so totally rude toward him.

We too often wander. Yet wanting Him and Him alone to fill our empty hearts, we pick up what is left of ourselves and head for home. With the help of other pilgrims, we soon catch our pace, and the nearer we draw, the more familiar the landmarks become. There's the church we attended, and as we pass we see the days gone by when our hearts were filled with joy in the fellowship of His Word and His people. There's the park bench where we used to sit and feel His closeness as we contemplated the beauty and wonder of His creation. And our Bible is still sitting there. We remember how our hearts were often comforted, tuned, and trimmed by His Word.

Who is that running to meet us? Could it be God? We've been away so long, and our choice to live in the far country has been such a sadness, such an offense to Him. Yet with open arms He kisses us with His forgiving mercy, and we fall before Him, stunned by His grace, vowing to stay home and never roam again.

Turn your heart toward Him and He will turn His face toward you! (Hebrews 11:6).

PSALM 62

I wait quietly before God,
for my salvation comes from him.
He alone is my rock and my salvation,
my fortress where I will never be shaken.
So many enemies against one man—
all of them trying to kill me.
To them I'm just a broken-down wall
or a tottering fence.
They plan to topple me from my high position.
They delight in telling lies about me.
They are friendly to my face,
but they curse me in their hearts.
I wait quietly before God, for my hope is in him.
He alone is my rock and my salvation,
my fortress where I will not be shaken.
My salvation and my honor come from God alone.
He is my refuge, a rock where no enemy can reach me.
O my people, trust in him at all times.
Pour out your heart to him, for God is our refuge.
From the greatest to the lowliest—all are nothing in his sight.
If you weigh them on the scales, they are lighter than a puff of air.
Don't try to get rich by extortion or robbery.
And if your wealth increases, don't make it the center of your life.
God has spoken plainly, and I have heard it many times:
Power, O God, belongs to you; unfailing love, O Lord, is yours.
Surely you judge all people according to what they have done.

THE DIRECTION OF DESIRE

When Lust Has Conceived, . . . It Brings Forth Death.
—James 1:15 NASB

*J*ames recognized our tendency to cave in to the lures of the world and give in to our lusts. "Let no one say when he is tempted, 'I am being tempted by God'; for God . . . does not tempt anyone. But each one is tempted when he is carried away and enticed by his *own* lust" (James 1:13–14 NASB, italics added).

Lust is desire that is out of balance or out of bounds. John spoke of three levels of desire: "the lust of the flesh, and the lust of the eyes, and the pride of life" (1 John 2:16 KJV). When Scripture speaks of our *flesh*, it is speaking of our normal physical, emotional, and sensual impulses apart from God in our fallen condition. Our *eyes* are the windows that put all the seductive stuff of this world into clear view. The *pride of life* is the impulse that drives us to elevate ourselves.

We all feel the tension. The tension between living to glorify God and placating our fallen impulses. How quickly our eyes focus on all that enhances, empowers, and brings pleasure to us. And our self-focused pride reaches out to grab all that will elevate our sense of significance. The price for all of this? The betrayal of our love and loyalty to God.

Loyal followers are content with what they have and are grateful for what they gain from their love and loyalty to God. They gladly affirm that the gratification of their flesh—all that their eyes can see and all that will advance their image, fame, or fortune—is not worth trading for their allegiance to their King, who is preparing a place for them and who showers them with incomparable blessings on this side of eternity. We are liberated from the death wish of our lusts when we realize that we are in this world to serve the King—not ourselves or the things this present world offers.

Loyal lovers are satisfied with the One who is all we need.

Is there a lust that entices you? Deal with the little ones . . . they tend to grow up.

DELIVER US FROM EVIL

THAT I MAY KNOW HIM AND THE POWER OF HIS RESURRECTION.
—Philippians 3:10 NASB

Temptations . . . all of us have them. They dominate our thought life and our relationships; show up in moments of victory and in the midst of despair. They dress like money, wear fine perfume and rich cologne, go high tech on the Internet, make anger seem sweet, and offer bitterness as a five-star luxury. Temptations lure us to give in to our doubts and to live to do what seems right at the moment. They love what feels good. In short, they offer the sizzle of sin—for a season.

So to think that we experience Jesus in the realm of temptations is an unlikely thought. But temptation is, in fact, one of the places where we meet and experience Him. Given the frequency of temptations, it becomes our opportunity to meet Him on a regular basis.

When was the last time you looked for Jesus in the midst of a pressing temptation? Most of the time we try on our own power to break the spell of sin. We try to defeat sin by learning to fear the consequences, bucking up to be good, finding an accountability partner, or a dozen other good but inadequate mechanisms. But only He can deliver you. He was tempted in every way like we are. He understands our struggle and promises to give us grace and mercy to help in our time of need (Hebrew 4:14–16).

In every temptation there is a choice between pleasing yourself or pleasing Jesus. Need to lie to avoid a problem? Trust Him to care for the consequences of telling the truth. Feel like cheating to gain an extra advantage? He will meet all your needs—miraculously, if necessary. Attracted by the buzz of some sensual fulfillment? He will bring you long-term pleasure without polluting your soul. Tempted to give in to revenge? Let Him teach you to love. Want your own way? He'll lead you to consider others as more important than yourself. Learn to look for Him the moment temptation moves in on your desires. He always offers something of greater value than the lure being trolled by your heart.

When Jesus rose from the dead He defeated all of sin and hell. Take advantage of His power.

CLOSE ENCOUNTERS OF THE ANGELIC KIND

THE ANGEL OF THE LORD ENCAMPS AROUND THOSE WHO FEAR HIM, AND
RESCUES THEM. O TASTE AND SEE THAT THE LORD IS GOOD.
—Psalm 34:7–8 NASB

*I*n his best-selling book *Angels,* evangelist Billy Graham tells a moving story about John G. Paton, pioneer missionary in the New Hebrides islands. Paton and his wife went to this cannibal-populated island in the face of great opposition from friends and family in Britain. They set up camp on the beach. Their first child died in childbirth, and they slept on its grave so the islanders wouldn't dig it up and take the body. One night, hostile natives surrounded the home of Paton and his wife, intending to set it on fire and kill the missionaries. During those long, terrifying hours, the Patons prayed for God's protection. But when morning came, they were relieved and amazed to find that their would-be attackers had left. God had delivered them.

After thirty years of ministry there, Paton headed home. He had come to the sound of savage drums, but now he was leaving to the sound of church bells. In saying good-bye to the chief of the tribe, who was now a believer, Paton asked the chief why they had not burned his house down. The chief responded in surprise, "Who were all those men you had with you there?" The missionary answered, "There were no men there; just my wife and I." The chief replied that they had seen hundreds of large men wearing shining garments and carrying drawn swords surrounding their home. The natives, seeing the imposing guards, had quietly withdrawn. God had sent His angels to protect His servants.

Maybe you haven't had an experience as dramatic as that of the Patons, but listen to the words of the psalmist, "If you make the Most High your dwelling —even the LORD, who is my refuge—then no harm will befall you, no disaster will come near your tent. For he will command his angels concerning you to guard you in all your ways" (Psalm 91:9–11).

Angels aren't out of business yet.

Do you feel that God hasn't done anything for you lately? Thank God today for the invisible ways that He has intervened for you.

KNOWING WHERE TO TINKER

For It Is God Who Works in You to Will and to Act According to His Good Purpose.

—Philippians 2:13

Most of us have that gnawing sense that there is something wrong in our lives and that there are areas in our lives that need to be dealt with. The problem is that we have a hard time putting our finger on them and often don't know where to start.

Henry Ford, the great automobile magnate, was advised by some of his colleagues at the Ford Motor Company to hire a consultant to solve some of the problems created by the phenomenal growth of the car industry. Ford never liked to spend money, but he reluctantly hired a consultant by the name of Charles Steinmetz. When Steinmetz's work was done, he sent Henry Ford a bill for $10,000—a huge sum of money in Ford's day. Ford was outraged. According to correspondence on display at the Henry Ford Museum, he wrote back to Steinmetz expressing his shock and disappointment at the cost of the consultation and requesting details concerning the cost. In his correspondence, Ford said, "This is an outrageous charge for just tinkering around."

Steinmetz wrote back that he was pleased to provide a detailed accounting of the cost. The itemized invoice stated $10 for tinkering around and $9,990 for knowing where to tinker.

Our problem is not that we don't spend time tinkering around with our Christianity. We may simply have not known *where* to tinker. Or, is it possible that we *know* but are *unwilling* to tinker there? If you are looking for a growing faith—the fullness of Jesus in and through your life, here are some places to tinker. No charge for the consultation!

- What does the Spirit convict you about most pointedly?
- What do your critics point out most consistently?
- What aspects of your life do your friends and/or spouse remind you of most often?
- What produces conflict in your life and relationships most regularly?
- What ongoing issues do you always complain about? Could God be saying something to you?

Make a list . . . take the issues one by one, and start letting God work in you to do His good pleasure!

GENEROUS GIVERS

REMEMBER THIS: WHOEVER SOWS SPARINGLY WILL ALSO REAP SPARINGLY,
AND WHOEVER SOWS GENEROUSLY WILL ALSO REAP GENEROUSLY.
—2 Corinthians 9:6

*I*f this were your last day on earth, what would you do with your money? Kingdom people know that today is ours to live for the kingdom and that tomorrow belongs to the King, who will provide and care for us when and if tomorrow comes. Interestingly, Jesus' teachings about money are more often mentioned in the Gospels than any other subject. He consistently puts money into the context of generously giving rather than greedily gaining it.

The great British preacher Charles H. Spurgeon once learned about this kind of trust while trying to raise money for poor children in London. He came to Bristol hoping to collect 300 pounds for London's homeless children. At the end of the week of meetings, many lives had been changed and his financial goal had been reached. That night, as he bowed in prayer, Spurgeon was clearly prompted to give the money to George Mueller.

"Oh, no, Lord," answered Spurgeon, "I need it for my own dear orphans." Yet Spurgeon couldn't shake the idea that God wanted him to part with it. Only when he said, "Yes, Lord, I will," could he find rest.

With great peace, he made his way the next morning to Mueller's orphanage and found that great man of prayer on his knees. The famous minister placed his hand on Mueller's shoulder and said, "George, God has told me to give you these 300 pounds I've collected."

"Oh, my dear brother," said Mueller, "I've just been asking Him for exactly that amount."

The two servants of the Lord wept and rejoiced! When Spurgeon returned to London, he found a letter on his desk containing more than the 300 pounds he had given to Mueller. "There," he cried with joy, "the Lord has returned my 300 pounds with 300 shillings interest."

Spurgeon learned what another generous believer once said: "I shovel out, and God shovels in, and He has a bigger shovel than I do."

Do you love and trust God enough to give generously and sacrificially to His cause?

INTIMACY THAT SATISFIES

LOVE THE LORD YOUR GOD WITH ALL YOUR HEART AND WITH ALL YOUR SOUL
AND WITH ALL YOUR STRENGTH.

—Deuteronomy 6:5

We live in a world that normally thinks of intimacy in terms of close encounters of the physical kind. The intimacy offered by our shallow, sometimes shabby, society is cast in terms of apparel, one-night stands, colognes, video titles, evenings of candlelight and red wine, luxury cars, and voyeuristic exchanges on the Internet or in some smoke-filled nightclub.

Our hearts, minds, and desires may be lured to these counterfeit offers of intimacy, but they are not what our soul craves. Every time we dip into these buckets, we eventually come up empty. And, I might add, not only disappointed but frequently injured. Peter warns us to abstain from fleshly lusts because they "wage war against the soul" (1 Peter 2:11 NASB).

The intimacy we long for is found in a growing relationship with the One who is perfectly suited to satisfy and sustain us. True intimacy is what we enjoy as we grow more deeply conscious of, connected to, and confident in God—and Him alone—as our unfailing resource in life. Intimacy is developed as we lean on, trust in, obey, and love our God. It can't be purchased at the corner newsstand. Nor can it be pursued in the market, on vacations, or through the hottest of social calendars. When it comes to the joy of intimacy, these are the small talk of life compared to the deep satisfaction that comes from profound, soulish interaction with the God who alone can fill our souls.

Our lives need to be aimed in the direction of a deepening love relationship with our Lord in every fiber of our being. We were built for intimacy with God. We were redeemed to enable our souls to reclaim the privilege. Remove the layers of life, lust, and distractedness that keep you from hearing the cry of your soul, "As the deer pants for the water brooks, so my soul pants for Thee, O God" (Psalm 42:1 NASB 1977).

Has your heart been longing and loving somewhere else?

Do you love God with all that you are and have? If not, what baggage must you get rid of to renew that relationship?

PSALM 66

Shout joyful praises to God, all the earth!

Sing about the glory of his name! Tell the world how glorious he is.

Say to God, "How awesome are your deeds!

Your enemies cringe before your mighty power.

Everything on earth will worship you; they will sing your praises,

shouting your name in glorious songs."

Come and see what our God has done, what awesome miracles he does for his people!

He made a dry path through the Red Sea, and his people went across on foot.

Come, let us rejoice in who he is.

For by his great power he rules forever. He watches every movement of the nations;

let no rebel rise in defiance.

Let the whole world bless our God and sing aloud his praises.

Our lives are in his hands, and he keeps our feet from stumbling.

You have tested us, O God; you have purified us like silver melted in a crucible.

You captured us in your net and laid the burden of slavery on our backs.

You sent troops to ride across our broken bodies.

We went through fire and flood. But you brought us to a place of great abundance.

Now I come to your Temple with burnt offerings to fulfill the vows I made to you—

yes, the sacred vows you heard me make when I was in deep trouble.

That is why I am sacrificing burnt offerings to you—

the best of my rams as a pleasing aroma.

And I will sacrifice bulls and goats.

Come and listen, all you who fear God, and I will tell you what he did for me.

For I cried out to him for help, praising him as I spoke.

If I had not confessed the sin in my heart, my Lord would not have listened.

But God did listen! He paid attention to my prayer.

Praise God, who did not ignore my prayer

and did not withdraw his unfailing love from me.

ANGER IN PERSPECTIVE

MAKE EVERY EFFORT TO LIVE IN PEACE WITH ALL MEN AND TO BE HOLY.
—Hebrews 12:14

*A*nger is a "signal emotion." It alerts us that something has gone "tilt" in life. Anger alerts us that justice or righteousness has been violated. That our rights and privileges have been trespassed. Anger always catches our attention. But once it catches our attention, the issue is, What should we do with it? If our anger is not responded to properly, it will quickly lead us into sin.

In Ephesians 4:26, Paul makes a clear distinction between anger and sin. Anger in and of itself is not sin. Sin is what happens when anger is permitted to manage our response to an offense. It's like temptation and sin. It is not a sin to be tempted; sin is what happens when temptation goes unchecked (James 1:14–15). If we *remain* angry and do not do what is right, sin is like a crouching beast waiting to devour us (Genesis 4:7), and Satan gets the advantage in our lives (Ephesians 4:26–27). Anger that remains becomes spoiled and turns into the self-destructive sins of bitterness and hatred. Anger is like mayonnaise—a sandwich without it loses its edge, but if it isn't eaten immediately, it spoils and produces major problems.

In fact, many sins are born from residual anger. Sins such as lying, gossip, slander, murmuring, threatening, cursing, taking God's name in vain, and contentious words are all products of anger gone sour. Murder, envy, immorality, division, strife, and revenge are common sins of an angry heart. The writer of the book of Hebrews encourages us to "make every effort to live in peace with all men and to be holy; without holiness no one will see the Lord. See to it that no one misses the grace of God and that no bitter root grows up to cause trouble and defile many" (Hebrews 12:14–15).

Romans 12:17–21 gives us the plan. Give the source of your anger to God, who handles wrath and justice perfectly. Then love your enemies in return. Sound radical? It is. Wonderfully radical!

How do you normally respond to your anger? Read Romans 12:17–22 prayerfully.

JULY 29 / 223

BACK TO THE FUTURE

"BUT SEEK FIRST HIS KINGDOM AND HIS RIGHTEOUSNESS, AND ALL THESE THINGS WILL BE GIVEN TO YOU AS WELL."
—Matthew 6:33

Periodically, it's important to stop long enough to measure where we are in life and to access the true significance of what we are devoting our time and attention to. I find myself wanting to reduce the regrets of life and to envision myself standing before our Lord with as much in my hands for Him as possible. While we often think of regrets in terms of sinful things, it is important to remember that many regrets will be directly attributable simply to things that, while good, were not of lasting value.

At the end of life, we'll want to be sure that the inevitable regrets of greed don't haunt our memories. Greed offers us nothing more than the empty shell of things that do not last and cannot satisfy. We need to keep self-centeredness in check because preoccupation with our own advancement and importance will evaporate in the all-consuming celebration of His preeminent presence on the other side.

If we are not careful, life can be poured into the bottomless bucket of all this world offers. And, after all is said and done, the bucket is still empty. Imagine stepping onto the shore on the other side and realizing that we have brought nothing with us of eternal worth. Think of looking into the face of our eternal God and realizing that our lives reflect only the wood, hay, and straw of earthside stuff and little of and for the kingdom (1 Corinthians 3:10–15).

Living with eternity as the driving force of our decisions and desires is the key. While it is easy to think, "Life now and heaven later," authentic followers see all of life in the long view and do all that they do *here* in the light of *there*.

Make the switch, and refuse to sacrifice the permanent on the altar of the temporary. And in case you think that you just might become so heavenly minded that you will be no earthly good . . . think again. You'll be surprised at how much "earthly good" you'll do when heaven is on your mind!

Can you think of something that you have done lately that will count in eternity? What can you do for eternity today?

AS WE FORGIVE OTHERS

As Far as the East Is from the West, so Far Has He Removed Our Transgressions from Us.

—Psalm 103:12

*H*ave you ever noticed how we are more prone to talk about other people's problems than we are to confront them? Which means that often the last person to know about the problem is the very one who has the problem. Love demands a better way.

Because God loved us, He took the initiative to come to us in our sin (Genesis 3:8–24; John 3:16–17). If we love, an important part of that love is the willingness to approach those who have sinned with the intent of restoring them. Since timing is important, we must bathe the encounter in prayer, asking God to provide the right opportunity and receptivity.

Galatians 6:1 gives us key instructions about our approach to the person who has sinned. First, we must be in tune with and in fellowship with God—gentle and without bitterness, revenge, or hostility in our hearts. We must be willing to see the problem from the other person's point of view and be cautious—taking care, lest, in the process, we too fall into sins like anger, bitterness, or sins of the tongue. As we humbly show the person his faults, it is important that we convey love for his best interests and avoid a judgmental, "holier than thou" attitude.

Matthew 18:15 gives instructions for the procedure to be followed. "Go and show him his fault, just between the two of you" (Matthew 18:15). There is great freedom in the interchange if we can assure the one we are talking to that we have discussed this with no one else!

If the person responds, he is restored to God's fellowship and to ours, and forgiveness removes the sin "as far as the east is from the west" (Psalm 103:12). If the person does not respond, Scripture encourages us to take another person back with us for another meeting, and then go to the church if that meeting is unsuccessful (Matthew 18:16–17).

What a joy it would be to live among fellow travelers who love each other enough to deal with sins instead of tolerating sin by simply talking about it behind each other's back.

Is there someone you need to approach concerning sin? Do it prayerfully, claiming God's grace to forgive one another.

MIRACLE GROW

FOR THE WORD OF GOD IS LIVING AND ACTIVE.
—Hebrews 4:12

*S*omeone has well said that God did not give us the Bible just to make us smart but to change our lives. So true! In fact, you have probably been around some fellow followers who have been in "Bible-world" for a long time but whose lives are unloving, crotchety, and rarely like Christ. Just in case you are headed in that direction, let's look at His Word in a different light.

As Paul told Timothy, the Word is intended to train us in righteousness (2 Timothy 3:16). In the same way a parent rears a child in what is right, so the Word rears us that we might grow up living according to His righteous standards. Righteousness in Scripture means conforming to "the correct standard." These benchmarks of conduct are not just measurements of our growth but also of our Christlikeness (Romans 8:28–30). If you want to know if you are a person of the Word, check to see if your life is more righteous, more like Christ's today than it was six months ago.

What can we expect when we submit to the Word? The Bible describes itself as a two-edged sword that goes past the externals, penetrates us to the very thoughts, intents, and motives of our heart (Hebrews 4:12). Christ said that the Word is like a seed that, when it falls on the receptive soil of "a noble and good heart," bears the fruits of righteousness (Luke 8:11–15). Or as James says, reading the Word is like looking into a mirror. It shows us what we are really like (James 1:22–25).

The life-changing power of the sword, the seed, and the mirror is only triggered when we submit to their influence in every area of our lives. Will you let the scalpel of His Word take you deep into your inner self? Does its seed take root in the soil of your heart? And when you have seen yourself as you really are . . . what then?

When you read God's Word, envision its work as a sword, seed, and mirror. Ask yourself, "Which of these influences is it exerting on my heart and life?"

FROM SIGNIFICANCE TO SERVANTHOOD

"JUST AS THE SON OF MAN DID NOT COME TO BE SERVED, BUT TO SERVE."
—Matthew 20:28

*L*iving to establish our own significance disables us from fulfilling our primary calling as followers of Jesus. It is clear from Jesus' teachings that we are called to serve Him and others rather than ourselves (Matthew 20:20–28). Yet living as a servant is obviously less than a "significant" calling. Which is just the point! If we live for our own significance, our ambitions will fight against His agenda at every turn. In fact, as Paul made clear in Philippians 2, we have to give up our right to significance before we can obey our Father, who often calls us to do things that seem to work against our own sense of self-esteem.

Followers forgive and humbly bear the reproach of a fallen world. They serve unnoticed and live to please someone besides themselves. They give of their possessions to the poor and surrender their wills to the will of their God. They submit to the needs and interests of others and refuse inner impulses that others consume with pleasure.

The choice is clear. Our lives will be about significance or servanthood. Jesus chose the latter. In becoming a servant Jesus accomplished significant things for God and others. And that's the twist. When I live for my own significance, it often ends in emptiness and loss . . . ultimately. But servanthood is satisfyingly productive.

Think about it. We wouldn't be redeemed from the ravages of sin with hell canceled and heaven guaranteed if it weren't for the fact that He served us all the way to the cross . . . nakedly bearing our shame as a despised criminal. If personal significance was His intention, redemption would have gone by the wayside.

Servants love their spouses regardless, sacrifice for their children, and consider personal integrity of higher value than their careers. They trust God to deal with their enemies, and they forgivingly serve their enemies in return. Servants give up their significance to do significant things, believing that in due time *He* will exalt them (1 Peter 5:6). Servanthood is our responsibility; significance is His.

Have you chosen your identity yet? How would others know?

LOVING HIM

"Abide in My Love . . . that My Joy May Be in You."
—John 15:10–11 NASB

*E*ver been in love? If so, you know what it means to be preoccupied. I met Martie in the fall of our freshman year at college. It didn't take long for me to know that my heart had become hopelessly lost to her. When summer came, she went home to Cleveland, and I went on the road for two and a half months with a team of musicians representing our college.

We had a great summer. Exciting experiences, interesting places to travel, and chances to meet all kinds of people filled our days. But no matter how new and exciting the trip, my mind kept returning to Martie. I hoped there would be a letter from her at the next church, that she would be home when I called. I wondered where she was, what she was doing, and what we'd be doing if we were together. And I was looking forward to the day we'd be together again.

It's like that for those of us who are developing an ever-deepening relationship with Jesus. Though busy in our daily routines, we find that He increasingly becomes the backdrop to all of life. We love to hear from Him in His Word, where we find out more about Him and more about what He wants us to know. We thrill to new discoveries about Him and His ways, and we listen carefully to His direction for our lives. We increasingly enjoy times of prayer, as we speak with Him and sense His communion with us. And we find ourselves longing for the day we will see Him.

Loving Jesus is not an escape from life, nor is it a brief encounter on some monastic retreat. It's the joy of staying in touch and the pleasure of knowing that, regardless of what a day may bring, the best day is still to come.

It's great to be alive . . . it's even better to be alive and in love with Him!

What preoccupies your heart? When was the last time Jesus had the privilege?

PSALM 67

May God be merciful and bless us.
May his face shine with favor upon us.
May your ways be known throughout the earth,
your saving power among people everywhere.
May the nations praise you, O God.
Yes, may all the nations praise you.
How glad the nations will be, singing for joy,
because you govern them with justice
and direct the actions of the whole world.
May the nations praise you, O God.
Yes, may all the nations praise you.
Then the earth will yield its harvests,
and God, our God, will richly bless us.
Yes, God will bless us,
and people all over the world will fear him.

ALL TALK IS HEART TALK

... The Mouth Speaks Out of That Which Fills the Heart.
—Matthew 12:34

We all remember the neighborhood tattletale. Not the most popular kid on the block—he took great delight in exposing deeds we were trying to hide. Unfortunately, our tongues play that much-despised role in our own lives. Jesus said that we speak "out of the heart" (Matthew 15:19). Which means that our speech often tells on the attitudes we would rather not have others know about.

Romans 3:13 is vivid. Paul writes that sinner's throats "are open graves," venting the smell of death. My friends in medicine tell me that certain sicknesses produce terrible breath odors. So it is with sinful hearts.

One of my early memories is of spouting off to my kindergarten teacher. I can't remember what stimulated the crisis, but I told my teacher to "shut up," then promptly left the room and started to walk home. As I walked down the block, I noticed that my mother was working in the backyard. I stopped dead in my tracks. What would I tell her?

My options sped before me—face my mother, face the teacher, or walk alone into the big, cruel world. I chose the least of the three evils and went back to school. My teacher met me at the door, took me by the arm, and marched me to the rest room, where she washed my mouth out with soap.

It was a never-to-be-forgotten lesson. But to be honest, I needed more than a mouthwash. I needed a heart wash. My little five-year-old spirit had shown up in my mouth. And if we aren't careful, the attitudes we have as adults will show up there as well! Anger, pride, fear, sensuality, and a host of other sins we harbor will eventually show up in the words we say.

In essence, all talk is heart talk. Groom your heart to growth in Christ and your words will show it. Neglect your heart, and your tongue will tell on you every time.

If you sense that your mouth needs washing, start with your heart.

THE REAL YOU

AFTER HIS SUFFERING, HE . . . GAVE MANY CONVINCING PROOFS THAT HE
WAS ALIVE.

—Acts 1:3

*M*ost of us think of our existence in eternity as some type of a blessed fantasy totally disconnected to reality. The trouble with that kind of thinking is that it makes heaven seem so unreal. Yet Scripture intends us to live looking forward to the reality of heaven. So Jesus did an extraordinary thing to help us understand that eternity is far more connected to our earthly experience than we thought.

Did it ever strike you as interesting that after Christ's resurrection He stayed on our planet for forty additional days in His resurrected body? In doing so, He gave us clues as to our existence in heaven as real people. If you wonder what your body will be like in heaven, look at Christ in Acts 1:3–4 and at the record of Christ's appearances at the close of the Gospels. Think specifically of all that the resurrected Christ was able to do with His built-for-heaven body.

It was recognizable and touchable. Mary recognized His voice in the garden. He invited a skeptical Thomas to touch His wounds that he might verify for himself the reality of the risen Lord. What is fascinating to me is that His resurrected body was transmaterial. He was able to appear in a room whose doors and windows were locked tight. (The only other person I've ever known to be transmaterial was my mother. She could appear from nowhere in an instant.)

Scripture records that He ate with His disciples in His postresurrection form. Think what eating on the other side might be like—calorie-free chocolate and fat-free sirloin steaks! And, while we probably won't need to eat there, it is a demonstration of how real His risen body was.

The point is that when we get there we will be real . . . really us in a very real place. But, I might add, far better, fully transformed into His likeness (1 John 3:2). Think of it, us without those dreadful imperfections!

Forget any thought that we will be unstructured ghosts or cosmic dust floating through an ethereal forever.

Eternity is real—look forward to it!

Envision a real, fully fixed "you" in heaven. How does this alter your view and anticipation of heaven?

AS THE DEER . . .

As the Deer Pants for the Waterbrooks . . .
—Psalm 42:1, 2

*M*artie and I went on a camel safari in the desert of the United Arab Emirates. We rocked on top of those ugly beasts for an hour as we perused the quiet of the desert. In the course of describing the attributes of camels, our guide mentioned that camels can go for three months without water. They are obviously built for the desert.

What a contrast these plodding animals are to the sleek, type "A" gazelle the psalmist had in mind when he said that his soul's desire for God was like the thirst the deer feels as it "pants for the water brooks" (Psalm 42:1 NKJV). Bounding through the meadows and the forests, the deer is satisfied and sustained on a regular basis with water. He needs it and yearns for it in his fast-paced existence.

After our intriguing desert experience, it crossed my mind how easy it is in the midst of our affluence to be far more like the camel than the deer. Rarely sensing our need for God, we go for months without desiring Him. For some of us, life has been a long stretch of religious and secular activity without any sense of dependence on or desire for God. The problem is that we weren't built for life in a spiritual desert. We were built—in fact, redeemed— for regular, satisfying access to the refreshing presence of God in our souls.

So what is it that keeps us from longing for and seeking Him?

For all the things that make us more like the camel, none is so glaring as the sin of self-sufficiency. And why are we self-sufficient? Because we think we have all that we need apart from Him. Jesus is little more than a highly valued fire escape and Someone to whom we love to belong. But cultivating Him as our soul mate and supreme necessity of life has somehow escaped us.

But it hasn't escaped Him. The One who calls us His friend still waits, knocking at your heart's door for the sweet fellowship that only relying on Jesus can deliver (John 15:15; Revelation 3:20).

Are you thirsty for God? Fresh water waits . . .

WHO WANTS TO CHANGE?

"Sanctify Them by the Truth; Your Word Is Truth."
—John 17:17

*H*ow many church members does it take to change a light bulb? *"Change . . .* who said anything about change!" Well, church members may resist change, but followers of Christ welcome it as the adventuresome part of the journey.

The adventure starts when we pray. In prayer, God usually changes more about us than about what we are praying for. Have you ever noticed that once you start a conversation with God, He often does a lot of the talking? So if we are going to become more like Him, we need to pray with increasing regularity and intensity.

Preaching is an agent of change, depending on our response to it. If we sit under teachers saying, "Here am I, Lord. Change me," He most likely will.

The indwelling Holy Spirit is yet another force for change. His is a wonderful, penetrating, often troubling voice. Yielding to Him positions us for change.

But it is the Word of God that buttresses all this power to change. Without the Bible, we would not know what prayer is, how to pray, or even that we should pray. Apart from the Scriptures, preaching—no matter how forceful or eloquent—has no life-changing authority. And the Word He has authored makes the ministry of the Holy Spirit effectual in changing our lives.

In John 17 Christ asked the Father to change us. When He prayed that we be sanctified, He prayed for our lives to be set apart that we might be unique and useful. Sanctified by what? "Sanctify them by the truth," our Lord prayed. "Your word is truth" (v. 17). Sanctification is the process of changing us from our own carelessly crafted lives to the likeness of Christ.

I'll never forget the seventy-six-year-old man who said to me, "Young man, if you come here to be our pastor, I am praying that the Lord will use your ministry to help me grow."

That old and that anxious to change!

As you pray, listen to preaching, hear the voice of the Spirit, and read the Word, what do you hear about change in your life?

LIVING IN THE LIGHT

WALK IN THE LIGHT, AS HE IS IN THE LIGHT.

—1 John 1:7

*J*ohn's first epistle was written to first-century Christians who were under the influence of the heretical doctrines of Gnosticism. The Gnostics believed that matter was evil and spirit alone was good. John's letter was an attempt to clarify the mistakes of the Gnostics and to encourage believers to stay in the light with Jesus.

The Gnostics believed (1) that knowledge was superior to virtue; (2) that only a privileged few were able to understand truth; (3) that evil in the world suggested that God was not the only creator; (4) that the Incarnation was not plausible, since that which is spiritual cannot unite with sinful flesh; and, finally, (5) that there is no such thing as the resurrection of the flesh.

Surprisingly, two thousand years later, Gnosticism is making a comeback. And, more troubling still, its tenets are tragically detouring many followers. Today, New Age theology claims that it is what you know, not how you live, that gives credibility. Truth is evasive and found only in the words of a few cross-legged Eastern mystics. Evil is good, and God is not really connected. Jesus is only a good person. If there is an afterlife, reincarnation is the accepted option.

Don't be deceived. Jesus lights our way with the preeminence of virtue and the confidence that in Him we find "true" truth. And while God is not the author of evil, He is not disconnected. He will ultimately judge all that is wrong and will make wrongs right for those who follow Him. And it is Jesus who physically conquered sin, death, and hell. He opens heaven's door to all who believe.

Do you want to believe that there is no cure for sin? That Jesus is not God, and that you can't really find solid truth? Do you want to believe that this is the only world we have, and that at best we will be little more than a recycling project?

I'd rather have Jesus! He forgives us and wonderfully assures us that He is the Way, the Truth, and the Life . . . that nobody gains access to the Father except through Him (John 14:6).

Stay in the light with Jesus and keep the darkness at bay!

LONG SHADOWS

"STILL OTHER SEED FELL ON GOOD SOIL, WHERE IT PRODUCED A CROP—A HUNDRED, SIXTY OR THIRTY TIMES WHAT WAS SOWN."
—Matthew 13:8

*O*n our twenty-fifth wedding anniversary, Martie and I stayed in a tiny, rustic bed-and-breakfast in the north Yorkshire Dales of England. We were there with four other couples—all British—whom we had never met before.

About halfway through the evening, one of them asked me, "What do you do?" Quite frankly, I didn't know how I would answer that question. It seemed to me that no one would know much about Moody Bible Institute, let alone what I do there. So I began by saying, "I'm with a group of ministries in Chicago known as the Moody Bible Institute." As I was getting ready to explain, I noticed the couples on the couch responding with interest, and one of them said, "Of Moody . . . Sankey? That Moody?" I was shocked. How could they have known about Moody and Sankey? I said in amazement, "Why, yes!" They replied, "We have Sankey hymnals that have been passed down through our families for generations." The older couple sitting to our right said, "So do we! Periodically on Sunday nights we gather around the piano and sing from the Sankey hymnal."

Moody and Sankey, his musician, were in the British Isles more than 120 years ago and ministered there for three years. The impact of their ministry lingers still. I walked out of that room that night saying to God that I wanted my life to be lived so faithfully that I too would cast long shadows for Him, far beyond my life. No one would have to remember my name or even what I have done. But I asked the Lord to help my life have long-term impact.

Long shadows come not by planning large, self-manufactured stages upon which to strut the stuff of life and ministry but rather through unflinching faithfulness and faith-focused perseverance to the tasks He has assigned, trusting Him to preserve and multiply the outcomes.

What are you doing today that will count for the long term? Parenting, witnessing, giving, serving, praying . . . ? Be faithful and cast "long shadows" for Him.

PSALMS 69:1–3, 16–18, 29–33; 70

Save me, O God, for the floodwaters are up to my neck.

Deeper and deeper I sink into the mire; I can't find a foothold to stand on.

I am in deep water, and the floods overwhelm me.

I am exhausted from crying for help; my throat is parched and dry.

My eyes are swollen with weeping, waiting for my God to help me. . . .

Answer my prayers, O LORD, for your unfailing love is wonderful.

Turn and take care of me, for your mercy is so plentiful.

Don't hide from your servant; answer me quickly, for I am in deep trouble!

Come and rescue me; free me from all my enemies. . . .

I am suffering and in pain. Rescue me, O God, by your saving power.

Then I will praise God's name with singing,

and I will honor him with thanksgiving.

For this will please the LORD more than sacrificing an ox

or presenting a bull with its horns and hooves.

The humble will see their God at work and be glad.

Let all who seek God's help live in joy.

For the LORD hears the cries of his needy ones;

he does not despise his people who are oppressed.

Please, God, rescue me! Come quickly, LORD, and help me.

May those who try to destroy me be humiliated and put to shame.

May those who take delight in my trouble be turned back in disgrace.

Let them be horrified by their shame, for they said, "Aha! We've got him now!"

But may all who search for you be filled with joy and gladness.

May those who love your salvation repeatedly shout, "God is great!"

But I am poor and needy; please hurry to my aid, O God.

You are my helper and my savior; O LORD, do not delay!

FINISHING WELL

"I Will Give You a Wise and Discerning Heart, so that There Will Never Have Been Anyone Like You, nor Will There Ever Be."
—1 Kings 3:12

When Solomon took his father's throne, he asked God for one thing—wisdom. He needed wisdom to rule the nation of Israel. Wisdom to distinguish right from wrong and guide his people in the ways of the Lord. God was pleased with Solomon's request.

"So God said to him, 'Since you have asked for this and not for long life or wealth for yourself, nor have asked for the death of your enemies but for discernment in administering justice, I will do what you have asked. I will give you a wise and discerning heart, so that there will never have been anyone like you, nor will there ever be'" (1 Kings 3:11–12).

Solomon did not ask for temporal things like money, influence, or respect. Instead, he asked for God's guidance, knowing that he could not be an effective king without God at his side. God granted Solomon's request and added to it what he had not asked for: riches and honor. And, if he walked according to the ways of God, he would be given a long life.

First Kings records the early days of his reign. Solomon was devoted to God, eager to follow in the footsteps of his father, and ambitious in his plans to build a magnificent temple to honor God.

But further into his reign, Solomon's life slowly began to shift. His love for, and marriage to, women from foreign countries eventually led to his falling from the ways of God. He became distracted and disoriented, his priorities askew. He gave in to idolatry and led his nation away from God.

Solomon's life is an example and a reminder to each of us that starting well is only the beginning. Keeping our priorities straight, aiming for goals that will ultimately satisfy our Lord, and seeking first God and His kingdom are all high-maintenance objectives for those of us who wish to finish well.

Drift is inevitable unless we monitor our hearts daily staying close to Jesus and obedient to His voice.

Mark the drift in your life.

IN OTHER WORLDS

IF ONLY FOR THIS LIFE WE HAVE HOPE IN CHRIST, WE ARE TO BE PITIED.
—1 Corinthians 15:19

*P*eggy Noonan, former speechwriter for President Reagan and for the first President Bush, insightfully observed in the September 14, 1992, issue of *Forbes* magazine:

> I think we have lost the old knowledge that happiness is overrated—that, in a way, life is overrated. We have lost, somehow, a sense of mystery—about us, our purpose, our meaning, our role. Our ancestors believed in two worlds, and understood this to be the solitary, poor, nasty, brutish and short one. We are the first generation of man that actually expected to find happiness here on earth, and our search for it has caused such unhappiness. The reason: If you do not believe in another, higher world, if you believe only in the flat material world around you, if you believe that this is your only chance at happiness—if that is what you believe, then you are not disappointed when the world does not give you a good measure of its riches, you are despairing.

When the apostle Paul wrote that we are to be pitied if we only have hope in Christ in this world, he was on to a very important truth. If this is the only world for us, then the misery of a passive pessimism is indeed our lot. Optimism dies and hope is deflated. If you ever feel like that has happened to you, then Paul has given a hint as to what may be wrong.

I have a camera that has a special setting for distance. The interesting thing is that when I set it there and take a picture of a mountain range, the closer landscape comes into focus as well. As C. S. Lewis said, "Aim at heaven and you get earth thrown in. Aim at earth and you get neither." Scripture constantly presses us to set our minds on things above. Heaven's world is to be the focus of our heart's attention and the realm from which we craft every decision and desire in this present, hollow, fallen, temporal world. Make sure your heart never feels at home here.

Do you expect what heaven promises in this "solitary, poor, nasty, brutish, and short" world? What is different about your life because you belong to the world to come?

TRUE SURVIVORS

WE ARE AFFLICTED IN EVERY WAY, BUT NOT CRUSHED; . . . STRUCK DOWN, BUT NOT DESTROYED.

—2 Corinthians 4:8–9 NASB

Television programmers made a killing when they created the smash-hit program *Survivor*. Staged in real-life settings, the program featured a select group competing to be the last one to survive in nearly impossible conditions. The prize? A moment of glory and a million dollars to spend.

But it's not a new idea. The Bible is full of "survivors." Take people like David, Esther, Job, and Paul. One look at this list tells you two very important things. First, God's idea of surviving and thriving has nothing to do with wanna-be millionaires, personality salesmen, and others who populate the cable TV channels. Second, you don't have to win every battle to win the war. These people weren't perfect, but they were triumphant.

Who wouldn't love to have the steadfastness of a Job or the spiritual legacy of a Paul? But when we see the "school of adversity" that God enrolls all of His saints in, we may want to say, "Thanks anyway, Lord. Do You have any electives?"

He doesn't, of course. Not if we want spiritual growth and maturity and power in prayer and service. Our four biblical heros remind us that adversity teaches lessons we can't learn any other way, that life's trials are not sent to overwhelm us, that God's grace is sufficient, that in Him we can be "more than conquerors" (Romans 8:37), and that we can have joy along the way (2 Corinthians 8:2).

You may wonder why we call our heroes "survivors," since we usually think of a survivor as someone who barely makes it. Think of the term in its best sense: someone who not only makes it but comes through the fire spiritually and emotionally stronger, ready for the next challenge. In this sense, I want to be a "survivor." And the prize is paid in the multiplying currency of personal growth and effectiveness. And the benefits that are "out of this world."

All you need is the confidence that He will provide all the grace you need to survive, will give you a purpose in your troubles, and will never waste your sorrows.

Pray for the staying power to make it through victoriously.

BE HAPPY

HIS DELIGHT IS IN THE LAW OF THE LORD, AND ON HIS LAW HE MEDITATES
DAY AND NIGHT.

—Psalm 1:2

*I*f you were given a choice between beauty, popularity, great wealth, or happiness, my guess is that happiness would win hands down. Especially if we understand happiness in its biblical sense as the deep inner sense that everything in life is in order and satisfying. But how can such peace be found? The psalmist tells us in Psalm 1:2, to our surprise, that happiness is experienced as we commit ourselves to live by God's rules. Unfortunately, a lot of us never quite get that straight. For many, God's rules are like divine handcuffs. We often see God's Word as a heavenly straitjacket, as though every time something seems fun or enjoyable, God says, "You can't do that." And when something seems difficult, God says, "That's what I want you to do."

Any thought that God gives us restrictions to oppress us and keep us sober and serious all the time is Satan's oldest lie. The earliest attack of Satan on the true, God-designed happiness of Adam and Eve shopped that lie in a tragically successful way (Genesis 3:1–6).

The key is to remember that the law of the Lord originates in God Himself. He cannot contradict Himself (2 Timothy 2:13). He could not possibly give us a set of laws that would be damaging, wicked, unkind, unloving, imperfect, or unrighteous. Remember that as the Israelites began the military campaigns that would lead to conquering Canaan, God in essence told them not to forsake His law because He had given it to them that they might prosper (Joshua 1:8).

Paul rightly declares that the law of God is "holy, righteous and good" (Romans 7:12). I am still waiting to meet the first person to tell me that his life has been totally devastated because they followed the laws of God for their life. But I've dealt with a lot of mixed-up, unhappy lives that are a direct result of having scorned God's directives.

When it's hard to obey, remember that His commands are an expression of His love and that Psalm 1:2 celebrates them as the key to a blessed, happy life.

Read Psalm 119:97–105.

PATIENCE UNDER PRESSURE

BEING STRENGTHENED WITH ALL POWER . . . SO THAT YOU MAY HAVE GREAT
ENDURANCE AND PATIENCE.

—Colossians 1:11

The biblical word *patience,* or *perseverance,* is often the translation of a Greek word that literally means to "remain under" (Colossians 1:11; Romans 5:3–4; Hebrews 12:1). It reminds me of the times my family has eaten ripe, juicy watermelons. Invariably, one of us presses our thumb on a seed. You guessed it—out it shoots! We are often like that. When pressure comes, we want a quick escape. Yet patience provides the staying power to remain under the pressure of the situation so that we can permit God to accomplish His work in us.

Patience works to keep us within the parameters of His plans. Because of Abraham and Sarah's impatience, Satan's kingdom had an opportunity to sabotage the promised line of the Messiah. If Ishmael had been Abraham's only son, the genealogical line of Jesus would have come to an end. It took God's intervention to override the threat of the impatient pair by rejecting Abraham's counterfeit seed (Genesis 17:17– 22) and miraculously providing His seed, Isaac, through Sarah (21:1–7).

Our impatience makes us vulnerable to be used and manipulated by Satan to accomplish his fallen purposes. Think of the anger, hurtful words, anxiety, and loss of testimony that impatience consistently breeds in our lives.

But we need not fail. God offers us the option of perseverance. Of "staying under" the pressure with a good spirit. Successful perseverance reflects God's strength and glory. As Paul wrote, "We pray this in order that you may live a life worthy of the Lord and may please him in every way: bearing fruit in every good work, growing in the knowledge of God, being strengthened with all power according to his glorious might so that you may have great endurance and patience, and joyfully giving thanks to the Father, who has qualified you to share in the inheritance of the saints in the kingdom of light" (Colossians 1:10–12).

What do you know about God that encourages you to persevere?

IMAGE BEARERS

Then God Said, "Let Us Make Man in Our Image."
—Genesis 1:26

*I*f you have wondered about "purpose" in your life, wonder no more. In 1 Corinthians 6:20 we read that we are "bought at a price" and therefore should "honor God" with our bodies. As the catechism says, it is the chief end of man to "glorify God and enjoy Him forever." But what does that mean?

God makes clear that His primary purpose in creating us was to demonstrate His qualities and His glory *through* us. As Genesis notes, "Then God said, 'Let Us make man in Our image, according to Our likeness'" (Genesis 1:26 NASB). So by divine design we are image bearers.

It is obvious that "in His image" cannot mean that we physically look like Him. God has no physical properties. Nobody looks like God, because "God is spirit" (John 4:24).

To be created in His image means that we were created with the potential to reflect His qualities through our lives. For instance, God has personality, will, and emotions. He created us with personality, will, and emotions so that we could connect with His and let His personality, will, and emotions flow through ours. His personality encompasses His character and attributes. His will reflects His plans; and His ways and His emotions reflect how He feels toward sin, sinners, His children, and His creation. When His character and attributes are reflected in our lives, when His will is manifest in how we live, and when we love what He loves and hate what He hates, we are in the process of fulfilling His intended purpose.

Psalm 19:1 tells us that "the heavens declare the glory of God." Romans 1:20 says that "God's invisible qualities—his eternal power and divine nature—have been clearly seen" in creation. But the fact that God is loving, righteous, merciful, and just can only be seen through us. As those around us watch the personality, emotions, and will of God flow from our lives, we give visibility and credibility to God.

That is what it means to "glorify God." Image bearing is our privileged purpose in life.

In what ways could you "glorify God" in your life today? Make a plan . . . be intentional!

PSALM 73:1–2a, 3–9, 12–17, 20b–28

Truly God is good to Israel, to those whose hearts are pure.

But as for me, I came so close to the edge of the cliff! . . .

For I envied the proud when I saw them prosper despite their wickedness.

They seem to live such a painless life; their bodies are so healthy and strong.

They aren't troubled like other people or plagued with problems like everyone else.

They wear pride like a jeweled necklace, and their clothing is woven of cruelty.

These fat cats have everything their hearts could ever wish for!

They scoff and speak only evil; in their pride they seek to crush others.

They boast against the very heavens, and their words strut throughout the earth. . . .

Look at these arrogant people enjoying a life of ease while their riches multiply.

Was it for nothing that I kept my heart pure and kept myself from doing wrong?

All I get is trouble all day long; every morning brings me pain.

If I had really spoken this way, I would have been a traitor to your people.

So I tried to understand why the wicked prosper. But what a difficult task it is!

Then one day I went into your sanctuary, O God,

and I thought about the destiny of the wicked. . . .

When you arise, O Lord, you will make them vanish from this life.

Then I realized how bitter I had become, how pained I had been by all I had seen.

I was so foolish and ignorant—I must have seemed like a senseless animal to you.

Yet I still belong to you; you are holding my right hand.

You will keep on guiding me with your counsel, leading me to a glorious destiny.

Whom have I in heaven but you? I desire you more than anything on earth.

My health may fail, and my spirit may grow weak,

but God remains the strength of my heart; he is mine forever.

But those who desert him will perish, for you destroy those who abandon you.

But as for me, how good it is to be near God!

I have made the Sovereign LORD my shelter,

and I will tell everyone about the wonderful things you do.

TONGUE IN CHECK

I Said, "I Will Watch My Ways and Keep My Tongue from Sin; I Will Put a Muzzle on My Mouth . . ."

—Psalm 39:1

When someone is about to tell you a juicy tidbit of gossip, you have the option of saying, "Tell me about the details," or of encouraging them not to violate God's principles. A short statement like "Don't tell me; I already have more negative thoughts than I know what to do with" should stop the bad news before it gets started.

Many times at social gatherings someone will get just far enough into a story to have everyone's attention and then say, "You know, I really shouldn't say this," to which we all respond, "Oh, come on—you can't stop now! We won't tell." It would be refreshing to hear someone say, "Good for you. Don't tell. I admire your self-control." If you "happen" to hear gossip, only repeat it to the Lord. Pray about . . . is appropriate.

The best way to avoid the embarrassment of being party to an uncontrolled tongue is to control your own tongue and let others know of your commitment to do so. Tactfully share your commitment with your family, friends, and church. Ask them to patiently encourage and pray for you. As others become aware of your personal desire to have a controlled tongue, they will be sensitive and not pass on the wrong information to you.

Nurturing our inner maturity, by restricting our conversation to good reports, and being constructive in the face of negative input will not only fortify and stimulate our growth but will infect others with an awareness of the benefit of a tongue in check.

Words fitly spoken are like "apples of gold in settings of silver," a "tree of life" to all who hear (Proverbs 25:11 followed by Proverbs 15:4). They are the Lord's delight!

If you "happen" to hear gossip, only repeat it to the Lord. Pray for healing, conviction, growth, reconciliation, wisdom, or whatever is appropriate.

LOVING THE LARGER FLOCK

THE BODY IS A UNIT, THOUGH IT IS MADE UP OF MANY PARTS; AND THOUGH ALL ITS PARTS ARE MANY, THEY FORM ONE BODY. SO IT IS WITH CHRIST.
—1 Corinthians 12:12

Why is it that we often view the body of Christ as the members of our own local congregation? While attending a conference, I met a layman who, in the course of our conversation, remarked about how wonderful it was that every Sunday his pastor prayed by name for other churches and their pastors. He prayed that the cause of Christ would be powerfully advanced through their ministries. I was struck by the fact that I had never thought of doing that and was particularly convicted that I had looked at some of my fellow ministers as competitors rather than colleagues. I resolved at that point to incorporate this practice in my own ministry. I realized what a powerful force this could be for reconciling and strengthening the body of Christ.

The next Sunday during my pastoral prayer, I included a church down the road and mentioned the pastor by name, asking God to be with the church as they met and worshiped and proclaimed the good news of Jesus Christ that Sunday.

That afternoon, at a nearby restaurant, the pastor of the other church and a couple of his people walked by the table of our church business manager. They had been longtime friends, and in the course of their greeting one another, our business manager said to him, "By the way, you'll never guess what our pastor did in church this morning." He went on to say that I had prayed that God would prosper the work of both the pastor and his church. That night, in the middle of the evening service, the pastor told his people what had happened at our church that morning and said, "We're going to take a moment now to pray specifically for Pastor Stowell and the church he pastors, that God would strengthen and use them for His glory." And they prayed for us.

Loving the larger flock by including them in our prayers begins to melt the barriers between us and contributes to the unity that God desires in His body.

Ask your church to pray for a fellow congregation and pastor.

FOR HEAVEN'S SAKE

For Our Citizenship Is in Heaven, from Which Also We Eagerly Wait for a Savior, the Lord Jesus Christ.

—Philippians 3:20 NASB

How quickly we forget that our Father is real right now, living in a real place called heaven, and sitting on His sovereign throne with His Son at His right hand. That from His throne He gives grace, perspective, mercy, and help in time of need and the confident hope of a better world in days to come (John 14:1–6, Hebrews 4:14–16).

It is so easy as earthlings to believe that heaven is there but not relevant enough to make a difference in our lives.

Maybe heaven seems far away because we weren't drawn to it in the first place. Some of us came to Christ because we feared hell. Some of us knew our need for a Savior because our lives had been destroyed by sin. Salvation was a last resort, and if Christ couldn't help us, no one could. Some of us were prompted to repentance because life was empty and He promised to fill us. Or we may simply have been honest seekers wondering if there were reasons beyond what we had been told about life and existence. We wondered if the marvel of the creation didn't have a designer after all and, if it does, if we should have taken that into account in case someday we had to face Him.

There are dozens of reasons why people come to Christ as Savior. But when we came to Him, Jesus had heaven on His mind. We were saved to be rescued from the domain of darkness and to be given something to live for beyond this tough, ruthless world. There is a special joy in turning our hearts toward heaven, to live here for all that He will give us there. Keeping in mind that heaven is actively at work in our lives even as we read this. The God who is there is with us—protecting, guiding, keeping, and teaching us. Living with the thought that all of life here on earth is but a preparation for, a pilgrimage toward, and an investment in heaven is transformingly relevant.

Are you living with heaven on your mind?

SEE YA IN HEAVEN

He Who Testifies to These Things Says, "Yes, I Am Coming Soon."
Amen. Come, Lord Jesus.

—Revelation 22:20

*J*n 1988, a Bible teacher announced in his booklet entitled *Eighty-Eight Reasons Why Christ Will Return in '88* that the second coming of Christ would occur that September. The book received much publicity and attracted a large following. A video was released that dramatized the detailed proof of the prediction, and people sent me copies of the booklet and video, hoping that, as president of Moody, I would help warn the church that Christ would be returning that year.

In light of the fact that Christ predicted that no man would know the time of His coming, I largely discounted the phenomenon.

On the September morning the author had pinpointed for the return of Christ, I rose from bed and, for a moment, wondered, *What if I am wrong and he is right? What if this is the day?* At the breakfast table, our family engaged in a lively discussion about it.

My daughter, Libby, walked down the driveway on the way to school, and as I headed for my car, Libby waved and said, "Hey, Dad . . . see ya in heaven!"

The date setter had been wrong, but the controversy had given rise to an increased awareness that Christ could come back at any time. The implications sent my mind heavenward.

My thoughts during that day were often of heaven.

Think of the difference it would make if each day heaven were so real to us that we anticipated being there by the day's end.

What difference would it make for you—today?

AUGUST 22 / 247

TEACH US TO TRUST

"THOUGH HE SLAY ME, YET WILL I TRUST HIM."
—Job 13:15 NKJV

None of us would want to trade places with Job. His problems are beyond our capacity to understand. But his trouble was not without a purpose. God permitted Job to prove a very important point—that God is worthy of our loyal allegiance regardless of what happens in our life. When his wife encouraged him to "curse God and die!" (Job 2:9), she was playing right into Satan's plan. If it were up to her, she would affirm Satan's slander of God that He had to buy the favor of men by being good to them (Job 1:9–11).

This past summer, I slipped into the back row of a small country church. After a season of praise and worship, the pastor asked a lady to come and lead the church in prayer. She asked all of us to bow and join her. It was a beautifully spoken prayer until she prayed, "And, Lord, we pray this morning for Susan and Peter . . ." At this point her voice broke, and, after failing to get the next couple of words out she stopped. It was one of those awkward moments when someone publicly starts to cry and can't continue.

But in a few moments she regained a measure of composure and brokenly prayed, "Lord, we don't know why You have seen fit to take three children from us this year." I gulped as I thought about the fact that three precious children had died that year in that tiny congregation. She continued with a prayer from her heart that I will never forget, "But, Lord, it's not ours to ask why but to trust You. So teach us to trust."

And while asking "why" is not wrong, the real issue is whether or not we can trust that whatever He does will ultimately be worthy of our praise.

The psalmist wrote, "My foes have trampled upon me all day long, for they are many who fight proudly against me. . . . In God I have put my trust; I shall not be afraid. What can mere man do to me?" (Psalm 56:2, 4 NASB).

Oswald Chambers wrote, "Faith is unutterable trust in God, trust which never dreams that He will not stand by us."

AGE-OLD THINKING IN A NEW AGE

SO WE MAKE IT OUR GOAL TO PLEASE HIM, WHETHER WE ARE AT HOME IN THE BODY OR AWAY FROM IT.

—2 Corinthians 5:9

Few philosophies in Western history have made a more profound impact on the thinking processes of a nation, especially in relation to individuals' concept of God, than the New Age movement. This movement encourages those who seek a transcendent experience to think of God as a depersonalized force existing within each of us. It promises that the seeker can discover this force, tap into its resources, and use its power for his own benefit. This force does not impose ethical standards. The only personalization occurs when we "realize" that because this force is in us and in everything around us, we ourselves can be gods.

The claim that we can be gods is nothing new. In Genesis 3:5 the serpent promised Eve that if she ate of the fruit, "You will be like God." Offering man equality with God and escape from accountability for sin are some of Satan's oldest and most effective strategies. And they continue to work today.

Viewing God as the generic "power base" of the universe leads to disastrous conclusions. Life and religion become no more than self-serving, slippery experiences manipulated and defined by our own desires.

True Christianity, by contrast, requires that I yield myself to a true, personal, solid God who holds me accountable for the good of others. When Christ was asked about the greatest command, He replied, "'You shall love the Lord your God with all your heart, and with all your soul, and with all your mind.' This is the great and foremost commandment. The second is like it, 'You shall love your neighbor as yourself'" (Matthew 22:37–39 NASB).

This is the true prescription for life the way it is meant to be.

Do you view God as a heavenly benefactor who exists for your own pleasure?

PSALM 80:1–14a, 18–19

Please listen, O Shepherd of Israel, you who lead Israel like a flock.

O God, enthroned above the cherubim, display your radiant glory

to Ephraim, Benjamin, and Manasseh.

Show us your mighty power. Come to rescue us!

Turn us again to yourself, O God. Make your face shine down upon us.

Only then will we be saved. O LORD God Almighty,

how long will you be angry and reject our prayers?

You have fed us with sorrow and made us drink tears by the bucketful.

You have made us the scorn of neighboring nations. Our enemies treat us as a joke.

Turn us again to yourself, O God Almighty.

Make your face shine down upon us. Only then will we be saved.

You brought us from Egypt as though we were a tender vine;

you drove away the pagan nations and transplanted us into your land.

You cleared the ground for us, and we took root and filled the land.

The mountains were covered with our shade;

the mighty cedars were covered with our branches.

We spread our branches west to the Mediterranean Sea,

our limbs east to the Euphrates River.

But now, why have you broken down our walls

so that all who pass may steal our fruit?

The boar from the forest devours us, and the wild animals feed on us.

Come back, we beg you, O God Almighty.

Look down from heaven and see our plight. . . .

Then we will never forsake you again.

Revive us so we can call on your name once more.

Turn us again to yourself, O LORD God Almighty.

Make your face shine down upon us. Only then will we be saved.

DEALING WITH DISCIPLINE

WHOM THE LORD LOVES HE REPROVES, EVEN AS A FATHER, THE SON IN
WHOM HE DELIGHTS.

—Proverbs 3:12 NASB 1977

When we contemplate or, worse yet, cling to known sin in our lives, God works every angle to make us aware of the sin and aggressively brings sufficient pressure to cause us to repent. God hates sin and loves us enough to bring reproofs into our lives that will turn us back from the certain destruction that sin brings. Though always troubling and often uncomfortable, God's discipline is our friend. Responding to His reproofs is the difference between deepening intimacy and a growing distance that jeopardizes our spiritual safety.

While many reproofs are external—a sermon, a broken relationship, a passage of Scripture that you "coincidentally" happen to read—the most frequent are those reproofs that resonate within, such as the voice of God's Spirit. This is almost always immediate in its arrival when we are contemplating or have committed a sin. It's the spiritual "tilt" that registers in our soul when we have violated God's rules for life. We hear that still—and sometimes not so still—small voice telling us that we have been wrong and calling us back to God.

God also uses shame to catch our attention. Shame is the gnawing awareness that we have lost our sense of worthiness. Our adversary loves to use sin to erode the spiritually appropriate confidence we have in ourselves as people of worth and dignity created in the image of God. When we allow sin to corrupt the quality of that image, the immediate reproof is shame.

And then there is guilt. Guilt is the alarm bell that rings in our souls with a clanging irritation until we deal with it. Unfortunately, many of us try to deal with the reproof of guilt with self-defeating rationalizations. "I couldn't help myself." "Everybody's doing it." "I owed it to myself." "One little sin isn't all that big a deal." "God will forgive me anyway."

Reproofs are wonderfully unpleasant. They interrupt the sense of peace, tranquillity, confidence, and security that intimacy with God provides. They are signals from God that something is drastically wrong. They require our attention.

Listen for the reproofs, however they come, and repentantly release each struggle to His purifying Spirit.

ALL THESE THINGS

"Do Not Store Up for Yourselves Treasures on Earth, Where Moth
and Rust Destroy, and Where Thieves Break in and Steal."
—Matthew 6:19

*M*adame Blueberry, VeggieTales heroine of materialism, loves shopping at the "stuff-mart." Her problem, however, is that her treetop cottage soon becomes so overstuffed that the tree collapses under the weight of it all.

It is not unlike that in many of our lives. Our families suffer as we place material gain above spouses and children. Double incomes relegate our children to day care centers and latchkey status. When the day is done, our energies are spent and there is little left to pour out at home.

The strength of the work of Christ is compromised as well. The promise of quick credit and plastic cash leaves us in bondage to debt, which disables our support of the kingdom. Living for financial and material gain means living for the realm of empty treasures, where, as Christ said, "moth and rust destroy, and . . . thieves break in and steal" (Matthew 6:19), leaving few "leftover" resources to support the kingdom of God.

Ultimately, sometimes too late, we realize that precious things have collapsed under the weight of our own greed. Thousands of missionaries retire each year. Who is going to replenish these troops? All over North America our children are growing up just like us, choosing their careers based on how they can make the most money and what will help them achieve the highest standard of living as quickly as possible. What of the legions of workers who will be needed to win the world to Christ? Who will go? Who will support them? Our pursuit of a hollow prosperity threatens to weaken the supply line of eternity.

According to Christ, true prosperity is about things that last forever. It is ours to live for the kingdom, and up to Him to supply our needs. As Christ said, "Seek ye the kingdom of God; and all these things shall be added unto you" (Luke 12:31 KJV).

What does your heart desire? The advance of His kingdom—or yours?

UNINTIMIDATED FAITH

—John 16:33

I am not an alarmist by nature and I cringe when I hear doom and gloom conspiracy theories about clandestine plans to discredit Christians and our values. But in spite of my unrepentant optimism, I have to admit that increasingly I notice that Christians who unashamedly identify themselves with Christ are often marginalized and maligned.

When Steve Jones won the U.S. Open in 1996, an irritated journalist wrote this of the victory: "Jones paid tribute to another source of inspiration —his religion. An avowed Christian, he was playing with Lehman, another Christian, and, somewhat to his surprise, Lehman turned to him on the first green and said: 'Steve, God wants us to be strong and courageous, for that is the will of the Lord.' Lehman said something similar on the 16th hole, too."

The story went on to censure Jones and Lehman: "Aside from expressing the old-fashioned concept that one player can encourage a rival, one has to say that the flaunting of God and religion is becoming wearing. . . . One does not know Jones' shoe, hat or glove size, nor the state of his bank account. Do we need to know his religion?"

Surprisingly, these reflections were not written in a personal opinion editorial, but rather in a lead article in the sports section of the *Times,* Great Britain's leading daily.

Do you ever wonder why the people least tolerated in our culture are those of us who believe that there is a right and a wrong and a God who will ultimately judge the rebellion mirrored in the hearts of mankind? That might seem like an odd bias in a culture that values tolerance above all else, but there is a reason for it. An unrighteous society is uncomfortable with reminders of God and His brand of righteousness.

What do we do when we feel the increasing press of a resistant culture? We don't fold; we don't get mad; we don't sulk or whine. We stay the course, remembering that Jesus said, "In this world you will have trouble. But take heart! I have overcome the world" (John 16:33).

Is the approval of man or the approval of Christ more compelling to you?

KINGDOM VALUES

OUR CITIZENSHIP IS IN HEAVEN.

—Philippians 3:20

*O*n a trip to West Africa, I was surprised to learn that a man's standing in the community was established not by how he looked but by how his wives dressed. If they showed up dripping precious gems and sporting the finest fashion and fabrics, he was automatically assumed to be a man of wealth and rank. It crossed my mind that this was not much different from the culture in which I lived. But what was radically different was the fact that the man's status was enhanced by the largeness of his wife. The larger his wife was, the more beautiful she was considered to be. In fact, a local proverb said, "If your wife sits on a camel and the camel cannot stand up or breaks its legs in the process, then she is truly a beautiful woman." Her size reflected well on him, given the fact that he was obviously wealthy enough to feed her abundantly.

Given these seemingly strange customs of sub-Saharan Africa, it is obvious that we march to a totally different drummer in our Western culture. Throughout my stay there, I was always mindful that I came from a different land, and I frankly felt no compulsion to blend in to their standards and values.

In case you hadn't noticed, the Scriptures are full of exhortations reminding us that we are foreigners and aliens in this world, people of the unique culture of the kingdom of Jesus. The purpose of these reminders is to call our attention to the fact that we are to do more than just enjoy the pleasures and privileges of this citizenship. We are to reflect the values of the land to which we truly belong.

What would that look like in your life? Kingdom people reflect the character of their King by regarding people above possessions, others above self, eternity above the present, righteousness above the temporary pleasures of sin, His will above our will, forgiveness above revenge, giving above receiving, children over careers, character above credentials, truth above falsehood, fact above feelings, commitment above comfort, and Christ above culture.

When others see your life, is it clear that you are a citizen of another country?

WHO'S THAT KNOCKING?

"Here I Am! I Stand at the Door and Knock. If Anyone Hears My Voice and Opens the Door, I Will Come in and Eat with Him, and He with Me."
—Revelation 3:20

*I*f you are not too busy, you can hear Him knocking at the door of your heart. Think of this for a moment—Christ intentionally, aggressively pursues fellowship with us. There are no qualifiers here. He isn't speaking just to the few select, highly spiritual, worthy people at Laodicea. And He isn't speaking here, as some may think, of standing outside unbelieving hearts. This is about us and His deep desire for intimacy with us.

We shouldn't be surprised. God has always pursued His own. He walked back into the sin-ravaged landscape of the Garden of Eden to find Adam and Eve. Throughout the history of Israel, God consistently pursued His people. Why would God want to live in the wilderness when He had heaven? Because His people were there. So He tabernacled in their midst, satisfying them with manna and protecting them from fierce enemies.

And then Immanuel was born. God with us. As John tells us, He "pitched his tent among us" (John 1:14 EMPH. NT). He touched the lame and the leper. He gave sight to the blind. One word to His entombed friend, and Lazarus walked from the grave. To His disciples He said, "Follow Me." And when He left, He told them, "I go to prepare a place for you. If I go . . . I will come again and receive you to Myself; that where I am, there you may be also" (John 14:2–3 NASB). The whole history of Scripture explodes with the fact that God is busy intentionally pursuing intimacy with us.

Then why haven't we heard Him knocking? It is possible that the business of life and the cares of this world, the sound of our own dreams dancing in our heads, or perhaps the noisy clutter of all the "stuff" in our lives has drowned out the sound of His knocking at our heart's door.

What obstacles do you need to clear away to get to the door? Is there anything you desire more than intimacy with God?

"JUST THE FACTS . . ."

"YOUR WORD IS TRUTH."

—John 17:17

A student came to me one day and said that he had seen a Porsche turn the corner in front of him with the license plate "MBI-1." His immediate conclusion was that it was my car. If he hadn't checked with me, he would have logged the "fact" in his brain that the president of Moody Bible Institute drives a Porsche! Sadly, it wasn't my car . . . but the process of verifying it kept his thinking straight and my reputation intact.

By nature, we possess a hunger for facts. Learning to count to five provides an early thrill. Throughout our lives, the joy of discovering new facts fuels the mind's hunger for information.

But equally as important is guaranteeing that the "facts" we store are true. This is particularly critical in a world managed and manipulated by Satan, who, as Christ said, is "the father of lies" (John 8:44). If you believe that success is about the car you drive and the kingdom you have built, you will live to succeed in that way. If your information base is programmed to conclude that life is first and foremost about you, that money is your sustaining commodity, that others exist to please and satisfy you, and that God is not good, you will live in distorted and often ungodly ways.

This is where the Word of God becomes an essential tool. The Bible is the final measurement for all data concerning every area of life. Second Timothy 3:16–17 states that "all Scripture is . . . profitable for teaching, for reproof, for correction, for training in righteousness; so that the man of God may be . . . equipped for every good work" (NASB). God's Word provides reliable data in a world that largely runs on fiction. The Word's data about relationships, Christ, history, people, money, the world around us, and eternity beyond the universe is reliable and true.

Gathering and guaranteeing reliable data is foundational for keeping life on target, which may be why Paul said, "Do not be conformed to this world, but be transformed by the renewing of your mind" (Romans 12:2 NASB).

If you thought God's thoughts, how would your life be different?

PSALM 84

How lovely is your dwelling place, O LORD Almighty.
I long, yes, I faint with longing to enter the courts of the LORD.
With my whole being, body and soul, I will shout joyfully to the living God.
Even the sparrow finds a home there, and the swallow builds her nest
and raises her young—at a place near your altar,
O LORD Almighty, my King and my God!
How happy are those who can live in your house,
always singing your praises.
Happy are those who are strong in the LORD,
who set their minds on a pilgrimage to Jerusalem.
When they walk through the Valley of Weeping,
it will become a place of refreshing springs,
where pools of blessing collect after the rains!
They will continue to grow stronger,
and each of them will appear before God in Jerusalem.
O LORD God Almighty, hear my prayer.
Listen, O God of Israel.
O God, look with favor upon the king, our protector!
Have mercy on the one you have anointed.
A single day in your courts is better than a thousand anywhere else!
I would rather be a gatekeeper in the house of my God
than live the good life in the homes of the wicked.
For the LORD God is our light and protector. He gives us grace and glory.
No good thing will the LORD withhold from those who do what is right.
O LORD Almighty, happy are those who trust in you.

NOTHING BETWEEN

I Count All Things to Be Loss in View of the Surpassing Value of
Knowing Christ Jesus My Lord.
—Philippians 3:8 NASB

We've all been to sporting events, parades, and gatherings where we want to get a glimpse of the action only to have someone plop themselves right in front of us, making it impossible to see. How frustrating and distracting. I'm reminded of the Scottish poet who got stuck in church behind a lady with a large and imposing hat that blocked his view. Seeing a flea jumping in the hat, he became distracted, lost interest in worship, and wrote a now-famous poem about the lady and her flea-infested hat.

What a metaphor of our dilemma. We are blessed with the gift of salvation that we might grow into an increasingly intimate relationship with Jesus. A relationship in which we can find solace, forgiveness, direction, purpose, companionship, and a dozen other pleasures that only He can provide. He is the action we are supposed to keep in clear view.

But there is so much that distracts us. And it's not just the sin in our lives that gets in the way. It's often innocent things and even good things. Paul knew that if He was to know and experience Jesus more fully there could be nothing between his heart and Jesus. So, he counted everything in his life—good, bad, and indifferent—to be secondary to the surpassing value of knowing Christ.

I love the words of that song I used to sing in church as a boy:

Nothing between my soul and the Saviour, Naught of the world's delusive dream;
I have renounced all sinful pleasure, Jesus is mine; there's nothing between.
Nothing between, like worldly pleasure, Habits of life though harmless they seem,
Must not my heart from Him e'er sever, He is my all; There's nothing between.
Nothing between like pride or station, Self or friends shall not intervene,
Tho' it may cost me much tribulation, I am resolved; there's nothing between.
Nothing between my soul and the Saviour, So that His blessed face may be seen;
Nothing preventing the least of His favor, Keep the way clear! Let nothing between.

Amen!

BODY LANGUAGE

Do You Not Know that Your Body Is a Temple of the Holy Spirit?
—1 Corinthians 6:19

There is a dramatic shift from Old Testament worship to the worship we express today. In the Old Testament, God's people worshiped in a place —the place where God dwelt. It was filled with somber, purified priests; vessels that had been set aside; and rituals of cleansing.

In the new covenant, however, God now dwells in our bodies (1 Corinthians 3:16–17; 6:19). Second Timothy 2:21 says that our bodies are the vessels purified for use in worship and God's service. We have become His temple! And we are the priests who manage the system of worship (1 Peter 2:9). Worship for us is both internal and intimate. And given the fact that we are His temple, worship is an everyday expression, not just something that happens on Sunday morning.

This is why Paul wrote, "Therefore . . . present your bodies a living and holy sacrifice" (Romans 12:1 NASB). Don't miss the fact that Paul called for a *living* and *holy* sacrifice. The sacrifice Paul refers to in this verse is the total surrender and purification of all that we are, from the inside out, as a daily expression of the worth and worthiness of our God.

Placing our bodies on the altar means giving ourselves to Him totally, without reservation, in the place of the lambs, doves, and goats of the Old Testament. God wants *us,* not just our gifts and possessions. That is a great compliment. And it goes without saying that if He has all of us, He will also have all that we have.

Why would we do this? Because God has reached down and touched helpless, hopeless persons such as us, cleansed us of our sin, and made us His own. For this we live to worship Him with all of our being—with our actions, our attitudes, and our possessions.

The only issue remaining is, are we purified sacrifices? He not only wants us, but He want us to come with clean hands and a pure heart (Psalm 24:3–4).

I have a friend who says, "The trouble with living sacrifices is that they tend to crawl off the altar!" Does this apply to your life?

TENACITY IN TROUBLE

"Go, Gather Together All the Jews . . . and Fast for Me. Do Not Eat or Drink for Three Days, Night or Day. I and My Maids Will Fast as You Do. When This Is Done, I Will Go to the King. . . . And if I Perish, I Perish."

—Esther 4:16

When difficult circumstances hit our lives, they inevitably bring the unwelcome companions of despair, hurt, revenge, self-pity, anger, sorrow, fear, and a dozen other feelings that can, if we permit, distract us and defeat God's intended purposes. God permits crises for our good and the gain of His kingdom. So it is no surprise that Satan consistently seeks to turn the tables on God by using trouble to defeat us.

Esther refused to fold under phenomenal pressure. Her tenacious faith in what she knew to be true and right gave her strength in her devastating situation. Deciding to risk her life and face the king's wrath to rescue her people, she asked others to cover her in prayer. For three days she fasted, seeking the face of God for the courage and strength to do what God required of her. Fear, cowardice, and her love for life would not distract her from a surrendered response to her God.

If we learn anything from the life of Esther, it is that our resource in times of trouble must not be what we feel but rather what and whom we know. We know that God has a purpose in our pain. That He will provide the grace and wisdom to endure victoriously. That He permits only those things into our lives that He can turn to good and glory. We know that He is a God of accurate timing, consistent presence, certain purpose, unfailing love, and productive empathy.

What we know is the advantage. Which is why James was confident that based on all that we know, we could without compromise consider trouble as something that would bring ultimate joy. Therefore we can welcome it as a friend and not resist it as an enemy (James 1:1–5).

What truths do you cling to in times of crisis?

ABSOLUTELY

"For My Thoughts Are Not Your Thoughts, Neither Are Your Ways My Ways," Declares the Lord.

—Isaiah 55:8

*D*uring the days of my grandfather's and my father's ministries, there was basic cultural assent to the absolutes of Scripture. Divorce was wrong. Homosexual acts were clearly seen as sin. Adultery, pornography, and a host of other social evils were out of bounds. This made preaching about righteousness and godliness far more palatable even to the unbelieving listener. But today, the clear and nonnegotiable teaching of absolutes that determine what is right and wrong is often greeted by both saint and sinner as being "too bigoted," "too intolerant," or "too culturally insensitive." Decades ago, God was banished from the center of life, leaving us free to decide what was good and right for ourselves.

While waiting for my shirts at the dry cleaners recently, I heard on the radio a scholar who was delivering a lecture on fundamentalism. He stated that the one thing that was true about fundamentalists was that they believed in absolutes. And then, in a cynical aside, he said, "And to top that, they believe they know what the absolutes are."

While he felt that clinging to the absolutes was arrogant, the truth is that Christians do not arbitrarily choose the absolutes they adhere to. It goes deeper than that. The more important issue is that Christians believe in a God who is absolute and true. And since there is a God who has revealed His truth to us, Christians humbly affirm the truths that are grounded in His nature and revealed in His Word. The absolutes we affirm find their source in the essence of the God we serve.

But in a world of skeptics, the most powerful argument is the argument of our lives. When we live up to the absolutes we profess, even the harshest critics will have to admit that the fruits of righteousness are the enviable results of our allegiance to God's absolutes. As St. Francis of Assisi said, "Preach the gospel every day; if necessary, use words."

Cling to the truth and let your life do the talking.

WHO CARES?

Now the Tax Collectors and "Sinners" Were All Gathering Around to
Hear Him.

—Luke 15:1

Those of us who are committed to righteousness typically have a hard
time mustering up a heart of compassion toward those who flaunt their
own will and desires in the face of what we know to be true and good.

In Christ's day, the tax gatherers were the charlatans of society. They were
Jews who for personal gain had sold out to the oppressing empire of Rome.
They not only collected the exorbitant taxes, but they pocketed additional fees.
In short, it was government-approved extortion. To any upstanding Jew in
Jesus' day, tax collectors were the ultimate traitors. Sinners, according to Jewish
religious law, were those who willfully lived apart from the laws of God.

So it came as a surprise—at least it did to the Pharisees—that Jesus often
spent time with such people and even ate with them. Luke didn't shy away
from the tension. He noted that "tax collectors and 'sinners'" were at the core
of the crowd listening attentively to Jesus' teaching, while the religious folk
stood around the fringe of the crowd, grumbling that this One who claimed
to be God associated with such disreputable people. To counter their complaint, Christ told three stories about caring for things of value that were lost.
The point was clear. God cares for the lost—all of them. In fact, Jesus would
soon demonstrate His love for them on the cross.

The issue for us is, Do we care about the lost? The worst kind of the lost?
Are we at the core of the crowd with Christ, or are we standing at the edge
with other grumpy religious folk complaining about sinners? When was the
last time you prayed for "bad" people who aren't like you and sought ways to
win them to Christ?

If our hearts are with His, we will applaud and support groups working
with homosexuals, drug addicts, AIDS victims, prostitutes, and the undeserv-
ing homeless. Whether it is aimed at the best or the worst, compassion is the
appropriate expression of a follower of Christ in a dark world.

*Is there a "tax-collector" or "sinner" in your life? In your town? Plan a compas-
sionate action—today.*

CHEERING THE ADVANCE OF THE CAUSE

BUT WHAT DOES IT MATTER? THE IMPORTANT THING IS THAT . . . CHRIST IS
PREACHED. AND BECAUSE OF THIS I REJOICE.

—Philippians 1:18

*O*ne thing we have to get over if we are going to honor Christ in our work
is our competitive spirit. The goal of serving Him is to advance His
cause, not our reputation or ministry.

One Easter Sunday, a church across town decided to set a record attendance by having a "Friends Day" and throwing an Easter egg roll on their
front lawn for all the kids who came. To be candid, I felt a sense of competi-
tion with this particular church and was quietly critical of its approach to
ministry.

What really bothered me was the fact that many of the friends their people called to invite to their service were members of our church. My heart was
reproved by Paul's attitude in Philippians 1:18, where he spoke about others
who were more successful than he, even though the motivation for their ministry was competitive and less than pure.

A woman in our church came to me one Sunday evening in great frustration as she blurted out, "Pastor, do you know how many they had at Temple
Baptist Church this morning? They had more than fifteen hundred there, and
many of them were our own people. I don't think that's right or fair, do you?"
It was a test of my motives. I wish I could always be this on target, but thankfully the Word had done a remedial work on my carnal perspectives and I
found myself saying, "Are you telling me that more than fifteen hundred people in our town heard the gospel of Jesus Christ this morning? Isn't that the
best news you've heard in a long time?" She was stunned and verbally back-
pedaled to "Well . . . well . . . yes, I guess it is."

When our focus is on the glory of Christ and the gain of His kingdom, it
doesn't make a whole lot of difference who facilitates the goal. If Jesus is lifted up, our hearts should rejoice—unless we think our life and ministry are all
about us.

*Are you a competitor with other Christians or a colleague in the cause? Do you
rejoice when they succeed?*

PSALM 86

Bend down, O LORD, and hear my prayer; answer me, for I need your help.

Protect me, for I am devoted to you.

Save me, for I serve you and trust you. You are my God.

Be merciful, O Lord, for I am calling on you constantly.

Give me happiness, O Lord, for my life depends on you.

O Lord, you are so good, so ready to forgive,

so full of unfailing love for all who ask your aid.

Listen closely to my prayer, O LORD; hear my urgent cry.

I will call to you whenever trouble strikes, and you will answer me.

Nowhere among the pagan gods is there a god like you, O Lord.

There are no other miracles like yours.

All the nations—and you made each one—will come and bow before you, Lord;

they will praise your great and holy name.

For you are great and perform great miracles. You alone are God.

Teach me your ways, O LORD, that I may live according to your truth!

Grant me purity of heart, that I may honor you.

With all my heart I will praise you, O Lord my God.

I will give glory to your name forever,

for your love for me is very great.

You have rescued me from the depths of death!

O God, insolent people rise up against me; violent people are trying to kill me.

And you mean nothing to them.

But you, O Lord, are a merciful and gracious God, slow to get angry,

full of unfailing love and truth.

Look down and have mercy on me. Give strength to your servant;

yes, save me, for I am your servant. Send me a sign of your favor.

Then those who hate me will be put to shame,

for you, O LORD, help and comfort me.

OUR FIRST LOVE

"YET I HOLD THIS AGAINST YOU: YOU HAVE FORSAKEN YOUR FIRST LOVE."
—Revelation 2:4

At first blush, we'd vote for the church at Ephesus as described in Revelation 2:1–3 to receive the "Church of the Year" award. In His first letter to the churches of Asia Minor, Jesus showered the Ephesians with bouquets of affirmation for their faithfulness, doctrinal purity, and perseverance. But before we voted, we would need to hear what else Christ had to say. He added, "Yet I hold this against you" (v. 4). That's an unsettling charge. We revel in the claim in Romans 8:31, "If God is for us, who can be against us?" but what if the reverse is true?

Christ's complaint? "You have forsaken your first love" (Revelation 2:4). The Greek word for "first" here doesn't mean first in terms of time. It's not referring to how they felt the first day they were saved. We'll never feel the same way again until we get Home. He meant first in terms of priority or preeminence. Christ was saying that the Ephesians had abandoned Him as the priority of their love. They were busy doing all the right religious things, but they were not doing them because they loved Him.

Which leads us to ask some important questions of ourselves. Why do you resist temptation? Because you might get caught or because you fear the consequences? Why do you give your money? So He will bless you in return? Why do you teach or serve on committees and boards? For your own glory? Do you sing in the choir because you love to sing? When we do what we do for God for any reason other than the expression of our love for Christ, we become busy for all the wrong reasons. That was Christ's point. All we do should be about Him, for Him, and because of Him.

Jesus calls us to repent and cultivate hearts that serve Him for one central reason: because we love Him. Happily, doing all we do because we love Him keeps us at it regardless of who sees or affirms or what the outcomes might be. Loving Him makes serving Him worth it, regardless.

Do you serve Christ because you love him, or has He gotten lost in your good works?

BEYOND OURSELVES

HE WHO WINS SOULS IS WISE.

—Proverbs 11:30

*I*n case you are weary in well-doing and discouraged because it seems that your life and ministry are about unnoticed things, be encouraged. Your impact in seemingly insignificant acts of obedience can cause spiritual repercussions far beyond what you've ever dreamed. Dwight Lyman Moody, in the course of his ministry, led Wilbur Chapman to the Lord. Wilbur Chapman became a great national evangelist in the generation succeeding Moody's.

During Wilbur Chapman's ministry in Chicago, a baseball player with the Whitestockings was standing in front of a bar on State Street when people in a gospel wagon from the Pacific Garden Mission came by playing hymns and inviting people to the afternoon service down the street. This ballplayer, recognizing the hymns as ones his mom used to sing, attended the service and received Christ as his personal Savior.

That afternoon encounter with Christ dramatically changed the life of Billy Sunday. He played ball for two more years and then left professional sports to minister in the YMCA in Chicago. Wilbur Chapman invited Billy Sunday to join his crusade team as an advance man to help organize the pastors and set up Chapman's meetings. Billy Sunday enthusiastically agreed.

Billy Sunday soon began scheduling his own meetings, which launched his ministry across America for the cause of Christ. In one of those meetings, a young man by the name of Mordecai Hamm accepted Christ. Mordecai Hamm became a great evangelist in the southeastern United States, ministering to massive crowds south of the Mason-Dixon line. One night at one of those large tent meetings, a young man and his friend came forward to accept Christ. The name of that young man? Billy Graham.

But as spectacular a chain of impact as this is, the amazing thing is that it was all started by an unknown Sunday school teacher named Edward Kimball. One Saturday, Kimball decided to visit the boys in his class to be sure they knew Jesus as their Savior. He called on D. L. Moody and led him to the Lord in the back of a shoe store in Boston operated by Moody's uncle. Hardly anyone knows who Edward Kimball is, but heaven's population swells today because of his routine faithfulness to Christ.

Just be faithful!

SEPTEMBER 11, 2001

Be Still, and Know that I Am God; I Will Be Exalted Among the Nations.

—Psalm 46:10

We all remember where we were and what we were doing. It was a day none of us will ever forget. Terrorists using our own planes as incendiary bombs brutally murdered thousands of innocent civilians in the worst attack on America in its history. Through the grief and shock questions begged for answers. Questions about security, terrorism, war and personal safety haunted us. But none were more troubling than the questions about God. Where was He? If He is a loving God, why didn't He stop this?

Thankfully, there are answers. And the answers lie in the very nature of God Himself. He is *transcendent* which means that His wisdom and thoughts are far beyond our ability to grasp. With our limited perspectives, we can't hope to fully understand His ways. Our brains aren't big enough to get all the way around Him. To stand as His judge, having only incomplete information, would be folly. What we do know however is that He is a just, righteous, and loving God. Which means that justice will ultimately be done, wrongs will be made right, and love prevail. When we can't fully understand Him, it is comforting to know that we can trust Him.

Throughout history, God has proved that He is able to take the worst acts of mankind and turn them to good and glory. The Cross stands as the prime example. In that terrorist attack of hell against heaven, God watched from a distance as His innocent Son died an agonizing death in the public square. For three long days His followers brokenly wondered why a loving God would not stop such injustice. In fact, His enemies, at the foot of the cross, mocked the seeming inability of God to save Jesus. But in God's wise time He intervened. The empty tomb is forever a reminder that God is good and that He lovingly permits only that which in the end will bring glory to His name and good to those who follow Him.

It must be frustrating for Satan to realize that even in his finest hour, God still ruled!

It is well with our souls . . .

CHOICES

She Took From Its Fruit and Ate; and She Gave Also to Her Husband with Her, and He Ate.

—Genesis 3:6

*N*ever before were we so pressed to respond to the age-old question, "If God is a loving God, then why is there evil in this world?" than in the aftermath of the attacks on the World Trade Center and the Pentagon.

Though we may not fully understand now, ultimately there is a clear and just answer. God's infinite wisdom is without fault. Yet the Bible does help us get a grip on the question.

In His wisdom, God created an environment for mankind in which people can choose to love and surrender to Him or to go their own way and live life on their own terms. This, then, allows the possibility of both good and evil. God's other option would have been to create everyone as a mechanical being, preprogrammed to act out His will. That would have been a world without joy, love, feeling, romance, friendships, plans, ideas, or dreams. It would have been a world where our relationship with the Creator would have been wooden and sterile. It would have been a world in which few of us would want to live. God chose, instead, to create a race with whom He could have a loving relationship. The fact that man has abused the privilege of choice to perpetrate evil is an abuse of God's good plan.

Thankfully, God offered a remedy for our foolish and destructive choices. Choices for evil instead of good leave us guilty before Him and liable for eternal judgment. God came to earth in the person of Jesus Christ, with the ultimate purpose of dying in our place so that our sinfulness could be covered by His love—so that even the worst among us could be forgiven and restored to Him (John 3:16). As Paul noted, "God demonstrates His own love toward us, in that while we were yet sinners, Christ died for us" (Romans 5:8 NASB).

God is not responsible for events like the terrorist attacks on that dark Tuesday in 2001. God created Eden. And the love of Jesus seeks to restore us to Eden again—an eternal Eden, safe and unscathed by Satan's destructive schemes.

To the only wise God be honor and glory forever. Amen.

GOD OF THE ORDINARY

"Never Will I Leave You; Never Will I Forsake You."
—Hebrews 13:5

*H*ave you ever felt that if God were to show up as regularly as He did in the lives of people in Bible times that you too could be a spiritual hero? Unfortunately, this mind-set assumes that the quality of our relationship to Him is measured by how many times He drops into our lives and does something spectacular.

When this is our expectation, we grow quickly discouraged in our walk with Him. I often feel cheated when I hear someone talk about an extraordinary intervention of God in their life. If I am not careful, I can go into a spiritual funk wondering why God "never does anything like that for me."

It's easy to feel spiritually abnormal because God doesn't seem to be doing a lot for us, or to suffer from a lack of spiritual self-esteem, as though you're not all that important to God. It's not unlike Lewis Carroll's *Alice in Wonderland,* where the complaint is lodged: "Cake yesterday, cake tomorrow, but no cake today!"

I think that's why a lot of us are easily seduced by "spectacular" forms of spirituality. We miss the fact that God's presence is most often expressed in quiet, unseen movings of the Spirit below the surface of our situations. Rather than continuing to faithfully take the routine steps toward God in our pilgrimage, we wait by the side of the road hoping for a holy handout. We opt for the quick hit, the rush of spiritual adrenaline.

Recently I time-tabled Abraham's life and noted that God "showed up" only about once every fifteen years. Abraham had no Bible, no small group fellowship, no exhilarating worship experiences, but his steadfast faith is celebrated in Hebrews 11:8–19. Joseph was unrelentingly faithful against great odds. Yet for many years, God didn't "show up" . . . Joseph experienced repeated setbacks. What we do know, however, is that "the LORD was with Joseph"; wherever he served in Egypt, the Lord gave him success, even though freedom from servitude and prison did not come for a long time (Genesis 39:2–6, 20–23).

Faith claims that our God is with us all the time (Hebrews 13:5–6)—even if He doesn't always "show up."

Are you willing to be routinely faithful regardless? Stay the course! He really is there.

LOVING THOSE YOU'D RATHER NOT

"IF YOU OBEY MY COMMANDS, YOU WILL REMAIN IN MY LOVE."
—John 15:10

*L*ucy reproved Linus after he had said that it was his life goal to be a doctor by retorting, "Linus, you can't be a doctor. You hate mankind!" To which Linus replied, "Oh no, I love mankind. It's people I can't stand." Most of us have spent a considerable amount of time around "mankind" and have noticed that people are often a major problem. Which makes Christ's command to "love your neighbor as yourself" a serious challenge (Matthew 22:39).

Challenging because our "neighbors" may not be worth loving.

So what is the reason we should love people? First, let's consider what are definitely *not* reasons for loving people. It is *not* because people deserve it. They usually don't. It's *not* because people are easy to love. Our wounds and scars assure us that is not the case. It's *not* because they will always love us back, they probably won't. Rather, Scripture teaches us that the true motivation for loving people is our love for God. Which means that people are not the reason we love people. Loving them is just another way we tell God how much we love Him!

In Matthew 22:37–39, the first and second commandments are inseparable: "'Love the Lord your God with all your heart and with all your soul and with all your mind.' This is the first and greatest commandment. And the second is like it: 'Love your neighbor as yourself.'"

Jesus said that He knows we love Him if we do the things He commands (John 15:10). Which means that He knows we love Him by the way we treat others—all of them. Of course, our response to that is usually, "Lord, you don't know the people I know. I'll double-tithe, but please don't ask me to start loving these people!"

But God still says, "If you really love Me, reach out and love people." And, since He is always worthy of our love, we are free to consistently help, forgive, serve, pray for, and minister to *everyone* who comes across the path of our lives. Not necessarily because they deserve it, but because He does. What a liberating thought!

Whom could you love today for Christ's sake?

PSALM 91

Those who live in the shelter of the Most High
will find rest in the shadow of the Almighty.
This I declare of the LORD: He alone is my refuge, my place of safety;
he is my God, and I am trusting him.
For he will rescue you from every trap and protect you from the fatal plague.
He will shield you with his wings.
He will shelter you with his feathers.
His faithful promises are your armor and protection.
Do not be afraid of the terrors of the night, nor fear the dangers of the day,
nor dread the plague that stalks in darkness,
nor the disaster that strikes at midday.
Though a thousand fall at your side, though ten thousand are dying around you,
these evils will not touch you.
But you will see it with your eyes; you will see how the wicked are punished.
If you make the LORD your refuge, if you make the Most High your shelter,
no evil will conquer you; no plague will come near your dwelling.
For he orders his angels to protect you wherever you go.
They will hold you with their hands to keep you from striking your foot on a stone.
You will trample down lions and poisonous snakes;
you will crush fierce lions and serpents under your feet!
The LORD says, "I will rescue those who love me.
I will protect those who trust in my name.
When they call on me, I will answer; I will be with them in trouble.
I will rescue them and honor them.
I will satisfy them with a long life and give them my salvation."

INTIMACY WITH GOD

Jesus Replied: "Love the Lord Your God with All Your Heart and with All Your Soul and with All Your Mind.'"
—Matthew 22:37

*I*t would be impossible to enjoy intimacy in an earthside relationship if we were living in continuing offense toward the one whom we say we love. Many marriages suffer a loss of intimacy because one of the partners has ceased to be loyal. Lying to or cheating on a spouse, ignoring the other's needs, using the relationship for our own benefit when it's convenient but not when it costs something, and generally neglecting responsibilities are all recipes for a distancing between two hearts.

So it is with God. All through Scripture, God requires that we surrender to Him the totality of our beings. We are to love the Lord our God with all our heart, soul, mind, and strength (Deuteronomy 6:5; Matthew 22:37; Mark 12:30, 33). In the letters Christ wrote to the churches in the early chapters of the book of Revelation, it was their ongoing, undealt-with sin and shortcomings that diminished their relationship with Christ.

We cannot expect intimacy when we negotiate what we will give to Him and take from Him. Too often we are like the person who said:

> I'd like to buy three dollars' worth of God. Please, not enough to explode my soul or disturb my sleep, but just enough to equal a cup of warm milk or a snooze in the sunshine. I don't want enough of Him to make me love a black man or pick beets with a migrant. I want ecstasy, not transformation. I want the warmth of the womb, not a new birth. I want about a pound of the eternal in a paper sack. I'd like to buy about three dollars' worth of God, please.

Do you long for that coveted closer walk with Him? He needs all of you, and you need all of Him. Love Him with the nonnegotiated commitment of your whole self, and He will satisfy the deepest recesses of your soul with the fullness of His presence.

List how you love the Lord in the areas of heart, strength, and mind. Is there anything that He doesn't have?

A LIAR FROM THE BEGINNING

"THERE IS NO TRUTH IN HIM. WHEN HE LIES, HE SPEAKS HIS NATIVE LANGUAGE, FOR HE IS A LIAR AND THE FATHER OF LIES."
—John 8:44

*S*atan established his rule on earth when he turned the minds of Adam and Eve against God. In order to pull this off, he had to lie to them about God and, more importantly, they had to believe his lies. In that strategic moment in the Garden of Eden, he lied to them about God's goodness, God's word, and God's intentions for their lives. In essence he said that God was not good but stingy and repressive in restricting them from eating of the Tree of the Knowledge of Good and Evil. Moreover, Satan said, God's word was not true. They really wouldn't die if they ate. And, he claimed, God's intentions were not for their good but rather to oppress them and hold them back from experiencing life at its fullest. If they would go ahead and eat the fruit, they would be truly fulfilled.

Sound familiar? Satan still seeks to capture our minds through the same basic lies. And though the players and the settings have changed dramatically since that first "mind assault," the strategy is the same.

When trouble interrupts our lives he whispers, "God is not good." When we are asked to sacrifice things that are precious to us he whispers, "God is stingy and repressive." When God asks for obedience and requires that we walk in His way, Satan whispers that God's Word is oppressive, robbing us of life the way we really want it to be. But the lies are not the problem. It's that we tend to—no, that we *want* to—believe them, and when we do, love and loyalty to God are compromised, leaving us at the mercy of our Enemy. And he will soon slither off to his next assignment, leave us alone in our misery and sorrow to face the sad realization that his lies have seduced us away from our truest and dearest friend . . . who indeed is "the way, the truth and the life" (John 14:6 KJV)!

Are there any lies that have determined your attitudes and behavior? Do you really want to trust the Enemy?

THE LONG SPOON

Now the Serpent Was More Crafty Than Any Beast of the Field. . . .
The Serpent Said to the Woman, "You Surely Will Not Die!"
—Genesis 3:1–4 NASB

When I was a freshman in college, T. I. Evans, a sophomore, would gather the freshman in our dorm and help us plot mischievous adventures that we could carry out under the cover of night. Unfortunately, most of these schemes meant breaking some of the rules in the handbook. But the plans were too compellingly fun. The challenge to pull them off and not get caught was a temptation that few of us could resist. So after hours, we would execute our clandestine plots, only to get caught on a regular basis. One night, it dawned on us that T. I. never went with us. He got his kicks by setting up naive freshman. We had been duped, and his joy was not in the plan but in watching us get snagged.

With all due apologies to Mr. Evans, I have often thought that Satan is just like that. He offers us schemes that we can hardly resist and then slithers off into the weeds to watch us destroy ourselves in the aftermath of his seduction. He laughs at our sorrows and delights in our pain. Have we forgotten that his intent is to devour us, not to make us happy (1 Peter 5:8)? For Adam and Eve, the serpent offered fulfillment apart from God. But under the seduction he intended to shroud their lives in shame and to alienate them from their true source of hope and satisfaction. Talk about bait and switch. He is the master of the trade!

Ask King David about the aftermath of Satan's plans. Or, better yet, check with Judas, who reaped a sorrow beyond comfort as his reward.

Peter Berger writes, "He who sups with the devil had better have a long spoon, because he who sups with the devil will find that his spoon gets shorter and shorter until that last supper in which he is left alone at the table with no spoon at all and an empty plate. But the devil, one may guess, will have by then gone on to more interesting company."

Be alert—Satan's intentions are not as they seem.

THE PERSEVERANCE OF THE SAINTS

"The Lord Gave and the Lord Has Taken Away; May the Name of the Lord Be Praised."

—Job 1:21

One of the frustrating things about problems and pain is that it's usually impossible to walk away from them. The only option is how you will respond. Will the pain embitter your spirit and destroy hope? Or will you seek to survive—better yet, to *succeed*—in the midst of trouble? If your choice is success, it requires what the Bible calls *perseverance*.

When I left seminary, I had an unflinching commitment to the doctrine of the perseverance of the saints. I soon discovered that, on a practical level, the saints don't "persevere" all that well.

As a young pastor, I noted that God's flock was sometimes more committed to comfort than to character; to convenience than to commitment; and to cash rather than to Christ. It was a brand of disposable discipleship, a Christianity that prospered in pleasure but not in pain. So I hammered away in the pulpit, trying to call God's people to perseverance. In time, I encountered a few difficulties of my own. To my surprise, I didn't persevere all that well. When the going got tough, I was prone to wander—spiritually, mentally, and emotionally.

We all need a fresh call to the perseverance of the saints. We need to be followers of Christ who refuse to deny God in pain. Who reject bitterness as an option. Who cling to the reality that He has a purpose in our trouble, that He never wastes our sorrows. We need to refuse to buy the recommendations and remedies of the world, and to claim righteousness and faithfulness as our ultimate commitment in every situation. We need to be followers who say with Job, "The Lord gave and the Lord has taken away; may the name of the Lord be praised" (Job 1:21).

Perseverance is staying under the pressure with a good spirit; with an unflinching trust in the wisdom and goodness of our God.

What are the realities about God that you can cling to in the midst of trouble? Be specific.

A GREAT POWER PLAY

WHO, BEING IN VERY NATURE GOD . . . MADE HIMSELF NOTHING, TAKING THE
VERY NATURE OF A SERVANT.

—Philippians 2:6–7

When Lord Acton said, "Absolute power corrupts absolutely," he was not speaking of Jesus. Jesus never used His power for His own benefit. Instead, His power was spent to empower others for their good and for the glory of His Father. As such, He leaves an important legacy about our use of power.

I will never grow accustomed to the fact that when Jesus came to our planet and could have chosen any identity He wished, He chose the identity of a servant. He served us all the way to the cross, where He used His power to provide offensive sinners with the gift of redemption (Philippians 2:7–8).

Whatever power God has given us—as parent, husband, wife, foreman, teacher, executive, or friend—can you imagine the dramatic impact of saying, "I will use my power to serve the best interests of others for their good, growth, and the glory of God through their lives"?

When I first came to serve at Moody Bible Institute, a well-meaning friend said, "You really took a step up." I knew what he meant, but in reality there are no "steps up" in the kingdom. It is a vast vineyard, and we are all servants sovereignly assigned to our places in His field. As a servant, I am called to use whatever power I've been given to serve students and associates toward what is best for them. As a husband and dad, I am to use the influence of my life to advance the lives of my wife and children. Using the power and position God has given for personal gain aborts and distorts God's purpose for power.

Success is measured not by how much power we have but by how we use our power. It is not what we have, but how well we serve with what we have. Which is exactly why Paul began the passage above with the words "Have this attitude in yourselves which was also in Christ Jesus" (Philippians 2:5 NASB).

Envision ways to use your power to bless and empower others.

BEYOND FAILURE

FOR ALL HAVE SINNED AND FALL SHORT OF THE GLORY OF GOD.
—Romans 3:23

*W*hen we are honest with ourselves, we are aware that we cannot hope to save ourselves by being good. Consistently living up to the ten rules in the Decalogue is an impossible challenge. In fact, that is why God's Word pictures the law as a testimony to the fact that we are sinners unable to measure up on a consistent basis. The proof that we are sinners underscores the amazing love of Jesus in that He was willing to die for us to close the gap between our obvious failures and the holiness of God. But given the uselessness of the law to save does not mean that we disparage the importance of the commandments. Nor does it mean that we have license to bail out on their requirements. The commandments are God's will for our lives, and the closer we stay to them the more satisfying our lives become.

Valuing His commands is not easy in a world that celebrates disobedience. The first ad in a recent advertising campaign depicted a glitzy new car decked out with an emerald finish. The copy read "ENVY." The second ad in the series, featuring a red car, was titled "LUST." Both fly in the face of two of the ten commands. Movies, music, and merchandising portray in the most compelling of terms the desire to satisfy self and the disregard of God's laws.

By contrast, followers of Jesus are clear about sin and righteousness. Without an awareness of God's perfect standard and our own shortcomings, we cannot hope to understand our personal need for God and the depth of His marvelous grace.

Thankfully, He doesn't expect us to be perfect. The Ten Commandments attest to that fact. We must instead turn our attention to the righteous Judge, who sees us as we truly are. He knows our failures. He sees our shortcomings. And—beyond our wildest dreams, beyond our most irrational hopes—He has redeemed us still. "Amazing grace! how sweet the sound."

Think through the commandments. Have you rationalized them or abused God's grace by willfully violating them? In what areas of your life do you need to clarify the standard of righteousness?

PSALM 92

It is good to give thanks to the LORD, to sing praises to the Most High.

It is good to proclaim your unfailing love in the morning,
your faithfulness in the evening,
accompanied by the harp and lute and the harmony of the lyre.
You thrill me, LORD, with all you have done for me!
I sing for joy because of what you have done.
O LORD, what great miracles you do!
And how deep are your thoughts.
Only an ignorant person would not know this!
Only a fool would not understand it.
Although the wicked flourish like weeds,
and evildoers blossom with success,
there is only eternal destruction ahead of them.
But you are exalted in the heavens.
You, O LORD, continue forever.
Your enemies, LORD, will surely perish; all evildoers will be scattered.
But you have made me as strong as a wild bull.
How refreshed I am by your power!
With my own eyes I have seen the downfall of my enemies;
with my own ears I have heard the defeat of my wicked opponents.
But the godly will flourish like palm trees
and grow strong like the cedars of Lebanon.
For they are transplanted into the LORD's own house.
They flourish in the courts of our God.
Even in old age they will still produce fruit;
they will remain vital and green.
They will declare, "The LORD is just!
He is my rock! There is nothing but goodness in him!"

OUR FATHER'S GLORY

They Will Speak of the Glorious Splendor of Your Majesty, and I Will Meditate on Your Wonderful Works.

—Psalm 145:5

*I*n the intriguing French film titled *My Father's Glory*, a husband and wife living in Paris vacation in the countryside with their two boys and the boys' aunt and uncle. It becomes apparent that Marcel, the older boy, deeply admires his dad. He is embarrassed that his uncle dominates and intimidates his father. Early one morning, the two men go hunting. Marcel begs to go with them and, although his father seems to be weakening, his uncle firmly says that this is not something for a boy to be doing. As the men leave, Marcel sneaks off and follows them from a distance.

As the hunters walk through the valley, chatting and looking for quail, he walks along the ridge, hiding behind bushes when he thinks they might see him. Quite by accident, Marcel flushes two royal partridges out of a bush. As they rise, his father spots them and raises his gun, as does his uncle. But Marcel's father is faster, and he fires twice. Both birds come plummeting to the ground at Marcel's feet.

Ecstatic at his father's triumph, forgetting that he is not supposed to be there, Marcel grabs the birds in each hand and stands up, lifting them high, one in each hand. His unrestrained shouts echo through the hills: "He killed them, both of them. He did it!" As the camera zooms away from the boy, the gorgeous beauty of the hills and valley envelops him as he stands, arms lifted high, raising his father's glory to the sky.

It is that kind of pride that marks authentic believers. We cease to be arrogant, insolent, and self-absorbed. No longer consumed with ourselves, we are consumed with the marvel of our Father's works, and our hearts swell with pride that He is our Father and we are His children.

Those of us who are taken with the goodness and glory of our Father lift our voices instinctively in worship and praise without fear. What a joy to brag on God in a world that regularly disdains His presence and power.

When was the last time you "bragged" on God?

"YIELD"

DRAW NEAR TO GOD AND HE WILL DRAW NEAR TO YOU.
—James 4:8 NASB

*O*ne traffic sign important to notice is that upside-down triangle that means it's time to "yield." It is a clear warning that the other lane has the right of way and that refusing to yield may create a problem. Yielding when an eighteen-wheeler is bearing down at 60 mph is a wise thing to do, unless you don't really care much about your car or your health. But, yielding in traffic sometimes means swallowing my pride and letting someone go ahead of me. I am usually in a hurry when I drive, and yielding tends to make me late. But there is little doubt that on a scale of values, yielding holds top priority given the consequences of refusing to yield.

It's important to keep the same dynamics in mind when God requires that we yield to His ways and His will. Refusing to prioritize His wise plans for our lives carries significant downsides . . . like the consequences of sin. Admittedly, it is not always easy to yield. His ways are full of challenging requirements. Forgiving cruel offenses and offenders; saying no to passions that seem so satisfying; transitioning from greed to generosity and from self-centeredness to servanthood often seem like inconvenient and unwanted places to yield. Nevertheless, given the danger of not yielding, yielding is a good and wise thing to do regardless of how tough it may be. But surrendering to God is more than self-preservation.

Yielding my will for the sake of His will is the ultimate statement of how much I love Him. He is not as interested in love that is merely expressed in words, ritual, or habits. He wants us to love Him by choosing His way with our whole hearts. He wants us to prove to Him that He is truly worth more than anything else to us. When I lay the baggage of my selfish and sinful choices at the base of the yield sign and merge with His will and way, He knows that my heart belongs to Him.

Are you stuck at a "yield" sign in your spiritual journey?

THE PRIORITY OF CHARACTER

WE KNOW THAT SUFFERING PRODUCES PERSEVERANCE; PERSEVERANCE, CHARACTER; AND CHARACTER, HOPE.

—Romans 5:3–4

I don't know if you've noticed, but character is increasingly devalued in our culture and eclipsed by credentials and the pragmatic lure of prosperity. It no longer makes much difference how you get there, just so you get your turn at the brass ring of life at its best.

Before Martie and I moved to the city, I sometimes commuted to Moody by train. Joined by masses of other businesspeople on their way into the city, I found it fascinating to watch us try to out-credential each other. Lower management used Bic pens; middle management, Cross pens; upper management, Mont Blancs. The upper management guys rarely wore button-downs, but always stiff, straight white collars. Then there were the guys with the alligator briefcases and the ones with laptop computers. The ultimate stroke of credentialed significance was the commuter with the cellular phone who did business all the way into the train station.

This is a world where it's not what you are as a person that counts but the title you hold, the floor your office is on, and the look of your business card. If you and I were on a panel discussion with preeminently successful people, no one would ever think of asking, "Now, I know that you are successful in your own right, but I'm more concerned about how you got there. Tell me how your integrity, commitment to ethical principles, compassion, and justice helped you succeed. And while you're at it, tell me a little bit about your home life—what kind of a spouse and parent are you?" No one would dream of asking questions about character, because performance and subsequent credentials are more highly regarded than the process by which they were obtained.

But followers of Jesus are not taken in by the hype. Character counts. In fact, it is job number one in terms of His work in our life. It is His plan that our lives reflect the richness of His character regardless of position, prosperity and prestige.

In what ways do you cooperate with the Spirit's priority of character development in your life? How does your life measure up with the list in Galatians 5:22–26?

TRUE WORSHIP

And Every Created Thing ... I Heard Saying, "To Him Who Sits on the Throne ... Be Blessing and Honor and Glory and Dominion Forever and Ever," and the Four Living Creatures Kept Saying, "Amen." And the Elders Fell Down and Worshiped.

—Revelation 5:13–14 NASB

In our language, the word *worship* comes from the root word *worth*. Thus, worship is the ongoing declaration of the worth of God in my life.

A traditional favorite at Christmastime is the classic film *Little Lord Fauntleroy*. When the film opens, his widowed mother in the slums of Boston is raising little Fauntleroy. His father was an English aristocrat who had married an American and was therefore disowned. After he was killed in the war, his widow and young son were left to fend for themselves. However, one day his grandfather who lived in England, realizing that apart from his grandson he has no heir, sets out to find his grandson in America. He finds the boy playing "kick-the-can" in the slums of Boston, and elevates him to the English aristocracy. From slum child to Lord Fauntleroy. Dressed up and paraded through the streets, he is surprised to find both servant and merchant bowing to him and saying, "Good morning, your lordship."

How much more does the Lord Jesus, as He walks through the streets of our lives, deserve our respect? It is right and proper—it is our obligation, in fact—to bow before Him and say, "Good morning, your Worth-ship."

What is God's worth to you? How does He know? Does anybody know? When was the last time you proved His worth by surrendering or sacrificing for Him? Obedience proves His worth, giving proves His worth, serving proves His worth, and living to please Him alone proves His worth.

Worship is our everyday opportunity to demonstrate that there is nothing in our lives that is more valuable or precious then He. Worship is far more than verbal expressions on a Sunday morning. How well we worship throughout the week is the proof of the sincerity of our worship on the weekend.

What have you done to prove His worth to you lately?

COMPARTMENTALIZING RELIGION

See if There Is Any Offensive Way in Me, and Lead Me in the Way Everlasting.

—Psalm 139:24

*S*enate confirmation hearings on Supreme Court nominees often focus on the candidate's view of privacy. This has been a veiled way to ask the candidate about his or her views on the hot topics of abortion and gay rights.

The cascading effect of this is that Americans are increasingly coming to believe that there are areas in their lives into which no one else has the right to intervene. If we permit this attitude to seep into the way we exercise our faith, it will threaten fundamental issues such as surrender, submission, and the lordship of Christ. Privatism leads to lives that are compartmentalized, in which God occupies several unrelated and often isolated segments of our lives but not all segments. It gives us permission to set up other compartments where no one, including God, has the right to enter. Harvard professor Stephen Carter pointed out in *The Culture of Disbelief* that society finds it easy to tolerate "people whose religion consists of nothing but a few private sessions of worship and prayer, but who are too secularized to let their faith influence the rest of their week." He insightfully concludes, "This attitude exerts pressure to treat religion as a hobby."

Privatizing our faith dilutes the work of the Spirit and stymies the process of becoming holy as He is holy. Outwardly, it leads to blatant contradictions and inconsistencies in how we live out our faith. It threatens to write graffiti on the face of Christ through our lives.

David was aware that there should be no private sectors in his life when it came to God's right to enter and morally cleanse his life. He prayed, "Search me, O God, and know my heart; try me and know my anxious thoughts; and see if there be any hurtful way in me, and lead me in the everlasting way" (Psalm 139:23–24 NASB). He held nothing back.

Anything short of inviting our Lord's full involvement in every area of our lives is something less than authentic Christianity.

What private areas do you need to expose to the cleansing work of Jesus?

SATISFIED

I Shall Not Want.

—Psalm 23:1 NASB

*W*hen David wrote, "The Lord is my shepherd, I shall not want" (Psalm 23:1 NASB), He was celebrating the reality that if we have the Lord we have all that we need. He knew what he was talking about. Having spent much of his life as a shepherd, he knew that a good shepherd supplied for every need of the sheep. If the shepherd was there, the sheep had all they needed and nothing to fear.

Contentment is a tough virtue to cultivate in a world that offers so much more than we can ever hope to have. But the peace of true contentment is the companion of those who have become fully satisfied with God. Nowhere is the complete care of our Lord more exquisitely described than in this psalm.

The picture of God's *securing* work is particularly profound. It is reflected in the psalmist's response to facing his enemies in "the valley of the shadow of death." He testifies that God has made him so secure that he can dine in the presence of his enemies and fearlessly walk through the valley of death if that would be necessary. Why? Because God is with him.

The presence of God brings with it all that God is. He blesses us with the fullness of His partnership in our lives. His presence guarantees His protecting power, His sovereign direction, His unsurpassed wisdom, His tender-loving care, and His just involvement in our lives. Embracing by faith the reality of His presence convinces us that He will fully secure us, regardless.

The psalmist concluded with God's *sustaining* work. The reality of His rod (protecting work) and His staff (providing work) sustained the psalmist. The psalmist spoke of God's sustaining work in his life as an overflowing cup, and he marveled that the goodness and loving-kindness of God would follow him every day of his life. The psalmist concluded with a celebration of ultimate provision as he anticipated the day that he would "dwell in the house of the Lord forever."

How has God protected and provided for you? Rejoice!

PSALM 96

Sing a new song to the LORD!
Let the whole earth sing to the LORD!
Sing to the LORD; bless his name.
Each day proclaim the good news that he saves.
Publish his glorious deeds among the nations.
Tell everyone about the amazing things he does.
Great is the LORD! He is most worthy of praise!
He is to be revered above all the gods.
The gods of other nations are merely idols,
but the LORD made the heavens!
Honor and majesty surround him;
strength and beauty are in his sanctuary.
O nations of the world, recognize the LORD;
recognize that the LORD is glorious and strong.
Give to the LORD the glory he deserves!
Bring your offering and come to worship him.
Worship the LORD in all his holy splendor.
Let all the earth tremble before him.
Tell all the nations that the LORD is king.
The world is firmly established and cannot be shaken.
He will judge all peoples fairly.
Let the heavens be glad, and let the earth rejoice!
Let the sea and everything in it shout his praise!
Let the fields and their crops burst forth with joy!
Let the trees of the forest rustle with praise before the LORD!
For the LORD is coming! He is coming to judge the earth.
He will judge the world with righteousness
and all the nations with his truth.

HOW CAN I HELP?

Do Not Use Your Freedom to Indulge the Sinful Nature; Rather, Serve One Another in Love.

—Galatians 5:13

While I was pastoring in Detroit, the specific needs of the growing singles population in our church led most of us to conclude that we needed to hire a singles pastor. As we processed the vision, we ran into some resistance from the long-timers in our congregation, or, as we affectionately called them, "the lifers." According to them, in the late thirties and forties the church was serving fifteen hundred people in Sunday school and yet had only two pastors. "Why," they asked, "do we need so many pastors today?" Their question was insightful and difficult to field.

The reality was that the church was planted in a time when the work ethic was valued in America. In fact, the church was planted in the heart of Detroit, where immigrants from the Old Country brought their sense of the importance of hard work and community with them when they went to the automobile factories. There they planned to meet needs and give of themselves as much as they could. When they came to church, they came the same way, walking in with that "What can I do to help?" attitude.

As you're aware, we now live in a consumer-oriented society where we no longer ask, "What can I do to help?" but, "What will this church do for me?" We are more prone to come to church asking, "Do I like this pastor? Do I like the choir? Do I like the songs we sing? Are these my kind of people?"

When we understand the true nature of calling as servants and His plan for the growth of His church, our question will no longer be, "Will this church meet my needs?" but rather, "How can I use the gifts He has given me to make a contribution to the advance of His cause?" A diversity of pastors may be necessary, because of increasing special needs, but we all would do well to apply the old-fashioned work ethic to our spiritual lives if we hope to see His work prosper.

If you asked, "What can I do to help?" what might you end up doing?

GOD'S PERFECT TIMING

THE FRUIT OF THE SPIRIT IS . . . PATIENCE . . .

—Galatians 5:22

*W*e've all heard the prayer "Lord, make me more patient—and do it now!" If patience is a virtue, most of us have a way to go. Ask moms, those of us who get caught in traffic, teachers, and anyone who serves the public, and they will tell you that being patient is a challenge. And while learning to wait with a good spirit is hard, it's clear that God wants us to grow in this area. After all, patience is a fruit of the Spirit.

There is a good probability that our struggle with patience is unsuccessful because we have been trying to focus on being patient with people. But the issue is not the people who push us to the edge; it is rather our inability to focus on what God is doing when He puts us in His waiting room. God wants us to learn to wait patiently for Him because He is working as we wait. In reality, patience waits for Him.

God waits for the sake of our growth. We grow by crises. When everything is going well, I'm tempted to coast. But let some crisis impact me and immediately I become sensitive to God. When God "grows" us, it often takes pressure, and it always takes time (Romans 5:3–5; James 1:2–4).

God waits for the sake of His glory. God often seems to wait until we have moved into the arena of the impossible. Then He acts so that a watching world will know that He is the true and living God. In this way, we know firsthand the reality of His power on our behalf.

God waits because He works in our fallen world. He works His plans and purposes in our lives, through politics, economics, and the ordinary complexities and inconveniences of life in the midst of Satan's domain. No wonder it's slow going.

One thing we can be sure of . . . God's time is always the right time. Patience is not learning to wait for others; it is learning to wait on God and cooperating with His work in our lives.

When impatience threatens, ask what God is doing and willingly wait for Him to finish His work.

OCTOBER 1 / 287

UNDER NEW MANAGEMENT

THEREFORE, IF ANYONE IS IN CHRIST, HE IS A NEW CREATION; THE OLD HAS GONE, THE NEW HAS COME!

—2 Corinthians 5:17

*I*t's always an unsettling moment when you pull up to one of your favorite haunts only to see a sign plastered in the window that reads, Under New Management. A change in management means that the restaurant may not be the way it used to be. Different waiters, different menus, and a different décor all threaten our sense of familiarity and comfort. Seeing a sign like that rarely causes us to think that it might be a change for the better.

When we came to Jesus knowing that we desperately needed a Savior for the forgiveness of our sins, something dramatic happened. He moved in. We were not just handed a redemptive passport that guaranteed us freedom from hassle at the border of heaven, but we received the gift of the indwelling Spirit, who intends to put our entire life under His control. He simply looks for cooperative partners who fully believe that life under His control is far better than life under the old management.

The new management seeks to transition us from "gratifying the cravings of our sinful nature" (Ephesians 2:3) to craving what pleases and glorifies Christ. This transition, living to please Christ, explains why "new" people

- are faithful to their wives and husbands regardless of temptations or how they are treated;
- remain committed to integrity even when their careers are at risk;
- care for and contribute to the lives of the helpless and oppressed, who can do nothing in return; and
- live in the face of hostile environments with courage and confidence.

When we welcome Him as the new manager of our lives, He turns our desires to flow toward Him instead of ourselves. As this transition takes hold, it is happily a change for the better.

Who is in charge of your life?

WHEN GOD IS SILENT

. . . For He Himself Has Said, "I Will Never Desert You, Nor Will I Ever Forsake You," So that We Confidently Say, "The Lord Is My Helper, I Will Not Be Afraid. What Will Man Do to Me?"
—Hebrews 13:5–6 NASB

*J*t's easy to think we would be faithful if God intervened in our lives the way He did with Abraham. But we forget that the recorded interventions of God into Abraham's life averaged about one every fifteen years. Think about going fifteen years without a Bible, the indwelling Spirit, spiritual friends, or hearing from God. Yet Abraham lived a life of steadfast faithfulness to God.

Think about Joseph. When he was seventeen, God gave him two dreams showing that someday he would stand in great authority and even his brothers would bow to him (Genesis 37:5–7, 9–11). But those were the last dreams he had from God for many years. In the meantime, his jealous brothers sold him as a slave (vv. 14–36). His owner's wife tried day after day to seduce him and eventually falsely accused him of attempted rape (39:1–20). He was sent to jail, where he helped out a man who promised to repay the favor but then forgot about him (39:20; 40:9–23). Still, Joseph stayed faithful to God.

God could have appeared at any time and bailed Joseph out of a problem situation, but He didn't. Instead, He worked behind the scenes, silently arranging the time when Joseph would emerge humbled and refined. The Genesis story reminds us again and again that, though silent, "the LORD was with Joseph" (39:2, 23; see also vv. 3–6, 21). When Joseph was ready to be used by God, God delivered him. Joseph's simple, steadfast faithfulness led to effectiveness in his life (41:39–57).

Think of Job, who was clueless as to what God was doing in his life. I find it interesting that God never explained that the devil was actually behind Job's sufferings (Job 1:1–2:7). But after Job exemplified steadfast faithfulness, God intimately revealed Himself and helped Job resolve the conflict of his soul (Job 38:1–42:6).

We have a great advantage. The written Word of God, the presence of the indwelling Spirit, and the assurance of a better world to come should be more than adequate to keep us faithful, regardless of the twists and turns of life.

Do you still trust Him when He seems silent?

DEAD TO SIN AND ALIVE TO HIM

I Have Been Crucified with Christ and I No Longer Live, but Christ Lives in Me. The Life I Live in the Body, I Live by Faith in the Son of God, Who Loved Me and Gave Himself for Me.
—Galatians 2:20

Most of us are delighted with the reality that Jesus was willing to die for us, taking our sins on Himself that we might be forgiven and set free, forever. We revel in the works of grace that emanate from the finished work of Jesus on that fateful day on Golgotha. We rightly see it all as a free gift that we don't deserve but have received because of His love for us. Yet if this is all we have in our minds when we meditate on the Cross, it is easy to understand why we so quickly fall into sin.

Paul takes us to the necessary next step of realizing that we were "crucified with Christ" (Galatians 2:20) and, as such, need consider ourselves "dead to sin" (Romans 6:2 KJV). As authentic followers of Jesus, we live victorious lives because we have "crucified the sinful nature with its passions and desires" (Galatians 5:24) and are now alive to live in Christ. Every temptation should be the occasion for a crucifixion of that desire on the spot. As we consciously see ourselves hanging on the cross with Christ, we are compelled to see sin for what it really is and be released to live in resurrection power.

You've probably noticed that the trouble with all the daily crucifixions of the flesh is the fact that they tend to resurrect themselves to haunt us again. Crucifying them afresh is only a reminder to the devil that we are alive to Jesus and no longer in his grip.

At the beginning of each day, anticipate where the flesh will be the most alluring, and start each day praying through those ambush locations and crucifying each of them before they are encountered.

All of us should carry a pocket full of nails for those surprise temptations.

A LIFE VERSE

THY WORD IS A LAMP UNTO MY FEET, AND A LIGHT UNTO MY PATH.
—Psalm 119:105 KJV

*P*eriodically someone asks me what my "life verse" is. The trouble with answering that question is that I have had many through the years. Just when a passage becomes meaningful, another strikes my heart, and I have a new "life verse." We all have our favorite Bible verses. They may be verses that were taught to us as children, or handwritten verses stuffed into our wallets or pasted onto our mirrors to help us through a particular season of growth. These verses are gifts from God, pointers on the spiritual compass of our lives at important times.

I'll never forget Revelation 3:20, because that's the verse my dad shared with me when, as a child, I put my faith in Christ. Psalm 100 was another passage I memorized.

But as good as verses tucked away in the corner of our minds may be, what God is looking for most is whether or not our lives reflect the verses we treasure. The psalmist said it best when he wrote that for him the Word was a lamp to his feet and a light to his path. There is not much use to having special sections of Scripture if they don't illuminate, comfort, convict, and direct our lives. A true "life verse" is one that has marked or changed our lives in a significant way, not just a verse that we happen to like.

When my dad signs his name, he always adds Isaiah 58:10–11 below his signature. These verses speak of the blessing on a life that extends itself to the needs of those who are victimized, helpless, and oppressed. My childhood memories are full of seeing Isaiah 58:10–11 in action. Every Christmas afternoon, my dad would walk down the street to visit an elderly widow who had no family. He ministered to alcoholics and often quietly reached out to the downtrodden and poor. After watching his life for more than fifty years, I know that he has every right to claim that verse as his own.

Choose a verse or passage that you can use to transform some action or attitude. Keep it fresh until it has done its work.

OCTOBER 5 / 291

PSALM 100

Shout with joy to the LORD, O earth!
Worship the LORD with gladness.
Come before him, singing with joy.
Acknowledge that the LORD is God!
He made us, and we are his.
We are his people, the sheep of his pasture.
Enter his gates with thanksgiving;
go into his courts with praise.
Give thanks to him and bless his name.
For the LORD is good.
His unfailing love continues forever,
and his faithfulness continues to each generation.

TO GOD BE THE GLORY

HUMBLE YOURSELVES, THEREFORE, UNDER GOD'S MIGHTY HAND, THAT HE
MAY LIFT YOU UP IN DUE TIME.
—1 Peter 5:6

*J*ohann Sebastian Bach, who had a clear view of God's calling in life, lived, worked, and composed for the glory of God. If anyone had a right to gloat in his attainments, it was he. He came from a long line of musicians and achieved praise in his lifetime and lasting acclaim after his death. Yet at the end of every masterpiece, he sketched the letters SDG, which stand for *Soli Deo Gloria,* "To God alone be glory."

Unlike Bach, if we are not careful, we tend to live for our own acclaim and the praise and recognition of others. The net result is that we end up living for our own glory and not for Christ's. This is a serious offense to God, for He shares His glory with no one; and all we have and are able to do is totally because of His gifts and grace in our lives.

We are called to be servants, not superstars. Paul keys in on this principle when he observes that even Jesus came as a servant and served our needs all the way to the cross (Philippians 2:5–11). And when He served well, God exalted Jesus by giving Him "the name that is above every name" (v. 9).

If you are wondering what's in it for you . . . wonder no more. Peter writes that those of us who humble ourselves under the authority of God are, in due time, exalted by God. What we need to keep in mind is that affirmation and exaltation are not what we grab for; they are what God gives us in His time and in His way. For some of us, it may be the ultimate affirmation in eternity, "Well done, thou good and faithful servant" (Matthew 25:21 KJV).

A willingness to be faithful in all things regardless of recognition or acclaim liberates us to live lives that reflect Paul's words "So . . . whatever you do, do it all for the glory of God" (1 Corinthians 10:31).

Do something today intentionally for His glory. In fact, sign off on everything you do with the spirit of SDG.

PAGAN PASTIMES

*T*he list of followers of Jesus who have tragically derailed their lives trying to find satisfaction in our pagan world is long. The early Christians lived in a world full of elaborate and ornate temples where gods and goddesses offered to fulfill every desire. The lasting hallmark of the lives of those Christians testifies to the fact that they were not seduced by such claims and, when necessary, did without for the sake of unflinching loyalty to Christ and the ultimate rewards of eternity.

The seductions in our world are not much different. It is easy to feel that righteousness is a deterrent to wealth when we see others compromise their lives in the temple of gain. Early temples were palaces of pleasure where prostitutes offered themselves to worshipers as an act of loyalty to the goddesses. For us, pleasure palaces abound on the Internet, in the media, and in magazines. That flirtatious affair others find so satisfying easily threatens our loyalty to Jesus. It's easy to feel cheated when for His sake we deny ourselves unrestrained pleasure.

If all you see is the glitter and gain of the world, you might indeed falter in your commitment to Jesus. The allure of this world often veils His surpassing worth and our rewards in Him. Such was Asaph's problem; just read Psalm 73. He admits he almost fell until he looked toward God and regained his perspective. Just in the nick of time, Asaph saw the big picture. "It was oppressive to me till I entered the sanctuary of God; then I understood their final destiny" (vv. 16–17).

Destiny is the key word. Paul writes that when we sow to the flesh we will reap the destruction of the flesh (Galatians 6:8). Sin always has a final destiny, and when it comes, it's not a pretty picture. In the end, our destiny in Jesus will be far different from the destiny of the wicked. The steady follower revels with the psalmist in the satisfying reward of God's in-depth, long-range goodness.

What destiny are you headed for? Are your desires and decisions moving your life toward His rich rewards?

AS FOR ME AND MY HOUSE . . .

"IF THE WORLD HATES YOU, KEEP IN MIND THAT IT HATED ME FIRST."
—John 15:18

You probably are aware that America has turned a dramatic corner. As a culture we are no longer committed to the Judeo-Christian principles that undergirded our law and society from the beginning. Americans have now moved into a neopagan environment where the values that Christians hold to be nonnegotiable are no longer politically correct. In fact, they are culturally unacceptable. Our views on sexuality that promote abstinence until marriage and the importance of heterosexual relationships are often scorned. Our view of the sacredness of life and resistance to abortion as being morally wrong are dramatically out of step. Claiming that there is truth to which we will be held accountable and a clear set of rights and wrongs makes us sound bigoted and intolerant.

In a very real sense, we are becoming more and more of an underclass in our society. Our convictions are at best discounted and at worst mocked by the prevailing philosophies promoted by the media and other significant influences. Our choices are now clearer than ever before. We will either stay the course of righteousness, looking to Jesus as the highest value of our lives, or we will find our hearts silenced and intimidated by the forces of our day. The history of the church is littered with individual Christians and institutions that sought to remain "culturally relevant" and in the process eroded their distinctiveness in Christ.

Maintaining a thoughtful, balanced, and just posture within a pagan culture is a worthy goal, but there comes a time when standing for truth may invite rejection by a culture whose values are dramatically opposed to the values of God's kingdom. Our Lord warned clearly in John 15:18–20 that if this world rejected Him, His followers would suffer the same fate.

Christ needs followers whose hearts are focused on pleasing Him even if it means rejection by friends and associates. This commitment, held in a spirit of compassion and love, is our only hope for becoming lights in the deepening darkness.

In what ways are you intimidated by the changing values of our culture? Are you willing to embrace Christ's values, regardless of the cost?

GOOD NEWS

For I Am Not Ashamed of the Gospel of Christ, for It Is the Power of God to Salvation for Everyone Who Believes.
—Romans 1:16 NKJV

*W*e all know how easy it is to be intimidated by others when we have an opportunity to speak about Jesus. But letting that happen ignores the deep hunger that many have for God and the supernatural power that waits to transform their lives.

Historian Will Durant, who was often contemptuous of or amused by Christianity, wrote in the book *Caesar and Christ* of the power of the gospel in the early centuries of the church and of the powerful spread of its good news.

All in all, no more attractive religion has ever been presented to mankind. It offered itself without restrictions to all individuals, classes, and nations; it was not limited to one people, like Judaism, nor to the free-men of one state, like the official cults of Greece and Rome. By making all men heirs of Christ's victory over death, Christianity announced the basic equality of men, and made transiently trivial all differences of earthly degree. To the miserable, maimed, bereaved, disheartened, and humiliated it brought the new virtue of compassion, and an ennobling dignity; it gave them the inspiring figure, story, and ethic of Christ; it brightened their lives with the hope of the coming Kingdom, and of endless happiness beyond the grave. To even the greatest sinners it promised forgiveness, and their full acceptance into the community of the saved. To minds harassed with the insoluble problems of origin and destiny, evil and suffering, it brought a system of divinely revealed doctrine in which the simplest soul could find mental rest. . . . Into the moral vacuum of a dying paganism, into the coldness of Stoicism and the corruption of Epicureanism, into a world sick of brutality, cruelty, oppression, and sexual chaos, into a pacified empire that seemed no longer to need the masculine virtues of the gods of war, it brought a new morality of brotherhood, kindliness, decency, and peace. So molded to men's wants, the new faith spread with fluid readiness. Nearly every convert, with the ardor of a revolutionary, made himself an office of propaganda.

Is there anyone you know who needs the good news?

PERSPECTIVES ON PAIN

FOR IT IS COMMENDABLE IF A MAN BEARS UP UNDER THE PAIN OF UNJUST
SUFFERING BECAUSE HE IS CONSCIOUS OF GOD.

—1 Peter 2:19

Although it is true that all pain comes through the sovereign permission of God and that He permits nothing that He cannot turn to His glory and our good, the sources of our pain may vary. There are at least four sources of suffering. First, we live in a fallen place among a fallen race. In a sense, "pain happens." Second, some pain is caused directly by Satan. Job's experience is the classic example. Third, pain may come to us because of our own disobedience or carelessness (1 Peter 2:20). Jonah purposely disobeyed, and the trauma of suffering a three-day blackout in a sleazy underwater hotel was the result (Jonah 1:1–3, 12–17). Fourth, and this is important to note, some problems may arise out of our obedience. The disciples obediently took the boat across the lake and met a storm that threatened their lives (Mark 4:35–41).

Understanding that nothing enters our lives that escapes His permission is important. Yet in and of itself, that knowledge is not enough. Without a second certainty, we may be tempted to think that God is cruel, unfair, and insensitive in permitting pain into our lives.

That second certainty is that all that God permits is guaranteed by His nature. God's goodness, power, justice, holiness, total knowledge, accurate timing, consistent presence, certain purpose, unfailing love, and productive empathy are fundamental to His character. And "he cannot deny himself" (2 Timothy 2:13 KJV). This truth has relevance to the problem of pain and the certainty of His permission. Since God cannot violate His nature, all that He permits must be consistent with what He is. This guarantees that God is never destructive, malicious, or wrong in what He permits.

Where is God when it hurts? Right in the midst of it all, working it out, guarding the gate, and restricting the adversary. And in all He permits, He guarantees that there is purpose and that good and glory will soon emerge. All He asks from us is that we cooperate and not resist.

Troubles are inevitable; responding to them well is the issue.

SHARING IN HIS SUFFERINGS

THAT I MAY KNOW HIM, . . . AND THE FELLOWSHIP OF HIS SUFFERINGS.
—Philippians 3:10 NKJV

The transatlantic connection was filled with static, but the sound of a broken heart on the other end of the line was clear. It was Craig's wife, Martha. As she spoke, everything inside me felt crushed.

Craig and I grew up together. After attending the same college, I went off to seminary. Craig married Martha and enlisted in the Air Force.

Our paths merged, as I assumed my first pastorate. Craig taught our high school boys, and she taught the girls. It wasn't long before God led them to work with troubled teens on the island of Haiti. They had been in Haiti only a week, and now Martha was telling me that Craig had suffered a serious injury while diving into a pool. He didn't make it through the night. She was there alone. Younger than thirty—and already a widow.

Questions plagued all of our minds. *Why, God? Why now? Why them?* But God's grace strengthened Martha's heart. As the hurt began to subside, she chose to see the suffering as a shared experience with Jesus. A few months after Craig's death, she wrote,

> Thank You, Lord, for choosing me to view Your pain at Calvary.
> Your tearstained paths of grief You share with me these days because You care.
> Thank You for the time I cried within the garden, by Your side,
> "If it be possible for Thee, please, God, this cup remove from Me."
> Thank You, too, for the burden I bear, for the loneliness, and for the despair,
> For beneath this cross, and on this road I feel, in part, Your heavy load.
> Thank You for the desperate plea, "God, why hast Thou forsaken me?"
> "Because," You answer tenderly, "I have a special plan for thee."
> Thank You for the hope You've given, for the truth that You have risen.
> I, too, from suffering shall rise as I fulfill Your plan so wise.
> Thank You, Lord, for letting me say, "By grace I've suffered in Your way."
> And, may I nevermore depart from this, the center of Your heart.

There is a special solace in meeting Jesus in your pain.

PSALM 103

Praise the LORD, I tell myself; with my whole heart, I will praise his holy name.

Praise the LORD, I tell myself, and never forget the good things he does for me.

He forgives all my sins and heals all my diseases.

He ransoms me from death and surrounds me with love and tender mercies.

He fills my life with good things. My youth is renewed like the eagle's!

The LORD gives righteousness and justice to all who are treated unfairly.

He revealed his character to Moses and his deeds to the people of Israel.

The LORD is merciful and gracious;

he is slow to get angry and full of unfailing love.

He will not constantly accuse us, nor remain angry forever.

He has not punished us for all our sins, nor does he deal with us as we deserve.

For his unfailing love toward those who fear him

is as great as the height of the heavens above the earth.

He has removed our rebellious acts as far away from us as the east is from the west.

The LORD is like a father to his children,

tender and compassionate to those who fear him.

For he understands how weak we are; he knows we are only dust.

Our days on earth are like grass; like wildflowers, we bloom and die.

The wind blows, and we are gone—as though we had never been here.

But the love of the LORD remains forever with those who fear him.

His salvation extends to the children's children

of those who are faithful to his covenant, of those who obey his commandments!

The LORD has made the heavens his throne; from there he rules over everything.

Praise the LORD, you angels of his,

you mighty creatures who carry out his plans, listening for each of his commands.

Yes, praise the LORD, you armies of angels who serve him and do his will!

Praise the LORD, everything he has created, everywhere in his kingdom.

As for me—I, too, will praise the LORD.

MAKING THE EXCELLENT CHOICE

SOLID FOOD IS FOR THE MATURE, WHO BECAUSE OF PRACTICE HAVE THEIR
SENSES TRAINED TO DISCERN GOOD AND EVIL.
—Hebrews 5:14 NASB

*D*ealing with difficulty in constructive ways is not an easy assignment. More challenging yet is learning to deal with life when all is well. It is then that we are most prone to forget that we need God and His direction in our lives. So here are six guidelines from Scripture to keep our journey on compass in good times as well as bad.

1. *Love God.* What would most clearly demonstrate a total, sweet surrender to God (Matthew 22:34–40)?
2. *Be His temple.* What would most accurately reflect the fact that God dwells in me and would best fulfill my responsibility as a priest at the gate, protecting the purity of His dwelling place (1 Corinthians 6:19–20; 1 Peter 2:5)?
3. *Love others.* What would be most constructive in meeting the needs of those around me, even if it involves personal sacrifice (Matthew 22:34–40)?
4. *Build the body.* What would be of greatest benefit to my brothers and sisters in Christ as I seek to value their welfare and to promote love, joy, peace, righteousness, and their edification within the body of Christ (John 13:34–35; Romans 14:10–15; 1 Corinthians 13:4–8; James 2:8–9)?
5. *Make right choices.* What would prove to be the excellent choice as a result of committing my life to true love based on knowledge and insight (Philippians 1:9–11)?
6. *Reach for eternity.* What would be most effective in maximizing my impact on eternity (Matthew 5:3–16, 38–48; 6:25–34; Luke 12:13–40; Colossians 1:9–13)?

As life is run through the grid of these standards, discernment and righteousness will be the result. The answers may not be easy, nor will the demands they make always be convienient, but our lives will be better positioned to glorify God and to be used by Him.

Master the list!

DON'T FORGET THIS PIECE!

WITH THIS IN VIEW, BE ON THE ALERT WITH ALL PERSEVERANCE AND
PETITION FOR ALL THE SAINTS, AND PRAY ON MY BEHALF.

—Ephesians 6:18–19 NASB

*M*ost of us, if we have grown up in "Bible-world," can name the pieces of armor God has provided for our success in the warfare (Ephesians 6:10–20). But for all the times I have heard them listed, I am surprised how often prayer has been excluded from the discussion. Particularly since Paul closes the section on spiritual warfare with a call to use prayer as an offensive weapon by praying for one another.

I can't help but wonder if there wouldn't be fewer casualties if we took that admonition seriously.

My hand froze to the phone as I heard myself say, "Impossible!" I was a young pastor, and this man had been a model to me. Now the news that he had left his family and his flock rang in my ears. Moral failure. *No one is exempt,* I thought. *I'll never be surprised again.*

Life is full of exemptions. Tax exemptions, a bye in the first round of tournament play, a test waived, diplomatic immunity. Knowing the right people, being in the right place at the right time. These are the loopholes of life. But when it comes to sin and its ravaging effects, there are no byes for anyone. All of us face the same spiritual warfare and are in the crosshairs of the "devil's schemes" (Ephesians 6:11).

So, when Paul cataloged our defenses against Satan, praying diligently for one another was an important part. Think of the protective power of combined prayers for one another's integrity, purity, and safety. If we prayed more and criticized less, the grace of God would camp around us in greater defense against the Enemy. I have a friend who prays for me every Thursday. Periodically, someone says to me that he prays for me every day. There have been days when I have dodged the darts and settled in for a good night's rest victoriously because someone was praying.

Share the power!

Choose a leader, friend, or fellow follower to pray for every day for the rest of the month. Let him or her know about it.

LOVING GOD

WE LOVE BECAUSE HE FIRST LOVED US.

—1 John 4:19

When we fall in love, we learn quickly how to express it. Whether it is flowers, little surprises, sweet notes, a wink across a crowded room, a midmorning phone call, a listening ear, or a word of encouragement, nothing is too good or too much.

Love is the most precious thing we give in a relationship. We give it to our friends, our marriage partners, our children, our coworkers, and even our cats and dogs. So it should come as no surprise that love is the central issue in our relationship with God (Matthew 22:34–40).

Loving God starts by understanding the profound truth that God loves us. As God's Word states, "we love because he first loved us" (1 John 4:19). Not only is it true that He is love (1 John 4:8, 16), it is transformingly true that He is busy loving you as you read this. And if you doubt that you are loved by Him, think of the overwhelming proof expressed in Jesus' death for you.

God is the initiator; He simply asks us to reciprocate. He wants our responses to His love to be natural, spontaneous, and free—not forced.

Early in our ministry, our mode of transportation was marginal, to say the least. At the close of one Thanksgiving Eve service, the members of our church, much to our surprise, gave us a set of keys to a new car they had leased for us. I drove away that night with a deep gratefulness toward the flock that had been so sensitive and generous toward us. I had always sought to be faithful in shepherding them, but their love for our family stimulated me to seek new ways to express how much I loved them in return.

We have been and are loved by God in far deeper and more enduring ways than anyone else has ever loved us. When we get a grip on this, our lives will search for ways to love and please Him as a thankful response rather than a grudging responsibility. Acts of loyalty, obedience, sacrifice, and service to others all say, "I love You, God," in clear and compelling ways.

How does He know that you love Him?

BEING IN LOVE

Love the Lord Your God with All Your Heart and with All Your Soul and with All Your Mind.

—Matthew 22:37

J f we aren't careful, we may assume that loving God is measured by how we feel. While there are times when we feel we love Him, more often our relationship with God is measured by faithfulness and obedience in the routines of everyday life. If we wait to feel good about God before we lovingly respond to Him, our Christianity will be sporadic at best. Nothing else of importance in life is dependent on how we feel. We go to work whether we feel like it or not. We make valiant efforts to be good spouses in spite of how we feel. We feed the kids and mow the lawn even when we don't feel like it.

In his book, *The Problem of Pain,* C. S. Lewis wrote of the importance of living beyond feelings in our love relationships here on earth.

Being in love is a good thing, but it is not the best thing. It is a noble feeling, but still a feeling . . . who could bear to live in this excitement for even five years? But, of course, ceasing to "be in love" need not mean ceasing to love. Love in a second sense, love as distinct from being in love is not merely a feeling. It is a deep unity, maintained by the will and deliberately strengthened by habit; reinforced by the grace which both partners ask and receive from God. They can have this love for each other even at those moments when they do not like each other; as you love yourself even when you do not like yourself. . . . "Being in love" first moved you to promise fidelity; this love enables you to keep the promise. It is on this love that the engine of marriage is run; being in love was the explosion that started it.

Thankfully, loving God with the totality of our lives is driven by choice, not feeling. It is "a deep unity maintained by the will . . . strengthened by habit . . . reinforced by . . . grace." Seek His grace to live to love Him, and enjoy the deep resultant unity!

Choose to love Him, and the feelings of love will fill your heart more often.

BRAGGIN' RIGHTS

FINALLY, MY BROTHERS, REJOICE IN THE LORD!
—Philippians 3:1

*P*hilippians 3 was written in response to the Judaizers, people who discounted grace and emphasized the law as a requirement to be fully acceptable to Christ. This heresy had a devastating impact on the Philippian church. It created a caste system between those who conformed to the rites and rituals of the law and were proud of it and those who believed that Christ had fulfilled the requirements of the law at the cross. Those who conformed to the law boasted of their advanced status and looked down on those who did not. Here was pride busy at work in the early church.

Paul warned in Philippians 3:2 against the prideful teaching of the Judaizers. Then he affirmed that authentic followers were those who "worship by the Spirit of God, who glory in Christ Jesus, and who put no confidence in the flesh" (v. 3). His intent was to instruct us to resist the sense of pride that comes when we place our confidence in human accomplishments and instead fix our pride in Jesus Christ as we glory in Him.

Paul then listed his credentials, of which he could have been proud. He was "circumcised on the eighth day, of the people of Israel, of the tribe of Benjamin, a Hebrew of Hebrews; in regard to the law, a Pharisee; as for zeal, persecuting the church; as for legalistic righteousness, faultless" (vv. 5–6). But he refused to allow those things to become a platform for pride and one-upmanship.

Paul counted gaining Jesus and growing to know Him more intimately to be of far greater value than any personal attainment, pedigree, or possession. No longer willing to rejoice in himself, Paul lived to rejoice in Christ. The wonderful possibility is that if all of us who are followers of Jesus focused our pride on Him and made Him our "braggin' rights," we would find blessed release from the competitiveness and the divisiveness of striving for position and celebrating our own accomplishments. Lord, haste the day!

What accomplishments do you need to count as loss in order to rejoice in Christ instead of yourself?

SHRINKING THE DISTANCE

LET US DRAW NEAR TO GOD WITH A SINCERE HEART IN FULL ASSURANCE OF FAITH, HAVING OUR HEARTS SPRINKLED TO CLEANSE US FROM A GUILTY CONSCIENCE.

—Hebrews 10:22

When I was dating, I always enjoyed the sense of anticipation when it came time to pick her up for that special evening together. I'd walk up the sidewalk and press the doorbell—and when she answered, we'd walk down the sidewalk together, and, being the gentleman that I am, I'd open the car door for her. As she slid in, I'd shut the door and hope that she was in the process of sliding over to be as close to me as possible. (Of course, this was back in those no-seat-belt, pre-bucket-seat days.) But instead of sliding over, sometimes she'd be hugging her door. What a blow! I knew something had happened between us, and job number one for me was to fix it.

I find myself wondering if that's how God feels about us. He's courted us, redeemed us, and made us His own. Yet to His disappointment, He discovers that while we are content to ride with Him, there's a significant and increasing distance between us. Someone has well said, "If God seems far away, guess who has moved?" Distance between our heart and His is never His problem. What, then, can we do to shrink the distance?

- Keep short accounts with sin (1 John 1:9).
- Stay in communication with Him through the Word and prayer (Colossians 3:16; 1 Thessalonians 5:16–22).
- Refuse to let bitterness toward Him or others occupy our heart (Ephesians 4:31).
- Live in awareness of His presence, and keep a spirit of gratitude and praise alive and well in our spirit (Colossians 3:15–17).
- Find someone who seems closer to God than we do and learn from them (Galatians 6:2; Philippians 2:1–4).

I always find that keeping company with a friend who is farther down the road than I, stimulates my heart to get closer to Jesus as well.

That old hymn that speaks to the issue. "Nothing between my soul and the Saviour, naught of this world's delusive dream; I have renounced all sinful pleasure, Jesus is mine; there's nothing between."

What should you do today to shrink the distance?

PSALM 107:1–22

Give thanks to the LORD, for he is good! His faithful love endures forever.

Has the LORD redeemed you? Then speak out!

Tell others he has saved you from your enemies.

For he has gathered the exiles from many lands,

from east and west, from north and south.

Some wandered in the desert, lost and homeless.

Hungry and thirsty, they nearly died.

"LORD, help!" they cried in their trouble, and he rescued them from their distress.

He led them straight to safety, to a city where they could live.

Let them praise the LORD for his great love

and for all his wonderful deeds to them.

For he satisfies the thirsty and fills the hungry with good things.

Some sat in darkness and deepest gloom, miserable prisoners in chains.

They rebelled against the words of God, scorning the counsel of the Most High.

That is why he broke them with hard labor;

they fell, and no one helped them rise again.

"LORD, help!" they cried in their trouble, and he saved them from their distress.

He led them from the darkness and deepest gloom; he snapped their chains.

Let them praise the LORD for his great love

and for all his wonderful deeds to them.

For he broke down their prison gates of bronze; he cut apart their bars of iron.

Some were fools in their rebellion; they suffered for their sins.

Their appetites were gone, and death was near.

"LORD, help!" they cried in their trouble, and he saved them from their distress.

He spoke, and they were healed—snatched from the door of death.

Let them praise the LORD for his great love

and for all his wonderful deeds to them.

Let them offer sacrifices of thanksgiving and sing joyfully about his glorious acts.

ENJOY!

BLESSED IS THE MAN WHO DOES NOT WALK IN THE COUNSEL OF THE WICKED.
—Psalm 1:1

*A*s we follow in the footsteps of Jesus, not only do we conform our lives to what He intends for us to do but we find unspoiled joy as well. While it is tempting to be diverted periodically toward the distracting pleasures offered to us along the way, those who stay the course experience the kind of happiness and joy that only God can give. The psalmist declared that God desires to bestow pleasure on His own. Psalm 16:11 says, "You have made known to me the path of life; you will fill me with joy in your presence, with eternal pleasures at your right hand." In Psalm 36:8, David said of God's faithfulness to men, "They feast on the abundance of your house; you give them drink from your river of delights."

The themes of happiness and joy as outgrowths of a faithful, obedient life are underscored in Christ's words to His disciples in John 15:10–11: "If you obey my commands, you will remain in my love, just as I have obeyed my Father's commands and remain in his love. I have told you this so that my joy may be in you and that your joy may be complete."

The pleasure that is a by-product of living to please God is not simply a package of quick thrills. It is, rather, the deep satisfaction that comes to a life that is "straight," or "correct." Not straight in the sense of strict or stoic but clean, without pretense or hypocrisy, and free from the clutter of shame, loss, and regret.

Satan appeals to our pleasure instinct with momentary highs that are fraught with devastating downsides. True pleasure is experienced in the rightness of a life committed to God's glory and gain.

The righteous laugh more heartily, enjoy more fully, and find good times more lasting because their pleasure is ultimately pure and centered in Him.

J. I. Packer writes, "God values pleasure, both His and ours, and it is His pleasure to give us pleasure as a fruit of His saving love"

Have you been looking for pleasure in the wrong places?

OCTOBER 21 / 307

HATE IS HORRIBLE

SEE TO IT THAT NO ONE COMES SHORT OF THE GRACE OF GOD; THAT NO ROOT
OF BITTERNESS SPRINGING UP CAUSES TROUBLE, AND BY IT MANY BE DEFILED.
—Hebrews 12:15 NASB

*I*f we learn anything from the memory of the terrorist attack on New York City and our nation's capital, it is that hate is a horrible thing. None of us will soon forget the horror we felt as we watched people jumping out of the windows of the World Trade Center. Or the heart wrenching pictures of loved ones who wandered the streets of New York for days carrying pictures of a dad, sister, mom, or friend whom they hoped might still be alive. The temperatures of the fires in the Trade towers rose to well over 1000 degrees, as the jet fuel melted the steel of the towers. It became a massive crematorium, a holocaust of a different kind. I'll never forget the gripping story of a little girl wiping ashes off a car into a shoe box because, as she said, her cousin had died in the flames and she thought that maybe these were the ashes of her cousin. The human pain and tragedy is immeasurable. If you went to three funerals a day of those who lost their lives, it would take you nearly six years to attend them all.

It seems beyond comprehension that anyone could be capable of such an evil act. Yet there is an explanation. And it isn't that the terrorists wanted to rule our land or possess our natural resources. Simply put, they hated us. So they struck. Hatred is a horrible thing, and we saw it in all of its ghastly potential on that memorable day.

Any of us who harbor hate in our hearts need to take note. This is a wake-up call. Hate is a terrorist emotion. It deludes our minds, and unless it is dealt with, it does irreparable damage to homes, treasured relationships, businesses, and, most important, our own souls. It is an emotional luxury no one can afford. Now is the time to learn the freedom of forgiveness and the overriding benefit of living to love.

If the terror of hate lurks in your life, declare war until grace and love have been victorious.

THE BAD SIDE OF PRIDE

PRIDE GOES BEFORE DESTRUCTION, A HAUGHTY SPIRIT BEFORE A FALL.
—Proverbs 16:18

*P*ride is why we never say we're sorry. It is why we take the credit for ourselves and belittle others. It drives us to establish our credentials at any cost and claim our rights and privileges even to the detriment of those around us.

If left to itself, pride will dominate every thought, every situation, every relationship, and every conversation. Clearly, it is a major detriment to an intimate and growing relationship with God. In fact, we learn from Proverbs 6:16–17 that pride is first on the list of seven things that are "detestable" to God. Anything that creates such hostility in the heart of God is serious. Peter confirmed God's hostility to the proud when he said that God "opposes the proud" (1 Peter 5:5).

Here's the rub. Pride elevates us as though we are not debtors to God's grace. It is all about us and never about Him. It crowns us as the creator of our lives and acts like we are worthy to be worshiped. It declares us as the god of our lives.

Pride was one of the signature attitudes of the former heavyweight boxing champion, Muhammad Ali, whose athletic success took him to such heights that he was once called the most recognizable athlete in the world. He proudly proclaimed, "I am the greatest," and then set out to prove it. But today, Ali is a middle-aged Parkinson's disease victim, an overweight ex-fighter whose hands shake and whose once-flying feet now shuffle painfully. The most telling thing to me, however, is Ali's appraisal of his scintillating career: "I had the world," he declared recently, "and it wasn't nothin'."

To be properly managed, pride must hear the counsel of the psalmist, who declared, "Know that the Lord Himself is God; it is He who has made us, and not we ourselves; we are His people and the sheep of His pasture" (Psalm 100:3 NASB).

Humility puts God back at the center as the reason for all we are and all we do.

What are the pride points of your life that you can turn over to God and gratefully give Him the credit?

UNWAVERING TRUST

*W*hen trials interrupt our tranquil and well-ordered lives, Satan would love to have us blame God and disconnect from the very source that we need in the midst of trouble. His first and successful strategy in the Garden of Eden was crafted to get Adam and Eve to believe that God was not good and to go it on their own. We all know the rest of that story.

Few moments in history better display the tension between our experience with life and our view of God than the exchange between Job and his wife. Although both had ample reason to see life from Satan's point of view, it was his wife whose heart had been turned against God by their shared tragedy.

Her counsel: "Curse God and die!" (Job 2:9). His perspective: "Though he slay me, yet will I hope in him" (13:15). Job had an intimate connection with God that could not be severed by life's circumstances, regardless of how wrenching they were. The tougher life got, the more Job felt he needed God. As Peter Kreeft pointed out in his book *Three Philosophies of Life,* "Job has everything, even though he has nothing," in contrast to the godless man, who has "nothing even though he has everything."

The psalmist confidently embraced God and testified in the midst of the calamities in his life, "Though an army besiege me, my heart will not fear; though war break out against me, even then will I be confident. . . . For in the day of trouble . . . he will hide me in the shelter of his tabernacle and set me high upon a rock" (Psalm 27:3, 5).

Responding to difficult times in light of these certainties keeps our hearts and minds in touch with God and enables us to resist any wedge the Enemy seeks to drive between our heart and His. Regardless of circumstances, we can place our unwavering trust in God, who deserves our highest allegiance. He cares intensely for us and does all things well.

How does Satan use a crisis to drive a wedge between you and your God?

THE TROUBLE WITH GOOD PEOPLE

... WOE TO YOU, ... HYPOCRITES.

—Matthew 23:13–15

The sobering thing about Christ's terse condemnation of hypocrites is that He was indicting the really good people of His day, people who knew the law in every nuance and kept it precisely. These were the people who, as Christ said, honored Him with their lips though their hearts were far from Him (Matthew 15:7–8).

The trouble with being good is that the better we get the worse we might become. Keeping all the rules, going to all the right places, and saying all the right things has a nasty way of making us feel smug about ourselves. Our Christianity soon becomes more about ourselves than Jesus. And as that happens, pride takes its place on center stage, and anyone who is not "our kind" is looked down on and condemned.

I have been taken with the story in Luke 7, where the town prostitute crashes the party held in the home of Simon the Pharisee, where Jesus is a guest. She falls at His feet to gratefully worship Him for the forgiveness He has extended to her. Simon is aghast. Offended by her presence, he distances himself from both Jesus and the woman. Can it be that we can become so good that we don't even recognize Jesus as He really is and rejoice in His love and mercy for the worst of the lost?

As one author noted, Simon was typical of a whole group of "good" people. Describing Simon, he wrote:

> [Simon is] humorless, prudish, constrained in his affections, incapable of enjoying himself, repressed, inhibited, pouting and censorious.
>
> There are hundreds of people like that today: respectable, conventional, good people. They look down their noses at the permissive society. They curl their lip at the decay in moral standards. They think they're good but they are not; they're simply dull. They think they're being moral, but they are not; they're simply feeling sanctimonious.

What an important warning to those of us who value righteousness and truth. Humility, compassion, love, and righteous tolerance mark true followers. We can never forget that we are debtors to grace who, in the presence of Jesus, know we still have a long way to go.

Pray for the humility to know that you have not yet arrived.

CAN YOU SEE HER?

AND BEHOLD, THERE WAS A WOMAN IN THE CITY WHO WAS A SINNER.
—Luke 7:37 NASB 1977

What a contrast. Jesus loved and forgave the town prostitute. Simon, the good person in town, was repulsed by her presence.

Lisa DePalma, a recent Moody grad, ministers to prostitutes on Chicago's West and North Sides. Always used and never loved, they hear—some of them for the first time—that God has wonderfully loved them in Jesus Christ.

Recently, I sat in a small gathering where Lisa was describing her work with these women. We sat stunned, gripped by the awfulness of her stories of shattered throwaway lives. For most of us, prostitutes are some distant reality, a repulsive part of the dark underside of society. Few of us have ever thought about them, let alone of taking the love of Jesus to them.

My guess is that more often than not we think of prostitutes with Simon's kind of sanctimonious aloofness—the aloofness that often plagues our kind of Christianity.

Lisa wrote these pleading lines:

Can you see her? Will you let God show you?
Her face instead of her clothes? Her eyes instead of her body?
Can you see her? Will you let God show you?
She has a name instead of a label, A broken heart instead of a hard one
Can you see her? Will you let God show you?
The image of God instead of an object of scorn
Her worth to the Savior instead of her worthlessness to the world
Can you see her? Will you let God show you?
His heart of forgiveness instead of your heart that judges
His blood that covers instead of your rules that condemn
Can you see her? Will you let God show you?
And when you do see, what then?

I wish Lisa had been there to whisper these words to Simon as he watched with revulsion the outpouring of the prostitute's love at Jesus' feet. His well-conformed life had shut her out. Christ welcomed her in.

Are there any sinners that you could love in Jesus' name?

PSALM 111

Praise the LORD!
I will thank the LORD with all my heart
as I meet with his godly people.
How amazing are the deeds of the LORD!
All who delight in him should ponder them.
Everything he does reveals his glory and majesty.
His righteousness never fails.
Who can forget the wonders he performs?
How gracious and merciful is our LORD!
He gives food to those who trust him;
he always remembers his covenant.
He has shown his great power to his people
by giving them the lands of other nations.
All he does is just and good,
and all his commandments are trustworthy.
They are forever true,
to be obeyed faithfully and with integrity.
He has paid a full ransom for his people.
He has guaranteed his covenant with them forever.
What a holy, awe-inspiring name he has!
Reverence for the LORD is the foundation of true wisdom.
The rewards of wisdom come to all who obey him.
Praise his name forever!

SETTING UP RESIDENCE

"I AM THE LORD YOUR GOD; CONSECRATE YOURSELVES AND BE HOLY, BECAUSE
I AM HOLY."
>   —Leviticus 11:44

*I*n seminary, I worked as a bellman in a luxury hotel in Dallas. During that time, the vice president of the United States was coming to the city and chose to stay at our hotel. It was no longer business as usual. He reserved an entire floor. Security agents swarmed the hotel to guard him. The whole city knew where he was staying, and it made all of us proud to be working there. I found that I worked a little harder, looked a little sharper, and operated a little more efficiently. My job had an entirely new focus and atmosphere. When we realize that God dwells in us, His residency should prompt us to reevaluate how we manage our lives (1 Corinthians 6:12–20).

God is a holy God—perfect and undefiled. He expresses holiness in everything He does. His holiness demands a similar atmosphere in which to dwell. The fact that He dwells within us needs to stimulate us to behave and respond in a different way from those who don't "temple" God (1 Peter 1:13–16).

The tabernacle of the Old Testament provides the most graphic picture of what God's templing requires of us. All the regulations regarding the use of the tabernacle were instituted to honor the presence of a holy God. The Israelites had to undergo ceremonial cleansings from the defilement of the world in order to come into His presence. There were sacrifices of worship and praise, and there were sacrifices that foreshadowed the sacrifice of Christ. They allowed for forgiveness of sin as the people came to fellowship with their God. The Old Testament tabernacle had priests who were entrusted with serving the Lord and guarding His holiness. All those things were required to make a fit place for God to dwell.

Today we have the privilege of Christ dwelling within us. We don't have to go to a temple—we *are* the temple. And since we are, how much more we should be careful to guard and magnify His holy glory by keeping it fit for His residence.

What difference does it make on a practical level that you are the temple of the holy God?

VAST RICHES IN CHRIST

IF ANYONE LOVES THE WORLD, THE LOVE OF THE FATHER IS NOT IN HIM.
—1 John 2:15

*H*ave you ever dreamed about what you would do if you hit the jackpot on *Who Wants to Be a Millionaire?* Money is magic . . . it promises to make all our dreams come true. Those who believe it is worth pursuing run the risk of more problems than pleasure. Paul wrote, "People who want to get rich fall into . . . many foolish and harmful desires that plunge men into ruin and destruction" (1 Timothy 6:9). How easy it is to cheat at work to get ahead financially, to waste major amounts of money on the lottery, to risk what you do have to "get rich quick." History is full of tragic stories of the devastation that has ruined families, relationships, businesses, and governments just because money had become the god of someone's heart.

Money was obviously the problem in the family of the man who called from the crowd asking Jesus to tell his brother to divide the inheritance with him. Jesus answered, "Take heed and beware of covetousness, for one's life does not consist in the abundance of the things he possesses" (Luke 12:15 NKJV). He then told the story of a rich fool who had everything but God (vv. 16–21). He followed that by telling His followers that they should not be distracted by a concern about material provisions, for "your Father knows that you need them" (v. 30). Instead, they should "seek his kingdom," and all that they needed would be given to them (v. 31).

For authentic followers, money is no longer the major interest of our lives. Needless to say, it is important. Bills must be paid. What is true about the follower is that serving Christ instead of money is the goal of his heart. We are released to do this when we get a firm grip on two truths: we are already rich in Jesus, and He will supply all we need as we turn our hearts to serve the prosperity of the kingdom and eternity (Philippians 4:19).

Do you worry about money? What steps could you take to be content with what you have and turn your heart to serving the kingdom, trusting Him to supply your needs?

ULTIMATE SURRENDER

"TAKE NOW YOUR SON, YOUR ONLY SON, WHOM YOU LOVE . . ."

—Genesis 22:2 NASB

I've always been fascinated by the requirement God made of Abraham when He asked him to sacrifice his son as an act of obedient worship (Genesis 22:1–2). From Abraham's perspective, this was an unreasonably wrenching request. God had already asked Abraham to leave the security of his affluent surroundings to travel to a distant land where He would give him a son. This son was to become the father of a great nation through whom all the earth would be blessed. Isaac embodied the heartbeat of what God had planned for Abraham and the whole reason Abraham had left Ur of the Chaldeans in the first place (Genesis 11:27–31; 12:1–5). And, if that weren't enough, this was the miracle child, born to Sarah after she was too old to conceive (Genesis 21:7). Yet God was now asking Abraham to place this son whom he loved on an altar of sacrifice.

In an unprecedented stroke of unflinching obedience, Abraham agreed. So unshaken was his confidence in God that he believed that God would raise Isaac from the dead if necessary (Hebrews 11:17–19). But as he lifted the knife with trembling hands, God stopped him and provided a substitute sacrifice (Genesis 22:10–14). It was a test. Would Abraham love the gift more than the Giver? Would the center of Abraham's affections be his son or his God? Abraham lived in a Canaanite civilization that practiced child sacrifice as the supreme expression of consecration to gods of wood and stone. Would Abraham be willing to love the true God with the dedication pagans felt toward their gods? He passed the test! He had more confidence in the promises of the provider than in the pleasure of the provision.

There will be times that we face similar tests. These tests will prove how loosely we hold what God has supplied. When God requires a dearly held commodity, will you give it up for Him? Could your money be His? Could your children be sacrificed to the front lines of global evangelism if they were called? Could He have your business? Could He have your heart?

Is there anything that stands between you and unconditional loyalty to God?

CHOOSING GOOD FRUIT

BUT THE FRUIT OF THE SPIRIT IS LOVE, JOY, PEACE, PATIENCE, KINDNESS, GOODNESS, FAITHFULNESS, GENTLENESS AND SELF-CONTROL. AGAINST SUCH THINGS THERE IS NO LAW.

—Galatians 5:22–23

A friend of mine who was struggling with a sin problem said that whenever his particular sin came up in social conversation or was mentioned in a sermon, he felt like a spotlight had been beamed on him, exposing his sin. The sin he refused to conquer held territory in his soul. It's a terrible thing to live with guilt. When we do, our lives become fearful, dishonest, critical, angry, and bitter. But a choice for righteousness protects us from these inevitable liabilities. It keeps fingers from pointing in our direction and blesses us with the joy of a clear conscience.

Choosing to live righteously is not the boring dead-end street we often assume it to be. Quite the opposite. Righteousness produces results in our lives that not only glorify God and bring us personal pleasure but also shower blessings on others as well. Think of the qualities in a life committed to living out the righteousness of Christ. God's Word describes the fruit of righteousness in terms of "love, joy, peace, patience, kindness, goodness, faithfulness, gentleness and self-control" (Galatians 5:22–23). By contrast, choices that emanate from the flesh produce "sexual immorality, impurity and debauchery; idolatry and witchcraft; hatred, discord, jealousy, fits of rage, selfish ambition, dissensions, factions and envy; drunkenness, orgies, and the like" (vv. 19–21).

Take your pick. What kind of life are you looking for?

Choosing fruit has never been one of my better skills. Melons are the toughest. I tap them, smell them, and stare at them, trying to find a good one —usually without much success. I am thankful that bearing the good fruit of righteousness is more predictable and controllable.

Keep short accounts. Righteous living is not about perfection. It's about progress. Say yes to what is right before God, regardless, and enjoy the deep and abiding peace that only a clear conscience can produce.

Cultivate your fruit with a submissive and honest heart, careful Bible study, and intensive prayer, and let God feed His people with the quality of your life.

NEEDING HIM

*"I Counsel You to Buy from Me Gold Refined in the Fire . . . White
Clothes to Wear . . . and Salve to Put on Your Eyes, so You Can See."*
—Revelation 3:18

We always desire what we need. Whether it's sleep, food, or companionship, when we need them we seek them. Perhaps that is why we don't desire Jesus. Having all that we think we need, we don't feel as though we need Him. It is the sin of self-sufficiency, and it robs us of the intimacy with Jesus that our hearts long for. We can't neglect the fact that self-sufficiency is a deep offense to Jesus. In fact, He told the Laodiceans their sin was so revolting it made Him sick.

The Laodiceans thought they had need of nothing because they had everything (Revelation 3:14–22). But, as Christ so graphically told them, though rich, they were really "wretched, pitiful, poor, blind and naked" (v. 17). Christ invited them to abandon their preoccupation with the gifts and turn their hearts to the Giver of their gifts and seek from Him what they really needed. "Gold refined in the fire" refers to character forged by His work in our lives; "white clothes" refers to His righteousness; and "salve" is for the wisdom to see life from His point of view (v. 18). What we really need is what only He can give.

He then called the Laodiceans to repent of their self-sufficiency. He closed the letter with a striking picture. Jesus is standing on the outside of our lives, knocking to come in and have fellowship with us. We are so taken with the noise and clutter of our lives, we barely hear Him knocking until we realize that the gold, garments, and salve He offers are what we desperately need. When we wake up to the fact that we need them, we let Him in and find sweet fellowship as He meets our needs and fondest expectations.

Take a moment to repent of being taken with all that He has given you, and turn your heart to needing what only He can give.

QUALITY CONTROL

But the Fruit of the Spirit Is Love, Joy, Peace, Patience, Kindness, Goodness, Faithfulness, Gentleness and Self-control.
—Galatians 5:22–23

George Sweeting served as the sixth president of Moody Bible Institute for sixteen years. Not only had he been an outstanding leader, but also he looked like the quintessential president. His wavy white hair, soft eyes, and sensitive yet determined countenance made him look like the consummate president. His pulpit mannerisms were impeccable; his representation of Moody, superb. As good as he was in these arenas, those were not the qualities that marked his ministry. I'll never forget one of the broadcasting people at Moody saying to me that in his sixteen years of service at Moody, Dr. Sweeting never gave them any reason to be ashamed. He not only had the look, but he had the character to back it up; and it was the quality of his life that made and marked his ministry.

You don't have to be the leader of an organization to realize that developing and expressing godly character is a high priority. We all are called to manage our own world to the glory of God (1 Corinthians 10:23–31). The worlds of homemaking, child-rearing, career tracking, friend building, and a dozen other enterprises in which we engage throughout life need the qualities of Jesus expressed through our lives. True followers commit themselves to reflect the character of Christ in all that we do, everywhere we go, regardless of the environment we find ourselves in. But we do need to know what we are aiming at. To think that we need to be totally like Jesus could be an overwhelming thought. Where would you ever start?

Galatians 5:22–23 lists the kingdom fashions that adorn pilgrims who are committed to character. Second Peter 1:5–8 also gives us another good target list. He writes that qualities such as moral excellence, knowledge, self-control, perseverance, godliness, brotherly kindness, and love will render our lives useful and fruitful.

Where would you like to start?

Chose one—perhaps two, if you are brave—of the qualities from Galatians 5:22–23 or 2 Peter 1:5–8 you feel you need to grow in. Patiently apply this quality to every situation of life today . . . and tomorrow.

PSALM 112

Praise the LORD!

Happy are those who fear the LORD.

Yes, happy are those who delight in doing what he commands.

Their children will be successful everywhere;

an entire generation of godly people will be blessed.

They themselves will be wealthy,

and their good deeds will never be forgotten.

When darkness overtakes the godly, light will come bursting in.

They are generous, compassionate, and righteous.

All goes well for those who are generous,

who lend freely and conduct their business fairly.

Such people will not be overcome by evil circumstances.

Those who are righteous will be long remembered.

They do not fear bad news;

they confidently trust the LORD to care for them.

They are confident and fearless

and can face their foes triumphantly.

They give generously to those in need.

Their good deeds will never be forgotten.

They will have influence and honor.

The wicked will be infuriated when they see this.

They will grind their teeth in anger;

they will slink away, their hopes thwarted.

GREAT IS THY FAITHFULNESS

THY FAITHFULNESS CONTINUES THROUGHOUT ALL GENERATIONS.
—Psalm 119:90 NASB 1977

*J*im and Carol Cymbala went through a wrenching season of grief in their lives when their daughter turned her back on them and ran away from home. For months, they heard nothing from her. Every attempt to find her and to communicate was rebuffed. You can imagine the fear, anxiety, and despair that shrouded the Cymbalas' hearts. Through their tears and with shattered hearts, they worried, wondered, and prayed, seemingly to no avail.

Where do you go when life hurts that much? Jim and Carol fled to the arms of Jesus and counted on His faithfulness. They knew that when all of earth has forsaken us, God is faithful still. Since He is faithful, He cannot be unfaithful to Himself. His love, mercy, justice, grace are all guaranteed. He cannot deny Himself. And, more wonderful yet, He cannot be unfaithful to us. His grace in the time of need never fails. His promises are secure, and His wise plans are unfailing.

Because of this, Carol sat down one day and penned these words that since have become bulwarks of strength for thousands of hurting hearts who have heard the Brooklyn Tabernacle Choir sing these words all over the world.

> In my moment of fear,
> Through every pain, every tear,
> There's a God Who's been faithful to me. . . .
> When my strength was all gone,
> When my heart had no song,
> Still in love He's proved faithful to me.
> Every word He's promised is true;
> What I thought was impossible, I see my God do.
> *Chorus:*
> He's been faithful, faithful to me.
> Looking back His loving mercy I see
> Though in my heart I have questioned,
> Even failed to believe,
> Yet He's been faithful, faithful to me.

As the hymn "Great Is Thy Faithfulness" assures, God's faithfulness provides "strength for today and bright hope for tomorrow."

Count on Him . . . He never fails.

SURRENDER

THAT I MAY KNOW HIM . . . BEING CONFORMED TO HIS DEATH.
—Philippians 3:10 NASB

*I*n Gethsemane, Jesus knelt in agony at the rock praying that the prospect of the cross could be lifted from Him. It is not surprising that Jesus in His humanity shrank from the horror—but in the end, broken and weary, through lips parched with anxiety, with a voice heavy with the weight of the cross to come, he uttered these words that now ring through history with a strength of unparalleled resolve, "Not My will, but Yours be done!"

This is the 'image of His death', and being conformed to the image of His death means *full surrender* to our Father's will . . . regardless. No excuses. No escape clauses. No negotiation. And not only is it surrender for the moment, it is about *persevering* in the resolve until we have fully obeyed. As Jesus rose from the rock exhausted, the torch lit lynch mob was approaching.

But Jesus would not be deterred.

When Peter unsheathed his sword and slashed the side of the soldiers face leaving his ear on the ground, Jesus had the perfect excuse to escalate the conflict. It's one thing to surrender. It's quite another to persevere when opportunities to justifiably slide out of our resolve present themselves.

Through all of those horrible hours to follow, when Jesus was dragged through the halls of the kangaroo courts, He refused to return their accusations and slander. Years later Peter would pen, "Christ also suffered for you, leaving an example that you should follow in His steps" (1 Peter 2:23).

Regardless of what He requires, those of us who want to draw close to Him meet Him at that sweat stained rock in the garden brokenly repeating His words after Him: "Not My will but Yours be done." It is a resolve that covers the whole waterfront of our existence. Nothing is exempt. Relationships, real estate, financial resources, spouses, children, grandchildren, desires, dreams, plans, attitudes, and actions all are included. It demands no flirting around the edges of sensuality. It requires the expulsion of jealousy, residual anger, and the bitterness that tears at our relationships.

Gethsemane asks for it all.

Is there anything in your life that is unsurrendered to the will of the Father?

EMOTIONAL BAGGAGE

CONSIDER IT PURE JOY, MY BROTHERS, WHENEVER YOU FACE TRIALS OF
MANY KINDS.

—James 1:2

*I*t is God's command to *consider every trial to be a thing of joy.* Initially, that seems unreasonable because trials do not feel joyous. If we are to respond constructively, we must understand that the text does not tell us to "*feel* it a thing of joy." For that we can be thankful, since it is impossible for us to manipulate our emotions. Emotions are a result of circumstances, body chemistry, how we have slept, what we have dreamed, or even what we may have eaten the night before. None of us have a joy button that we can press to make us feel wonderful. Although we are usually able to keep our emotions in check, it is impossible to change them dramatically.

Emotions are the baggage that comes with our difficulty. The emotions that swirl in our hearts are legitimate and normal. We should not feel guilty about feeling down. Even Jesus wept (John 11:35).

What we must do, however, is refuse to permit how we feel to dictate how we respond. If you have traveled through the mountains, you may have seen ramps for runaway trucks. They are for drivers who have lost their brakes and are careening dangerously down the road, out of control. At that point, trucks are driven by the weight of their baggage. It's disaster waiting to happen. Letting our emotions dictate our actions is like letting the baggage do the driving.

This is exactly why James says to count it a "joy" thing "because you know . . ." (James 1:3). We can reckon trials as a source of joy when we *know* that God is working in it for our good, that trials will refine us, that they will be used to accomplish good results that would not happen otherwise.

Responding to trouble based on what we know to be true is the only way to keep life on the road toward God's productive purposes. When we do this we can count any difficulty to ultimately be a thing of joy.

What are the emotions that tend to drive your attitudes and decisions in times of trouble? Counter them with what you know to be true.

THE CHILDREN'S NEW CLOTHES

HONOR AND GLORY FOR EVER AND EVER. AMEN.
—1 Timothy 1:17

H onoring God is an important part of living out His glory in our lives. He clearly deserves it. It's just that often we aren't quite sure how to extend it. Or, worse yet, we would rather live to honor ourselves.

One night, Martie and the children came home from the mall bearing new clothes for the summer. A style show ensued, and excitement ran high. I began to feel good about how I had earned the money to provide for my family. *I'm a pretty good dad!* crossed my mind as I wondered if anyone in the room who was sporting the new clothes would recognize it! While I was patting myself on the back, the Lord reminded me that all I was able to provide was really because of His gracious provision in my life. Suddenly I felt small for basking in the honor that was His. As I tucked the kids into bed, I asked them if they knew where their new clothes had come from. My youngest said, "God gave you the job that gave us the money to buy our clothes." Good answer! God got the credit He deserved (1 Timothy 1:12–17).

Honoring Him is giving Him the credit for what He does in and through our lives. God takes it seriously when we take credit for His glory. Moses was denied entrance to the Promised Land because he claimed that he and Aaron would provide water from a rock. In reality, the water was God's provision (Numbers 20:1–12). Nebuchadnezzar was banished to the field to roam as a wild beast because he claimed the glory for his kingdom (Daniel 4:30–37). Herod was struck dead for accepting praise as a god (Acts 12:21–23).

President Reagan kept a sign on his desk that read, "There is no limit to what a man can do if he doesn't care who gets the credit." Biblically, there is no limit to what God can do through us if we are willing to give Him the credit. Which is exactly what it means to honor Him.

Look for God's hand in your achievements. Let your world know!

THE WARFARE

"NEITHER DO MEN POUR NEW WINE INTO OLD WINESKINS. IF THEY DO, THE SKINS WILL BURST, THE WINE WILL RUN OUT AND THE WINESKINS WILL BE RUINED. NO, THEY POUR NEW WINE INTO NEW WINESKINS, AND BOTH ARE PRESERVED."

—Matthew 9:17

*C*hrist used the metaphor of new wineskins to call us to live out our newness in Him in the freshness of His teachings rather than in the old traditions of our past. He said these things in response to one of John the Baptist's disciples, who asked Him why His disciples did not fast like they did. Christ said that a new order had come and that trying to live by the old ways in this new world order would create major problems.

My generation saw an unforgettable example of this principle at work as we watched former prisoners of war return from Vietnam in the early 1970s. I'll never forget seeing these men step off planes—some crippled, and all with weary, drawn faces, but still smiling as they received the salutes of their comrades. Several of these men stooped to kiss American soil. Then came the happiest moment of all: the rush of waiting family members to embrace each prisoner and welcome him home.

Heroic stories emerged of men who held fast to their loyalty in the face of incredible suffering and pain. These men had fought in an alien, hostile environment that called for a whole new way of thinking, acting and responding. To succeed in the battle they couldn't live like they did at home.

We too are in a war. Living as though we are in a comfortable, unthreatening environment is a sure prescription for spiritual failure. We need to pour our lives into the new wineskin of all that He has taught us, not just about the joys but about the inevitable dangers of following Him and the crosses we may have to bear (1 Peter 4:12–19). Always bearing in mind the day when we will arrive "home" and kiss the ground of heaven, hoping to hear, "Well done, thou good and faithful servant"(Matthew 25:21 KJV).

Read Ephesians 6:10–20. What pieces of the armor need to be put on in your life?

HEADY STUFF

I Am Astonished that You Are So Quickly Deserting the One Who Called You.

—Galatians 1:6

*T*here is a wonderful prayer that begins, "Christ be in my head . . ." The first time I heard it I thought it sounded too cute for good doctrine. But after reflecting on it I was convinced that it is a prayer we should say on a regular basis. When we think of good "religion," we often think of our heart, emotions, and experience. Heady, intellectual religion seems suspect, dull, and proud. So we tend to want to check our brains at the door and hope that Jesus goes straight for the heart.

But that has always proved dangerous. Early Christians were endangered by false teachers who filled their heads with misinformation. They taught that salvation and subsequent spiritual growth could be attained only through keeping all the requirements of the law. When Paul heard of this, he remarked, "I am astonished that you are so quickly deserting the one who called you" (Galatians 1:6). The Galatians were off track because they thought incorrectly about what it means to live a life pleasing to Christ through love and not the law.

And it's not just false teachers. The world around us is full of attractive thoughts that are in the end devastating. It really isn't good to do whatever you want to do. Nor is it good to think that sin and evil should be tolerated in the name of cultural propriety. Nor is success measured in wealth and status. Since we live by our definitions, we'd better have them straight (2 Corinthians 10:1–5).

Christianity begins in our heads. In fact, the very first item on the list for fully surrendered followers in Romans 12 is the transformation that comes from the renewing of our minds (v. 2). It's vitally important to check every thought, not by how it feels or if it has heart, but rather by asking, Is it true?

Memorize God's Word, think His thoughts, give the Holy Spirit control of all that happens in your mind, and then let your heart and emotions feel Him in the fullness of His power.

Check every thought today by the standard of what you know to be true. Make it a habit!

PSALM 115

Not to us, O LORD, but to you goes all the glory
for your unfailing love and faithfulness.
Why let the nations say, "Where is their God?"
For our God is in the heavens, and he does as he wishes.
Their idols are merely things of silver and gold, shaped by human hands.
They cannot talk, though they have mouths, or see, though they have eyes!
They cannot hear with their ears, or smell with their noses,
or feel with their hands, or walk with their feet,
or utter sounds with their throats!
And those who make them are just like them, as are all who trust in them.
O Israel, trust the LORD! He is your helper; he is your shield.
O priests of Aaron, trust the LORD! He is your helper; he is your shield.
All you who fear the LORD, trust the LORD!
He is your helper; he is your shield.
The LORD remembers us, and he will surely bless us.
He will bless the people of Israel and the family of Aaron, the priests.
He will bless those who fear the LORD, both great and small.
May the LORD richly bless both you and your children.
May you be blessed by the LORD, who made heaven and earth.
The heavens belong to the LORD, but he has given the earth to all humanity.
The dead cannot sing praises to the LORD,
for they have gone into the silence of the grave.
But we can praise the LORD both now and forever!
Praise the LORD!

THE STRENGTH OF MEEKNESS

WHILE BEING REVILED, HE DID NOT REVILE IN RETURN . . . BUT KEPT
ENTRUSTING HIMSELF TO HIM WHO JUDGES RIGHTEOUSLY.
—1 Peter 2:23 NASB

Meekness is the ability to be offended, give the offense and the offender back to God, and then love the offender in return. If you feel that meekness is weakness, think again. It's much easier and seemingly more gratifying to go after our enemies. But followers of Jesus stay in the power of the meekness He so clearly modeled for us. When confronted by lies, distortions, and temptations, He trusted His Father to ultimately vindicate His life and ministry. When the temple guard and the elders came to arrest Him, Jesus submitted readily, even though He had the power to call more than a dozen legions of angels to aid Him (Matthew 26:50–53). Even as Peter drew a sword to defend Jesus, Christ yielded to His Father's will because He trusted His Father's ability to see Him through to the "joy set before Him" (Hebrews 12:2).

Before an amazed Pilate, Jesus remained silent, refusing to argue with His accusers (Mark 15:3–5). The charges were trumped-up lies by false witnesses, but Jesus trusted God to ultimately defend His reputation (Philippians 2:9–11). He humbly trusted God the Father to do what was best, which freed Him to walk the road to Calvary, the road that led to death—but also to resurrection power. Peter reminds us, He did this "leaving [us] an example, that [we] should follow in his steps" (1 Peter 2:21).

Meekness sees even our worst enemies as tools in the hand of God to accomplish His will in our lives. Meekness releases us to say, with Jesus, "Father, forgive them; for they know not what they do" (Luke 23:34 KJV). Trusting God to work "all things . . . together for good" gives us release from the nagging defeat of anger and bitterness (Romans 8:28 KJV). Trusting Him to do justice toward those who have treated us unjustly releases us from acts of revenge and enables us to humbly love and serve even our enemies.

Troubled by an offense and struggling with God's command to forgive and love? Trust God to care for your enemy and in meekness cover the situation with His grace.

NEVER ALONE

—John 14:1

*W*e have all had times when we feel alone and are troubled by the fact that no one really understands our fears and struggles. In these times, it is important to focus on the fact that God has provided meaningful sources of comfort. His resources are available to all who tap in to the companionship and counsel He provides.

His Word. I find it particularly helpful to read the Psalms when my spirits are low. The psalmist is often despairing but consistently finds hope in his God. Survey several psalms, and go deep in the ones that minister to your heart, especially Psalms 13, 27, and 42. The many praise psalms offer weary hearts something to be thankful for. A good dose of gratitude always helps!

Prayer. As my Pentecostal friends often say, sometimes we need to "pray through," staying on our knees until Jesus breaks through and we are given the comfort, wisdom, and peace He promises. Pray psalms back to God, and spend seasons of silent prayer where you wait for Him to dawn upon your spirit until you are ready to face another day . . . but not alone.

His Spirit. His Spirit dwells in you for the express purpose of bringing comfort and illuminating the Word of God. He prays on our behalf and understands our infirmities better than we do (Hebrews 4:15). Cultivating a sensitivity to His inner promptings and counsel, based on God's Word, brings the comfort He promised.

His people. When Jesus left His disciples, He commanded them to love each other as He had loved them (John 15:12). Find a fellow cross-bearer. Even if they don't fully understand your troubles, their listening ear and prayer support will bring comfort.

Heaven. As Jesus told His despairing followers, "Let not your heart be troubled. . . . I go to prepare a place for you" (John 14:1–2 KJV). Many of our problems are simply the outcomes of living among a fallen race in a fallen place. But, thanks to Jesus, the best is yet to come. Hearts fixed on heaven are hearts looking forward to home. No matter how bad it gets here, it's not forever . . . that's what heaven is!

Meditate, memorize, and believe what He has promised. Claim something for your own soul.

TOUGH TIMES

CONSIDER IT ALL JOY.

—James 1:2 NASB

rouble is so indiscriminate. Good people suffer. Bad people prosper. Children are victimized by crack addict parents, and old people end up being neglected and marginalized. We have a wonderful neighbor who is in her eighties. She is admittedly crusty and makes a life out of being just a touch out of sorts about most things. It's her "gig," and we love her for it. She claims that her gin every day and the cigarettes she consumes keep her fresh. Her sister, on the other hand, was as proper as they come. She didn't drink or smoke. She exercised faithfully at the local pool and complained about nothing. Last winter, while swimming, she was taken ill and lay in a coma in the hospital for days until she finally died. Our neighbor was stunned. All she could say in the days following her sister's death was, "I don't understand it. It should have been me. My sister was such a good person."

So it's time to get real. You're not exempt—none of us are—and you can count on it, lurking just around the corner is some kind of trouble waiting for your arrival.

Thankfully, for those of us who seek the face of God in the midst of trouble, we discover that He is not surprised by arrival of our pain and is ready to protect us against our destructive instincts by showing us a better way. We have the advantage of discovering that our loving Father uses trouble to refine and shape our lives into the likeness of His Son. As in surgery, some things simply can't be removed or changed without a fair amount of well-intended pain. So our biblically tutored instincts tell us that we no longer need to resist trouble as an enemy but rather welcome it as a friend and even count it to be a source of joy. Not the pain; we'll never feel good about that. But joy in the prospect of the development of our character and the refinement of our faith. No more pity parties!

As Paul wrote, "We are afflicted in every way, but not crushed; perplexed but not despairing; . . . struck down, but not destroyed" (2 Corinthians 4:8–9 NASB 1977).

THE PROBLEM WITH PLEASURE

He Chose to Be Mistreated Along with the People of God Rather than to Enjoy the Pleasures of Sin for a Short Time.
—Hebrews 11:25

*E*very schoolchild knows that the Declaration of Independence grants us "the pursuit of happiness" as an inalienable right. Yet pleasure, in God's terms, is not a pursuit but rather the reward He gives for obeying and pleasing Him. Keeping that distinction is vitally important in a society that glorifies the pursuit of pleasure over anything else.

The Greek word for *pleasure* is the root of the word we translate as *hedonism*. Hedonism's theme is "I'll do whatever makes me happy." When hedonism becomes a compelling drive, we are immediately vulnerable to a horde of seductions. From the allure of an affair to the lure of more things—or any other pleasure offered us—there are many forbidden fruits the adversary offers. Hedonists have been around forever, but it was in my generation that Hugh Hefner codified hedonism into the "Playboy Philosophy." Hefner's basic premise: "We reject any philosophy which holds that a man must deny himself for others."

Granted, pleasure is fulfilling and often satisfying. In fact, God has intended many things to bring us pleasure. But when pleasure is pursued by betraying obedience to God, it ultimately brings sorrow. Moses recognized this, so he chose to suffer affliction with the people of God "rather than to enjoy the pleasures of sin for a short time" (Hebrews 11:25).

Let's face it. Sin would have no appeal if there were no pleasure offered as bait. How boring it would be to cheat in business if not for the pleasure of pounding your competitor one more time or watching your bank account grow. If there were no pleasure in sin, it would be seen as the dragon it is, and there would be fewer takers. But sin *is* pleasurable—for a short time. When the pleasure expires—and it always does—we are left with the sorrow, shame, and loss that sin brings. This may be part of what Proverbs 21:17 means when it warns, "He who loves pleasure will become poor."

In what ways does the pursuit of pleasure distort your life?

TRUE SIGNIFICANCE

He Is Before All Things, and by Him All Things Consist.
—Colossians 1:17

*I*f we all were honest, we would have to admit that living for Jesus' significance and not our own is an ongoing challenge. But a worthy challenge nonetheless. Particularly when we remember that living for our own significance inevitably eclipses His, and upstaging Jesus is not a compelling thought. When Paul lists Christ's unparalleled credentials in Colossians 1, he concludes that Jesus has the right to the preeminence in all things. If that is your goal, remember that you can't have it both ways—life cannot be about Him and about me at the same time.

Refusing to use our lives to celebrate His significance leaves us vulnerable to a host of sins. Hearts that are hungry for significance will be easily seduced. A lie that elevates us, a slanderous word that puts another person down, an affair that makes us finally feel significant to someone, or a bragging attitude that continually features "us" in conversations are all the ready companions of self-launching egos. Living to beat out competitors and having the best possessions to prove our importance will lure us to violate honesty and good stewardship.

But followers who are committed to His significance escape the jaws of this kind of defeat. When life is about Jesus, nothing is more important than following and pleasing Him. We will gladly promote His significance by giving Him the credit for all that we are and have. As a child of God, we are fully vested with an irrevocable inheritance, a temple where God dwells, and have insider information when it comes to truth that the world is clueless about concerning life, happiness, peace, and eternity. It doesn't get more significant than that. For us, significance is no longer a search; it has been secured for us by His loving grace.

Since significance is secured for you in Jesus, what can you do to magnify His significance in your life?

DEVOTION TO CHRIST

BUT I AM AFRAID THAT JUST AS EVE WAS DECEIVED BY THE SERPENT'S
CUNNING, YOUR MINDS MAY . . . BE LED ASTRAY FROM YOUR . . . DEVOTION
TO CHRIST.

—2 Corinthians 11:3

*Y*ou've probably noticed that Christianity subtly, yet surely, slips from relationship to ritual, from passion to project, from devotion to duty, running the risk of a faith that becomes burdensome and boring. If that is where you are, it's not Jesus' fault. He has done all that is necessary and more to fill your walk with the joy of a fulfilling relationship with Him.

In Revelation 2:4 Jesus speaks of wanting our "first love" (see also John 21:15–17). The word *first* in this text refers to priority. It is a love that motivates and drives all that we do. We have been loved with the deepest love possible. After all, who would go to the cross for offensive sinners if it weren't the purest kind of love? And being loved with such amazing love, the only response our heart can have is, "How can I love You in return?"

Jesus knows we love Him when we serve others, give of our resources to advance His cause, exercise our spiritual gifts in service to the church, love our wives and cooperate with our husbands, say no to temptation, help the poor and oppressed, hate sin, and reject prejudice. Christ-lovers do all this and more for Him and Him alone.

When our children were babies, they brought additional duties into our lives—like changing diapers. Why did I do diaper duty? Because that's what fathers do? Because the child would stop crying if I did? Those reasons may have been part of it, but the greatest joy in duty came when I did it because I cared about my wife, Martie, and wanted to express my love for her. Devotion always adds delight to duty!

What a liberating truth! With Christ at the core of our lives, we can parent, teach, serve, help, play—everything to express our love for Him (2 Corinthians 5:14–21).

Plan to do one thing today to express your love for Him. Be intentional. How about two?

PSALM 116

I love the LORD because he hears and answers my prayers.
Because he bends down and listens, I will pray as long as I have breath!
Death had its hands around my throat; the terrors of the grave overtook me.
I saw only trouble and sorrow.
Then I called on the name of the LORD: "Please, LORD, save me!"
How kind the LORD is! How good he is! So merciful, this God of ours!
The LORD protects those of childlike faith;
I was facing death, and then he saved me.
Now I can rest again, for the LORD has been so good to me.
He has saved me from death,
my eyes from tears, my feet from stumbling.
And so I walk in the LORD's presence as I live here on earth!
I believed in you, so I prayed, "I am deeply troubled, LORD."
In my anxiety I cried out to you, "These people are all liars!"
What can I offer the LORD for all he has done for me?
I will lift up a cup symbolizing his salvation;
I will praise the LORD's name for saving me.
I will keep my promises to the LORD in the presence of all his people.
The LORD's loved ones are precious to him; it grieves him when they die.
O LORD, I am your servant; yes, I am your servant, the son of your handmaid,
and you have freed me from my bonds!
I will offer you a sacrifice of thanksgiving and call on the name of the LORD.
I will keep my promises to the LORD in the presence of all his people,
in the house of the LORD, in the heart of Jerusalem.
Praise the LORD!

CLOSET CHRISTIANS

"Be Careful Not to Do Your 'Acts of Righteousness' Before Men, to Be Seen by Them. If You Do, You Will Have No Reward from Your Father in Heaven."

—Matthew 6:1

*I*nteresting, isn't it, that what can be used for good can be dangerous as well? It is unsettling to note that Christ's label for people who gave, prayed, and fasted in order to be noticed and publicly affirmed was *hypocrite*. A hypocrite is someone whose life contradicts the essence of what he says he believes. When we say we are serving God, yet our intent is to serve ourselves, we qualify for the dubious distinction. More troubling still is that doing God's work for our advantage robs God of the glory due to Him. And, as Christ taught, the result of serving ourselves while appearing to serve heaven is that we lose our eternal reward, since we have already rewarded ourselves here on earth. The advantage of giving, praying, and fasting in secret is that it tests our true intentions. Practicing spiritual disciplines behind closed doors proves the sincerity of our worship.

Prayer done in secret tests the true intent of our prayers. The praise of others is a nonissue. It is important to note that when Christ taught His disciples to pray, the first half of the prayer focused not on our needs but on the needs of the kingdom and the Father's glory (Matthew 6:9–13). Our needs and interests are addressed secondarily. Note too that the closing focus of the Lord's Prayer affirms that the glory is always His (Matthew 6:13 NKJV).

And, Christ adds, when we fast, we are not to advertise how spiritual we are by our gaunt and frail appearance (Matthew 6:16–18). Because fasting is a personal thing between our Father and ourselves, we are to do it in secret, disguising the fact from public notice. Only God needs to know. Subjects of the kingdom value the intimate relationship they have with their King and practice piety for His glory and not their own.

It is not always easy to discern motives, but practicing our faith privately is a great way to verify authenticity.

Do you practice more of your faith in public than you do in private?

SHARE THE WEALTH

Do Good . . . Be Rich in Good Deeds . . . Be Generous and Willing to Share.
                                        —1 Timothy 6:18

*I*f you had a choice between contentment, character, and cash (lots of it!), what would you choose? Think carefully. Be honest. Or, to ask it another way, if you could have all three, in what order would they come? If cash rules, then character and contentment will be seriously damaged under its reign. But if character and contentment rule, we are willing to give, are not overly concerned when we lose, and are never interested in cheating on God's standards in our lives for gain. It will be obvious that character and contentment rule when we transition from greed to generosity.

God has blessed many of His people with significant amounts of wealth. The world has one basic message for people like this: Be proud! Guard what you have, grow it, spend it. But God's principle is to "store up for yourselves treasures in heaven" (Matthew 6:20).

One of the ways we can do this is to change our view of riches. In God's economy, true riches are not measured in terms of cash. Riches are what we have in Him, what we do for eternity, and the good works we do on earth. Paul knew how important it was for those of us who have been given much to keep our perspectives straight. So he exhorted those who are "rich in this present world" not to become spiritually dysfunctional by becoming conceited, trusting in the uncertainty of riches and hoarding what we have. Instead, we are to be "rich in good deeds," generous, and looking for ways we can share (1 Timothy 6:17–18).

If your spiritual goal is contentment and character, then it will show in how much you are committed to contribution. God's way is for us to place our trust in Him, who "richly provides us with everything for our enjoyment" and then look for ways "to be generous and willing to share" what He has given us with His cause and those in need (1 Timothy 6:17–18).

What a purifying delight it is to use our riches to bless and benefit others!

Measure your management of wealth by the standards of 1 Timothy 6:17–19. Make adjustments where necessary.

DO RIGHT . . . REGARDLESS

AS OBEDIENT CHILDREN . . . BE HOLY ALSO YOURSELVES IN ALL YOUR BEHAVIOR.
—1 Peter 1:14–15 NASB

*H*ave you ever been tempted to do something wrong, thinking that it really is all right since the results will be good? Like playing the lottery and telling God that you will give Him half if you win big. Or like cheating someone because he has cheated you and he needs to learn a lesson. Or perhaps it's just a matter of telling one of those "little white lies" to help someone feel better. While the outcomes may seem worthy, we need to know that God is not impressed. He values who we are far more than what we do, and when we erode our integrity He is concerned, regardless of the outcomes.

I recall as a boy wanting to go to camp with my friends but having to recite Psalm 100 by heart in order to qualify. The deadline approached, and I hadn't committed it to memory yet, so I called my teacher on the phone, told him I was ready to recite the psalm, and proceeded to read the passage impeccably. At the end, he complimented me on a job well done but then said, "It sounded like you were reading it. Were you?" I was so embarrassed and have never forgotten the poignant lesson that it is important to do the right things in the right way.

God commanded Moses to speak to the rock, but instead he struck it in anger and suffered the consequence (Numbers 20:2–12). Saul sacrificed to God, yet did it in the wrong spirit and in violation of the prophet's instruction. Samuel's response was classic, "To obey is better than sacrifice" (1 Samuel 15:22; see also Proverbs 21:3; Mark 12:32–33).

If we do what is right in wrong ways, we teach our hearts to value performance over character. And we deceive ourselves into thinking that our good works validate our standing before God when actually nothing could be further from the truth. It is important to remember that while "man looks at the outward appearance . . . the LORD looks at the heart" (1 Samuel 16:7).

Commit yourself to doing all you do under the guidance of the values of truth, integrity, justice, fairness, love, and purity. Don't ever fudge, regardless of how compelling the outcomes appear to be.

ALL FOR JESUS

According to My Earnest Expectation and Hope . . . that with All Boldness, Christ Will Even Now, as Always, Be Exalted in My Body, Whether by Life or by Death.

—Philippians 1:20 NASB

*S*cripture makes clear that our rescue from sin, death, and hell was about far more than our own gain. And while having hell canceled and heaven guaranteed is great gain, we must never lose sight of the fact that we have been saved for other reasons as well. Out of gratitude for all He has done for us, God asks that we live our lives here to proclaim His glory and advance His cause. God's glory through us is the visible expression of His marvelous character in our lives (1 Corinthians 6:19–20; Ephesians 1:11–14). We display God's glory when His mercy, grace, love, justice, and righteousness are actively evident. As we live to glorify Him, He becomes evident through us and His cause is advanced. In Philippians 1:20 Paul declared: "I eagerly expect and hope that I will in no way be ashamed, but will have sufficient courage so that now as always Christ will be exalted in my body, whether by life or by death."

Sadly, given our tendency to be taken with ourselves, we are more prone to live for our own glory. The goal is to follow the example of Paul, who said, "For to me, to live is Christ . . ." (Philippians 1:21).

Michelangelo is said to have often painted with a brush in one hand and a shielded candle in the other to prevent his shadow from covering the masterpiece he was creating. As God works through us to craft His glory and gain, we must be careful that our shadows are not cast across the canvas of His work.

In what ways does your life reflect His glory and advance His cause? Do you need to adjust?

THANKSGIVING

In Everything Give Thanks.

—1 Thessalonians 5:18 NKJV

Thanksgiving is my favorite holiday—bar none. I love it for the smell of the turkey in the oven, the pungent taste of the cranberry sauce, and the comfort of the dressing. It's quiet, family, fallish, and fun. But more than that, it's a reminder to me of the importance of a thankful spirit, that it is "a good thing to give thanks unto the Lord" (Psalm 92:1 KJV).

Good for a lot of reasons. It keeps us mindful that the Lord is the source of all we are and have. It keeps our hearts and minds on the positive side of the ledger of life and keeps our bent to pessimism in check.

But what about those all-too-frequent days when we have every right to feel pessimistic? When a healthy dose of pessimistic grousing seems therapeutic? Actually, grumpy responses to life add to the burden. Satan would love to compound your pain by throwing you a colossal pity party.

It's thankfulness that is therapeutic. Which is exactly why Scripture commands us to give thanks *in everything*. And, thankfully, it's not asking you to get lost in some wah-wah land of denial.

The command simply asks us to believe that God is intimately involved in our lives. That He never leaves us, and that He doesn't forsake us. It affirms that, even in the worst of situations, He is working all things together for good and will use the struggle to refine and groom us. It recognizes that His grace is abundantly sufficient to carry us through. In the midst of the suffering we have the opportunity to identify and understand how He felt when He suffered for us. Thankfulness admits that He is God and knows what He is doing with our lives. It rejoices with Jeremiah, who declared what God had said: "I know the plans I have for you, . . . plans for welfare and not for calamity to give you a future and a hope" (Jeremiah 29:11 NASB).

A thankful spirit recognizes that God, not the devil, is in the details of a follower's life. To refuse to give thanks in everything is to deny the presence, the goodness, and the greatness of God—something I'm not ready to do.

In everything give thanks!

THE MALADY OF MURMURING

Do All Things Without Murmurings and Disputings.
—Philippians 2:14 KJV

I have a sign in my conference room that has one of those red circles with a diagonal line through it over the word *whining*. Whining is never constructive. It tires those who have to listen to it, and it plants negative thoughts in otherwise clear and open minds. Every parent knows how irritating it is to be around whiny kids. So it's no wonder that God isn't enthused when He hears the droning sounds of murmuring followers.

In fact, if you want to know how He feels about murmurers, Jude gives us a clue. After a description of the ungodly, he concludes, "These are murmurers, complainers" (Jude 16 KJV). Whining is a direct offense against God. Let me explain.

The wandering children of Israel are the forefathers of all who like to complain. In fact, they never made it out of the wilderness precisely because of their whining (Numbers 14:26–30). They whined when God took them into the wilderness. They whined about their lack of food. And they whined about God's generous provision of manna. If it wasn't the lack of water, it was the giants in the land. They had murmuring down to a science.

Moses and Aaron rightly warned the people that their grumbling was not "against us, but against the Lord" (Exodus 16:8). After all, who had taken them out there? Who was in charge of their food supply? Who was the provider of water? Who was it who ultimately determined their life situation? Who parted the Red Sea, defeated mighty armies, granted long life to their sandals, and gave them a hundred other graces? The answer is simple: God! God is the primary mover beneath every aspect of our lives. He supplies, withholds, permits, and oversees. Murmuring is a direct affront to Him and a deep offense to His wise work in our lives. And not only does it reflect poorly on God, it reflects on us. Murmuring thrives in faithless, ungrateful, discontented, and unyielding hearts. That alone would be enough to cause God to be concerned.

The remedy? Trust in His wisdom and goodness, be patient for Him to complete His work in His way . . .

And be thankful!

PSALM 119:1–24

Happy are people of integrity, who follow the law of the LORD.

Happy are those who obey his decrees and search for him with all their hearts.

They do not compromise with evil, and they walk only in his paths.

You have charged us to keep your commandments carefully.

Oh, that my actions would consistently reflect your principles!

Then I will not be disgraced when I compare my life with your commands.

When I learn your righteous laws, I will thank you by living as I should!

I will obey your principles. Please don't give up on me!

How can a young person stay pure? By obeying your word and following its rules.

I have tried my best to find you—don't let me wander from your commands.

I have hidden your word in my heart, that I might not sin against you.

Blessed are you, O LORD; teach me your principles.

I have recited aloud all the laws you have given us.

I have rejoiced in your decrees as much as in riches.

I will study your commandments and reflect on your ways.

I will delight in your principles and not forget your word.

Be good to your servant, that I may live and obey your word.

Open my eyes to see the wonderful truths in your law.

I am but a foreigner here on earth; I need the guidance of your commands.

Don't hide them from me!

I am overwhelmed continually with a desire for your laws.

You rebuke those cursed proud ones who wander from your commands.

Don't let them scorn and insult me, for I have obeyed your decrees.

Even princes sit and speak against me, but I will meditate on your principles.

Your decrees please me; they give me wise advice.

PUTTING PASSION IN ITS PLACE

THE ONE WHO SOWS TO PLEASE THE SPIRIT, FROM THE SPIRIT WILL REAP
ETERNAL LIFE.

—Galatians 6:8

*J*ohn wrote that those who love the world and all that is in the world—
"the lust of the flesh and the lust of the eyes and the boastful pride of
life"—are incapable of loving God (1 John 2:16 NASB). Loving God and living to experience the mismanaged passions of our souls are mutually exclusive.
But when we surrender in love to Him, He helps us manage our passions and
their relationship to the people and things that surround us.

Choosing to love God with our passions keeps us within safe boundaries
and opens up the world of all that is pleasurably legitimate yet without shame
and regret. If we live to experience the urges of our passions apart from the
guiding hand of God, our love for Him is only a charade. We must remember that for the believer every choice to fulfill our own wants and needs apart
from God inevitably ends in sorrow and sin. "The one who sows to please his
sinful nature, from that nature will reap destruction" (Galatians 6:8).

John called our passions apart from God "the lust of the flesh." *Flesh* is
used in the New Testament as a metaphor for our sinful nature. Galatians 5:17
tells us that our flesh and the Holy Spirit are set in opposition to each other.
The closing portion of the verse sums up our struggle: "They are in conflict
with each other, so that you do not do what you want." As we seek to bring
our passions back into line with their intended purpose and to turn them to
serve God, we will always feel the tension . . . a tension that affirms that we
are moving in the right direction.

Transitioning from yielding to the flesh to gladly surrendering to the Holy
Spirit is the fundamental goal of every follower. When we succeed in permitting God's Spirit to redirect our passions, we will know the true fulfillment
that comes from using our inner drives to please Him and satisfy our own
souls.

Does your love for God or love for self manage your inner urges?

UNCOMFORTED SORROW

Do Not Be Deceived, God Is Not Mocked; for Whatever a Man Sows, This He Will Also Reap. For the One Who Sows to His Own Flesh Will from the Flesh Reap Corruption.

—Galatians 6:7–8 NASB

When the Bible speaks of the flesh it is referencing our natural instincts apart from God. Galatians 5:16–21 explains that the instincts of the flesh are in direct tension with the desires of the Holy Spirit in our lives. Although the text assures us that a life yielded to the Spirit produces qualities such as love, joy, and peace in our lives, it also warns that the flesh has its own set of rewards. Rewards such as immorality, impurity, hatred, strife, anger, divisions, envy, and drunkenness are the inevitable results of living to please the flesh.

Oscar Wilde was arguably one of Britain's greatest playwrights. Toward the end of his life, in *De Profundis,* he wrote to his homosexual lover, for whom he has left a wife and two children. His testimony should be a sufficient warning to all of us who would like to give the flesh room to run in our lives.

> The gods have given me almost everything but I let myself be lured into long spells of senseless sensualities. I surrounded myself with the smaller natures. . . . I became the spendthrift of my own genius. And to waste an eternal youth gave me a curious joy. Tired of being on the heights I deliberately went to the depths and searched for new sensations. Desire, at the end, was a malady for me, or a madness or both. I grew careless of the lives of others. I took pleasure where it pleased me. . . . I forgot that every low action of the common day makes or unmakes character and therefore, what one has done in the secret chamber one has someday to cry aloud on the housetop. I ceased to be lord over myself. I was no longer the captain over my own soul and I did not even know it. I allowed pleasure to dominate me and I ended in horrible disgrace.

Irreversible regret is the inevitable fruit of the flesh. In the end it is far better living to please Jesus.

Follow the lead of Moses, who chose to follow God rather than to "enjoy the passing pleasures of sin" (Hebrews 11:25 NASB).

AMAZING GRACE

SEEK THE LORD WHILE HE MAY BE FOUND; CALL UPON HIM WHILE HE IS
NEAR. LET THE WICKED FORSAKE HIS WAY AND . . . RETURN TO THE LORD
. . . AND TO OUR GOD, FOR HE WILL ABUNDANTLY PARDON.
—Isaiah 55:6–7 NASB

*O*scar Wilde was imprisoned for his homosexuality in the latter years of his life. There he had time to reflect on his years of wanton pleasure. In that reflection his heart turned toward God. Perhaps he had grown up in a godly home; or, had been a faithful church-goer in his early years. Someone may have befriended him in prison and told him of God's amazing grace to cover the worst sinner's faults. We don't know. But after writing the sobering words of *De Profundis* to his gay lover, he later wrote the poem, "The Ballad of Reading Gaol." In that poem he penned some of the most exquisite words about the marvelous grace of Jesus to rescue those of a broken, repentant heart. Speaking of life in prison, he wrote:

And thus we rust life's iron chain Degraded and alone;
And some men curse, and some men weep, And some men make no moan:
But God's eternal laws are kind And break the heart of stone.

And every human heart that breaks, In prison-cell or yard,
Is as that broken box that gave Its treasure to the Lord,
And filled the unclean leper's house With the scent of costliest nard.

Ah! happy they whose hearts can break And peace of pardon win!
How else may man make straight his plan And cleanse his soul from Sin?
How else but through a broken heart May Lord Christ enter in?

And he of the swollen purple throat, And the stark and staring eyes,
Waits for the holy hands that took The Thief to Paradise;
And a broken and a contrite heart The Lord will not despise.

Though we do not know if Wilde ever personalized these treasured thoughts, his poem reminds us once again that there is a wonderful wideness in God's mercy.

Meditate on the rich truth that God abundantly pardons. Take it personally.

A DIM VIEW OF HEAVEN

"HE WILL WIPE EVERY TEAR FROM THEIR EYES. THERE WILL BE NO MORE
DEATH OR MOURNING OR CRYING OR PAIN."

—Revelation 21:4

*I*t seems strange that Christians so often look at the end times with a
hesitant ambivalence. For some of us, there is either little or no thought
about His return or the inadmissible hope that He won't come back just yet.
It would ruin our earthside plans and interrupt our dreams. We still have
things to take care of. There's that great vacation coming. Retirement is just
another year or two away. The last child is about to marry. You name it, but
a lot of born-again Christians would be very happy for Him to come back
later, thank you.

Of course, there are exceptions: college students in the midst of final exams
long for His imminent return; people in debt they can't handle look for the
divine escape route. And far more seriously, people in great physical or emotional suffering long for His deliverance. One doctrine that the suffering
church always celebrates is the hope of His soon return.

The Bible suggests that this latter group is very much in line with God's
thinking. When the Bible talks about Christ's return for His own, the text is
full of hope. "He will wipe every tear from their eyes. There will be no more
death or mourning or crying or pain" (Revelation 21:4). Indeed, we are to
"encourage each other with these words" (1 Thessalonians 4:18).

Unfortunately, the first doctrine to be quickly forgotten among believers
who prosper and enjoy good times is the importance of living in the everyday
anticipation of His coming. It is only a commentary on the shallowness of our
perspective and the fact that in finding our satisfaction here we have ceased in
some measure to find our satisfaction in Him. Paul had it right when he said
that to go and be with Jesus was "far better" (Philippians 1:23 KJV). Notice
that he didn't qualify the statement. It is just far better . . . than anything.

Is there an earthside intrigue that has dimmed your view of heaven?

PROGRESSIVE FOLLOWERS

Be Diligent in These Matters . . . so that Everyone May See Your Progress.

—1 Timothy 4:12–16

I'm reminded of the husband who gloated that he and his wife didn't have a perfect relationship, but he was certainly doing his part. Like the typical male, he was totally self-deceived. "Perfect" is what God will make us when we step across the threshold into heaven. What Christ is looking for is "progress." But if we feel that we are just about perfect and that the few faults in our lives are attributable to everyone else, we make little or no progress.

I am so thankful that perfection is not what God expects. Progress is something I can get my life and hands around. It doesn't have to be dramatic. It just has to be progress. And, I might add, there is power in progress. Whether we are parents, pastors, leaders in the marketplace, or in any way an influencer of others, progress is our main asset. While most of us recoil from admitting our imperfections, the real power is in admitting that we are not perfect and showing those who are around us that we are making progress.

I love to be around people who are farther down the road with Jesus than I am. They stimulate my heart to say, *I want to grow like they are.* Their progress is magnetic and it gives me hope that I too can grow. When I envision perfection, I shrug my shoulders and say, "I can't get there!" But progress motivates me.

Followers who are making progress humbly admit their failures, refuse the mediocrity of getting stuck in the same faults, make friends with followers who are out in front of them, and ask for the grace, wisdom, and courage to grow in accelerated ways toward the likeness of Jesus. We will know that we are making progress when people say of us, "You know, they're more like Christ today than they were six months . . . two years ago."

Has anyone noticed the progress you have made in your life recently . . . or are you stuck?

SEDUCED BY SIDESHOWS

For Everything in the World—the Cravings of Sinful Man, the Lust of His Eyes and the Boasting of What He Has and Does—Comes Not from the Father but from the World.

—1 John 2:16

When I was a boy, one of the biggest annual events in town was the circus. My dad would take us early in the morning to watch the circus trains unload the tigers, lions, elephants, monkeys, and all the paraphernalia that made the circus so intriguing.

Once the circus was set up, great attractions were lined along the "midway." The midway was the walk leading to the big tent. Vendors hawked their wares, happy music played, the smell of hot dogs and cotton candy mingled in the air, and multicolored balloons bounced in the wind. With bursts of laughter and screams, customers twisted and turned on amusement rides. The midway was almost more than a boy could take.

The most intriguing sights of all for me were the "sideshows." Large posters advertised all kinds of physical deformity and daring feats of bravery— a man with three eyes, a bearded woman, sword swallowers and fire-eaters, a man with no arms and no legs. I would pull on my dad's hand and beg him to take me behind the posters so I could see for myself only to hear, "Joe, it's a waste of money. It's not all it's cracked up to be."

The world is a lot like the midway. There is much of it that is exciting. But as our Father walks us through the experience, He warns us of what will disappoint us, waste our resources, and distort and destroy us. It's the sideshows that seduce us and endanger our experience here.

Our world constantly puts us in tension with all that it offers. This tension forces us to make up our minds about whom we will believe and follow—our Father or the sideshow.

When I grew up and went to the circus on my own, I couldn't wait to put up my money and see the sideshows, only to find out that my father had been right and my money had been wasted. It's like that in life, but the stakes are far greater.

In which sideshows do you live?

PSALM 119:97–112

Oh, how I love your law!
I think about it all day long.
Your commands make me wiser than my enemies,
for your commands are my constant guide.
Yes, I have more insight than my teachers,
for I am always thinking of your decrees.
I am even wiser than my elders,
for I have kept your commandments.
I have refused to walk on any path of evil,
that I may remain obedient to your word.
I haven't turned away from your laws,
for you have taught me well.
How sweet are your words to my taste;
they are sweeter than honey.
Your commandments give me understanding;
no wonder I hate every false way of life.
Your word is a lamp for my feet and a light for my path.
I've promised it once, and I'll promise again:
I will obey your wonderful laws.
I have suffered much, O LORD;
restore my life again, just as you promised.
LORD, accept my grateful thanks and teach me your laws.
My life constantly hangs in the balance,
but I will not stop obeying your law.
The wicked have set their traps for me along your path,
but I will not turn from your commandments.
Your decrees are my treasure; they are truly my heart's delight.
I am determined to keep your principles, even forever, to the very end.

ALWAYS WINTER?

WHY ARE YOU IN DESPAIR, O MY SOUL? AND WHY HAVE YOU BECOME TROUBLED WITHIN ME? HOPE IN GOD, FOR I SHALL AGAIN PRAISE HIM FOR THE HELP OF HIS PRESENCE.

—Psalm 42:5 NASB

I love winter! I hate winter! And that "love-hate" relationship is an annual experience since, for some reason, best known to God, I have lived most of my life in the bleakness of northern winters. I hate winters because they are too long. Because it gets dark early. And I can do without winter when the snow turns into slush and the temperature is damply neither cold nor hot. Yet there are some things I love about winter. I like the beautiful variety it brings to the changing seasons. I like curling up on the couch with a good book, a crackling fire, and a snowfall proving its presence as it softly drifts past the streetlight. I love winter because it makes spring so much more wonderful.

But most of all I love winter for Christmas. When I was a child, Christmas was wonderful because of the toys and games. In my latter years, I have come to love Christmas because it celebrates the reality that, in the bleak and chilly darkness of my world, God broke through to give me hope in the place of despair, peace in the midst of conflict, and forgiveness in the place of guilt and judgment. If there were no Christmas, winter would be a horrible place in which to be stuck.

That must have been what C. S. Lewis had in mind. In *The Lion, the Witch and the Wardrobe,* the children go through the wardrobe into the land of winter. Upon arrival, they are told by the inhabitants of this cold, dark land that for them it is always winter and never Christmas. Thankfully, for us life is no longer like that. No matter how dark, cold, and bleak life may become, the Christ of Christmas takes us through with His reassuring promises, the light of His Word, and the comforting warmth of His presence. Best of all, He assures us that an eternal spring will someday be ours!

This Christmas give thanks that in the winter of your life Christmas is coming.

LOVING JESUS

"YET I HOLD THIS AGAINST YOU: YOU HAVE FORSAKEN YOUR FIRST LOVE."
—Revelation 2:4

Feeling good about Jesus is not what He had in mind when He reproved the believers at Ephesus for not making Him their "first love." Loving Jesus is not an issue of manipulating our emotions to always "be in love with Him." It is rather a transaction that takes place in our wills . . . in the choices we make. Obviously, the emotional dimension of our relationship with Christ is very satisfying. But the central issue in a thriving relationship with Him is to love Him by choosing to make Him our absolute priority —the consuming center of all that we are and do. Loving Jesus like this will cause something down deep inside to resist because placing Christ at the core threatens the sin, the false security systems we have constructed, the importance of some valued relationships, and the fulfilling of some desires. It is far more comfortable to have Him along for the ride than sitting in the driver's seat.

In fact Satan would be delighted if you felt "in love with Jesus" while continuing to manage your own life. So delighted that he offers a whole menu of things as substitute priorities. You can name them—goods, friends, pleasures, business, plans, and dozens of other delights. But, in the end, wouldn't you rather have Jesus?

And, it must be noted, a "first love" commitment is not a one-time, never-to-be-repeated experience. As my friend who, when teaching Romans 12:1, says that the trouble with living sacrifices is that they keep climbing off the altar. Having Christ at the core is like marriage; it is not the original investment but the maintenance that makes the long-term difference.

Putting Christ first in our choices fuels the burners of our emotions for Him. When we live lives that are directed into righteous ways by Him, joy is the promised result (John 15:11). The more He is in charge, the closer we get to Him; and in that closeness is potential for falling in love with Him afresh.

What would it take to make Him your "first love"?

MARVEL-WORLD

WHAT THE EYES SEE IS BETTER THAN WHAT THE SOUL DESIRES. THIS TOO
IS FUTILITY AND A STRIVING AFTER WIND.

—Ecclesiastes 6:9 NASB

We live in a world that offers us new and intriguing toys that scintillate us at megabyte speed. High definition TV; wireless communications; videophones; e-mail; speedier Internet connectivity; on-line shopping; on-line education; on-line anything. Special effects stretch our imaginations beyond the bounds of reality, and virtual experiences of every kind are available at the touch of a finger. In-car voice-activated navigational systems enable men never to have to humble themselves to ask directions, and futurists speak glibly about the day we will be able to laser beam 3-D images of ourselves, or anything else for that matter, to wherever technology exists.

Still, our hearts hunger. The fancier we get, the more alone we feel. Awe and wonder no longer exist. We have seen and experienced it all in marvel-world. The dullness we feel reminds us that we have lost something of life. God and His satisfying power have been eclipsed by the fleeting glitz of technology.

Peter Kreeft speaks to the loss when he writes,

If we are typically modern . . . we are bored, jaded, cynical, flat, and burnt out. When the skies roll back like a scroll and the angelic trump sounds, many will simply yawn and say, "Pretty good special effects, but the plot's too traditional." If we were not so bored and empty, we would not have to stimulate ourselves with increasing dosages of sex and violence—or just constant busyness. Here we are in the most fantastic fun and games factory ever invented—modern technological society—and we are bored. . . . Medieval people by comparison were like peasants in toy-less hovels—and they were fascinated. Occasions for awe and wonder seemed to abound: birth and death and love and light and darkness and wind and sea and fire and sunrise and star and tree and bird and human mind—and God and Heaven. But all these things have not changed; we have. The universe has not become empty and we, full; it has remained full and we have become empty, insensitive to its fullness, cold hearted.

Let your "soul . . . delight itself in the richest of abundance" (Isaiah 55:2 NKJV).

THE BEST OF TIMES

The Night Is Nearly Over; the Day Is Almost Here. So Let Us Put Aside the Deeds Of Darkness and Put On the Armor of Light.
—Romans 13:12

Charles Dickens opened his classic *A Tale of Two Cities* with the now-familiar line, "It was the best of times; it was the worst of times." Nothing could be more true for us as at the dawn of the twenty-first century.

Although "these days" often seem like "the worst of times," they offer a strategic opportunity to present the clarity of the gospel to a world that has an ever-increasing awareness of its needs and the emptiness of life without God. As paganism matures, the despair, disorientation, and disenfranchisement deepens as life gets worse when godless solutions prove ineffective. Like the early Christians, in the face of the debilitating effects of paganism, we have the opportunity to show our world the remedy of a better life in Christ. Jesus said, "You are the light of the world. A city set on a hill cannot be hidden; nor does anyone light a lamp and put it under a basket, but on the lampstand, and it gives light to all who are in the house. Let your light shine before men in such a way that they may see your good works, and glorify your Father who is in heaven" (Matthew 5:14–16 NASB).

Even a casual review of church history shows that the worst of times have actually been the best of times for the church. When the pressure comes, true disciples of Jesus rise with clear and unwavering convictions, assured of their identity in Christ and the unsurpassed value of His eternal cause. They are unflinchingly willing to be rejected, misunderstood, and underclassed for Christ. A generation committed to compassion and community. Followers with such an undaunted and tenacious grasp of truth and righteousness that their lives, families, and actions are noticeably different and far more satisfying than the lives of those around them. Different in stability, peace, success, productivity, hope, and confidence. Of whom the world is not worthy.

These noticeable differences become compelling beams of light that a dark and despairing world cannot ignore.

What is in your life that shines as a laser beam in the darkness around you?

TRUTH TO THE RESCUE

CONSIDER IT ALL JOY . . . WHEN YOU ENCOUNTER VARIOUS TRIALS, KNOWING THAT THE TESTING OF YOUR FAITH PRODUCES ENDURANCE.

—James 1:2–3 NASB

Trials have a way of wrenching our emotions and jading our perspective. Regardless of how we feel in pain, God's Word is still true. Letting what we know manage how we feel is a key to endurance in difficulty. When life gets in our face, God's truth may very well be the only solid rock to which we can cling.

So, what do we know? We know that God works in our suffering toward our growth and His glory. We know there are the foolproof, unconditional certainties of His goodness, creative power, justice, holiness, and total awareness of our dilemma. We know that He is a God of accurate timing, consistent presence, certain purpose, unfailing love, and productive empathy.

We know that trouble develops character (Romans 5:3–5) and that trials equip us to be more useful (James 1:2–4). Because of Romans 8:28, we know that good is the ultimate purpose of the process of pain. We know that God never wastes our sorrows. Knowing and clinging to what we know make the difference. Truth is our sure footing in the slippery places of trouble.

A friend told me about devastating months of depression she had gone through. Nothing seemed to help. She told me that the only thing that kept her from breaking was "the truth that heaven is real." That basic bit of knowledge kept her head above the swirling flood of her emotional despair.

Another friend, whose child had died two months before, told me as his voice broke, "It hurts more now than it did then. All we have is the fact that God is sovereign and omniscient." That's pretty basic, but it's huge, and it was enough to get him through.

We are people of the truth—use it. Though tears may cloud your eyes and the brokenness of your heart may seem overwhelming, hold on to the truth of God. Let it get to your heart and free it to manage all of life. It's our advantage in trouble. Don't let go.

List the emotions that defeat you in trouble. Next to each one write the truth that puts the emotion in perspective.

"IT'S A PLEASURE"

You Will Fill Me with Joy in Your Presence, with Eternal Pleasures
at Your Right Hand.

—Psalm 16:11

Words like *pride, pleasure,* and *passion* are often viewed with suspicion by those of us who follow Jesus. The problem with that suspicion when it is unthoughtfully applied is that we end up believing that God is pleased with prideless, pleasureless, passionless Christians. Thankfully, nothing could be further from the truth. He created these instincts for us to take an appropriate sense of pride in Him rather than ourselves (Jeremiah 9:23–24; Philippians 3:1–11). To find our pleasure in all that He has given us and in our fellowship with Him. And to be passionate about His kingdom and the advance of His cause (Luke 12:22–34). Because these instincts are divinely implanted, there is a danger in trying to stifle them. If we are not careful, we will end up taking pleasure in our pleasurelessness, feeling proud of our humility, and secretly succumbing to the seductive passions of our world.

We must resist fostering an attitude that inflicts unwarranted guilt when we feel too exuberant and repent of having sanctified, stoical sobriety, doormat humility, and placid emotions. TV's *Saturday Night Live* didn't miss the opportunity to mock Christians who sanctify a sour brand of stoicism when they created "church woman."

If we are not careful, we will be like the sad-faced man on a bus. After several days of watching this somber chap board the bus, a curious fellow rider asked him, "Excuse me, but are you a minister?" As someone well said, "If you have joy in your heart, please telephone your face!"

C. S. Lewis told about a schoolboy who was asked what he thought God was like. The lad replied that as far as he could make out, God was "the sort of person who is always snooping 'round to see if anyone is enjoying himself and then trying to stop it."

It is not the eradication, suppression, or flogging of these inner energies that is required. Rather, what is needed is their redirection from serving self to using them to fully experience all that's good in life and all of God in fresh ways. They will either compete with or become our allies to aid and empower the glory and gain of Christ through us.

What is the focus of your pleasure, pride, and passion?

DECEMBER 7 / 354

PSALMS 121; 123; 124

I look up to the mountains—does my help come from there?

My help comes from the LORD, who made the heavens and the earth!

He will not let you stumble and fall; the one who watches over you will not sleep.

Indeed, he who watches over Israel never tires and never sleeps.

The LORD himself watches over you!

The LORD stands beside you as your protective shade.

The sun will not hurt you by day, nor the moon at night.

The LORD keeps you from all evil and preserves your life.

The LORD keeps watch over you as you come and go, both now and forever.

————————

I lift my eyes to you, O God, enthroned in heaven.

We look to the LORD our God for his mercy,

just as servants keep their eyes on their master,

as a slave girl watches her mistress for the slightest signal.

Have mercy on us, LORD, have mercy, for we have had our fill of contempt.

We have had our fill of the scoffing of the proud and the contempt of the arrogant.

————————

If the LORD had not been on our side—let Israel now say—

if the LORD had not been on our side when people rose up against us,

they would have swallowed us alive because of their burning anger against us.

The waters would have engulfed us; a torrent would have overwhelmed us.

Yes, the raging waters of their fury would have overwhelmed our very lives.

Blessed be the LORD, who did not let their teeth tear us apart!

We escaped like a bird from a hunter's trap. The trap is broken, and we are free!

Our help is from the LORD, who made the heavens and the earth.

TRUE SUCCESS

Just as the Son of Man Did Not Come to Be Served, but to Serve, and to Give His Life as a Ransom for Many.
—Matthew 20:28

If you were asked to define success, what would you say? Most of us would answer in terms of houses, neighborhoods, cars, influence, clothes, and what it says on our business card. And while there is nothing wrong with being successful in these ways, according to Jesus true success is measured on a far different scale. When James and John came with their mother asking to be "big shots" in the kingdom, Christ did not reprove the disciples' desire for success. He simply redirected their thinking about what success is and held Himself up as the model.

Success, according to Jesus, is not about credentials but rather character. It is not measured in what you have but in who you are. And in this text it is the Christlike character of servanthood that spells success. True success dedicates itself to others by serving their needs and enabling them to grow and prosper, just as Christ came to serve our needs and gave Himself to us to guarantee our success against sin.

What, then, of those elements of secular success we tend to be so addicted to? What about people who hold rank and possess the credentials of earthly prosperity? For Jesus, the issue is not how many earthside symbols of success we have piled up; it is how we use them and whether or not we use our "success" to serve and empower others for God's glory and their gain.

No one has ever equaled the power and position, nor possessed the resources that Christ did. Yet Philippians 2:5–9 says that He used His power to serve our need for salvation and growth.

Only those who see their true identity as that of a servant have the potential for real success. If we live up to this level of success, we may hear Him say to us, "Well done, thou good and faithful servant" (Matthew 25:21 KJV). That's what I call true success!

What could you do to serve your way to success?

A HEART-CONTROLLED TONGUE

EVEN A FOOL IS THOUGHT WISE IF HE KEEPS SILENT, AND DISCERNING IF HE
HOLDS HIS TONGUE.

—Proverbs 17:28

When I took the pastorate at the Highland Park Baptist Church, I
quickly became aware that the first pastor had been a giant of a man.
Although he had long before gone to heaven, his hallowed memory and the
effects of his ministry remained. He served the church with distinction for
forty-one years and left a legacy that was evident. I often wondered what it
took to do so well over that span of time. One day when talking with Betty
Green, who had served for years as his secretary, I came to understand why he
had been so effective. Betty told me, "In all the years I worked for him I never
heard him say a bad word about anyone!"

Interesting, isn't it, that of all her memories it was his heart-controlled
tongue that she remembered most. He had been a shepherd whose speech
directly reflected the character of Jesus Christ, and that quality contributed to
an exemplary life worthy of respect.

A good rule of thumb when it comes to talking about others is, When in
doubt . . . don't. It's better to slow down, engage the brain, check with the
indwelling Christ, the manager of our souls, and carefully ponder before
speaking. In fact, continued silence is not a bad option on occasion. It's no
wonder that Paul wrote to Timothy that the key to gaining the respect of others is to be an exemplary believer in speech (1 Timothy 4:12).

Appoint love to be the guard at the gate of your lips.

ADVENT PEOPLE

A VOICE OF ONE CALLING: "IN THE DESERT PREPARE THE WAY FOR THE LORD;
MAKE STRAIGHT IN THE WILDERNESS A HIGHWAY FOR OUR GOD."
—Isaiah 40:3

*B*efore long, friends will be asking, "Are you ready for Christmas?" For people of the Advent, there is more to that question than most of us realize.

Throughout the history of the church Christmas has been referred to as the Advent of Christ. The word *advent* means "coming," and there has never been, in the history of the world, a more strategic coming than His. The Old Testament heralds His coming, and John the Baptist fulfilled the words of Isaiah the prophet when he called Israel to prepare the way for the arrival of their King.

While He has already come and conquered, the celebration of Christmas is a perfect time to make a highway for our Lord in the confused and often difficult wilderness of our own lives. What better time than Christmas for us to focus on the gifts and profound grace that surround His coming and to "strike up the band" of our hearts to celebrate Him as our King; to renew our desire to make a way for Him in our relationships, wills, plans, hopes, and dreams.

And while we are thinking of Advent, it's hard to escape the thought that He is coming back again and will once and for all put away sorrow, pain, failure, and confusion; and take us to His home, where there is joy forever in His presence. Advent people purify their lives to prepare for this glorious event (1 John 3:1–3).

The next time you are asked, "Are you ready for Christmas?" remember that being "ready" is about much more than your "to do" list. So set down those packages and that tangled string of Christmas lights. Fix your heart on the wonder of God's visiting our planet, and remember that the tiny baby who entered the world so quietly on that first Christmas Day will one day come again triumphantly to take you home at last.

What can you do to make ready the way of the Lord in the wilderness of your life? Be specific.

LIFE IN THE LONG VIEW

"SELL YOUR POSSESSIONS AND GIVE TO THE POOR. PROVIDE PURSES FOR
YOURSELVES THAT WILL NOT WEAR OUT, A TREASURE IN HEAVEN THAT WILL
NOT BE EXHAUSTED, WHERE NO THIEF COMES NEAR AND NO MOTH
DESTROYS."

—Luke 12:33

*M*ost of us suffer from a dreadful case of shortsightedness.
Psalm 73 tells us of Asaph, who, though he was a man of God,
found that his "feet had almost slipped" when he envied the "prosperity of the
wicked" (vv. 2–3). This envy of those who had so much while they were so
godless was only remedied in verses 16–17. He entered the sanctuary of the
Lord and saw the wicked from God's point of view: "It was troublesome in my
sight until I came into the sanctuary of God; then I perceived their end"
(NASB). Before Asaph transitioned to God's eternal perspective, his limited
point of view had skewed his perspective and he almost bailed out on God.
When he saw the bigger picture, he concluded that he was more blessed in his
trouble than the wicked are in their prosperity. As Christ said, "For what is a
man profited if he gains the whole world, and loses or forfeits himself?" (Luke
9:25 NASB).

It was to an anxious group of disciples, distracted by earthside stuff, that
Christ said, "Your heavenly Father knows that you need all these things. But
seek first His kingdom and His righteousness, and all these things will be
added to you" (Matthew 6:32–33 NASB). He also said, "Sell your possessions
and give to charity; make yourselves money belts which do not wear out, an
unfailing treasure in heaven, where no thief comes near nor moth destroys"
(Luke 12:33 NASB).

When we really believe in the other side, everything on this side is radically, wonderfully changed. We need to believe, with the British writer and
social critic Malcolm Muggeridge, that "the only ultimate tragedy in life is to
feel at home here."

What could you do during this Christmas season to invest in treasures in heaven?

WHATEVER HAPPENED TO VIRTUE?

AND OVER ALL THESE VIRTUES PUT ON LOVE, WHICH BINDS THEM ALL
TOGETHER IN PERFECT UNITY.

—Colossians 3:14

William Bennett wrote, "Today we speak about values and how important it is for us to 'have them' as if they were beads on a string or marbles in a pouch." He said that virtues are not something to be possessed but "something to be, the most important thing to be."

Historian Gertrude Himmelfarb added that "the shift from 'virtue' to 'values' has had other unfortunate consequences," including confining the idea of virtue to the idea of "chastity and marital fidelity," while forgetting to emphasize "the classical virtues of wisdom, justice, temperance, and courage, or the Christian ones of faith, hope, and charity."

When Bennett's *Book of Virtues* first came out, I went to my local bookstore to acquire a copy. After leafing through it, I took it to the counter, where a trendy, bookish-type clerk took my money. As he did, I naively said, "This looks like it could be a bestseller," to which he replied caustically, "I hope not." I was puzzled until I realized that the thought of virtues and moral absolutes that define character and behavior are unwelcome in our world. Long ago, it became intellectually fashionable to deny that there was ultimate truth or that anyone really knew what was right and wrong. Once we embraced the notion that there was no God and no accountability to His righteousness, virtue became a non-issue and those who espoused it were seen as bigoted and intolerant.

Yet, as pilgrims we commit ourselves to the moral absolutes of the King and strive to emulate those virtues in the midst of varying and often conflicting values in the hostile world around us. A kingdom mind-set elevates eternal virtues as the highest point of success, admiration, and personal affirmation. And among fellow travelers, respectability and honor belong not necessarily to those with status and visibility but to those whose lives reflect the virtues of the King. The poorest, least credentialed of us who is a virtuous kingdom traveler is the noblest of all.

Read 1 Corinthians 13; Colossians 3:12–17; and 2 Peter 1:3–10. List the virtues you find in these texts and target them for application in your life.

PURITY IN PERSPECTIVE

HE WILL KEEP YOU STRONG TO THE END.

—1 Corinthians 1:8

*B*eing committed to biblical purity is a tremendous challenge, particularly given the "liberated" sensuality of our world. Abstinence is a "bad word," homosexual behavior is a validated lifestyle, and affairs and divorce are now as common in the church as they are among the unchurched. Pornography and voyeuristic opportunities are readily available in the secrecy of your own home. And it is in this world that Jesus asks us to keep ourselves pure and spotless before Him as a bride adorned for her husband.

You may think that it was easy for apostles in New Testament times to tell us to toe the line given their relatively primitive and innocent culture. Think again. Most early Christians thrived in a sex-crazed environment. When Paul wrote to followers of Jesus in Corinth, he was writing to a church planted in the center of a city known for its rampant sensuality and unbridled lust. The city was home to the cult of Aphrodite, the goddess of love; and her temple housed literally thousands of prostitutes, both male and female, heterosexual and homosexual. The highest form of religious expression was to cohabit with these servants of the goddess. It was out of this kind of world that believers in Corinth had come to Jesus. Paul's letters were written to lead them from their former ways to lives that pleased Christ in purity.

In many respects, the first century was more challenging than ours, when it came to living pure and holy lives. At least in our culture, the vast majority of pagans reject the notions of wanton sexual exploits and disloyalty in marriage. The Roman Empire knew no such restraints.

It is in that context that I particularly like Paul's opening encouragement to the Corinthians as he writes, "Eagerly wait for our Lord Jesus Christ. . . . He will keep you strong to the end, so that you will be blameless on the day of our Lord Jesus Christ. God, who has called you into fellowship with his Son Jesus Christ our Lord, is faithful" (1 Corinthians 1:7–9).

Strong to the end. Blameless. Make these your goals and hold yourself, your family, and your friends accountable.

PSALM 139:1–10, 12b–18, 23–24

O LORD, you have examined my heart and know everything about me.

You know when I sit down or stand up.

You know my every thought when far away.

You chart the path ahead of me and tell me where to stop and rest.

Every moment you know where I am.

You know what I am going to say even before I say it, LORD.

You both precede and follow me. You place your hand of blessing on my head.

Such knowledge is too wonderful for me, too great for me to know!

I can never escape from your spirit! I can never get away from your presence!

If I go up to heaven, you are there;

if I go down to the place of the dead, you are there.

If I ride the wings of the morning, if I dwell by the farthest oceans,

even there your hand will guide me, and your strength will support me. . . .

To you the night shines as bright as day. Darkness and light are both alike to you.

You made all the delicate, inner parts of my body

and knit me together in my mother's womb.

Thank you for making me so wonderfully complex!

Your workmanship is marvelous—and how well I know it.

You watched me as I was being formed in utter seclusion,

as I was woven together in the dark of the womb.

You saw me before I was born. Every day of my life was recorded in your book.

Every moment was laid out before a single day had passed.

How precious are your thoughts about me, O God! They are innumerable!

I can't even count them; they outnumber the grains of sand!

And when I wake up in the morning, you are still with me! . . .

Search me, O God, and know my heart; test me and know my thoughts.

Point out anything in me that offends you,

and lead me along the path of everlasting life.

FAITH UNDER FIRE

I Consider that Our Present Sufferings Are Not Worth Comparing with the Glory that Will Be Revealed in Us.

—Romans 8:18

After the cold war, one of the last regimes to fall in Eastern Europe was the government in Romania, led by the dictator Nicolae Ceausescu. The flash point of his overthrow occurred when a pastor, Laslo Tokes, refused to obey politically motivated orders to leave his church and take an assignment elsewhere. He stayed inside the church building, and his congregation surrounded the building with their bodies, creating a human shield against the security forces who sought to take the pastor prisoner.

Most of these Christians did not fear death, even when the soldiers threatened brute force. After all, they knew they were bound for heaven. What did the temporary loss of life matter? Their courage and faith stopped the soldiers in their tracks. They could not—would not—challenge these people to get to their pastor.

The song of the revolution that filled the streets was a hymn of the Romanian church. Its words proclaimed the victory of the Second Coming of Jesus Christ. It had been a hallmark in those dark and terrible days when they were called on to suffer much. Now it would be their victory song as they streamed through the streets.

Throughout the history of the persevering church, courage in pain has been grounded in the reality of heaven. When threatened, heaven-focused Christians knew that dying was gain. When their treasures were taken, they were not shaken because they knew that the true treasures were in heaven. When threatened with torture, they bore up under it, knowing that the sufferings of this present time were not worthy to be compared with the glory that shall be revealed on the other side. To the suffering church at Smyrna Jesus said, "I know your afflictions and your poverty—yet you are rich!" (Revelation 2:9). They knew it as well and didn't flinch.

When German theologian Dietrich Bonhoeffer was hanged for his commitment to righteousness in the face of Nazi atrocities, he confidently spoke these last words: "For me this is the end but also the beginning."

Is there anything you wouldn't sacrifice, knowing that heaven is your eternal reward?

THE COST OF CHRISTMAS

HE . . . EMPTIED HIMSELF, TAKING THE FORM OF A BOND-SERVANT.
—Philippians 2:6–7 NASB

*I*f you think Christmas is expensive, think of what it cost Jesus. He willingly gave everything up that stood in the way of His coming. Although we will never understand fully all that this tremendous sacrifice meant for Christ, we can get a glimpse of its extent in Philippians 2.

When Christ came into our world, He forfeited His privileges and rights as the God of the universe. Emptying Himself meant that He had to give up the voluntary use of many of His attributes (Philippians 2:5–11). He yielded His omnipresence to be confined in the body of a baby, and His omnipotence to endure the Cross without overpowering His enemies with ten thousand angels. He sacrificed the "perks of paradise": the glory, praise, and honor bestowed upon Him by the angelic hosts. He forfeited His rightful recognition as Creator, Sustainer, and Ruler of the universe—all of this, to be born in a lowly stable while the world slept unaware.

Jesus even sacrificed things that ordinary humans expect to enjoy in the course of life: the reliability of intimate friendships, being understood and accepted for who He was, having a place to lay His head and a little money in His pocket. Ultimately, Christ paid the greatest price by surrendering His body on the cross, having the sins of humanity heaped upon Him and dying the death of a despised outcast.

The bottom line is this: Jesus voluntarily emptied Himself of anything and everything that stood in the way of accomplishing His Father's will through His life.

This poses a penetrating question for us. Rights, privileges, pleasures, possessions, expectations, relationships, and deep desires may not be inherently wrong. But are we willing to hold them loosely and let them go if emptying ourselves of them will enable us to surrender to God's will for our lives (Romans 12:1–2)?

"Let this mind be in you . . ." (Philippians 2:5 KJV).

Is there a price you need to pay so that God can do His will in your life?

HABITS OF HEAVEN

The favorite word to throw at Christians when people want to discredit us is *hypocrite*. From my point of view, the attack is a sham—a smoke screen to excuse their rejection of Christ. Do they really expect perfection from God's people? Even secularists periodically contradict their own philosophy of life. Yet the stinging charge, in spite of my objection, is more often than not well founded. We possess an uncanny ability to put graffiti on the face of Jesus with lives that contradict what we say we believe.

Too often, we have defined the difference between "us and them" in shallow, inconsistent codes of behavior. For instance, in days gone by the distinctions of a Christian often focused on things to avoid: Don't drink, dance, smoke, chew, or go with those who do. The model of what it meant to be a Christian looked something like this: Be faithful to church, tithe, and avoid doubtful work on Sunday. As important as they may have been, these lists distracted us from the authentic distinctions of our identity in Christ, giving us a false sense of spiritual accomplishment. Satisfied that we had conformed to the list of dos and don'ts, it was easy to ignore the more genuine marks of eternity—the habits of heaven that make us truly unique.

Today, in our more liberated Christian environment, where many have discarded codes of behavior that smack of legalism, we continue to miss the genuine marks of eternity. We live our liberated lives to the point that pagans wonder if there is really any difference at all.

It's time to demonstrate the true habits of heaven for a watching world to see. Values such as generosity over greed, servanthood over self-centeredness, people over things, the eternal over the temporal, purity over unrestrained lusts, and pleasing God over self-satisfaction will convince the world that we mean business for Jesus. Add commodities like compassion, truth, and a loving sense of community and we might just catch someone's attention.

What are you doing to show the world true habits of heaven?

BIGGER-PICTURE PEOPLE

By Faith Abraham . . . Obeyed . . . Even Though He Did Not Know
Where He Was Going.

—Hebrews 11:8–19

*D*o you ever feel that God has asked you to do something unreasonable or, worse yet, unknown in terms of the outcome of your obedience? Like forgiving a wrenching offense, or giving your children to His service in some remote part of the world? Perhaps He asks for a prized relationship or the refusal of a long-awaited promotion. Can you trust that God knows what He is doing, that He will prosper your faithfulness, and that in the end His way is best?

God asked Abraham to move his whole family and all their earthly goods without telling him where they were going (Genesis 12:1–3). The unknown is full of unsettling, insecure, distracting, and defeating thoughts of "What if . . . ?" Yet the unknown is territory He often asks us to occupy for Him.

For Abraham it wasn't just the haunting unknown. God asked Abraham to be faithful in the midst of what seemed to be impossible. God promised that He would give Abraham and Sarah a son. Then He let Sarah pass the age of childbearing. God asked them to faithfully persevere in obedience when the pull of past comforts sought to seduce them back to the comfort zone of Ur of the Chaldeans. He asked them to faithfully, routinely persevere in the task with no instant feedback on their progress toward the goal. In fact, when the book of Hebrews talks about Old Testament heroes, including Abraham, it says, "All these died in faith, without receiving the promises" (Hebrews 11:13 NASB). Nevertheless, they obeyed! How did they persevere in the face of unknown, impossible, and unrewarding circumstances?

The secret of their success was that they were bigger-picture people. They remained steadfast because they believed that God would not waste their investment in His will for them. In His time and in His way, He would keep His promise to them, even if that day came beyond their lifetime.

I love how the text in Hebrews notes that because they had faith in the bigger picture—faith in God's Word even beyond the span of their lifetime—God was "not ashamed to be called their God" (Hebrews 11:16 NASB).

Are you willing to obey, trusting that He will never mislead you?

SIGNIFICANT AT LAST

HE CHOSE US . . . AS SONS THROUGH JESUS CHRIST . . . TO THE PRAISE OF THE GLORY OF HIS GRACE.

—Ephesians 1:4–6

No amount of significance in terms of material posessions, fame, power, or position can compare to being a child of the eternal King and belonging to the kingdom of Christ before whom all the powers of this world will ultimately bow their knees (Philippians 2:9–11). Even those who are thought of as significant from the world's point of view need the true significance found only in Him, and those of us who feel less than important in this passing world are fully significant in Him. When we are children of the King, we are all the same. For us significance is no longer a search. It has been fully secured at Calvary.

My dad was the most important person in my world when I was a boy. He was the pastor of a large, successful church, a good preacher, and a kind and gentle leader. His gifts were recognized by several boards upon which he served. He was a household name in our denomination. Wheaton College recognized his stellar service to Christ with an honorary doctorate when he was in his early forties. People often said, "Oh, you're Joe Stowell's son" or introduced me as "the son of Dr. Stowell." I was proud of my dad and was so honored to be his son that to be known as his child was my source of significance. I was happy and satisfied to find my worth in him.

That is but a glimpse of what it means to be satisfied with the significance that comes with being a child of the King. There is no greater honor, affirmation of worth and value, or earthbound significance that can compare. When we get a grip on this reality, we are set free from the temptations that tyrannize our lives as we try to establish our place in the heap of humanity are free and to be servants of the One who has made us His own. When you belong to the King, you need no other bragging rights!

In what or whom have you sought to find importance?

THE CHRISTMAS COALITION

The End Will Come, When He . . . Has Destroyed All Dominion, Authority and Power. For He Must Reign Until He Has Put All His Enemies Under His Feet.

—1 Corinthians 15:24–25

*A*s happy as Christmas may be for all of us, it was not a good day for Satan. The birth of Jesus marked the beginning of the end for him. Jesus came not just as Savior but as conquering King.

As loyal subjects of the King, our responsibility is to get our lives in line with the King's agenda. The ultimate objective of the kingdom of Christ is the final, ultimate, and unchallenged defeat of Satan and his plans. Until that final moment when our King has "put all his enemies under his feet," Satan creates stealth skirmishes at the borders of our lives. He does so not only to defeat and destroy whatever he can but to use our lives as platforms to demonstrate his power and bring shame and discredit to the name of the King. But every time we marshal the forces of our heart, mind, and strength to defeat Satan's advances against us, we reflect the glory of the King's power and the central work of the kingdom. We do this by submitting to the authority of the King. Every time I say yes to the King, Satan is defeated again. Temptations of greed, sensual satisfaction, pride, gain, and the dishonorable use of power create arenas for us to demonstrate our allegiance to Christ. Saying to the adversary in the face of attack, "I would rather serve the King than reach for what you offer," leads us to conquest in even the strongest of assaults. Though the battle is sometimes intense, overcoming is just as simple as that.

It is a privilege as a kingdom follower to carry the flag of conquest as an early warning to the Enemy that his doom is sure. As Martin Luther said, "One little word shall fell him." For kingdom persons, that word is *yes* to the authority of the King.

Join the Christmas Coalition. Ask Christ for the strength to say yes to Him in every situation today. When you do, you demonstrate that Satan's "doom is sure."

PSALM 106:47; LUKE 1:76–77, 2:10–11, 1:79, 1:68–75. 2:29–32

O LORD our God, save us! Gather us back from among the nations,

so we can thank your holy name and rejoice and praise you.

———————

And you, my little son, will be called the prophet of the Most High,

because you will prepare the way for the Lord.

You will tell his people how to find salvation through forgiveness of their sins. . . .

But the angel reassured them. "Don't be afraid!" he said.

"I bring you good news of great joy for everyone!

The Savior—yes, the Messiah, the Lord— has been

born tonight in Bethlehem, the city of David! . . .

to give light to those who sit in darkness and in the shadow of death,

and to guide us to the path of peace." . . .

"Praise the Lord, the God of Israel,

because he has visited his people and redeemed them.

He has sent us a mighty Savior from the royal line of his servant David,

just as he promised through his holy prophets long ago.

Now we will be saved from our enemies and from all who hate us.

He has been merciful to our ancestors

by remembering his sacred covenant with them,

the covenant he gave to our ancestor Abraham.

We have been rescued from our enemies,

so we can serve God without fear, in holiness and righteousness forever. . . ."

"Lord, now I can die in peace!

As you promised me, I have seen the Savior you have given to all people.

He is a light to reveal God to the nations,

and he is the glory of your people Israel!"

POOR LITTLE JESUS BOY

THOUGH HE WAS RICH, YET FOR YOUR SAKES HE BECAME POOR.
—2 Corinthians 8:9

It seems strange, doesn't it, to be talking about poverty at a season like this, with all the abundance of gifts, food, friends, and celebration? It seems strange unless we're thinking about the middle of January when all the Christmas bills come due. Then we might understand what poverty is all about.

How would you know if you were poor? If you had two cars instead of three; one instead of two; a bike instead of a car? Would that make you poor? If you had one bedroom instead of three bedrooms, or if you had just one room in your house? If you were never able to buy a steak dinner again in your life?

What does it mean to be poor? It means lacking the resources to be able to provide for and meet basic needs. Which must be what God had in mind when in His Word He said, "Woe unto you who think you are rich but yet you are poor" (see Revelation 3:17). When we stand before God, we are guilty in our sin and we do not have the resources to deal with the problem. None of us can be rich enough to buy away the debt of our sin. None of us can be good enough to deserve to have our sins canceled before a holy God.

So, like divine alms given to a planet of people impoverished by sin, He came. He gave up His home in heaven to become a homeless, itinerant preacher. He gave up the comfort and all the glory of His surroundings to be born in a smelly stable and die on a cruel cross. He did all of that so that He would pay the price and be the resource to cancel my sin so that I could be rich in Him, sins forgiven.

How would you know if you were rich? If you were a child of a King, would you be rich? If you had hope in the midst of the worst despair of life? If you had peace in the midst of the most troubling times in life? Would you be rich if death, for you, were not a dread but a door to all that is far better? You have all of that and more in Jesus Christ, who became poor so that we might become rich.

By this the love of God was manifested in us, that God has sent His only begotten Son . . . so that we might live through Him (1 John 4:9 NASB)

LOVE CAME DOWN AT CHRISTMAS

THE WORD BECAME FLESH AND MADE HIS DWELLING AMONG US.
—John 1:14

I never liked board games much, so when our children were too old for "Chutes and Ladders," I was ecstatic. Only to find that meeting them in their world required evenings at elementary school band concerts. Why did I deny myself to spend time with my kids? Because I knew that they could not come into my world until I first met them in theirs and slowly led them to mine.

Come to think of it, that's just what God does for us.

From His world of supreme glory, the Almighty moved into our world. Compared to His world, ours is frightfully small and insignificant. But it is our world. And He knows that I can't get to His world until He first comes to mine.

And so He did in the person of Jesus Christ, and He remains here in the Spirit. It was here that He found me and adopted me as His child.

It is an astounding thought that "the Word became flesh and made his dwelling among us" (John 1:14). And all because He loved us (John 3:16).

Who of us would have been willing to leave the pleasures and privileges of heaven to run the risk of dwelling in a fallen, hostile world? And to add to the unlikely drama, He entered our world in "the very nature of a servant, being made in human likeness. And being found in appearance as a man, he humbled himself and became obedient to death—even death on a cross!" (Philippians 2:7–8).

Frankly, moving into the world of our children isn't always easy or convenient. It can sometimes be painful. Have you ever tried to ride a skateboard after forty? But for God, it meant sending His Son to a death on the cross—a death that took place so that those who respond to Him in faith might have life; so that He might take us by the hand and lead us to grow out of our world and follow Him to His far better world.

It's no wonder we call Him Father.

Whom do you meet in their world to help them to the world of our Father?

NIGHT VISITORS

NOW THERE WERE . . . SHEPHERDS LIVING . . . IN THE FIELDS, KEEPING WATCH OVER THEIR FLOCK BY NIGHT. AND BEHOLD, AN ANGEL OF THE LORD STOOD BEFORE THEM.

—Luke 2:8–9 NKJV

*I*f I had been given the assignment to choreograph the arrival of Jesus, I'm sure that I would not have let it happen the way it did. I'd want the finest surroundings, a thousand herald trumpeters, and to be sure the VIP list of visitors would have included the world's most important people. Money would be no object when it came to welcoming this King. Which may be why it never crossed God's mind to put me in charge of the script.

Did it ever strike you as highly unusual that He was born in a barn? Equally strange is the fact that shepherds were the first to hear the news and the first to visit baby Jesus. Often despised, shepherds were at the bottom of the social ladder in Israel. So, to think that shepherds, and the night crew at that, were chosen to receive an invitation heralded by a sky full of angels is the last thing I would have expected God to do.

Unless God wanted to make a point. If He wanted to prove that His coming was not an elitist thing but that He would be friend and Savior to even the lowest of people, then this is a brilliant move. Israel's religious leadership was wealthy, aloof, and out of touch with the needs of the average person. So, at the very beginning, God made a statement. A statement that Jesus affirmed throughout His ministry. From outcast beggars, to prostitutes, to Samaritans, Jesus proved that He had come for those society had pushed aside.

And just in case anyone would think that powerful, wealthy persons were out of the loop, later an entourage of Gentile kings came, bearing precious gifts.

The point is clear. Jesus came for all of us. Regardless. Which is something to be thankful for. If it hadn't been that way, you and I might not have been invited to the cross.

There is a marvelous wideness in God's mercy. . . . Rejoice!

THE GIFT THAT KEEPS ON GIVING

Jesus Christ Is the Same Yesterday and Today and Forever.
—Hebrews 13:8

*A*t a recent dinner, Martie and I were seated next to Billy Graham. In the course of the evening I asked Him, "Of all the experiences you have had in ministry what have you enjoyed the most?" And then, as though he might have trouble thinking of something, I suggested that perhaps it was having influence on kings and presidents or the privilege of preaching the gospel to countless millions around the world. But I had hardly finished, when he took his hand and brushed it across the linen tablecloth as though to push those suggestions aside and replied, "By far the greatest joy of my life has been my fellowship with Jesus. Having Him guide me, hearing His voice in my heart, to be blessed with His presence and power. This has been my highest pleasure."

It was spontaneous, unrehearsed, and obviously sincere.

I will never forget the moment. It struck me afresh that Jesus is indeed the most important gift we have ever been given, and that for those who honor His presence in their lives, He proves Himself wonderful all the way to the end.

Dr. Graham's words took on additional meaning against the backdrop of the words of Chuck Templeton. Templeton was an early friend of Billy's. They founded Youth for Christ in Canada together. Chuck Templeton was the pastor in a leading church in Toronto and a household name in evangelical circles. But years ago, to everyone's shock, Templeton openly rejected God, left his church and family, and launched a stellar career in Canada's media and political scene.

When Templeton was in his eighties, he granted an interview to Lee Strobel, who was writing his book *A Case for Faith*. In the interview, Strobel asked Templeton if he had ever regretted turning his back on God. Templeton's answer was a resolute no. Then Strobel asked him, "What about Jesus?" Templeton began to weep, put his face in his hands, and, as he sobbed, said, "I miss Him."

Two friends. Two divergent paths. One weeps over the loss of Jesus. One rejoices in Jesus as the greatest gift in his life.

I'd rather have Jesus!

GOOD WORKS AND GOD'S GRACE

FOR IT IS BY GRACE YOU HAVE BEEN SAVED . . . IT IS THE GIFT OF GOD.
—Ephesians 2:8

The great artist Michelangelo produced masterpieces that are among the best works of art in the world. His sculpture of David and the ceiling of the Sistine Chapel are among the greatest creations of all time. Nearly all of his subject matter was religious, and he often worked at the bidding of the Pope. Since he was a devout man, we should not be surprised that he took appropriate pride in what he was doing for God, hoping that somehow he might obtain favor with God.

Toward the end of his life, he became intrigued with what the Reformers were teaching about making peace with God through faith apart from works. Accepting the reality that all of his good works could do nothing to remove his sin, he embraced Christ as his forgiving Savior. It changed the meaning of life for him. Michelangelo now realized that what he had supposedly done for God had actually eclipsed God in his life. In a sonnet he confessed, "Whence the loving fancy that made of art my idol | and my king, | I know now well that it was full of wrong. . . . | Painting and sculpture shall no longer calm | the soul turned to that love divine | that spread its arms on the cross to take us in."

As taken as he was with Christ, he never stopped expressing himself through art. But now he did it for another reason—not for merit but for love. As one observer notes, "Michelangelo worked down to the end. . . . Nonetheless, the change was a radical one: art, which had become the primary interest, the 'idol and king' of his life, now becomes a means to serve God humbly."

His response is a lesson even for those of us who have believed with all of our hearts that our salvation is by His grace and grace alone. A lesson, because we often do good works hoping to impress and gain favor with God when He intended that all we do is an expression of gratitude for the complete favor we have received because of His grace.

Do you search for ways to do good deeds as a response to his abundant grace in your life?

AFTER ALL HE'S DONE FOR ME

WHO SHALL SEPARATE US FROM THE LOVE OF CHRIST? . . . IN ALL THESE THINGS WE OVERWHELMINGLY CONQUER THROUGH HIM WHO LOVED US.
—Romans 8:35, 37 NASB

*A*s you know, Hitler was obsessed with the eradication of the Jewish race. To be a Jew in Europe in the 1940s was a dangerous calling. They were hunted relentlessly. Their crime? They were born Jewish. When the Germans took Denmark, Hitler demanded that all the Jewish Danes wear a yellow armband to mark them for the express purpose of deportation to a concentration camp. Legend has it that the king of Denmark, Christian X, was forced to read the decree from the balcony of Amalienborg Royal Palace. At the conclusion of the announcement, with tears in his eyes, he proceeded to put a yellow armband on his own arm for all to see. Tradition has it that all the Danish people followed, making it impossible for the German forces to carry out their horrid intent against the Jewish race.

We have been born sinners. With the mark of sin indelibly imprinted into our lives, our adversary hunts and intends to destroy us. He would, except for the stunning reality that the King of heaven came to live among us. And, with tears in His eyes, He put the armband of our sin on Himself as He hung on a cruel cross that we might forever be hidden in Him. Rescued from the awful intent of our Enemy and the eternal ravages of hell. Free at last . . . free indeed . . . free forever!

For this we can do nothing less than love Him . . . with all of our life. The hymn writer William R. Featherstone expressed it well:

> My Jesus, I love Thee, I know Thou art mine;
> For Thee all the follies of sin I resign;
> My gracious Redeemer, my Saviour art Thou;
> If ever I loved Thee, my Jesus 'tis now. . . .

Or as Isaac Watts put it,

> Love so amazing, so divine,
> Demands my life, my soul, my all.

PSALM 145

I will praise you, my God and King, and bless your name forever and ever.

I will bless you every day, and I will praise you forever.

Great is the LORD! He is most worthy of praise! His greatness is beyond discovery!

Let each generation tell its children of your mighty acts.

I will meditate on your majestic, glorious splendor and your wonderful miracles.

Your awe-inspiring deeds will be on every tongue; I will proclaim your greatness.

Everyone will share the story of your wonderful goodness;

they will sing with joy of your righteousness.

The LORD is kind and merciful, slow to get angry, full of unfailing love.

The LORD is good to everyone. He showers compassion on all his creation.

All of your works will thank you, LORD, and your faithful followers will bless you.

They will talk together about the glory of your kingdom;

they will celebrate examples of your power.

They will tell about your mighty deeds

and about the majesty and glory of your reign.

For your kingdom is an everlasting kingdom.

You rule generation after generation.

The LORD is faithful in all he says; he is gracious in all he does.

The LORD helps the fallen and lifts up those bent beneath their loads.

All eyes look to you for help; you give them their food as they need it.

When you open your hand, you satisfy the hunger and thirst of every living thing.

The LORD is righteous in everything he does; he is filled with kindness.

The LORD is close to all who call on him, yes, to all who call on him sincerely.

He fulfills the desires of those who fear him;

he hears their cries for help and rescues them.

The LORD protects all those who love him, but he destroys the wicked.

I will praise the LORD, and everyone on earth will bless his holy name

forever and forever.

FINISHING WELL

Do You Not Know that in a Race All the Runners Run, but Only One Gets the Prize? Run in Such a Way as to Get the Prize.

—1 Corinthians 9:24

I don't know that I have ever met anyone who doesn't want to finish well. Ending life with as few regrets as possible and a minimum of shame is what I have my heart set on. But any athlete will tell you that finishing well is the most difficult part of the race. It is easy to start with a burst of speed and determination. But, as we go on, our initial desire inevitably cools. We get tired and burned out. Life distracts us with worries, concerns, and just plain busyness. We forget our goal. We lose sight of the end, and soon interruptions, trials, setbacks, and seductions lure us to quick hits of temporary satisfaction that promise to soothe our weariness.

I'm not surprised that Paul compared the Christian life to a race. In 1 Corinthians 9:24–25, he wrote: "Do you not know that in a race all the runners run, but only one gets the prize? Run in such a way as to get the prize. Everyone who competes in the games goes into strict training. They do it to get a crown that will not last; but we do it to get a crown that will last forever." And in Hebrews 12:1–2, we read: "Therefore, since we are surrounded by such a great cloud of witnesses, let us throw off everything that hinders and the sin that so easily entangles, and let us run with perseverance the race marked out for us. Let us fix our eyes on Jesus . . . who for the joy set before him endured the cross, scorning its shame, and sat down at the right hand of the throne of God."

What better example do we have of finishing well than our Lord Himself? From His humble beginning in the feeding trough of animals, He endured hardship—even death on the cross—to finish not just well but extraordinarily well, so that we could follow His example as He cheers us on from the emperor's box!

What is hindering your race? Hand it off and go for the prize.

THROUGH IT ALL

He Himself Has Said, "I Will Never Desert You, nor Will I Ever Forsake You," so that We May Confidently Say, "The Lord Is My Helper, I Will Not Be Afraid."

—Hebrews 13:5–6 NASB

As we come to the end of another year, it's important to look through the rearview mirror to take note of all that has transpired.

If we were to sit in a room and share our stories, they would all be different. For many of us, this past year has brought opportunities for joy and celebration. Unexpected blessings have been showered on us by His grace. For others, this has been a year of disappointment and difficulty. Tragedy is inevitable, and life has a way of bringing it in bunches. But for all of us who have faithfully followed Him in good times and bad, there is a recurring theme in our stories that is the same.

Through it all, Jesus has been there.

He alone has been the source of our blessings and our strength in pain. His Spirit has been our Comforter. His Word has given us guidance and solace. He has often repeated in our hearts that He is in the process of working "all things" together for good. Even when we haven't been aware of it, He has shielded us from the schemes of our adversary that would have done us in, provided abundant and sufficient grace for what He has allowed to come into our lives, and carried us over the terrain of trouble when it was too rugged for us to get through alone.

He has been patient with our failures, ready to mercifully forgive, and available whatever our need.

By far He has been our most important treasure.

As Peter Kreeft has noted,

> The world's purest gold is only dung without Christ. But with Christ, the basest metal is transformed into the purest gold. . . . With him, poverty is riches, weakness is power, suffering is joy, to be despised is glory. Without him, riches are poverty, power is impotence, happiness is misery, glory is despised.

Amen!

As the hymn writer penned, "In a love which cannot cease, I am His, and He is mine."

PROVERBS

NEW LIVING TRANSLATION

PROVERBS 1

¹These are the proverbs of Solomon, David's son, king of Israel.

²The purpose of these proverbs is to teach people wisdom and discipline, and to help them understand wise sayings.

³Through these proverbs, people will receive instruction in discipline, good conduct, and doing what is right, just, and fair.

⁴These proverbs will make the simpleminded clever. They will give knowledge and purpose to young people.

⁵Let those who are wise listen to these proverbs and become even wiser. And let those who understand receive guidance

⁶by exploring the depth of meaning in these proverbs, parables, wise sayings, and riddles.

⁷Fear of the LORD is the beginning of knowledge. Only fools despise wisdom and discipline.

⁸Listen, my child,¹ to what your father teaches you. Don't neglect your mother's teaching.

⁹What you learn from them will crown you with grace and clothe you with honor.

¹⁰My child, if sinners entice you, turn your back on them!

¹¹They may say, "Come and join us. Let's hide and kill someone! Let's ambush the innocent!

¹²Let's swallow them alive as the grave swallows its victims. Though they are in the prime of life, they will go down into the pit of death.

¹³And the loot we'll get! We'll fill our houses with all kinds of things!

¹⁴Come on, throw in your lot with us; we'll split our loot with you."

¹⁵Don't go along with them, my child! Stay far away from their paths.

¹⁶They rush to commit crimes. They hurry to commit murder.

¹⁷When a bird sees a trap being set, it stays away.

¹⁸But not these people! They set an ambush for themselves; they booby-trap their own lives!

¹⁹Such is the fate of all who are greedy for gain. It ends up robbing them of life.

²⁰Wisdom shouts in the streets. She cries out in the public square.

²¹She calls out to the crowds along the main street, and to those in front of city hall.

1. 1:18 Hebrew *my son;* also in 1:10, 15.

22"You simpletons!" she cries. "How long will you go on being simpleminded? How long will you mockers relish your mocking? How long will you fools fight the facts?

23Come here and listen to me! I'll pour out the spirit of wisdom upon you and make you wise.

24"I called you so often, but you didn't come. I reached out to you, but you paid no attention.

25You ignored my advice and rejected the correction I offered.

26So I will laugh when you are in trouble! I will mock you when disaster overtakes you—

27when calamity overcomes you like a storm, when you are engulfed by trouble, and when anguish and distress overwhelm you.

28"I will not answer when they cry for help. Even though they anxiously search for me, they will not find me.

29For they hated knowledge and chose not to fear the LORD.

30They rejected my advice and paid no attention when I corrected them.

31That is why they must eat the bitter fruit of living their own way. They must experience the full terror of the path they have chosen.

32For they are simpletons who turn away from me—to death. They are fools, and their own complacency will destroy them.

33But all who listen to me will live in peace and safety, unafraid of harm."

PROVERBS 2

1My child,1 listen to me and treasure my instructions.

2Tune your ears to wisdom, and concentrate on understanding.

3Cry out for insight and understanding.

4Search for them as you would for lost money or hidden treasure.

5Then you will understand what it means to fear the LORD, and you will gain knowledge of God.

6For the LORD grants wisdom! From his mouth come knowledge and understanding.

7He grants a treasure of good sense to the godly. He is their shield, protecting those who walk with integrity.

8He guards the paths of justice and protects those who are faithful to him.

1. 2:1 Hebrew *My son.*

9Then you will understand what is right, just, and fair, and you will know how to find the right course of action every time.

10For wisdom will enter your heart, and knowledge will fill you with joy.

11Wise planning will watch over you. Understanding will keep you safe.

12Wisdom will save you from evil people, from those whose speech is corrupt.

13These people turn from right ways to walk down dark and evil paths.

14They rejoice in doing wrong, and they enjoy evil as it turns things upside down.

15What they do is crooked, and their ways are wrong.

16Wisdom will save you from the immoral woman, from the flattery of the adulterous woman.

17She has abandoned her husband and ignores the covenant she made before God.

18Entering her house leads to death; it is the road to hell.[2]

19The man who visits her is doomed. He will never reach the paths of life.

20Follow the steps of good men instead, and stay on the paths of the righteous.

21For only the upright will live in the land, and those who have integrity will remain in it.

22But the wicked will be removed from the land, and the treacherous will be destroyed.

2. 2:18 Hebrew *to the spirits of the dead.*

PROVERBS 3

1My child,[1] never forget the things I have taught you. Store my commands in your heart,

2for they will give you a long and satisfying life.

3Never let loyalty and kindness get away from you! Wear them like a necklace; write them deep within your heart.

4Then you will find favor with both God and people, and you will gain a good reputation.

5Trust in the LORD with all your heart; do not depend on your own understanding.

6Seek his will in all you do, and he will direct your paths.

1. 3:1 Hebrew *My son;* also in 3:11, 21.

7Don't be impressed with your own wisdom. Instead, fear the LORD and turn your back on evil.

8Then you will gain renewed health and vitality.

9Honor the LORD with your wealth and with the best part of everything your land produces.

10Then he will fill your barns with grain, and your vats will overflow with the finest wine.

11My child, don't ignore it when the LORD disciplines you, and don't be discouraged when he corrects you.

12For the LORD corrects those he loves, just as a father corrects a child[2] in whom he delights.

13Happy is the person who finds wisdom and gains understanding.

14For the profit of wisdom is better than silver, and her wages are better than gold.

15Wisdom is more precious than rubies; nothing you desire can compare with her.

16She offers you life in her right hand, and riches and honor in her left.

17She will guide you down delightful paths; all her ways are satisfying.

18Wisdom is a tree of life to those who embrace her; happy are those who hold her tightly.

19By wisdom the LORD founded the earth; by understanding he established the heavens.

20By his knowledge the deep fountains of the earth burst forth, and the clouds poured down rain.

21My child, don't lose sight of good planning and insight. Hang on to them,

22for they fill you with life and bring you honor and respect.

23They keep you safe on your way and keep your feet from stumbling.

24You can lie down without fear and enjoy pleasant dreams.

25You need not be afraid of disaster or the destruction that comes upon the wicked,

26for the LORD is your security. He will keep your foot from being caught in a trap.

27Do not withhold good from those who deserve it when it's in your power to help them.

28If you can help your neighbor now, don't say, "Come back tomorrow, and then I'll help you."

2. 3:12 Hebrew *a son.*

[29]Do not plot against your neighbors, for they trust you.

[30]Don't make accusations against someone who hasn't wronged you.

[31]Do not envy violent people; don't copy their ways.

[32]Such wicked people are an abomination to the LORD, but he offers his friendship to the godly.

[33]The curse of the LORD is on the house of the wicked, but his blessing is on the home of the upright.

[34]The LORD mocks at mockers, but he shows favor to the humble.

[35]The wise inherit honor, but fools are put to shame!

PROVERBS 4

[1]My children,[1] listen to me. Listen to your father's instruction. Pay attention and grow wise,

[2]for I am giving you good guidance. Don't turn away from my teaching.

[3]For I, too, was once my father's son, tenderly loved by my mother as an only child.

[4]My father told me, "Take my words to heart. Follow my instructions and you will live.

[5]Learn to be wise, and develop good judgment. Don't forget or turn away from my words.

[6]Don't turn your back on wisdom, for she will protect you. Love her, and she will guard you.

[7]Getting wisdom is the most important thing you can do! And whatever else you do, get good judgment.

[8]If you prize wisdom, she will exalt you. Embrace her and she will honor you.

[9]She will place a lovely wreath on your head; she will present you with a beautiful crown."

[10]My child,[2] listen to me and do as I say, and you will have a long, good life.

[11]I will teach you wisdom's ways and lead you in straight paths.

[12]If you live a life guided by wisdom, you won't limp or stumble as you run.

[13]Carry out my instructions; don't forsake them. Guard them, for they will lead you to a fulfilled life.

[14]Do not do as the wicked do or follow the path of evildoers.

1. 4:1 Hebrew *My sons.*
2. 4:10 Hebrew *My son;* also in 4:20.

[15]Avoid their haunts. Turn away and go somewhere else,

[16]for evil people cannot sleep until they have done their evil deed for the day. They cannot rest unless they have caused someone to stumble.

[17]They eat wickedness and drink violence!

[18]The way of the righteous is like the first gleam of dawn, which shines ever brighter until the full light of day.

[19]But the way of the wicked is like complete darkness. Those who follow it have no idea what they are stumbling over.

[20]Pay attention, my child, to what I say. Listen carefully.

[21]Don't lose sight of my words. Let them penetrate deep within your heart,

[22]for they bring life and radiant health to anyone who discovers their meaning.

[23]Above all else, guard your heart, for it affects everything you do.[3]

[24]Avoid all perverse talk; stay far from corrupt speech.

[25]Look straight ahead, and fix your eyes on what lies before you.

[26]Mark out a straight path for your feet; then stick to the path and stay safe.

[27]Don't get sidetracked; keep your feet from following evil.

3. 4:23 Hebrew *for from it flow the springs of life.*

PROVERBS 5

[1]My son, pay attention to my wisdom; listen carefully to my wise counsel.

[2]Then you will learn to be discreet and will store up knowledge.

[3]The lips of an immoral woman are as sweet as honey, and her mouth is smoother than oil.

[4]But the result is as bitter as poison, sharp as a double-edged sword.

[5]Her feet go down to death; her steps lead straight to the grave.[1]

[6]For she does not care about the path to life. She staggers down a crooked trail and doesn't even realize where it leads.

[7]So now, my sons, listen to me. Never stray from what I am about to say:

[8]Run from her! Don't go near the door of her house!

[9]If you do, you will lose your honor and hand over to merciless people everything you have achieved in life.

[10]Strangers will obtain your wealth, and someone else will enjoy the fruit of your labor.

[11]Afterward you will groan in anguish when disease consumes your body,

1. 5:5 Hebrew *to Sheol.*

¹²and you will say, "How I hated discipline! If only I had not demanded my own way!

¹³Oh, why didn't I listen to my teachers? Why didn't I pay attention to those who gave me instruction?

¹⁴I have come to the brink of utter ruin, and now I must face public disgrace."

¹⁵Drink water from your own well—share your love only with your wife.²

¹⁶Why spill the water of your springs in public, having sex with just anyone?³

¹⁷You should reserve it for yourselves. Don't share it with strangers.

¹⁸Let your wife be a fountain of blessing for you. Rejoice in the wife of your youth.

¹⁹She is a loving doe, a graceful deer. Let her breasts satisfy you always. May you always be captivated by her love.

²⁰Why be captivated, my son, with an immoral woman, or embrace the breasts of an adulterous woman?

²¹For the LORD sees clearly what a man does, examining every path he takes.

²²An evil man is held captive by his own sins; they are ropes that catch and hold him.

²³He will die for lack of self-control; he will be lost because of his incredible folly.

2. 5:15 Hebrew *Drink water from your own cistern, flowing water from your own well.*
3. 5:16 Hebrew *Why spill your springs in public, your streams in the streets?*

PROVERBS 6

¹My child,¹ if you co-sign a loan for a friend or guarantee the debt of someone you hardly know—

²if you have trapped yourself by your agreement and are caught by what you said—

³quick, get out of it if you possibly can! You have placed yourself at your friend's mercy. Now swallow your pride; go and beg to have your name erased.

⁴Don't put it off. Do it now! Don't rest until you do.

⁵Save yourself like a deer escaping from a hunter, like a bird fleeing from a net.

⁶Take a lesson from the ants, you lazybones. Learn from their ways and be wise!

⁷Even though they have no prince, governor, or ruler to make them work,

1. 6:1 Hebrew *My son.*

8they labor hard all summer, gathering food for the winter.

9But you, lazybones, how long will you sleep? When will you wake up? I want you to learn this lesson:

10A little extra sleep, a little more slumber, a little folding of the hands to rest—

11and poverty will pounce on you like a bandit; scarcity will attack you like an armed robber.

12Here is a description of worthless and wicked people: They are constant liars,

13signaling their true intentions to their friends by making signs with their eyes and feet and fingers.

14Their perverted hearts plot evil. They stir up trouble constantly.

15But they will be destroyed suddenly, broken beyond all hope of healing.

16There are six things the LORD hates—no, seven things he detests:

17   haughty eyes,

     a lying tongue,

     hands that kill the innocent,

18   a heart that plots evil,

     feet that race to do wrong,

19   a false witness who pours out lies,

     a person who sows discord among brothers.

20My son, obey your father's commands, and don't neglect your mother's teaching.

21Keep their words always in your heart. Tie them around your neck.

22Wherever you walk, their counsel can lead you. When you sleep, they will protect you. When you wake up in the morning, they will advise you.

23For these commands and this teaching are a lamp to light the way ahead of you. The correction of discipline is the way to life.

24These commands and this teaching will keep you from the immoral woman, from the smooth tongue of an adulterous woman.

25Don't lust for her beauty. Don't let her coyness seduce you.

26For a prostitute will bring you to poverty, and sleeping with another man's wife may cost you your very life.

27Can a man scoop fire into his lap and not be burned?

28Can he walk on hot coals and not blister his feet?

29So it is with the man who sleeps with another man's wife. He who embraces her will not go unpunished.

30Excuses might be found for a thief who steals because he is starving.

³¹But if he is caught, he will be fined seven times as much as he stole, even if it means selling everything in his house to pay it back.

³²But the man who commits adultery is an utter fool, for he destroys his own soul.

³³Wounds and constant disgrace are his lot. His shame will never be erased.

³⁴For the woman's husband will be furious in his jealousy, and he will have no mercy in his day of vengeance.

³⁵There is no compensation or bribe that will satisfy him.

PROVERBS 7

¹Follow my advice, my son; always treasure my commands.

²Obey them and live! Guard my teachings as your most precious possession.¹

³Tie them on your fingers as a reminder. Write them deep within your heart.

⁴Love wisdom like a sister; make insight a beloved member of your family.

⁵Let them hold you back from an affair with an immoral woman, from listening to the flattery of an adulterous woman.

⁶I was looking out the window of my house one day

⁷and saw a simpleminded young man who lacked common sense.

⁸He was crossing the street near the house of an immoral woman. He was strolling down the path by her house

⁹at twilight, as the day was fading, as the dark of night set in.

¹⁰The woman approached him, dressed seductively and sly of heart.

¹¹She was the brash, rebellious type who never stays at home.

¹²She is often seen in the streets and markets, soliciting at every corner.

¹³She threw her arms around him and kissed him, and with a brazen look she said,

¹⁴"I've offered my sacrifices and just finished my vows.

¹⁵It's you I was looking for! I came out to find you, and here you are!

¹⁶My bed is spread with colored sheets of finest linen imported from Egypt.

¹⁷I've perfumed my bed with myrrh, aloes, and cinnamon.

¹⁸Come, let's drink our fill of love until morning. Let's enjoy each other's caresses,

¹⁹for my husband is not home. He's away on a long trip.

---

1. 7:2 Hebrew *as the apple of your eye.*

²⁰He has taken a wallet full of money with him, and he won't return until later in the month."

²¹So she seduced him with her pretty speech. With her flattery she enticed him.

²²He followed her at once, like an ox going to the slaughter or like a trapped stag,

²³awaiting the arrow that would pierce its heart. He was like a bird flying into a snare, little knowing it would cost him his life.

²⁴Listen to me, my sons, and pay attention to my words.

²⁵Don't let your hearts stray away toward her. Don't wander down her wayward path.

²⁶For she has been the ruin of many; numerous men have been her victims.

²⁷Her house is the road to the grave. Her bedroom is the den of death.²

PROVERBS 8

¹Listen as wisdom calls out! Hear as understanding raises her voice!

²She stands on the hilltop and at the crossroads.

³At the entrance to the city, at the city gates, she cries aloud,

⁴"I call to you, to all of you! I am raising my voice to all people.

⁵How naive you are! Let me give you common sense. O foolish ones, let me give you understanding.

⁶Listen to me! For I have excellent things to tell you.
    Everything I say is right,

⁷for I speak the truth and hate every kind of deception.

⁸My advice is wholesome and good. There is nothing crooked or twisted in it.

⁹My words are plain to anyone with understanding, clear to those who want to learn.

¹⁰"Choose my instruction rather than silver, and knowledge over pure gold.

¹¹For wisdom is far more valuable than rubies. Nothing you desire can be compared with it.

¹²"I, Wisdom, live together with good judgment. I know where to discover knowledge and discernment.

¹³All who fear the LORD will hate evil. That is why I hate pride, arrogance, corruption, and perverted speech.

¹⁴Good advice and success belong to me. Insight and strength are mine.

2. 7:27 Hebrew *to Sheol.*

¹⁵Because of me, kings reign, and rulers make just laws.

¹⁶Rulers lead with my help, and nobles make righteous judgments.

¹⁷"I love all who love me. Those who search for me will surely find me.

¹⁸Unending riches, honor, wealth, and justice are mine to distribute.

¹⁹My gifts are better than the purest gold, my wages better than sterling silver!

²⁰I walk in righteousness, in paths of justice.

²¹Those who love me inherit wealth, for I fill their treasuries.

²²"The LORD formed me from the beginning, before he created anything else.

²³I was appointed in ages past, at the very first, before the earth began.

²⁴I was born before the oceans were created, before the springs bubbled forth their waters.

²⁵Before the mountains and the hills were formed, I was born—

²⁶before he had made the earth and fields and the first handfuls of soil.

²⁷"I was there when he established the heavens, when he drew the horizon on the oceans.

²⁸I was there when he set the clouds above, when he established the deep fountains of the earth.

²⁹I was there when he set the limits of the seas, so they would not spread beyond their boundaries. And when he marked off the earth's foundations,

³⁰I was the architect at his side. I was his constant delight, rejoicing always in his presence.

³¹And how happy I was with what he created—his wide world and all the human family!

³²"And so, my children,¹ listen to me, for happy are all who follow my ways.

³³Listen to my counsel and be wise. Don't ignore it.

³⁴"Happy are those who listen to me, watching for me daily at my gates, waiting for me outside my home!

³⁵For whoever finds me finds life and wins approval from the LORD.

³⁶But those who miss me have injured themselves. All who hate me love death."

PROVERBS 9

¹Wisdom has built her spacious house with seven pillars.

²She has prepared a great banquet, mixed the wines, and set the table.

1. 8:32 Hebrew *my sons.*

³She has sent her servants to invite everyone to come. She calls out from the heights overlooking the city.

⁴"Come home with me," she urges the simple. To those without good judgment, she says,

⁵"Come, eat my food, and drink the wine I have mixed.

⁶Leave your foolish ways behind, and begin to live; learn how to be wise."

⁷Anyone who rebukes a mocker will get a smart retort. Anyone who rebukes the wicked will get hurt.

⁸So don't bother rebuking mockers; they will only hate you. But the wise, when rebuked, will love you all the more.

⁹Teach the wise, and they will be wiser. Teach the righteous, and they will learn more.

¹⁰Fear of the LORD is the beginning of wisdom. Knowledge of the Holy One results in understanding.

¹¹Wisdom will multiply your days and add years to your life.

¹²If you become wise, you will be the one to benefit. If you scorn wisdom, you will be the one to suffer.

¹³The woman named Folly is loud and brash. She is ignorant and doesn't even know it.

¹⁴She sits in her doorway on the heights overlooking the city.

¹⁵She calls out to men going by who are minding their own business.

¹⁶"Come home with me," she urges the simple. To those without good judgment, she says,

¹⁷"Stolen water is refreshing; food eaten in secret tastes the best!"

¹⁸But the men don't realize that her former guests are now in the grave.¹

1. 9:18 Hebrew in *Sheol.*

PROVERBS 10

¹The proverbs of Solomon:

A wise child¹ brings joy to a father; a foolish child brings grief to a mother.

²Ill-gotten gain has no lasting value, but right living can save your life.

³The LORD will not let the godly starve to death, but he refuses to satisfy the craving of the wicked.

⁴Lazy people are soon poor; hard workers get rich.

1. 10:1 Hebrew *son;* also in 10:1b.

⁵A wise youth works hard all summer; a youth who sleeps away the hour of opportunity brings shame.

⁶The godly are showered with blessings; evil people cover up their harmful intentions.

⁷We all have happy memories of the godly, but the name of a wicked person rots away.

⁸The wise are glad to be instructed, but babbling fools fall flat on their faces.

⁹People with integrity have firm footing, but those who follow crooked paths will slip and fall.

¹⁰People who wink at wrong cause trouble, but a bold reproof promotes peace.²

¹¹The words of the godly lead to life; evil people cover up their harmful intentions.

¹²Hatred stirs up quarrels, but love covers all offenses.

¹³Wise words come from the lips of people with understanding, but fools will be punished with a rod.

¹⁴Wise people treasure knowledge, but the babbling of a fool invites trouble.

¹⁵The wealth of the rich is their fortress; the poverty of the poor is their calamity.

¹⁶The earnings of the godly enhance their lives, but evil people squander their money on sin.

¹⁷People who accept correction are on the pathway to life, but those who ignore it will lead others astray.

¹⁸To hide hatred is to be a liar; to slander is to be a fool.

¹⁹Don't talk too much, for it fosters sin. Be sensible and turn off the flow!

²⁰The words of the godly are like sterling silver; the heart of a fool is worthless.

²¹The godly give good advice, but fools are destroyed by their lack of common sense.

²²The blessing of the LORD makes a person rich, and he adds no sorrow with it.

²³Doing wrong is fun for a fool, while wise conduct is a pleasure to the wise.

²⁴The fears of the wicked will all come true; so will the hopes of the godly.

²⁵Disaster strikes like a cyclone, whirling the wicked away, but the godly have a lasting foundation.

²⁶Lazy people are a pain to their employer. They are like smoke in the eyes or vinegar that sets the teeth on edge.

2. 10:10 As in Greek version; Hebrew reads *but babbling fools fall flat on their faces.*

27Fear of the LORD lengthens one's life, but the years of the wicked are cut short.

28The hopes of the godly result in happiness, but the expectations of the wicked are all in vain.

29The LORD protects the upright but destroys the wicked.

30The godly will never be disturbed, but the wicked will be removed from the land.

31The godly person gives wise advice, but the tongue that deceives will be cut off.

32The godly speak words that are helpful, but the wicked speak only what is corrupt.

PROVERBS 11

1The LORD hates cheating, but he delights in honesty.

2Pride leads to disgrace, but with humility comes wisdom.

3Good people are guided by their honesty; treacherous people are destroyed by their dishonesty.

4Riches won't help on the day of judgment, but right living is a safeguard against death.

5The godly are directed by their honesty; the wicked fall beneath their load of sin.

6The godliness of good people rescues them; the ambition of treacherous people traps them.

7When the wicked die, their hopes all perish, for they rely on their own feeble strength.

8God rescues the godly from danger, but he lets the wicked fall into trouble.

9Evil words destroy one's friends; wise discernment rescues the godly.

10The whole city celebrates when the godly succeed; they shout for joy when the godless die.

11Upright citizens bless a city and make it prosper, but the talk of the wicked tears it apart.

12It is foolish to belittle a neighbor; a person with good sense remains silent.

13A gossip goes around revealing secrets, but those who are trustworthy can keep a confidence.

14Without wise leadership, a nation falls; with many counselors, there is safety.

¹⁵Guaranteeing a loan for a stranger is dangerous; it is better to refuse than to suffer later.

¹⁶Beautiful women obtain wealth, and violent men get rich.

¹⁷Your own soul is nourished when you are kind, but you destroy yourself when you are cruel.

¹⁸Evil people get rich for the moment, but the reward of the godly will last.

¹⁹Godly people find life; evil people find death.

²⁰The LORD hates people with twisted hearts, but he delights in those who have integrity.

²¹You can be sure that evil people will be punished, but the children of the godly will go free.

²²A woman who is beautiful but lacks discretion is like a gold ring in a pig's snout.

²³The godly can look forward to happiness, while the wicked can expect only wrath.

²⁴It is possible to give freely and become more wealthy, but those who are stingy will lose everything.

²⁵The generous prosper and are satisfied; those who refresh others will themselves be refreshed.

²⁶People curse those who hold their grain for higher prices, but they bless the one who sells to them in their time of need.

²⁷If you search for good, you will find favor; but if you search for evil, it will find you!

²⁸Trust in your money and down you go! But the godly flourish like leaves in spring.

²⁹Those who bring trouble on their families inherit only the wind. The fool will be a servant to the wise.

³⁰The godly are like trees that bear life-giving fruit, and those who save lives are wise.

³¹If the righteous are rewarded here on earth, how much more true that the wicked and the sinner will get what they deserve!

PROVERBS 12

¹To learn, you must love discipline; it is stupid to hate correction.

²The LORD approves of those who are good, but he condemns those who plan wickedness.

³Wickedness never brings stability; only the godly have deep roots.

⁴A worthy wife is her husband's joy and crown; a shameful wife saps his strength.

⁵The plans of the godly are just; the advice of the wicked is treacherous.

⁶The words of the wicked are like a murderous ambush, but the words of the godly save lives.

⁷The wicked perish and are gone, but the children of the godly stand firm.

⁸Everyone admires a person with good sense, but a warped mind is despised.

⁹It is better to be a nobody with a servant than to be self-important but have no food.

¹⁰The godly are concerned for the welfare of their animals, but even the kindness of the wicked is cruel.

¹¹Hard work means prosperity; only fools idle away their time.

¹²Thieves are jealous of each other's loot, while the godly bear their own fruit.

¹³The wicked are trapped by their own words, but the godly escape such trouble.

¹⁴People can get many good things by the words they say; the work of their hands also gives them many benefits.

¹⁵Fools think they need no advice, but the wise listen to others.

¹⁶A fool is quick-tempered, but a wise person stays calm when insulted.

¹⁷An honest witness tells the truth; a false witness tells lies.

¹⁸Some people make cutting remarks, but the words of the wise bring healing.

¹⁹Truth stands the test of time; lies are soon exposed.

²⁰Deceit fills hearts that are plotting evil; joy fills hearts that are planning peace!

²¹No real harm befalls the godly, but the wicked have their fill of trouble.

²²The LORD hates those who don't keep their word, but he delights in those who do.

²³Wise people don't make a show of their knowledge, but fools broadcast their folly.

²⁴Work hard and become a leader; be lazy and become a slave.

²⁵Worry weighs a person down; an encouraging word cheers a person up.

²⁶The godly give good advice to their friends;¹ the wicked lead them astray.

²⁷Lazy people don't even cook the game they catch, but the diligent make use of everything they find.

²⁸The way of the godly leads to life; their path does not lead to death.

1. 12:26 Or *The godly are cautious in friendship,* or *the godly are freed from evil.* The meaning of the Hebrew is uncertain.

[1]A wise child[1] accepts a parent's discipline; a young mocker refuses to listen.

[2]Good people enjoy the positive results of their words, but those who are treacherous crave violence.

[3]Those who control their tongue will have a long life; a quick retort can ruin everything.

[4]Lazy people want much but get little, but those who work hard will prosper and be satisfied.

[5]Those who are godly hate lies; the wicked come to shame and disgrace.

[6]Godliness helps people all through life, while the evil are destroyed by their wickedness.

[7]Some who are poor pretend to be rich; others who are rich pretend to be poor.

[8]The rich can pay a ransom, but the poor won't even get threatened.

[9]The life of the godly is full of light and joy, but the sinner's light is snuffed out.

[10]Pride leads to arguments; those who take advice are wise.

[11]Wealth from get-rich-quick schemes quickly disappears; wealth from hard work grows.

[12]Hope deferred makes the heart sick, but when dreams come true, there is life and joy.

[13]People who despise advice will find themselves in trouble; those who respect it will succeed.

[14]The advice of the wise is like a life-giving fountain; those who accept it avoid the snares of death.

[15]A person with good sense is respected; a treacherous person walks a rocky road.

[16]Wise people think before they act; fools don't and even brag about it!

[17]An unreliable messenger stumbles into trouble, but a reliable messenger brings healing.

[18]If you ignore criticism, you will end in poverty and disgrace; if you accept criticism, you will be honored.

[19]It is pleasant to see dreams come true, but fools will not turn from evil to attain them.

1. 13:1 Hebrew *son*.

²⁰Whoever walks with the wise will become wise; whoever walks with fools will suffer harm.

²¹Trouble chases sinners, while blessings chase the righteous!

²²Good people leave an inheritance to their grandchildren, but the sinner's wealth passes to the godly.

²³A poor person's farm may produce much food, but injustice sweeps it all away.

²⁴If you refuse to discipline your children, it proves you don't love them; if you love your children, you will be prompt to discipline them.

²⁵The godly eat to their hearts' content, but the belly of the wicked goes hungry.

PROVERBS 14

¹A wise woman builds her house; a foolish woman tears hers down with her own hands.

²Those who follow the right path fear the LORD; those who take the wrong path despise him.

³The talk of fools is a rod for their backs,¹ but the words of the wise keep them out of trouble.

⁴An empty stable stays clean, but no income comes from an empty stable.

⁵A truthful witness does not lie; a false witness breathes lies.

⁶A mocker seeks wisdom and never finds it, but knowledge comes easily to those with understanding.

⁷Stay away from fools, for you won't find knowledge there.

⁸The wise look ahead to see what is coming, but fools deceive themselves.

⁹Fools make fun of guilt, but the godly acknowledge it and seek reconciliation.

¹⁰Each heart knows its own bitterness, and no one else can fully share its joy.

¹¹The house of the wicked will perish, but the tent of the godly will flourish.

¹²There is a path before each person that seems right, but it ends in death.

¹³Laughter can conceal a heavy heart; when the laughter ends, the grief remains.

¹⁴Backsliders get what they deserve; good people receive their reward.

¹⁵Only simpletons believe everything they are told! The prudent carefully consider their steps.

¹⁶The wise are cautious² and avoid danger; fools plunge ahead with great confidence.

1. 14:3 Hebrew *a rod of pride.*
2. 14:16 Hebrew *The wise fear.*

¹⁷Those who are short-tempered do foolish things, and schemers are hated.

¹⁸The simpleton is clothed with folly, but the wise person is crowned with knowledge.

¹⁹Evil people will bow before good people; the wicked will bow at the gates of the godly.

²⁰The poor are despised even by their neighbors, while the rich have many "friends."

²¹It is sin to despise one's neighbors; blessed are those who help the poor.

²²If you plot evil, you will be lost; but if you plan good, you will be granted unfailing love and faithfulness.

²³Work brings profit, but mere talk leads to poverty!

²⁴Wealth is a crown for the wise; the effort of fools yields only folly.

²⁵A truthful witness saves lives, but a false witness is a traitor.

²⁶Those who fear the LORD are secure; he will be a place of refuge for their children.

²⁷Fear of the LORD is a life-giving fountain; it offers escape from the snares of death.

²⁸A growing population is a king's glory; a dwindling nation is his doom.

²⁹Those who control their anger have great understanding; those with a hasty temper will make mistakes.

³⁰A relaxed attitude lengthens life; jealousy rots it away.

³¹Those who oppress the poor insult their Maker, but those who help the poor honor him.

³²The wicked are crushed by their sins, but the godly have a refuge when they die.

³³Wisdom is enshrined in an understanding heart; wisdom is not[3] found among fools.

³⁴Godliness exalts a nation, but sin is a disgrace to any people.

³⁵A king rejoices in servants who know what they are doing; he is angry with those who cause trouble.

PROVERBS 15

¹A gentle answer turns away wrath, but harsh words stir up anger.

²The wise person makes learning a joy; fools spout only foolishness.

3. 14:33 As in Greek version; Hebrew *lacks not.*

[3]The LORD is watching everywhere, keeping his eye on both the evil and the good.

[4]Gentle words bring life and health; a deceitful tongue crushes the spirit.

[5]Only a fool despises a parent's discipline; whoever learns from correction is wise.

[6]There is treasure in the house of the godly, but the earnings of the wicked bring trouble.

[7]Only the wise can give good advice; fools cannot do so.

[8]The LORD hates the sacrifice of the wicked, but he delights in the prayers of the upright.

[9]The LORD despises the way of the wicked, but he loves those who pursue godliness.

[10]Whoever abandons the right path will be severely punished; whoever hates correction will die.

[11]Even the depths of Death and Destruction[1] are known by the LORD. How much more does he know the human heart!

[12]Mockers don't love those who rebuke them, so they stay away from the wise.

[13]A glad heart makes a happy face; a broken heart crushes the spirit.

[14]A wise person is hungry for truth, while the fool feeds on trash.

[15]For the poor, every day brings trouble; for the happy heart, life is a continual feast.

[16]It is better to have little with fear for the LORD than to have great treasure with turmoil.

[17]A bowl of soup with someone you love is better than steak with someone you hate.

[18]A hothead starts fights; a cool-tempered person tries to stop them.

[19]A lazy person has trouble all through life; the path of the upright is easy!

[20]Sensible children bring joy to their father; foolish children despise their mother.

[21]Foolishness brings joy to those who have no sense; a sensible person stays on the right path.

[22]Plans go wrong for lack of advice; many counselors bring success.

[23]Everyone enjoys a fitting reply; it is wonderful to say the right thing at the right time!

[24]The path of the wise leads to life above; they leave the grave[2] behind.

---

1. 15:11 Hebrew *Sheol and Abaddon.*
2. 15:24 Hebrew *Sheol.*

²⁵The LORD destroys the house of the proud, but he protects the property of widows.

²⁶The LORD despises the thoughts of the wicked, but he delights in pure words.

²⁷Dishonest money brings grief to the whole family, but those who hate bribes will live.

²⁸The godly think before speaking; the wicked spout evil words.

²⁹The LORD is far from the wicked, but he hears the prayers of the righteous.

³⁰A cheerful look brings joy to the heart; good news makes for good health.

³¹If you listen to constructive criticism, you will be at home among the wise.

³²If you reject criticism, you only harm yourself; but if you listen to correction, you grow in understanding.

³³Fear of the LORD teaches a person to be wise; humility precedes honor.

PROVERBS 16

¹We can gather our thoughts, but the LORD gives the right answer.

²People may be pure in their own eyes, but the LORD examines their motives.

³Commit your work to the LORD, and then your plans will succeed.

⁴The LORD has made everything for his own purposes, even the wicked for punishment.

⁵The LORD despises pride; be assured that the proud will be punished.

⁶Unfailing love and faithfulness cover sin; evil is avoided by fear of the LORD.

⁷When the ways of people please the LORD, he makes even their enemies live at peace with them.

⁸It is better to be poor and godly than rich and dishonest.

⁹We can make our plans, but the LORD determines our steps.

¹⁰The king speaks with divine wisdom; he must never judge unfairly.

¹¹The LORD demands fairness in every business deal; he sets the standard.

¹²A king despises wrongdoing, for his rule depends on his justice.

¹³The king is pleased with righteous lips; he loves those who speak honestly.

¹⁴The anger of the king is a deadly threat; the wise do what they can to appease it.

¹⁵When the king smiles, there is life; his favor refreshes like a gentle rain.

¹⁶How much better to get wisdom than gold, and understanding than silver!

¹⁷The path of the upright leads away from evil; whoever follows that path is safe.

¹⁸Pride goes before destruction, and haughtiness before a fall.

¹⁹It is better to live humbly with the poor than to share plunder with the proud.

²⁰Those who listen to instruction will prosper; those who trust the LORD will be happy.

²¹The wise are known for their understanding, and instruction is appreciated if it's well presented.

²²Discretion is a life-giving fountain to those who possess it, but discipline is wasted on fools.

²³From a wise mind comes wise speech; the words of the wise are persuasive.

²⁴Kind words are like honey—sweet to the soul and healthy for the body.

²⁵There is a path before each person that seems right, but it ends in death.

²⁶It is good for workers to have an appetite; an empty stomach drives them on.

²⁷Scoundrels hunt for scandal; their words are a destructive blaze.

²⁸A troublemaker plants seeds of strife; gossip separates the best of friends.

²⁹Violent people deceive their companions, leading them down a harmful path.

³⁰With narrowed eyes, they plot evil; without a word, they plan their mischief.

³¹Gray hair is a crown of glory; it is gained by living a godly life.

³²It is better to be patient than powerful; it is better to have self-control than to conquer a city.

³³We may throw the dice, but the LORD determines how they fall.

PROVERBS 17

¹A dry crust eaten in peace is better than a great feast with strife.

²A wise slave will rule over the master's shameful sons and will share their inheritance.

³Fire tests the purity of silver and gold, but the LORD tests the heart.

⁴Wrongdoers listen to wicked talk; liars pay attention to destructive words.

⁵Those who mock the poor insult their Maker; those who rejoice at the misfortune of others will be punished.

⁶Grandchildren are the crowning glory of the aged; parents are the pride of their children.

⁷Eloquent speech is not fitting for a fool; even less are lies fitting for a ruler.

⁸A bribe seems to work like magic for those who give it; they succeed in all they do.

⁹Disregarding another person's faults preserves love; telling about them separates close friends.

¹⁰A single rebuke does more for a person of understanding than a hundred lashes on the back of a fool.

¹¹Evil people seek rebellion, but they will be severely punished.

¹²It is safer to meet a bear robbed of her cubs than to confront a fool caught in folly.

¹³If you repay evil for good, evil will never leave your house.

¹⁴Beginning a quarrel is like opening a floodgate, so drop the matter before a dispute breaks out.

¹⁵The LORD despises those who acquit the guilty and condemn the innocent.

¹⁶It is senseless to pay tuition to educate a fool who has no heart for wisdom.

¹⁷A friend is always loyal, and a brother is born to help in time of need.

¹⁸It is poor judgment to co-sign a friend's note, to become responsible for a neighbor's debts.

¹⁹Anyone who loves to quarrel loves sin; anyone who speaks boastfully[1] invites disaster.

²⁰The crooked heart will not prosper; the twisted tongue tumbles into trouble.

²¹It is painful to be the parent of a fool; there is no joy for the father of a rebel.

²²A cheerful heart is good medicine, but a broken spirit saps a person's strength.

²³The wicked accept secret bribes to pervert justice.

²⁴Sensible people keep their eyes glued on wisdom, but a fool's eyes wander to the ends of the earth.

²⁵A foolish child[2] brings grief to a father and bitterness to a mother.

²⁶It is wrong to fine the godly for being good or to punish nobles for being honest!

²⁷A truly wise person uses few words; a person with understanding is even-tempered.

²⁸Even fools are thought to be wise when they keep silent; when they keep their mouths shut, they seem intelligent.

PROVERBS 18

¹A recluse is self-indulgent, snarling at every sound principle of conduct.

1. 17:19 Or *who builds up defenses;* Hebrew reads *who makes a high gate.*
2. 17:25 Hebrew *son.*

²Fools have no interest in understanding; they only want to air their own opinions.

³When the wicked arrive, contempt, shame, and disgrace are sure to follow.

⁴A person's words can be life-giving water; words of true wisdom are as refreshing as a bubbling brook.

⁵It is wrong for a judge to favor the guilty or condemn the innocent.

⁶Fools get into constant quarrels; they are asking for a beating.

⁷The mouths of fools are their ruin; their lips get them into trouble.

⁸What dainty morsels rumors are—but they sink deep into one's heart.

⁹A lazy person is as bad as someone who destroys things.

¹⁰The name of the LORD is a strong fortress; the godly run to him and are safe.

¹¹The rich think of their wealth as an impregnable defense; they imagine it is a high wall of safety.

¹²Haughtiness goes before destruction; humility precedes honor.

¹³What a shame, what folly, to give advice before listening to the facts!

¹⁴The human spirit can endure a sick body, but who can bear it if the spirit is crushed?

¹⁵Intelligent people are always open to new ideas. In fact, they look for them.

¹⁶Giving a gift works wonders; it may bring you before important people!

¹⁷Any story sounds true until someone sets the record straight.

¹⁸Casting lots can end arguments and settle disputes between powerful opponents.

¹⁹It's harder to make amends with an offended friend than to capture a fortified city. Arguments separate friends like a gate locked with iron bars.

²⁰Words satisfy the soul as food satisfies the stomach; the right words on a person's lips bring satisfaction.

²¹Those who love to talk will experience the consequences, for the tongue can kill or nourish life.

²²The man who finds a wife finds a treasure and receives favor from the LORD.

²³The poor plead for mercy; the rich answer with insults.

²⁴There are "friends" who destroy each other, but a real friend sticks closer than a brother.

PROVERBS 19

¹It is better to be poor and honest than to be a fool and dishonest.

²Zeal without knowledge is not good; a person who moves too quickly may go the wrong way.

³People ruin their lives by their own foolishness and then are angry at the LORD.

⁴Wealth makes many "friends"; poverty drives them away.

⁵A false witness will not go unpunished, nor will a liar escape.

⁶Many beg favors from a prince; everyone is the friend of a person who gives gifts!

⁷If the relatives of the poor despise them, how much more will their friends avoid them. The poor call after them, but they are gone.

⁸To acquire wisdom is to love oneself; people who cherish understanding will prosper.

⁹A false witness will not go unpunished, and a liar will be destroyed.

¹⁰It isn't right for a fool to live in luxury or for a slave to rule over princes!

¹¹People with good sense restrain their anger; they earn esteem by overlooking wrongs.

¹²The king's anger is like a lion's roar, but his favor is like dew on the grass.

¹³A foolish child[1] is a calamity to a father; a nagging wife annoys like a constant dripping.

¹⁴Parents can provide their sons with an inheritance of houses and wealth, but only the LORD can give an understanding wife.

¹⁵A lazy person sleeps soundly—and goes hungry.

¹⁶Keep the commandments and keep your life; despising them leads to death.

¹⁷If you help the poor, you are lending to the LORD—and he will repay you!

¹⁸Discipline your children while there is hope. If you don't, you will ruin their lives.

¹⁹Short-tempered people must pay their own penalty. If you rescue them once, you will have to do it again.

²⁰Get all the advice and instruction you can, and be wise the rest of your life.

²¹You can make many plans, but the LORD's purpose will prevail.

²²Loyalty makes a person attractive. And it is better to be poor than dishonest.

²³Fear of the LORD gives life, security, and protection from harm.

²⁴Some people are so lazy that they won't even lift a finger to feed themselves.

²⁵If you punish a mocker, the simpleminded will learn a lesson; if you reprove the wise, they will be all the wiser.

²⁶Children who mistreat their father or chase away their mother are a public disgrace and an embarrassment.

²⁷If you stop listening to instruction, my child, you have turned your back on knowledge.

---

1. 19:13 Hebrew *son;* also in 19:27.

²⁸A corrupt witness makes a mockery of justice; the mouth of the wicked gulps down evil.

²⁹Mockers will be punished, and the backs of fools will be beaten.

PROVERBS 20

¹Wine produces mockers; liquor leads to brawls. Whoever is led astray by drink cannot be wise.

²The king's fury is like a lion's roar; to rouse his anger is to risk your life.

³Avoiding a fight is a mark of honor; only fools insist on quarreling.

⁴If you are too lazy to plow in the right season, you will have no food at the harvest.

⁵Though good advice lies deep within a person's heart, the wise will draw it out.

⁶Many will say they are loyal friends, but who can find one who is really faithful?

⁷The godly walk with integrity; blessed are their children after them.

⁸When a king judges, he carefully weighs all the evidence, distinguishing the bad from the good.

⁹Who can say, "I have cleansed my heart; I am pure and free from sin"?

¹⁰The LORD despises double standards of every kind.

¹¹Even children are known by the way they act, whether their conduct is pure and right.

¹²Ears to hear and eyes to see—both are gifts from the LORD.

¹³If you love sleep, you will end in poverty. Keep your eyes open, and there will be plenty to eat!

¹⁴The buyer haggles over the price, saying, "It's worthless," then brags about getting a bargain!

¹⁵Wise speech is rarer and more valuable than gold and rubies.

¹⁶Be sure to get collateral from anyone who guarantees the debt of a stranger. Get a deposit if someone guarantees the debt of a foreigner.¹

¹⁷Stolen bread tastes sweet, but it turns to gravel in the mouth.

¹⁸Plans succeed through good counsel; don't go to war without the advice of others.

¹⁹A gossip tells secrets, so don't hang around with someone who talks too much.

1. 20:16 An alternate reading in the Hebrew text is *the debt of an adulterous woman;* compare 27:13.

²⁰If you curse your father or mother, the lamp of your life will be snuffed out.

²¹An inheritance obtained early in life is not a blessing in the end.

²²Don't say, "I will get even for this wrong." Wait for the LORD to handle the matter.

²³The LORD despises double standards; he is not pleased by dishonest scales.

²⁴How can we understand the road we travel? It is the LORD who directs our steps.

²⁵It is dangerous to make a rash promise to God before counting the cost.

²⁶A wise king finds the wicked, lays them out like wheat, then runs the crushing wheel over them.

²⁷The LORD's searchlight penetrates the human spirit,² exposing every hidden motive.

²⁸Unfailing love and faithfulness protect the king; his throne is made secure through love.

²⁹The glory of the young is their strength; the gray hair of experience is the splendor of the old.

³⁰Physical punishment cleanses away evil;³ such discipline purifies the heart.

2. 20:27 Or *The human spirit is the LORD's searchlight.*
3. 20:30 The meaning of the Hebrew is uncertain.

PROVERBS 21

¹The king's heart is like a stream of water directed by the LORD; he turns it wherever he pleases.

²People may think they are doing what is right, but the LORD examines the heart.

³The LORD is more pleased when we do what is just and right than when we give him sacrifices.

⁴Haughty eyes, a proud heart, and evil actions are all sin.

⁵Good planning and hard work lead to prosperity, but hasty shortcuts lead to poverty.

⁶Wealth created by lying is a vanishing mist and a deadly trap.¹

⁷Because the wicked refuse to do what is just, their violence boomerangs and destroys them.

⁸The guilty walk a crooked path; the innocent travel a straight road.

1. 21:6 As in Greek version; Hebrew reads *mist for those who seek death.*

9It is better to live alone in the corner of an attic than with a contentious wife in a lovely home.

10Evil people love to harm others; their neighbors get no mercy from them.

11A simpleton can learn only by seeing mockers punished; a wise person learns from instruction.

12The Righteous One[2] knows what is going on in the homes of the wicked; he will bring the wicked to disaster.

13Those who shut their ears to the cries of the poor will be ignored in their own time of need.

14A secret gift calms anger; a secret bribe pacifies fury.

15Justice is a joy to the godly, but it causes dismay among evildoers.

16The person who strays from common sense will end up in the company of the dead.

17Those who love pleasure become poor; wine and luxury are not the way to riches.

18Sometimes the wicked are punished to save the godly, and the treacherous for the upright.

19It is better to live alone in the desert than with a crabby, complaining wife.

20The wise have wealth and luxury, but fools spend whatever they get.

21Whoever pursues godliness and unfailing love will find life, godliness, and honor.

22The wise conquer the city of the strong and level the fortress in which they trust.

23If you keep your mouth shut, you will stay out of trouble.

24Mockers are proud and haughty; they act with boundless arrogance.

25The desires of lazy people will be their ruin, for their hands refuse to work.

26They are always greedy for more, while the godly love to give!

27God loathes the sacrifice of an evil person, especially when it is brought with ulterior motives.

28A false witness will be cut off, but an attentive witness will be allowed to speak.

29The wicked put up a bold front, but the upright proceed with care.

30Human plans, no matter how wise or well advised, cannot stand against the LORD.

31The horses are prepared for battle, but the victory belongs to the LORD.

2. 21:12 Or *The righteous man.*

¹Choose a good reputation over great riches, for being held in high esteem is better than having silver or gold.

²The rich and the poor have this in common: The LORD made them both.

³A prudent person foresees the danger ahead and takes precautions; the simpleton goes blindly on and suffers the consequences.

⁴True humility and fear of the LORD lead to riches, honor, and long life.

⁵The deceitful walk a thorny, treacherous road; whoever values life will stay away.

⁶Teach your children to choose the right path, and when they are older, they will remain upon it.

⁷Just as the rich rule the poor, so the borrower is servant to the lender.

⁸Those who plant seeds of injustice will harvest disaster, and their reign of terror will end.

⁹Blessed are those who are generous, because they feed the poor.

¹⁰Throw out the mocker, and fighting, quarrels, and insults will disappear.

¹¹Anyone who loves a pure heart and gracious speech is the king's friend.

¹²The LORD preserves knowledge, but he ruins the plans of the deceitful.

¹³The lazy person is full of excuses, saying, "If I go outside, I might meet a lion in the street and be killed!"

¹⁴The mouth of an immoral woman is a deep pit; those living under the LORD's displeasure will fall into it.

¹⁵A youngster's heart is filled with foolishness, but discipline will drive it away.

¹⁶A person who gets ahead by oppressing the poor or by showering gifts on the rich will end in poverty.

¹⁷Listen to the words of the wise; apply your heart to my instruction.

¹⁸For it is good to keep these sayings deep within yourself, always ready on your lips.

¹⁹I am teaching you today—yes, you—so you will trust in the LORD.

²⁰I have written thirty sayings for you, filled with advice and knowledge.

²¹In this way, you may know the truth and bring an accurate report to those who sent you.

²²Do not rob the poor because they are poor or exploit the needy in court.

²³For the LORD is their defender. He will injure anyone who injures them.

²⁴Keep away from angry, short-tempered people,

²⁵or you will learn to be like them and endanger your soul.

26Do not co-sign another person's note or put up a guarantee for someone else's loan.

27If you can't pay it, even your bed will be snatched from under you.

28Do not steal your neighbor's property by moving the ancient boundary markers set up by your ancestors.

29Do you see any truly competent workers? They will serve kings rather than ordinary people.

PROVERBS 23

1When dining with a ruler, pay attention to what is put before you.

2If you are a big eater, put a knife to your throat,

3and don't desire all the delicacies—deception may be involved.

4Don't weary yourself trying to get rich. Why waste your time?

5For riches can disappear as though they had the wings of a bird!

6Don't eat with people who are stingy; don't desire their delicacies.

7"Eat and drink," they say, but they don't mean it. They are always thinking about how much it costs.

8You will vomit up the delicious food they serve, and you will have to take back your words of appreciation for their "kindness."

9Don't waste your breath on fools, for they will despise the wisest advice.

10Don't steal the land of defenseless orphans by moving the ancient boundary markers,

11for their Redeemer is strong. He himself will bring their charges against you.

12Commit yourself to instruction; attune your ears to hear words of knowledge.

13Don't fail to correct your children. They won't die if you spank them.

14Physical discipline may well save them from death.[1]

15My child,[2] how I will rejoice if you become wise.

16Yes, my heart will thrill when you speak what is right and just.

17Don't envy sinners, but always continue to fear the LORD.

18For surely you have a future ahead of you; your hope will not be disappointed.

19My child, listen and be wise. Keep your heart on the right course.

20Do not carouse with drunkards and gluttons,

1. 23:14 Hebrew *from Sheol.*
2. 23:15 Hebrew *My son;* also in 23:19.

²¹for they are on their way to poverty. Too much sleep clothes a person with rags.

²²Listen to your father, who gave you life, and don't despise your mother's experience when she is old.

²³Get the truth and don't ever sell it; also get wisdom, discipline, and discernment.

²⁴The father of godly children has cause for joy. What a pleasure it is to have wise children.³

²⁵So give your parents joy! May she who gave you birth be happy.

²⁶O my son, give me your heart. May your eyes delight in my ways of wisdom.

²⁷A prostitute is a deep pit; an adulterous woman is treacherous.⁴

²⁸She hides and waits like a robber, looking for another victim who will be unfaithful to his wife.

²⁹Who has anguish? Who has sorrow? Who is always fighting? Who is always complaining? Who has unnecessary bruises? Who has bloodshot eyes?

³⁰It is the one who spends long hours in the taverns, trying out new drinks.

³¹Don't let the sparkle and smooth taste of wine deceive you.

³²For in the end it bites like a poisonous serpent; it stings like a viper.

³³You will see hallucinations, and you will say crazy things.

³⁴You will stagger like a sailor tossed at sea, clinging to a swaying mast.

³⁵And you will say, "They hit me, but I didn't feel it. I didn't even know it when they beat me up. When will I wake up so I can have another drink?"

3. 23:24 Hebrew *a wise son.*
4. 23:27 Hebrew *is a narrow well.*

PROVERBS 24

¹Don't envy evil people; don't desire their company.

²For they spend their days plotting violence, and their words are always stirring up trouble.

³A house is built by wisdom and becomes strong through good sense.

⁴Through knowledge its rooms are filled with all sorts of precious riches and valuables.

⁵A wise man is mightier than a strong man,¹ and a man of knowledge is more powerful than a strong man.

1. 24:5 As in Greek version; Hebrew reads *A wise man is strength.*

⁶So don't go to war without wise guidance; victory depends on having many counselors.

⁷Wisdom is too much for a fool. When the leaders gather, the fool has nothing to say.

⁸A person who plans evil will get a reputation as a troublemaker.

⁹The schemes of a fool are sinful; everyone despises a mocker.

¹⁰If you fail under pressure, your strength is not very great.

¹¹Rescue those who are unjustly sentenced to death; don't stand back and let them die.

¹²Don't try to avoid responsibility by saying you didn't know about it. For God knows all hearts, and he sees you.

He keeps watch over your soul, and he knows you knew! And he will judge all people according to what they have done.

¹³My child,² eat honey, for it is good, and the honeycomb is sweet to the taste.

¹⁴In the same way, wisdom is sweet to your soul. If you find it, you will have a bright future, and your hopes will not be cut short.

¹⁵Do not lie in wait like an outlaw at the home of the godly. And don't raid the house where the godly live.

¹⁶They may trip seven times, but each time they will rise again. But one calamity is enough to lay the wicked low.

¹⁷Do not rejoice when your enemies fall into trouble. Don't be happy when they stumble.

¹⁸For the LORD will be displeased with you and will turn his anger away from them.

¹⁹Do not fret because of evildoers; don't envy the wicked.

²⁰For the evil have no future; their light will be snuffed out.

²¹My child, fear the LORD and the king, and don't associate with rebels.

²²For you will go down with them to sudden disaster. Who knows where the punishment from the LORD and the king will end?

²³Here are some further sayings of the wise:

It is wrong to show favoritism when passing judgment.

²⁴A judge who says to the wicked, "You are innocent," will be cursed by many people and denounced by the nations.

²⁵But blessings are showered on those who convict the guilty.

²⁶It is an honor to receive an honest reply.

²⁷Develop your business first before building your house.

2. 24:13 Hebrew *My son;* also in 24:21.

²⁸Do not testify spitefully against innocent neighbors; don't lie about them.

²⁹And don't say, "Now I can pay them back for all their meanness to me! I'll get even!"

³⁰I walked by the field of a lazy person, the vineyard of one lacking sense.

³¹I saw that it was overgrown with thorns. It was covered with weeds, and its walls were broken down.

³²Then, as I looked and thought about it, I learned this lesson:

³³A little extra sleep, a little more slumber, a little folding of the hands to rest—

³⁴and poverty will pounce on you like a bandit; scarcity will attack you like an armed robber.

PROVERBS 25

¹These are more proverbs of Solomon, collected by the advisers of King Hezekiah of Judah.

²It is God's privilege to conceal things and the king's privilege to discover them.

³No one can discover the height of heaven, the depth of the earth, or all that goes on in the king's mind!

⁴Remove the dross from silver, and the sterling will be ready for the silversmith.

⁵Remove the wicked from the king's court, and his reign will be made secure by justice.

⁶Don't demand an audience with the king or push for a place among the great.

⁷It is better to wait for an invitation than to be sent to the end of the line, publicly disgraced!

Just because you see something,

⁸don't be in a hurry to go to court. You might go down before your neighbors in shameful defeat.

⁹So discuss the matter with them privately. Don't tell anyone else,

¹⁰or others may accuse you of gossip. Then you will never regain your good reputation.

¹¹Timely advice is as lovely as golden apples in a silver basket.

¹²Valid criticism is as treasured by the one who heeds it as jewelry made from finest gold.

¹³Faithful messengers are as refreshing as snow in the heat of summer. They revive the spirit of their employer.

¹⁴A person who doesn't give a promised gift is like clouds and wind that don't bring rain.

¹⁵Patience can persuade a prince, and soft speech can crush strong opposition.

¹⁶Do you like honey? Don't eat too much of it, or it will make you sick!

¹⁷Don't visit your neighbors too often, or you will wear out your welcome.

¹⁸Telling lies about others is as harmful as hitting them with an ax, wounding them with a sword, or shooting them with a sharp arrow.

¹⁹Putting confidence in an unreliable person is like chewing with a toothache or walking on a broken foot.

²⁰Singing cheerful songs to a person whose heart is heavy is as bad as stealing someone's jacket in cold weather or rubbing salt in a wound.

²¹If your enemies are hungry, give them food to eat. If they are thirsty, give them water to drink.

²²You will heap burning coals on their heads, and the LORD will reward you.

²³As surely as a wind from the north brings rain, so a gossiping tongue causes anger!

²⁴It is better to live alone in the corner of an attic than with a contentious wife in a lovely home.

²⁵Good news from far away is like cold water to the thirsty.

²⁶If the godly compromise with the wicked, it is like polluting a fountain or muddying a spring.

²⁷Just as it is not good to eat too much honey, it is not good for people to think about all the honors they deserve.

²⁸A person without self-control is as defenseless as a city with broken-down walls.

PROVERBS 26

¹Honor doesn't go with fools any more than snow with summer or rain with harvest.

²Like a fluttering sparrow or a darting swallow, an unfair curse will not land on its intended victim.

³Guide a horse with a whip, a donkey with a bridle, and a fool with a rod to his back!

⁴When arguing with fools, don't answer their foolish arguments, or you will become as foolish as they are.

⁵When arguing with fools, be sure to answer their foolish arguments, or they will become wise in their own estimation.

⁶Trusting a fool to convey a message is as foolish as cutting off one's feet or drinking poison!

⁷In the mouth of a fool, a proverb becomes as limp as a paralyzed leg.

⁸Honoring a fool is as foolish as tying a stone to a slingshot.

⁹A proverb in a fool's mouth is as dangerous as a thornbush brandished by a drunkard.

¹⁰An employer who hires a fool or a bystander is like an archer who shoots recklessly.

¹¹As a dog returns to its vomit, so a fool repeats his folly.

¹²There is more hope for fools than for people who think they are wise.

¹³The lazy person is full of excuses, saying, "I can't go outside because there might be a lion on the road! Yes, I'm sure there's a lion out there!"

¹⁴As a door turns back and forth on its hinges, so the lazy person turns over in bed.

¹⁵Some people are so lazy that they won't lift a finger to feed themselves.

¹⁶Lazy people consider themselves smarter than seven wise counselors.

¹⁷Yanking a dog's ears is as foolish as interfering in someone else's argument.

¹⁸Just as damaging as a mad man shooting a lethal weapon

¹⁹is someone who lies to a friend and then says, "I was only joking."

²⁰Fire goes out for lack of fuel, and quarrels disappear when gossip stops.

²¹A quarrelsome person starts fights as easily as hot embers light charcoal or fire lights wood.

²²What dainty morsels rumors are—but they sink deep into one's heart.

²³Smooth¹ words may hide a wicked heart, just as a pretty glaze covers a common clay pot.

²⁴People with hate in their hearts may sound pleasant enough, but don't believe them.

²⁵Though they pretend to be kind, their hearts are full of all kinds of evil.

²⁶While their hatred may be concealed by trickery, it will finally come to light for all to see.

²⁷If you set a trap for others, you will get caught in it yourself. If you roll a boulder down on others, it will roll back and crush you.

²⁸A lying tongue hates its victims, and flattery causes ruin.

1. 26:23 As in Greek version; Hebrew reads *Burning.*

¹Don't brag about tomorrow, since you don't know what the day will bring.

²Don't praise yourself; let others do it!

³A stone is heavy and sand is weighty, but the resentment caused by a fool is heavier than both.

⁴Anger is cruel, and wrath is like a flood, but who can survive the destructiveness of jealousy?

⁵An open rebuke is better than hidden love!

⁶Wounds from a friend are better than many kisses from an enemy.

⁷Honey seems tasteless to a person who is full, but even bitter food tastes sweet to the hungry.

⁸A person who strays from home is like a bird that strays from its nest.

⁹The heartfelt counsel of a friend is as sweet as perfume and incense.

¹⁰Never abandon a friend—either yours or your father's. Then in your time of need, you won't have to ask your relatives for assistance. It is better to go to a neighbor than to a relative who lives far away.

¹¹My child,[1] how happy I will be if you turn out to be wise! Then I will be able to answer my critics.

¹²A prudent person foresees the danger ahead and takes precautions. The simpleton goes blindly on and suffers the consequences.

¹³Be sure to get collateral from anyone who guarantees the debt of a stranger. Get a deposit if someone guarantees the debt of an adulterous woman.

¹⁴If you shout a pleasant greeting to your neighbor too early in the morning, it will be counted as a curse!

¹⁵A nagging wife is as annoying as the constant dripping on a rainy day.

¹⁶Trying to stop her complaints is like trying to stop the wind or hold something with greased hands.

¹⁷As iron sharpens iron, a friend sharpens a friend.

¹⁸Workers who tend a fig tree are allowed to eat its fruit. In the same way, workers who protect their employer's interests will be rewarded.

¹⁹As a face is reflected in water, so the heart reflects the person.

²⁰Just as Death and Destruction[2] are never satisfied, so human desire is never satisfied.

²¹Fire tests the purity of silver and gold, but a person is tested by being praised.

1. 27:11 Hebrew *My son.*
2. 27:20 Hebrew *Sheol and Abaddon.*

[22]You cannot separate fools from their foolishness, even though you grind them like grain with mortar and pestle.

[23]Know the state of your flocks, and put your heart into caring for your herds,

[24]for riches don't last forever, and the crown might not be secure for the next generation.

[25]After the hay is harvested, the new crop appears, and the mountain grasses are gathered in,

[26]your sheep will provide wool for clothing, and your goats will be sold for the price of a field.

[27]And you will have enough goats' milk for you, your family, and your servants.

PROVERBS 28

[1]The wicked run away when no one is chasing them, but the godly are as bold as lions.

[2]When there is moral rot within a nation, its government topples easily. But with wise and knowledgeable leaders, there is stability.

[3]A poor person who oppresses the poor is like a pounding rain that destroys the crops.

[4]To reject the law is to praise the wicked; to obey the law is to fight them.

[5]Evil people don't understand justice, but those who follow the LORD understand completely.

[6]It is better to be poor and honest than rich and crooked.

[7]Young people who obey the law are wise; those who seek out worthless companions bring shame to their parents.

[8]A person who makes money by charging interest will lose it. It will end up in the hands of someone who is kind to the poor.

[9]The prayers of a person who ignores the law are despised.

[10]Those who lead the upright into sin will fall into their own trap, but the honest will inherit good things.

[11]Rich people picture themselves as wise, but their real poverty is evident to the poor.

[12]When the godly succeed, everyone is glad. When the wicked take charge, people go into hiding.

¹³People who cover over their sins will not prosper. But if they confess and forsake them, they will receive mercy.

¹⁴Blessed are those who have a tender conscience,¹ but the stubborn are headed for serious trouble.

¹⁵A wicked ruler is as dangerous to the poor as a lion or bear attacking them.

¹⁶Only a stupid prince will oppress his people, but a king will have a long reign if he hates dishonesty and bribes.

¹⁷A murderer's tormented conscience will drive him into the grave. Don't protect him!

¹⁸The honest will be rescued from harm, but those who are crooked will be destroyed.

¹⁹Hard workers have plenty of food; playing around brings poverty.

²⁰The trustworthy will get a rich reward. But the person who wants to get rich quick will only get into trouble.

²¹Showing partiality is never good, yet some will do wrong for something as small as a piece of bread.

²²A greedy person tries to get rich quick, but it only leads to poverty.

²³In the end, people appreciate frankness more than flattery.

²⁴Robbing your parents and then saying, "What's wrong with that?" is as serious as committing murder.

²⁵Greed causes fighting; trusting the LORD leads to prosperity.

²⁶Trusting oneself is foolish, but those who walk in wisdom are safe.

²⁷Whoever gives to the poor will lack nothing. But a curse will come upon those who close their eyes to poverty.

²⁸When the wicked take charge, people hide. When the wicked meet disaster, the godly multiply.

PROVERBS 29

¹Whoever stubbornly refuses to accept criticism will suddenly be broken beyond repair.

²When the godly are in authority, the people rejoice. But when the wicked are in power, they groan.

³The man who loves wisdom brings joy to his father, but if he hangs around with prostitutes, his wealth is wasted.

⁴A just king gives stability to his nation, but one who demands bribes destroys it.

1. 28:14 Hebrew *those who fear.*

5To flatter people is to lay a trap for their feet.

6Evil people are trapped by sin, but the righteous escape, shouting for joy.

7The godly know the rights of the poor; the wicked don't care to know.

8Mockers can get a whole town agitated, but those who are wise will calm anger.

9If a wise person takes a fool to court, there will be ranting and ridicule but no satisfaction.

10The bloodthirsty hate the honest, but the upright seek out the honest.

11A fool gives full vent to anger, but a wise person quietly holds it back.

12If a ruler honors liars, all his advisers will be wicked.

13The poor and the oppressor have this in common—the LORD gives light to the eyes of both.

14A king who is fair to the poor will have a long reign.

15To discipline and reprimand a child produces wisdom, but a mother is disgraced by an undisciplined child.

16When the wicked are in authority, sin increases. But the godly will live to see the tyrant's downfall.

17Discipline your children, and they will give you happiness and peace of mind.

18When people do not accept divine guidance, they run wild. But whoever obeys the law is happy.

19For a servant, mere words are not enough—discipline is needed. For the words may be understood, but they are not heeded.

20There is more hope for a fool than for someone who speaks without thinking.

21A servant who is pampered from childhood will later become a rebel.

22A hot-tempered person starts fights and gets into all kinds of sin.

23Pride ends in humiliation, while humility brings honor.

24If you assist a thief, you are only hurting yourself. You will be punished if you report the crime, but you will be cursed if you don't.

25Fearing people is a dangerous trap, but to trust the LORD means safety.

26Many seek the ruler's favor, but justice comes from the LORD.

27The godly despise the wicked; the wicked despise the godly.

PROVERBS 30

1The message of Agur son of Jakeh. An oracle.[1]

I am weary, O God; I am weary and worn out, O God.[2]

1. 30:1a Or *son of Jakeh from Massa.*
2. 30:1b The Hebrew can also be translated *The man declares this to Ithiel, to Ithiel and to Ucal.*

²I am too ignorant to be human, and I lack common sense.
³I have not mastered human wisdom, nor do I know the Holy One.
⁴Who but God goes up to heaven and comes back down? Who holds the wind in his fists? Who wraps up the oceans in his cloak? Who has created the whole wide world? What is his name—and his son's name? Tell me if you know!
⁵Every word of God proves true. He defends all who come to him for protection.
⁶Do not add to his words, or he may rebuke you, and you will be found a liar.
⁷O God, I beg two favors from you before I die.
⁸First, help me never to tell a lie. Second, give me neither poverty nor riches! Give me just enough to satisfy my needs.
⁹For if I grow rich, I may deny you and say, "Who is the LORD?"
And if I am too poor, I may steal and thus insult God's holy name.
¹⁰Never slander a person to his employer. If you do, the person will curse you, and you will pay for it.
¹¹Some people curse their father and do not thank their mother.
¹²They feel pure, but they are filthy and unwashed.
¹³They are proud beyond description and disdainful.
¹⁴They devour the poor with teeth as sharp as swords or knives. They destroy the needy from the face of the earth.
¹⁵The leech has two suckers that cry out, "More, more!"³ There are three other things—no, four!—that are never satisfied:

16   the grave,
          the barren womb,
          the thirsty desert,
          the blazing fire.

¹⁷The eye that mocks a father and despises a mother will be plucked out by ravens of the valley and eaten by vultures.
¹⁸There are three things that amaze me—no, four things I do not understand:

19   how an eagle glides through the sky,
          how a snake slithers on a rock,
          how a ship navigates the ocean,
          how a man loves a woman.

²⁰Equally amazing is how an adulterous woman can satisfy her sexual appetite, shrug her shoulders, and then say, "What's wrong with that?"
²¹There are three things that make the earth tremble—no, four it cannot endure:

---

3. 30:15 Hebrew *two daughters who cry out, "Give, give!"*

22 a slave who becomes a king,
   an overbearing fool who prospers,
23 a bitter woman who finally gets a husband,
   a servant girl who supplants her mistress.

24There are four things on earth that are small but unusually wise:

25 Ants—they aren't strong,
   but they store up food for the winter.

26 Rock badgers[4]—they aren't powerful,
   but they make their homes among the rocky cliffs.

27 Locusts—they have no king,
   but they march like an army in ranks.

28 Lizards—they are easy to catch,
   but they are found even in kings' palaces.

29There are three stately monarchs on the earth—no, four:

30 the lion, king of animals, who won't turn aside for anything,

31 the strutting rooster,
   the male goat,
   a king as he leads his army.

32If you have been a fool by being proud or plotting evil, don't brag about it—cover your mouth with your hand in shame.

33As the beating of cream yields butter, and a blow to the nose causes bleeding, so anger causes quarrels.

4. 30:26 Or *coneys,* or *hyraxes.*

PROVERBS 31

1These are the sayings of King Lemuel, an oracle[1] that his mother taught him.

2O my son, O son of my womb, O son of my promises,

3do not spend your strength on women, on those who ruin kings.

4And it is not for kings, O Lemuel, to guzzle wine. Rulers should not crave liquor.

5For if they drink, they may forget their duties and be unable to give justice to those who are oppressed.

6Liquor is for the dying, and wine for those in deep depression.

7Let them drink to forget their poverty and remember their troubles no more.

1. 31:1 Or *of Lemuel, king of Massa.*

⁸Speak up for those who cannot speak for themselves; ensure justice for those who are perishing.

⁹Yes, speak up for the poor and helpless, and see that they get justice.

¹⁰Who can find a virtuous and capable wife? She is worth more than precious rubies.

¹¹Her husband can trust her, and she will greatly enrich his life.

¹²She will not hinder him but help him all her life.

¹³She finds wool and flax and busily spins it.

¹⁴She is like a merchant's ship; she brings her food from afar.

¹⁵She gets up before dawn to prepare breakfast for her household and plan the day's work for her servant girls.

¹⁶She goes out to inspect a field and buys it; with her earnings she plants a vineyard.

¹⁷She is energetic and strong, a hard worker.

¹⁸She watches for bargains; her lights burn late into the night.

¹⁹Her hands are busy spinning thread, her fingers twisting fiber.

²⁰She extends a helping hand to the poor and opens her arms to the needy.

²¹She has no fear of winter for her household because all of them have warm² clothes.

²²She quilts her own bedspreads. She dresses like royalty in gowns of finest cloth.

²³Her husband is well known, for he sits in the council meeting with the other civic leaders.

²⁴She makes belted linen garments and sashes to sell to the merchants.

²⁵She is clothed with strength and dignity, and she laughs with no fear of the future.

²⁶When she speaks, her words are wise, and kindness is the rule when she gives instructions.

²⁷She carefully watches all that goes on in her household and does not have to bear the consequences of laziness.

²⁸Her children stand and bless her. Her husband praises her:

²⁹"There are many virtuous and capable women in the world, but you surpass them all!"

³⁰Charm is deceptive, and beauty does not last; but a woman who fears the LORD will be greatly praised.

³¹Reward her for all she has done. Let her deeds publicly declare her praise.

2. 31:21 As in Greek version; Hebrew *scarlet.*

SUBJECT INDEX

SCRIPTURE INDEX